gift ($30)

W9-DDJ-265

CSS - Certified Customer Service Specialist - Study Guide - 3rd Edition

This book was developed and published by:
The Electronics Technicians Association, International, Inc.
Greencastle, IN 46135-8024

Printing by Greencastle Offset
Greencastle, IN 46135
Cover Design by: Bryan Allen

Edited by:
The staff of the Electronics Technicians Association, International

Written by:
Sixteen individual working electronics workers, educators, business owners, CSS holders, association staff and others representing a broad segment of the high tech society we live in today created this book. Check each chapter heading for the background on each of the authors.

The years of experience represented by the book's authors is great. The ages vary from those 20+ years old to one or more over 70! Most have had experience as authors of CSS 1 or 2002 or have served on the CSS Subject Matter Experts committee recently. No matter what area of human endeavor one is engaged in, this book brings together common sense guidelines for treating customers, co-workers, allied workers, employers and yourself in a considerate, friendly and rewarding manner. It is unusual to see a book with so many authors, located in widely scattered areas of North America. That produces some repeating of theories or advice. But, that is not bad. It only verifies that the first guy had it right.

With so many different views on topics that sometimes may not seem to be 100% related specifically to customer service, it may appear the book gets off track now and then. But part of the concept of the book is that the complete customer service specialist not only knows the face-to-face rules for dealing with the public, but also can do this better because his/her own personal job position, feelings towards coworkers and the company itself are not merely satisfactory, but enjoyable, and he/she feels secure in what he/she does.

Lastly, you will find the book is fun to read. It is not stuffy and you will easily place yourself in the position of one or another of the characters exposed in the text. You will also come away with a great deal of respect for all of the authors.

Table of Contents

Table of Contents, continued

The CSS Study Guide, 3rd Edition

Foreword

CSS 3 - the third edition of the popular CSS Study Guide (first released in 1997), is published by ETA-I to provide tested and proven guidance for all persons whose job it is to help people solve problems they may encounter with products or services.

Thousands of books, videos, CDs and other training materials have been offered to help workers learn how to fix, adjust or install hardware and software products. Few of these address the issues of how to respond to customer problems; to acquire valuable feedback in order to measure the quality of service; to mold the attitudes required of service personnel, and to successfully increase the number of satisfied and repeat customers. As numerous human relations experts have pointed out in the past, a person's success in life, in their job, in their community, church, family - - everywhere, is more often that person's ability to get along, to influence, to establish relationships, to be able to solve conflicts, than it is her or his technical expertise. This book works to help technical people avoid people problems and to gain people skills to enhance their technical abilities and knowledge.

The CSS Certification program, begun in 1990, has grown from its original concept of assisting electronics field technicians, to a much broader program. Today, hundreds of schools offer CSS certification testing. Thousands of study guides have been purchased by individuals preparing to become CSS's. Dozens of companies have purchased CSS books for their employees or students. Many educational institutions now offer specific courses to prepare individuals for the CSS exam and to become top-notch customer service professionals. CSS courses have become a logical add-on to computer, communications and electronics technical courses at both public and commercial educational institutions.

The new CSS study guide, *CSS-3rd Edition*, despite the success of its predecessors, has double the number of topics and double the pages. It has sixteen authors with diverse backgrounds and 'tons' of experience in the customer relations field. Once the valuable concepts, as written by Bob Ing in the first edition, became known, the benefits began to be seen. Several more definable attitude and behavior tools which could be taught, became a mandate for the new CSS Guide. Everything that made the first book great is in *CSS-3rd Edition*. The new topics have already generated responses like: "Why didn't we think of that before?" and "I'm giving a copy to each of our techs." "This book says what I can't say". If you or your company have ever wondered if you were doing your best, in both the short and the long term, to mold pleasant and profitable human relations, *CSS-3rd Edition* answers the question.

Our gratitude goes to Dr. Ing, for initiating the original guide, virtually all of which is still included in this book. Thanks also to the new authors and the ETA staff editors, for their hard work and dedication. Also thanks to the many industry and educational associations, schools and companies who provided encouragement and suggestions.

Dick Glass, CETsr

Chapter 1

CSS—Customer Service Specialist

History and Objectives

Dick Glass, CETsr

Dick Glass is an author of previous ETA publications as well as more than a dozen books dealing with electronics technology and business management, published by Howard W. Sams Co, TAB Books, McGraw-Hill and ETA. He has also written hundreds of articles in trade journals and other association publications. Dick is a former Navy Avionics Technician, Industrial Electronics Computer Technician, Technical Writer, FCC Commercial License examination modernization committee chairman, inductee into the Electronics Hall of Fame and currently President of ETA-I. He has a broad background in all phases of work performed by electronics technicians. He oversees ETA's 40-plus certification programs and the association's Training Course Approval system.

In the Beginning

In the beginning (let's say the early part of the last century) there was no CSS - Customer Service Specialist - program. In fact, until 1965, technical certification programs were unknown in the young and exciting electronics industry.

Schools, both state-run and commercial, were teaching electronics to a growing workforce of high tech workers. These were the radio and TV technicians who were doing their best to keep the exploding number and complexity of products working. In those days of electron tubes, this was not easy. Today, we often find precision resistors, specialized transistors and integrated circuit chips. Back in the 50's and 60's, it wasn't unusual to find a TV chassis in which the actual manufacturer used two resistors in parallel in many cases, rather than a single resistor, for cost or availability reasons. That would be unheard of today. Somehow, by sharing information and going to frequent technical meetings, the service technicians were able to make the TVs and radios of that day work.

There were a lot of one or two-man TV shops in those days. A majority of the service technicians were owners of their own businesses, or guys who worked on contract, but had an interest in their own work.

It is because of that demographic makeup of the electronic service business that customer relations were usually not a problem. Many TV men were well-known members of the community. They had an investment in the business, and thus were keenly aware of the value of keeping their customers, friends and relatives happy. They worked long hours to get the most difficult jobs done. Customers appreciated the extra effort. Repair parts were reasonably priced. Employees seemed to have a vision of the future and thus also treated their valued customers well.

Things Changed

In the 70's and 80's, the consumer electronics business changed. Electronic products were being produced in other countries, where labor costs were very low. Ways were found to reduce the costs of components and cabinets. Thus, many products were priced so low by the mass merchandisers that repair was not practical for most low-end equipment.

Product Sales Factor

In the 50's, 60's and 70's, sales of TVs and stereos, radios and auto electronics were a significant factor in the profitability of the consumer electronics entrepreneur. With the advent of the mass merchandisers, the institution of what might be called "Creative Marketing" by product makers came about. Also, the creation of large electronic servicing networks put pressure on the independent shops. Thus the relationship between neighbors and consumer electronics shops changed. The servicer now was probably a stranger, working on commission for a seemingly more efficient and larger service operation.

Computer Servicing

With the advent of the Apple II, Commodore and Radio Shack personal computers, the public found an even greater need for help, both for hardware problems and, more importantly, software and operator problems.

Operator manuals for computers were poorly written. Some product makers set a policy of attempting to do the very least to assist buyers of their computers and related products. The poor service offered by consumer electronics product makers and some service firms now seemed a lot better when compared with the new computer world.

No-Help Desks

A new term, 'Help Desk,' came into being. The availability of a factory expert seemed great.

But computers were even more complicated to use than radios, stereos and TV sets. As small independent businesses began to spring up selling computer equipment, they quickly realized that they could spend exorbitant amounts of valuable time, just trying to bring computer owners up to speed. That doesn't even count solving real hardware problems or the many incompatibility and software difficulties users were experiencing. So, local help for most people became nonexistent. Fortunately, the computer makers had help desk personnel available. Finally, there was a place where you could get technical help. But, alas, here too, the cost of helping people with real problems, due to the newness of computers and the lack of standards, was expensive. Apple Computer solved the problem by restricting their help desks to only genuine retailer inquiries. Later they were fined by the U.S. Government when it was found that the company had intentionally established a 'policy' of no-help for consumers. This was contrary to what Apple's advertising claimed.

People were expected to get help locally, or to just become computer 'gurus' themselves.

Mass Merchandisers

The product maker wasn't the only culprit in the change from helpful service to lip service. Mass merchandisers, taking over the retail 'world' from independents, also lived in a highly competitive world. To cut costs, they too found that having no help desks, or no-help desks, saved dollars. Some of these, like Wal-Mart, being large enough to receive sizable concessions from product makers, solved the service problem by offering to exchange products with 'no questions asked.' This became a burden on product makers who often found less-than-fair customers would return products after damaging them, and just as often, when they had no problem at all, but were simply tired of them.

So, 'authorized service centers' were set up to handle service on products sold by mass merchandisers. But in a highly competitive merchandising world, paying for service on complex electronics, computers and appliances became a very non-competitive thing, so far as the bottom line was concerned. This was frustrating because a product maker that offered adequate after-sale, or warranty service, often found his no-services competitor able to reduce costs. This put pressure on the legitimate company to also reduce costs, since buyers could not predict how good after-sale service might be, or even if they would ever need any.

With such pressure, independent and contract service firms found they were being squeezed on warranty service payments by product makers, and that many costs, such as service literature, training, and replacement parts were rising.

All of these factors worked to present the consumer with poor service, no service, and even arrogant service firms and workers. An underpaid service technician, help desk worker, delivery or other service person is not always in a good mood.

Recognition

It was a group of manufacturers from the Northwest (Washington and Oregon) that recognized in the late 70's that, technicians especially, but also all other service personnel, were sometimes a bit short on customer relations, coworker relations, personal appearance, hygiene and other 'soft skills.'

The public was running out of patience with companies who professed to have customer service departments, but too often hired the lowest paid workers and gave them a one-sheet trouble-fix chart and sat them at a phone to 'get rid' of customer problems.

The concept of keeping help-desk costs at their lowest level quickly resulted in companies realizing that it was to their advantage to have only a few help desk workers, even if the phones were ringing off the hooks and they really needed dozens or hundreds more phone workers.

So, Customer Service became an important part of business for companies that expected to exist for many years. Customer Relations Management became a corporate phrase. Books were written and consultants hired to improve the image of corporate America.

ETA Establishes CSS

Don Howell, CETsr, an electronics instructor at Lake Washington Technical College in Kirkland, Washington, heeding the words of the large electronics firms in the Seattle area, proposed a Customer Service Specialist Certification program. This was aimed at equipping electronics technicians with soft skills. With Don leading the way (he was Chairman of ETA at the time, 1990), ETA evolved competencies and an examination to test these soft skills.

The CSS wasn't so much an effort to give credentials to technicians who treated people decently, as it was a program to set standards for how one is supposed to act if he or she is working in customer service.

Others Like It

Shortly after beginning the CSS testing program, the

association found that companies and workers in non-electronic technologies had the same problems: workers needed more soft skills.

Responding to this need, ETA reduced the materials in the exams and study guides which were specific to electronics. Thus, CSS became a more universal program, equally valuable in the automotive, health, manufacturing, communications and all other industries.

CE Manufacturers

In the early 90's, the EIA (Electronic Industry Association) in Washington, DC, received a grant from the U.S. Dept. of Education, which was intended to initiate a new technical certification program for entry-level electronics technicians. The major difference in the EIA skills standards and those already existing in ETA and ISCET (Int'l. Society of CETs), was the inclusion of 'soft skills' with the technical competencies. The validation study done by that association appeared to show that there was universal recognition that these 'people skills' were becoming ever more important.

The EIA certification effort became known as the 'CEA Certification Program.' However, when it eventually began testing, surprisingly, the exam had no 'soft skills' questions in it, and the CEA study guide had no mention of people skills, customer relations, manners, etc.

While it might appear to the casual observer that perhaps afterwards these skills were not considered so important as first thought to be, it remains a mystery as to what happened to the EIA soft-skills portion of the program.

Schools Join In

In 1999, state-funded school systems in different states started a program to encourage formal training in CSS type concepts. Grants were applied for. Announcements were made about the 'Work Readiness' training concept. School conference attendees were exposed to speakers who urged inclusion of this type of training in with technical courses.

Thus, the concept is universally accepted. The product makers, schools, the public, and ETA all agree that CSS skills are as important as technical know-how.

The Difference

The difference between ETA's CSS program and others seems not to be in whether to teach and test for soft skills, but HOW to go about it.

There is no question that everyone is in favor of impressing students and workers with human relations skills. The discussion revolves around whether to attempt to include soft-skills training in with technical competencies, or to establish it as a separate category of training standing on its own. Would it be best to intermingle customer relations questions with technical skills and knowledge test items, or to mandate that technical students participate in a class specifically teaching soft skills at the conclusion of the technical courses?

In the early 90's, ETA remolded its technical competencies to attempt to include a representative portion of exam questions devoted to CSS principles of behavior, customer and coworker relations. This was an attempt to cooperate with what was assumed to be an all-industry initiative to raise the standards of conduct of electronics workers.

Soft Skills Take a Backseat

Despite the efforts of ETA to mesh soft skills with technical competencies, it was found that the committees invariably concentrated on technical knowledge and skills and spent little or no time on soft skills. The highly successful A+ certification program for computer keyboard workers found that while soft skills were 'nice,' it was difficult to devote much exam space to the topic. Thus, the customer service questions on their exams were not even graded! Soft skills were given 'lip service' but not really seriously considered in the exam program of the Computer Technology Industry Association (CompTia).

With no known programs in existence which do justice to the need for behavior and customer service training, and with only a cursory amount of space and test questions devoted to the topic, ETA has looked towards attempting to convince the 'world' that the CSS program needs to be taught as a separate course, have its own test and study, and that it should be seriously considered as mandatory and an adjunct to tech school courses.

Some colleges and commercial technical schools have implemented CSS training and have found it everything it is touted to be, and more. Employers invariably give more consideration to prospective employees who can show soft-skills training in addition to their technical schooling. Some companies offer  raises to employees who obtain CSS certification. General Dynamics, for example, has suggested to certain segments of its employees that the next raise may be difficult to get unless the person has obtained a CSS.

Chapter 1. CSS History and Objectives

Coming Into Focus

With over a dozen years of experience and a continual honing of the CSS program to make it more universal and to cover all of the necessary soft-skills topics, the conclusions are clear. CSS is extremely important to the world of commerce and industry. The public deserves not only good service, but professional servicers who understand good people relations and its value to the economy.

The Objective

The objective of CSS is to improve the life of employees in their interaction with the public, but also with fellow workers and allied personnel.

By offering real standards of behavior and extending the subject to include nuances which, at first, are possibly not thought of as CSS principles, the worker who becomes a CSS gains tremendous confidence. The schools which teach specific CSS classes, either as stand-alone short courses, or as addenda to technical courses, will find their graduates getting jobs easier and doing well in them. Companies that recognize the benefits of pre-approving candidates who already have shown they understand the importance of people skills, can save money as their workers fit in better and have less people conflicts at or away from work. The public is the big winner as CSS workers understand and try to give world class service.

The Exam

The current CSS written examination is 100 questions in length. The competencies for that exam are contained on the ETA website at www.eta-i.org.

The ETA CSS Exam committee is composed of experienced teachers, technicians and administrators in many walks of life. Their job: to continually find better ways to teach, to test and to provide study for the CSS program. That committee, in 2007, was composed of twenty-five individual members.

A CSS Course

Schools can set up CSS training courses, which can range in length from one to several weeks, or 40+ hours. CSS courses are simple to set up, compared with technical courses in which expensive hardware is needed. This book is the best study text on this topic in existence. Exam competencies are listed on the web (www.eta-i.org). ETA stands ready to assist any school in its implementation of a CSS course. Just call 800 288 3824 or e-mail for help at: **eta@eta -i.org.** You can also find the CSS Competencies posted on the NCEE website at: www.ncee-edu.org.

Chapter 1. CSS History and Objectives

Chapter Quiz

1. The CSS testing program was started in:

   a. 1980.
   b. 1990.
   c. 2000.
   d. 2002.

2. The CSS exam contains many electronics technical questions.

   a. True
   b. False

3. The CSS exam (in 2007) contained how many questions?

   a. 35
   b. 50
   c. 75
   d. 100

4. Nearly all adults already know all of the concepts of the CSS program, but just don't apply them.

   a. True
   b. False

5. The concept of offering a customer service skills program was originally proposed by:

   a. military educators.
   b. mass merchandiser companies.
   c. independent service shop owners.
   d. large manufacturing companies in Washington state.

6. Changes in the motivation to give good customer service occurred when high tech products proliferated.

   a. True
   b. False

7. Customer service problems were shifted around in the 70's and 80's as a cost-cutting policy by many major companies.

   a. True
   b. False

8. Soft skills such as those taught in CSS courses can't be learned.

   a. True
   b. False

9. Some companies pay those with CSS certificates more than ordinary workers.

   a. True
   b. False

10. Including CSS type training concepts in technical training programs usually short-changes CSS and soft skills.

    a. True
    b. False

Answers:

1-b, 2-b, 3-d, 4-b, 5-d, 6-a, 7-a, 8-b, 9-a, 10-a

Chapter 2

Sales, Marketing & Customer Service Relationships

Robert (Bob) Ing served as Chairman of ETA-I in 1998 and developed much of the material in the first edition of the CSS Study Guide. He is Director of King's Markham Forensic Services in Toronto, Canada; a project management contractor specializing in the validation and examination of digital technology. The author of nineteen professional publications, he has lectured and given workshops in both Canada and the United States.

Robert (Bob) Ing, DSc, CESma

"There is only one boss: the customer. And he can fire everybody from the Chairman on down, simply by spending his money somewhere else."
- Sam Walton

In order to provide excellent customer service, it is important to understand where customer service is in relationship to the "big picture" of getting, servicing and keeping customers. With many businesses offering "self-serve" and automated customer service functions, the opportunity to provide personalized customer service has been reduced by an average of 55% over the past five years. This, combined with the fact that most businesses offer the same or similar products and services, makes customer loyalty and retention even more critical to business success. The main reason why customers buy and stay with one company over another is the relationship they have with the sales, marketing and service people. It is the people who represent the personality of the business, and differentiate it over the competition. This, simply put, is why people will do business with you and stay with your company.

It is very important to ensure that any personal contact with a customer is a pleasurable and productive one, from the initial sales contact to the customer service call and the subsequent follow-up contact with the customer.

It is not uncommon to find sales, marketing, and front-line management staff performing customer service functions and customer service representatives performing sales and marketing functions during the course of their duties. Thus, customer service training for these staff members is essential, as would be sales and marketing training for customer service representatives. Traditionally, the lines between sales, marketing and customer service have been distinct in large corporations. However, these lines have become more dotted with company restructuring. In 85% of all businesses that are designated "small business," the line may be non-existent, as very often one person may be responsible for sales, marketing and customer service.

A successful business is founded not on the concept of "making money," but on the concept of getting and keeping customers in order to provide them with a product or service at a reasonable profit.

The process of getting and keeping customers entails three distinct, but important, functions: Business Development, Sales, and Customer Relationship Management.

Business Development

Business development concerns itself with attracting and qualifying prospective customers. Under the business development function lie the advertising and marketing operations of the business. Advertising campaigns usually attempt to get the prospective customer to voluntarily call the company in order to make a sale. Marketing campaigns attempt not only to get the prospective customer to call, but usually attempt to follow up or directly contact prospective customers.

Dissecting Business Development

Prior to starting a marketing campaign, a great deal of research must be done. This should include a study of the competition, in particular the pricing and marketing strategy employed. This 'competitive intelligence' should be analyzed and mapped to see what works and what doesn't.

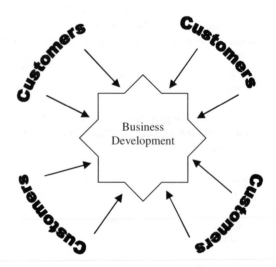

Chapter 2. Sales, Marketing & Customer Service Relationships

Avertising

A component of marketing, advertising is the broadcast message that goes out to all the nodes within a target group network. Efforts are directed towards everyone in your business arena to identify the potential customers and the location for the products and services to be marketed. By letting everyone know your company name and what you do, you inherently build a solid presence through word-of-mouth advertising. These default advertisers may not currently be in the market for the products or services being offered, but are happy to be of service to the network. A voluntary response, where the potential customer makes the first move, is indicative of the success of the strategy employed and leads into the main marketing phase.

Marketing

Follow-up is a key strategy in this phase. It is through the act of marketing that most new customers receive detailed information on the products and services being offered.

An effective marketing campaign utilizes different methods of product/service information delivery. Whatever the method, often referred to as 'media' (a newspaper or magazine ad would be referred to as "print media" because it is in print), it must grab the interest of potential customers. Hence, matching media to a particular target audience is critical. Here are some of the media used in a marketing campaign:

PRINT

- Advertisements in newspapers and magazines
- Flyers and handbills
- Brochures, catalogues and price lists
- Business cards

DIRECT MAIL

- Mailed letters of solicitation
- Advertisements and surveys
- Mail order catalogues or ads

TELEMARKETING

- Cold calls to potential customers. The first or initial unsolicited telephone or direct contact made in a marketing campaign to a potential customer is called a 'cold call' or 'cold calling.'

OUTDOOR

- Outdoor billboards and banners

PREMIUM & INCENTIVE

- Imprinted giveaways with your company name and telephone number, such as pens, refrigerator magnets, screwdrivers, rulers and mugs
- Contests or drawings
- Discount cards/programs
- Coupons, rebates and "buy one-get-one free" offers

ELECTRONIC

- Company Web Site, Internet links, banners, surveys

Key Marketing Strategies

1. CONDUCTING RESEARCH—Study, analyze and assess the market or need for a product or service. Don't reinvent the wheel. Use existing data to find out who and where are your customers and competitors. Extend that research to locate untapped areas or adapt it to suit the current trends.

2. SETTING THE TONE—Develop a cost efficient marketing campaign to reach these potential customers and to establish a solid business image.

3. RELATIONSHIP BUILDING—Develop a sound and sustainable method of follow-up for the campaign.

Sales

Sales is the process that gets your product or service into the hands of intended customers. A successful marketing campaign generates two types of sales activities:

Voluntary—A potential customer identifies him/herself by responding to your marketing campaign. This may be in the form of a request for more information or a sale or service appointment. Your next move here and the pace of your response are critical. Typical timeline: 24-48 hours.

Involuntary—A sales representative places a follow-up call, sends a letter or makes a personal visit to direct mail recipients. Typical timeline: 2-4 weeks.

Once a location or business arena has been identified, other methods can be revisited or employed. Sales people may utilize telemarketing and direct door-to-door visits to 'cold call' potential customers. At this point, sales personnel can further validate the benefits of products or services through the open endorsement of current clients. It is essential that clients who select to remain anonymous or who hold proprietary tools be afforded the option to do so.

Key Sales Strategies

1. Reaffirm information provided through the marketing campaign.

2. Respond promptly to any questions arising from the marketing material.

3. Provide additional information as required.

4. Discuss and conduct a continuous assessment of clients' needs and ways to fulfill them.

Customer Service

Customer service entails the relationship building aspect of an ongoing marketing campaign. Once a potential customer becomes a customer, customer service takes over.

> *The key to practical and effective customer service and marketing direction is the ability to interpret what the customer is relaying through attitudes, reactions and responses.*

It is the responsibility of the Business Development group to have clearly stated and governing principles that provide clear direction to the customer service personnel to aid in correct decision making. Subsequently, it is the responsibility of customer service to provide the human element that translates into good customer support during and after the sale of products and services.

Customer service functions can be divided into three distinct groups:

1. General Customer Support

   - Staffed primarily by generalists and non-technical personnel
   - Provides front-line assistance such as 'walking' the customer through the owner's manual, assessing the nature of interest— technical or non-technical, and responding to literature requests and other general issues

2. Technical Customer Support

   - Staffed by technicians and engineers
   - Provides technical assistance in the areas of application, installation, on-site repair and maintenance, user information, site repair and customer assistance

3. Customer Satisfaction Monitoring

   - Surveys and asks for feedback on products and services
   - Maintains a 'groan & moan' log of customer problems and complaints
   - Maintains a 'you're a genius' positive feedback log of customer praises and suggestions
   - Prepares and distributes customer satisfaction reports from surveys and logs for use in improving company products and services
   - Provides sensitivity or other targeted training as required

Key Customer Service Strategies

1. Listen and respond to customer issues promptly. The sustainability and longevity of your business depends on increased customer loyalty and retention.

2. Never put the customer on the defensive. *"A bird in the hand is worth two in the bush."* The goal here is to

increase goodwill and business reputation.

3. Keep competitors in focus. Provide the competitive advantage in securing new customers.

Such strategies can increase sales revenues (by up to 200%) through repeat and auxiliary product sales and service. Depending on the size of the company, sales, marketing and customer service functions may be handled by separate groups or by one individual. In any case, an understanding of how these three functions relate to each other is an important step towards obtaining and keeping customers.

World Class Customer Service

Techniques for evaluating a successful customer service operation:

1. Commitment to Quality

ETA-I has set a specific standard or level of customer service. The goal of this standard is to provide complete customer satisfaction, thus reducing, if not eliminating, many customer callbacks or recalls.

Through the surveys conducted and logs kept by individual companies, company standards can be revised to a level that accurately measures and improves upon customer satisfaction. This, however, can only be accomplished if the data from these test and measurement tools are converted into specific procedures for problem resolution and customer requests response.

2. Focused Customer Services

All customer services must be focused towards the resolution of customer requests and concerns. Compromise and apology, rather than quick resolution, must be the exception not the norm.

Customer frustration at company bureaucracy is one of the major roadblocks to achieving customer satisfaction.

Customer service is a person-to-person activity. Despite the advances in technology, the human element in this area is critical. **Reduce the number of people delivering service and support to your customers and, over time, the demand for your services and products will diminish.**

Focus Steps

a) Realize that you have external and internal

customers. *External* customers are the public: those who fall within your marketing campaign target area. *Internal* customers are departments or individuals within your company.

b) Prioritize customer concerns. It is the external customers who directly contribute to the welfare of the company, and so, should be everyone's first priority. It is the internal customers who support the infrastructure that supports the external customers. Their concerns may be secondary on the priority scale, but it must never appear to be so.

c) Training—Educate and involve internal customers in the process of customer prioritization and issue prioritization.

3. Customer Involvement

Feedback and suggestions regarding products and services should be obtained during each conversation with a customer.

Simple questions such as: How are we doing? How beneficial are our products and services to you? How do our products and/or services specifically meet your needs? These questions can help provide an unbiased practical and cost-efficient

> **INVEST YOUR MONEY IN THE AREAS OF HIGHEST RETURN**

customer satisfaction assessment tool for any company. Pay close attention to those customers who have issues with your products or services. Don't be afraid or dismissive of negative comments. *"There's no smoke without fire."* Remember that some companies spend literally millions of dollars each year commissioning special firms to do market studies. Get smart—reduce overhead, gain valuable customer/product/marketing information, and foster customer bonds.

4. Continuous Improvement

For the individual customer service specialist, continuous improvement means keeping current on customer service techniques, on new and emerging technology relevant to the company, and in having a very proactive attitude.

For the company, continuous improvement means taking all customer feedback seriously and using this feedback to improve the overall operations of the company, its products and services.

The key questions here are: What can I offer to customers that my competitors do not? How can I distinguish my company from its competitors?

Monthly or biweekly discussion groups, meetings or seminars on the performance of products or services could provide the ideas and strategies required to power the continuous improvement cycle.

5. Integrity

Integrity requires the authority and empowerment to make decisions and carry out tasks without requiring a superior's seal of approval. The customer service specialist should be able to authorize refunds, exchanges, repairs or upgrades based on established principles. This not only speeds up customer service response time, but also empowers and engages the specialist in the integral running and success of the company.

Key Strategies in Developing Integrity

a) The employee must receive awareness training on products, services, customer service principles, and company policy.

b) The employer must be willing to provide the employee with unrestricted access to the information and tools needed to get the job done.

c) The employer must be satisfied with the competency, reliability and trustworthiness of the individual.

Meeting these criteria aids in the development of mutual respect between the employee and the employer and, subsequently, between the employee and the customer. Company management must become cognizant of the fact that attitudes, work ethics, reliability, loyalty and other value-based behavior flow from the top down and eventually out through the pipeline of customer service.

Integrity is gained through empowerment, mutual respect and establishing clearly defined company policies and goals.

Chapter 2. Sales, Marketing & Customer Service Relationships

Chapter Quiz:

1. The main reason why customers buy and stay with one company over another is:

   a. relationship.
   b. service.
   c. products.
   d. brand.

2. A successful company is defined based on:

   a. money.
   b. customer retention.
   c. product upgrades.
   d. service contracts.

3. Business development concerns itself with:

   a. attracting and qualifying prospective customers.
   b. soliciting and qualifying prospective products.
   c. attracting and qualifying internal customers.
   d. empowering and aligning people.

4. A marketing tool such as cold calling is classified as a/an:

   a. premium and incentive.
   b. outdoor solicitation.
   c. telemarketing tool.
   d. discount program.

5. To ensure products and services reach intended customers, _____ is required.

   a. analysis
   b. technical skill
   c. pricing
   d. follow-up

6. Word-of-mouth advertising is defined as:

   a. people who have never seen your marketing campaign but like your internal customers.
   b. people who have never seen your marketing campaign but are currently in your business arena.
   c. people who have seen your marketing campaign and have heard good things about your services from other external customers.
   d. people who have seen your marketing campaign but may not necessarily know how to get your products.

7. Potential customers responding to your marketing campaign are called _____ sales.

   a. involuntary
   b. voluntary
   c. incidental
   d. general

8. Effective customer service operations will:

   a. increase customer loyalty and retention.
   b. increase overall sales revenues.
   c. provide competitive advantage.
   d. All of the above

9. Continuous improvement in the customer service picture means:

   a. using customer feedback to improve the overall operations of the company, its products and services.
   b. using customer feedback to increase customer callbacks and recalls.
   c. using customer feedback to extend overall company bureaucracy, its products and services.
   d. using customer feedback to avoid empowerment, discussion groups and exchanges.

10. Integrity requires:

   a. fully trained employees.
   b. unrestricted access to information and tools.
   c. Both A and B
   d. A only

Answers:

1-a, 2-b, 3-a, 4-c, 5-d, 6-c, 7-b, 8-d, 9-a, 10-c

Chapter 3

Pro-Profit Employees

Psychology of Success

Dick Glass is an author of previous ETA publications as well as more than a dozen books dealing with electronics technology and business management, published by Howard W. Sams Co, TAB Books, McGraw-Hill and ETA. He has also written hundreds of articles in trade journals and other association publications. Dick is a former Navy Avionics Technician, Industrial Electronics Computer Technician, Technical Writer, FCC Commercial License examination modernization committee chairman, inductee into the Electronics Hall of Fame and currently President of ETA-I. He has a broad background in all phases of work performed by electronics technicians. He oversees ETA's 40-plus certification programs and the training course approval system.

By Dick Glass, CETsr

Pro-Profit

Pro-Profit means 'for profit' or 'favoring' profit. Since most all forms of commercial business have the making of a profit as the number one goal, it might seem of little importance to include a chapter on the topic in a book aimed at helping employees succeed in their work place. After all, don't most all of us go to work our first day on the job, knowing that we were hired to assist the company in reaching its goals? We probably weren't hired with the idea that we would reduce profits, or that we were needed to help the company show a loss, perhaps for tax purposes. We are hired to help improve the efficiency and abilities of the company, whether it is a one person company that now needs a helper, or a large company which is filling a 'slot.'

Two Kinds Of Employees

Employees might be classified into two groups:

2 Kinds Of Employees

1. Employees who work to pick up a paycheck and who can't wait for 5 o'clock when they can go home

2. Employees who are part of the company team and who attempt to do their best to help the company meet its goals

It is no big sin to want to get off work. It is no sin to be working for a paycheck. Those two items are number one and two probably. We all like to have free time to pursue our family, home, hobby or other interests. Spending the best part of each day at a confining job interferes with our freedom.

But, we take a job because we must make money in order to pay for our car and its upkeep. We need clothes to maintain our lifestyle in the circles we move in. We get married and find our need for money is even greater; the kids come along and perhaps we want to purchase a home and so we need even more money. Not only that, but we may now be faced with having to make sufficient money or we could lose our car and home, ruin our credit, and even lose our family if we don't have a continuous income adequate to cover all of our needs.

So, we either start our own business, attempting to do work which will pay enough to cover all of our needs, or, more likely, we look for a job. After we graduate from school, perhaps tech school or college, we have accumulated some skills and knowledge. We offer these skills to an employer who is seeking workers, and we go to the job site to 'learn the ropes,' and then to apply our skills.

Some jobs are such that you have little ability to influence the profits of the company. An example might be a delivery person or a lifeguard or a ticket taker. In these jobs, the task is to get the package from point A to point B, or to observe, or to collect tickets and keep those without tickets from entering.

Each of the above examples has an influence on profits and each worker should do the job to the best of his or her ability, but the opportunity to influence profit may not be as great as the following examples:

1. A technician providing in-home service

2. A sales person

3. A help desk customer support person

The delivery person can influence profits downward by losing packages; not caring how much time it takes; being rude to recipients, and so forth.

The lifeguard can be so dictatorial that people quit

frequenting that swimming pool or area. He or she could create incidents or leave people to drown and subject the pool to legal suits.

The ticket taker might take his/her sweet time and let lines and impatience grow, or he or she might lose tickets, or in other ways cost the company money, thus forcing income down.

But, by and large, the delivery guy, lifeguard and ticket taker have less direct effect on profits than the technician, salesman or help-desk worker.

The Company is Rich

Employees may feel that the company has unlimited assets and makes jillions of dollars and thus, the individual worker is just a pawn. The company will continue to sell products or services, and the top brass will continue to make six or seven-figure salaries no matter what an individual does. So why make any serious efforts?

Companies come and go. One of the reasons they 'go' is because the workers, as well as management, assume that because the company has an organization, a history, or products or services that are in demand, that any one individual, or even a department, is not that important to the overall bottom line.

If management is cheating the stockholders, the retirees and current workers, then the company may deserve to fail. But many of the country's best known companies were started by one or two people who had a vision: Edison, Westinghouse, RCA, Sears & Roebuck, Boss Hotels, Woolworth department stores, Finco Antennas (Sears is still in business). After the originators turn the company over to other family members who really don't care; or after the founder is replaced by new Young Turks, companies get into a routine. The vision is no longer there. Only individual money- making becomes the goal. Arrogance and shortcut management ideas arise. No one is pro-profit. Everyone is pro-me. The company dies.

> **Mr. Fat Cat Runs This Company**

If the company retains the 'vision,' and if all of the employees are sharing in the success of the company, the sky is the limit so far as rewards for both management and workers are concerned. It is this type of company that can easily establish an atmosphere of cooperation and singleness of purpose which gets the maximum effort from employees. That maximum effort is not forced out of the workers. They give their best thinking, go the extra mile, and go home satisfied that they did their best because they wanted to. As Dale Carnegie taught early in the 20th century: "The only way to get people to do what you want is to make them *want* to do it."

Most companies don't have 'jillions' of dollars on hand. Less than 20% of start-up companies exist after five years. Competition, new technology, economical disasters and even accidents may put a company out of business. For example, how many motels and restaurants, auto repair shops and other highway businesses were forced out after the Interstate System bypassed them?

So 'making it' in business is not easy. Employees are the key to success. Disgruntled employees become inefficient workers and that, in turn, leads to poor morale and discouraged management and ownership. Understanding the mission of the company you work for is important. Management should ensure that you and all other employees understand the company's goals, its history and its products. If you do not have  the 'big picture' of your company, you may just come to work each day, doing as little as you can get by with and waiting for Friday when you are 'free' again. The company may be glad you are working for them and perhaps they expect no more than you give. Some companies are able to exist with that attitude.

So, you may be in the group which does as little as possible, just enough to 'get by,' or you may be an employee who feels a part of the team that is making a success of the business.

Psychology

Which is best—begrudgingly going to work each day of your life, not liking it, counting the minutes until you can clock out; or working at a job where the day seems to pass quickly—a job where you try to just 'look' busy, bored to tears, taking as many breaks as possible, sorting your tools, or a job where you are thrilled with the progress of the company and its products and you find your own knowledge and skills increasing; management noticing and commending you, and you gain a feeling of satisfaction because you know that you have contributed to a worthwhile cause?

Which is best? Doing the least work you can get by with, or working hard, earning your pay, knowing that you did 110% of what is expected?

Which is best? Making a repair in the home, making out the bill, collecting from the customer and walking out, or making the repair, explaining the job, establishing a friendly and professional relationship with the customer, suggesting the purchase of an exciting new product your company sells, making a good impression on the neighbor who happens to be visiting your customer at the time, and knowing that you have solidified one and possibly two families as customers, then efficiently moving to the next job, conserving minutes whenever possible?

Even if your job is the ticket-taker, lifeguard, or delivery person, you can make a difference. You can let the customers know that you enjoy your job. You can smile. You can offer to help. You can make the customer feel better for having dealt with you. People like to deal with workers who appear to enjoy their jobs and who show their concern for others. They come back to do business with cheerful people who try their best to make customers happy. A company with this type of employee usually does well.

Pro-Profit

Pro-profit doesn't mean just selling something at the price marked on it. Anyone can do that. Pro-profit means convincing a hesitant customer to buy the product. It means suggesting to other customers, your friends and relatives that they will benefit by buying the product. It means trying to sell the product while you are on the phone, out on an installation, delivery or service call.

Pro-Profit

Pro-profit means looking for ways to conserve your work time. If you can complete one additional service procedure, service call, installation, phone call or delivery each day, the difference in your productivity is enormous. The difference between completing four jobs and five is not simply a 25% increase in income. It is a larger increase in gross profits for the company. The reason for this is that when you ordinarily were able to complete four jobs, you had a certain amount of fixed costs. Those costs, such as rent, insurance, advertising, your wages and so forth are the same whether you make the four completions or more than four. Thus, adding one additional job, since the fixed costs are already covered, means a larger profit.

Work On Commission

One of the best educational experiences I had in my career as a technician came when I tried working for dealers on a commission basis. Prior to that, when working for myself, or for others for an hourly wage, my philosophy of work was different.

In my own business, or while working hourly, or during my military avionics technician days, there was always more work to do than hours to do it in, or so it seemed. Service work, especially troubleshooting, was a routine where you searched for service literature; got your soldering iron hot and located tools; then you sat at the bench and proceeded to find the suspected bad part. Perhaps you narrowed the problem down to one or two parts and found that you had to order one or another. You replaced the bad part if you were lucky and you buttoned up the unit, perhaps did a cleanup on it, made out the invoice and put the unit on a 'run' shelf and completed any details, such as calling the customer or ordering parts to replace any used on the repair.

The difference, when you are working on commission, is this:

1. You hurry to find service literature, unless you are familiar with the repair problem, in which case you can save time by not having to locate literature.

2. You hurry to get your soldering iron hot, to locate your tools, to make sure your equipment is in good repair and to locate parts.

3. You hurry to order parts, or you may work in a larger shop where you hurry to give the parts ordering person instructions on ordering the part you need--the exact part.

4. You hurry to phone the customer, if that is part of your duties.

5. You hurry up lunch or break time so that you can try to complete an additional repair before the too-short day comes to an end.

6. If you make service calls, you take the shortest route to the job. You make sure the address is correct and that the customer has given explicit instructions on how to find the home or business.

Chapter 3. Pro-Profit Employees

7. You attempt to do every job completely because if there is a recall, you will not get paid for doing that job.

8. If you have the authority, you are careful in accepting products for repair. If the product is so old it is practically guaranteed to have multiple troubles and is not likely to work as it did when new, and the customer, because of the product's age, doesn't want to spend the required repair costs, you try your best NOT to accept that type of repair job.

9. You will agree with management that every repair job should collect a minimum inspection fee up front. Thus, if the customer decides they can't afford to pick up the repair after you have done all of the work, you, at least, will make something for your work.

10. If you work by the hour, you may have an opposite attitude: You are willing to accept any repair job. After all, you want to remain busy or you might get laid off. You know the value of keeping old time customers happy, thus you may be willing to 'try' to fix some electrical unit for which you have no literature, parts, or more than a slim chance of repairing.

11. If you work on commission, you will do your best to make sure vehicle problems don't slow you down. You will try to make sure your truck, tools and replacement parts are in top shape, and you will even try to get needed maintenance done on Saturdays or at other times when not needed by you.

You will not allow your service vehicle to get 'messy.' Each time you jump into the vehicle, you will pick up trash and put loose tools or equipment back in their assigned locations. You will make sure that it is clean and that everything is in its place so that you are working at maximum efficiency. If you work by the hour you may not be too concerned with these things. What does it matter if you have to spend a few more minutes trying to find your hammer? So, you used the last 2-amp fuse a couple days ago and now there are none. Your simple repair now involved driving to a competitor's business to buy that simple, inexpensive but necessary part.

Okay, so, you only lost a couple bucks by buying the fuse retail. It only took you 15 minutes to go get it. Too bad you had to wait at the railroad crossing for 5 minutes while that slow freight train blocked your street. When you work on commission, you agonize while wasting time in traffic.

There are other things a pro-profit worker does. Things that ordinary workers don't do:

1. The paper rolls are down to nearly nothing in the bathroom. You replace them yourself in order that other workers won't be slowed down.

Pro-Profit Things You Can Do

2. You have a minute or two while waiting on a coworker to get his gear. You have just enough time to sharpen that screwdriver on the grinder.

3. You take the product operator manual home with you so that you can browse through it during TV commercials or timeouts, rather than spending the time during working hours.

4. You try to attend service technical seminars in every case where they can improve your abilities. You keep in contact with other workers in your field so that you have help you can call on when difficult repairs or situations come up.

5. You enthusiastically point out the services your company provides to the community.

6. You brag about other employees or company personnel when it is deserved.

7. If you are a union member at your work, you take part in as many decisions as possible, both for the good of the workers and to be fair with the company that pays you. If you feel the union is unfair, and you can't make it fairer, then you should consider working elsewhere. Unions can become bad, but only if the workers decide to let someone else make decisions. Unions are not any worse than management. If they are bad, it is because people let them degenerate. You have rights in this world, but you also have responsibilities in order to keep those rights. Unions are simply two or more employees joining together to attempt to speak with one voice in negotiations with management. Companies that treat their employees with respect and which realize their profits depend on their employees often have no unions. Those companies try to give the employees a voice and to create a sense of teamwork, rather than confrontation.

8. Pro-profit employees help fellow workers. They don't take satisfaction in seeing a coworker fail, or get reprimanded, or make a mistake. Pro-profit employees try to

15

help their fellow workers get each job done in the shortest time, at the least expense.

9. Pro-profit workers are always on the lookout for opportunities to increase the company's income. They make suggestions to customers for additional repair services. They are on the lookout for things which might make the business more efficient. A used service van goes on sale down the street and you realize it is a bargain, perhaps $500 less than comparable vans go for. Saving the company $500 might allow the company to reward you.

10. Pro-profit employees keep on the lookout for good people who may need a job at the company. To save the company recruitment dollars and time may lead to savings.

11. Pro-profit employees keep on the lookout for products or services that the competition may have started offering, and which your company should also provide.

12. Pro-profit employees try to keep up with the latest computer or networking advances in order to keep the company at top efficiency. The boss can't know everything there is to know. But the combined brain power of all the employees can provide an awareness that keeps the company ahead of the competition.

Anti Pro-Profit Employees

Smoking is an addiction. Sure, everyone wants to quit, especially now that tobacco is taxed so much. But, really, the social pressure to smoke is too much. If a person has no other good points, at least he or she can appear 'cool' by showing 'style' in how they manipulate a cigarette. It is nearly impossible to appear 'cool' when sitting at the bar with a beer in one hand, without properly lighting, waving, pointing, dangling, dousing or flicking a cigarette in the other hand.

People who smoke often do so because they do not know what else to do with themselves or their hands. People who smoke, but are not allowed to smoke in the workplace, will take a lot of time finding ways to take breaks and smoke.

I have noticed over the years that smokers seem to have accidents right after they light up. It may not be the nicotine that affects their brains. It may be simply that the mind is so overwhelmed with the desire to experience that 'lift' the

smoke temporarily gives, that attention and concentration suffer.

Also, smokers, if allowed to take a smoke break anytime they want (such as when working independently), will spend a lot of time smoking. Smokers also seem to drink more than non-smokers. The combination often results in lost work days due to health problems. Of course, if you are working on commission, only you lose. But most people work by the hour. Everyone loses.

Alcohol, drugs, tobacco, inability to do anything without a soft drink in hand, inability to concentrate due to an obsession with any of these, or with food, hampers your ability to accomplish tasks. You may well be bored with the job. That leads to snacking, smoking or wasting time. It may be that your job does not fit you well. Of course most of us don't have the luxury of choosing our jobs. Most times, we simply need a job and the 'ideal' one is not available at the moment. So, we take what we can get. A job may not be right for you. Some of us will continue in such a job, simply because we need to survive. We need money, and this job is better than none.

If you are in a dead-end job; if you are in a job that does not compensate you adequately, based on your value; if you cannot advance; if you cannot learn something new each day; if fellow workers are bad influences; if the boss is unfair; you should consider changing jobs as soon as a suitable opening elsewhere is available. If you are in the wrong job, you will have a hard time gaining the mindset of the pro-profit worker. You aren't doing your best for the company. The company may realize you are a bad fit and thus not pay you well, or may look over you at others for advancements.

Big Things

There are big things that can hurt a company. You can have your attention drawn to the person standing on the sidewalk and not see the stopped truck in front of you. You could cause the company a big lawsuit due to your negligence. You could cheat someone, causing a legal problem and penalties. You could embarrass the company by getting into serious trouble while on the job. You could write something that is libelous. As your employer, your

company could be made to pay damages. You could cheat your fellow workers, perhaps by trying to get them to work overtime for free. This could cause your company to be fined by wage-hour agencies. You could be negligent at a customer location and cause personal or property damage for which your company or its insurance firm must pay. You could discriminate against a customer or fellow worker and cause a legal action. You have less chance of falling into one of these traps if you are a fair and decent human being with respect for others.

You can also make sure your written work excels. If you have sloppy handwriting, or if you don't care about correcting misspelled words when you work at the computer, this will come home to haunt you.

You can't really do much to improve your handwriting. After your grade school years, it seems to remain the same the rest of your life. Since you can't improve it much, you must pay more attention to it. We can all slow down when writing. If a doctor scribbled the prescription down so poorly that the patient ended up taking poison and died, it wasn't cost-effective for the doctor to save the time by scribbling. Even poor writers can concentrate on forming letters which anyone can read. You waste time when the service van ends up going miles out of his way because you slopped over an important address ingredient, like putting down what looks like an "E" for east, when you really meant "W" for west.

Some people can type okay, but can't write longhand well enough to be understood. With the world now universally using keyboards and pads, that person can do most of his or her writing using them, thus solving part of the problem.

Technical people often are poor writers of letters or official documents. Technical writing is some students' worst part of a scientific or engineering class. But, it is part of your job. Rather than shying away from writing, wel-

Type if you can't Write

come the opportunity to learn to write better by practicing. I have known very smart technicians and managers who in their adult years print everything. Some learn to print well, knowing their handwriting is lousy. I also have known smart computer technicians who use only two fingers to type. If you simply can't force yourself to learn which keys should be hit with which finger, then use the 'hunt and peck method.' You can get fast at typing with only two fingers. Using two fingers may allow you to

communicate many times better than trying to get people to decipher your handwriting.

You may shy away from writing to a customer or a product maker, distributor or government agency because you aren't sure you write well. Or you may shy away because you don't spell well. You may have a technical solution to a problem, but keep it to yourself for fear that you might expose your poor grammar. Not communicating is not pro-profit. There are things, every day, that need to be written down. There are written communications which need to be made in order for your company, or your profession, or the country, to progress. If everything was already said, written and established, we would not need our brains for much. We would be more like sheep, reacting to events, unable to protect ourselves or to improve life.

The way to become Pro-Profit by improving your written communications is simple. Just do more of it. Try to make every note, invoice, requisition, Internet e-mail, party invitation, caption on a photo, or even a joke you are passing on, a work of art. If you are filling out an application form, make sure every letter is 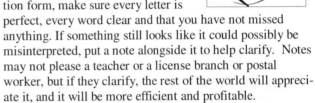 perfect, every word clear and that you have not missed anything. If something still looks like it could possibly be misinterpreted, put a note alongside it to help clarify. Notes may not please a teacher or a license branch or postal worker, but if they clarify, the rest of the world will appreciate it, and it will be more efficient and profitable.

Don't rely on memory. AVO is what you want to remember. It means Avoid Verbal Orders. General Motors has used AVO pads for decades, very successfully. Everyone in that company is encouraged to use AVOs. We all think we can remember well, but when our thoughts are put down on paper, we have two images—verbal and visual. The persons getting our communication have the exact wording you gave them. A written note is always asking for action. A verbal note gets forgotten and misinterpreted. Pro-Profit workers use written communications at every opportunity.

There are other ways to be a Pro-Profit person. If you acquire a Pro-Profit attitude at your work, you will become an efficiency expert. You will get in a habit of working towards your highest efficiency and that of your fellow workers and that of your company. The reward is one of the best of life: knowing you have done your best to improve yourself and the lives of others. To leave work at the end of the day or the week with a feeling that you really contributed, that you learned new methods and new ways to be more productive then begins to affect the way you live at home and at your social activities. You become a better scoutmaster, choir member, fishing partner, neighbor, town council member, Jaycee, soldier, manager and human being.

Chapter Quiz:

1. **The time at work seems to pass more quickly when you concentrate on the activities you are planning after quitting time than it does when you are deeply involved in a work project.**

    a.   True
    b.   False

2. **If the company doesn't seem to be paying you as much as you feel you are worth, there is no reason to devote your best efforts to your work.**

    a.   True
    b.   False

3. **Since a public library is usually a tax-supported service, the idea of being a pro-profit employee does not apply to that type of employee.**

    a.   True
    b.   False

4. **You work for a mass merchandiser. After parking in the large parking lot, you could take one of the shopping carts back into the building and put it in the cart pick-up area, but you don't. This is not an example of a pro-profit employee.**

    a.   True
    b.   False

5. **A good reason to do no more than absolutely required at your work is:**

    a.   management gets paid much more in proportion than the workers, so why help them out?
    b.   coworkers think you are stupid if you do little things, unrequired, which conserve time or resources.
    c.   unions discourage such helpful actions.
    d.   you are quite ill, but the boss wants you at work anyway if you can come in and he/she specifies that he/she doesn't want you to do any more than the minimum.

6. **Which of the following might be considered pro-profit actions?**

    a.   Making sure service literature or product catalogs are filed in proper order
    b.   Smoking in the rest room, rather than at your bench
    c.   Taking a bundle of ball point pens (which advertise the company's products) home for personal use
    d.   Stopping work in plenty of time to be prepared to clock out right at quitting time

7. **Which of the following would be considered pro-profit activities?**

    a.   Building relationships with fellow workers by discussing last evening's bowling
    b.   Submitting an employee suggestion for improving efficiency or safety
    c.   Leading your coworkers in asking management to relieve your department workers of clean-up details
    d.   Calling in sick because you can't be at your best with a hangover

8. **If you have poor handwriting, you should:**

    a.   always type your messages.
    b.   speed up in order to hurry through the unpleasant task of writing longhand.
    c.   slow down and try to improve the legibility.
    d.   ask others to do your writing.

9. **"AVO" stands for:**

    a.   Always Voice your Opinion.
    b.   Avoid Verbal Orders.
    c.   Anti Verifiable Operation.
    d.   A Very Obstinate person.

10. **If you aren't a good writer, because of bad grammar, spelling or punctuation, you should:**

    a.   avoid writing any more than necessary.
    b.   ask someone else to write it for you.
    c.   just tell people what you want, thus avoiding the embarrassment of not knowing the English language.
    d.   write as often as possible.

Answers:

1-b, 2-b, 3-b, 4-a, 5-d, 6-a, 7-b, 8-c, 9-b, 10-d

Chapter 4

Promoting Simplicity

Joe Sanfilippo, CET

Joseph Sanfilippo was born in Milwaukee, Wisconsin to a working class Italian family. He studied electronics at Custer High School , then took a job at a local consumer electronics service center sweeping floors and replacing picture tubes. After graduation from United Technical Institute in Milwaukee, he located a fabulous and interesting engineering lab job at Astronautics Corporation, an avionics development and production facility located downtown. He quit this job nine months later due to the daily drive on the freeway and returned to the service center until 1979 when he decided to leave the big city for the simple life of a rural area in northern Wisconsin. There, he started a family, opened Northern Technical Services and became involved in ETA. Servicing antennas, television and VCR's was his main work. In 2002 Joe eliminated the repair work, in part due to eroding profits, to concentrate on antenna and satellite service. He is grateful to be the antenna guy in a small town where things are simple, with plenty of fresh air. It's a good place to raise a family and there's enough income to get by.

Simplicity

Everything should be made as simple as possible, but not simpler.

In any occupation, as well as day-to-day living, keeping things simple is a key element to success. In our industry simplicity is a great challenge, considering the complexity of the equipment, systems, and people we work with. Simplifying something complex can be accomplished. I have found the most perplexing challenge is keeping up with changes. It would be easy if changes occurred yearly, but changes occur daily. I have found it necessary to focus on those changes that affect my business and let the rest go.

First, let's look at exactly what 'simplicity' means. According to the dictionary, the definition is: *The condition of being simple or free from difficulty.* What is the definition of 'simple?' Simple: *Not complicated or complex; easy to understand or do; plain.* We have no choice on 'not complicated or complex' as the high tech stuff around us *IS* complex and complicated. We can, however, make it easy to understand. This is a challenging task we as Customer Service Specialists have, nevertheless, keeping things easy to understand for your client is a must. Simplicity offers clarity, easiness, trustfulness and comfort, to name a few. Keeping things simple keeps customers happy and coming back.

Where Do We Start?

Where do we start? A good starting point is with ourselves. Do we make things simple in our own life, or are we constantly juggling so much stuff that we do not take time for ourselves? If we do not make time for exercise, relaxation, meditation and self-awareness, we have removed some critical elements that are essential to our well-

being. This keeps us out of balance, and we can become difficult to those around us. Try this simple task: Every day, take a 15 to 30 minute brisk walk. During the walk, mentally dwell on something in your life that needs finishing. Frequently, solutions find their way into your consciousness. With a solution at hand, things will appear simpler. Another daily activity to do is to give someone you care about a big hug and tell him/her how you feel about him/her. This can be very rewarding and help to maintain personal balance.

Reduce Clutter

Now, let's try making things simple for us at our workplace. Is our office cluttered? When I notice my office getting cluttered, I schedule some time to straighten it out. A lot of the "stuff" is magazines, tech notes and junk mail— stuff too interesting to throw out, but I probably will never make the time to look at it all. There is always new material arriving. Concentrate on the new. If you really believe some of the old stuff is too important to throw out, file it. If you do not make the time to do that, at least put it in a bag and set it in some dark closet. Leaving it on your desk makes your desk look too overwhelming, which can lead to anxiety, which leads to poor decision making, which inevitably complicates things. A neat desk is a sign of efficiency, which leads to good decision making and also simplifies things.

A simple tool that helps me stay organized is a pen and note pad. I jot down the duties and contacts that need to be tended to and organize them by level of importance. Once they are written down, I can remove them from my memory. Suspending things in memory uses energy. With less on my mind, I can put that spare energy to better use. The only thing I need to remember to do is look at the note pad. Using this method, I manage to get more done and forget about less. We all know that feeling when we realize something important did not get done. Whether it is a client we needed to contact or an order that needed to be filled, now we have to do it tomorrow. Tomorrow is now a little more complicated than it needed to be. Simple "post-it" notes can be a valuable tool.

For scheduling, a wall calendar is very handy. At a glance you can tell which days have openings for another appointment. Daily planners, whether they are the ingeniously laid-out notebook type or one of the rapidly appearing electronic types, are a must for the busy entrepreneur.

With ourselves in order now, we can focus on keeping things simple for our clients and coworkers. One essential item here is honesty. Nothing complicates things more than lying. Lies lead to more lies, becoming a self-perpetuating mess. It is difficult to keep track of untruths. This leads to anxiety. Anxiety leads to complications. We want to simplify, not complicate. Almost always, the truth is best. The truth does not change. There is less to keep track of with the truth. If you find yourself in a job that promotes lying, *go find a new job*. Things will not be simple there, and your well-being and integrity are at stake.

Develop A Routine

Develop routines and stick with them. Routines keep things simple by reducing irregularities. When I had a service shop and antenna business, I wasted a lot of time switching from in-shop repairs to antennas and back again. To reduce this inefficiency, I set up a routine where Monday, Wednesday and Friday were repair days. Tuesday and Thursday were set aside for antenna work. This routine made scheduling easier. I did my best to keep this routine and was flexible enough to vary from it when needed.

Then there is the guy who needs you to do something right away and tries to get you to break your routine, thus creating some inefficiency. It is nice

to be the good guy and help out, but it usually involves extra expense. You can absorb that expense or pass it on to the client. From a business perspective, you need to pass it on. My routine phrase at this point is, "I am scheduled with appointments for the next number of days. I can do it for you then, or we can do it sooner if we go after hours, which will involve higher service fees." Most people wait, and the ones who still insist make it worth your while by adding to your income.

Take advantage of technology. There is an abundance of bookkeeping and office management software that will make organizing your day-to-day elements easy and quick. Most come complete with inventory management sections. When tied to your job invoices, it automatically manages your supplies, alerting you when you're running low.

Although this software can be a little complicated, once you figure it out and put it to work, it will simplify your business by freeing up your time. There are also some terrific phone systems that help greatly at the office by allowing each employee to have their own message box and extension. It is easy for in-office and out-of-office calls to get routed to the correct person without interrupting others.

The Difficult Part

Now for the difficult part: helping people understand the electronic equipment and gadgets they have. This could be simple if there were only a few ways to do things. But with the multitude of manufacturers and models, we often scratch our own head trying to figure out how to operate the

stuff. A common call we receive is, "I can't get channel 36. My old TV got it fine, so I know it is not the antenna." I tell them new TV's are set up for cable, and you have to switch it to antenna in order to get UHF. "How do I do that?" The answer to that depends on the make and model they have. I do my best to help them on the phone, but often fail. I then recommend that they look at the owner's manual in 'setting up the channels' section or call the place they bought it from to ask for help. A short time later they call back, "I can't figure this out, and the guy at the discount store didn't know what I was talking about." It is time to sell myself. I tell them you need to hire a technician to visit and help you. Most people appreciate the help and are happy to pay for it.

A Better Way

There is a simpler way to deal with this scenario. The frequency of channel 36 is similar to cable channel 87. When I get that call I say, "try 87." They try 87 and a picture appears. Problem solved. Use 87 in place of 36.

The universal remote was developed to simplify things by having only one remote instead of two or more. For many folks this is great, but some people just don't get it and often become confused.

Chapter 4. Promoting Simplicity

I recommend they use a separate remote for each device they have. It is easier for them to understand.

I got a frantic call from some people trying to make it easy for their 80-year-old mother to watch TV. She was hard-of-hearing and could not see well. She was frequently pushing the wrong buttons on the universal remote and  losing control of her TV watching. Then, she would call her children to come over and straighten it out. The kids had a great idea. They bought mom a voice-controlled remote and called me to help them program it. The instruction manual was bigger and more complex than the operating manual of the Cessna 172 airplane I fly. It would take all morning to program this remote. Keeping in mind the whole point here was to make it easy for mom to watch TV, I came up with a simple solution. She mainly watched the satellite dish, which came in on channel 3 and sometimes watched channel 12 for local news. I programmed the TV channel list to only stop on 3 and 12. I recommended she operate the TV by the buttons on the set. This was not hard because she sat two feet from it. I put a piece of tape over the menu button so she would not accidentally press it.   Then I programmed the Satellite receiver favorite list to stop only on the channels she watched and made sure the remote did not operate the TV. Problem solved. They sent back the voice remote and got their $200 bucks back, and Mom was able to watch TV without bothering the kids.

Do not overcomplicate things by looking beyond their immediate needs. In the above case, the immediate need was making it simple for Mom to watch TV, not to operate a complicated remote. Use simple words whenever possible. Make  certain your clients understand what you just explained before moving on. I actually develop little quizzes and have the clients work them out, reassuring themselves that they understand.

Using simplicity frees up your time, allowing you to be your best. You will have time for yourself and time for others, time to relax and time to move forward. Keeping things simple is not always simple, but in the end, it is the best.

I leave you with a simple Swedish Proverb:

**Fear Less, Hope More;
Eat Less, Chew More;
Whine Less, Breathe More;
Talk Less, Say More;
Hate Less, Love More;
And All Good Things Are Yours.**

Chapter 4. Promoting Simplicity

Chapter Quiz:

1. You keep things simple to free up your time.

   a. True
   b. False

2. Using lies keeps client relations simple.

   a. True
   b. False

3. You cannot make complicated things simple.

   a. True
   b. False

4. Asking clients to demonstrate what they understand is not a good policy.

   a. True
   b. False

5. Going for a walk is a waste of your precious time.

   a. True
   b. False

6. A note pad with a pencil is a great tool for organizing your thoughts.

   a. True
   b. False

7. Universal remote controls are simple for everyone to understand.

   a. True
   b. False

8. Developing routines is a bad idea because you can get stuck in them.

   a. True
   b. False

9. Using a sophisticated phone message system can simplify office communications.

   a. True
   b. False

10. Most office/service center software is too costly to be effective.

    a. True
    b. False

Answers:

1-a, 2-b, 3-b, 4-b, 5-b, 6-a, 7-b, 8-b, 9-a, 10-b

Chapter 5

Business Leadership

Edward Bell, MBA, AAMS, CMFC, CSS is from Columbus, Ohio and graduated with honors in a course, "Writing for Children," from the Institute of Children's Literature. He has served as Contributing Editor of the Autograph Times. He won the 1999 award for best screenplay from the PEN American Center in New York and garnered the runner-up award for non-fiction writing in 2000. He earned his Masters in Business Administration from Hamilton University, and his Accredited Asset Management Specialist and Chartered Mutual Fund Counselor from the College for Financial Planning. He earned the ETA Certified Customer Service Specialist in August 2001.

Edward Bell, MBA, AAMS, CMFC, CSS

Vic Braden, the well-known tennis coach and television personality, often talks about a conversation he once overheard between a tournament promoter and the tennis champion, Jimmy Connors. The tournament director was trying to interest Connors in his tournament, and Connors wanted to know about the prize money.

"Well," said the tournament director, "If you come in first, you win $30,000. And if you come in second…" He never got a chance to finish the sentence. Said Connors, "I'm not interested in second place."

Indeed he was not. The fact is, if you talk to highly successful people in any field, from tennis to customer service, you will find substantially the same attitude: no special interest in second place. In fact, of all the attributes that characterize successful people in general and highly successful customer service specialists in particular, none is more universal than the simple *desire* to succeed. The one thing nearly all successful customer service specialists have in common is that they are not satisfied with the success they currently enjoy.

I am not suggesting here that, to be successful in customer service, the only thing you really need is a great *desire* to be successful – hardly. Customer service, after all, is a complex and demanding field. If you lack the intelligence, the judgment, the technical skills, and the discipline this complexity requires, you are not going to get very far, regardless of how ambitious you are. A lot of tennis players, remember, have as much competitive desire as Jimmy Connors had, but not too many of them could hit the backhand as hard.

On the other hand, what is lacking in most customer service specialists is not technical skills or intelligence, but the ability – and, in many cases, the desire – to direct these technical skills to a predetermined goal. What is lacking is a true commitment to success – to become a leader.

Let me point out here that, by "commitment to success – to become a leader," I do not mean that you need to be *compulsively* driven to succeed – driven to the point that you ignore everything else in your life, in particular, your family.

Regardless of your capabilities, however, you cannot take success for granted. You have to *want* it and you have  to go after it. You not only have to want success, you have to give your bosses and your customers what *they* want. "The mistake so many people make is that they believe that all people have the same requirements, and they therefore give them all the same service. It's important to determine what various people want, and then customize your service to satisfy each of them. Those who do that have a leg up on the ladder of success toward true business leadership.

You need what I like to think of as a "healthy" appetite for success (however you choose to define it) as an important goal for yourself, and you have to organize a good portion of your life toward that goal.

Nearly all successful customer service specialists are success-oriented in one-way or another. They have their own success goals. In some cases, it may be to become the best specialist. In other cases, it might be to become the department manager. Whatever it is, they are *aiming* for something.

I am not maintaining that the only way to become a successful leader is to work 80 hours a week. I recognize the crucial difference between being committed to success and being a workaholic: "someone who has nothing else in their life *except* work." Even so, it is important to recognize that success is not a game you can play now and then when the spirit moves you. You have to play the game on a constant basis, which is to say that the part of the mind concerned with success should be "on call" at all times.

When you take a vacation, for instance, I would be the last person to tell you to bring work with you. Then again, if, while you are on vacation, you meet someone who might be helpful to your career, you would be foolish not to establish contact and make arrangements to meet when the two of you are back at work.

Here is what I consider a valuable leadership tip. Perhaps you have an active leisure life. You travel. You play golf. You read. Whatever you are doing, always carry a small notebook and pen or mini-tape recorder with you. That way, if an idea should occur to you, you can write it down or record it immediately. You never know when you might wake up in the middle of the night with an idea or a solution to a problem you have been trying to solve all day.

These are little things, I grant you, and you may think of them as inconsequential. The point, though, is that success is often nothing more than the combined effect of a number of "inconsequentials."

Think about it a minute. Think about how much more productive you could be if you could train your mind to function 24 hours a day—not to be consumed with work 24 hours a day—but to be receptive at any time during the day to any idea or person who could be helpful in your career or to your customer.

Success Patterns in Customer Service

Over the past several years, there have been a number of studies on the traits that make people successful. No study that I know of has been done specifically on customer service specialists, but I have developed my own ideas on the subject. As far as I have been able to tell, most people at the top of the customer service profession share the following traits:

They view getting ahead as a goal unto itself.
They work very hard.
They are not afraid to put themselves on the line.
They have a great deal of intellectual curiosity.
They like what they do and are guided by "internal" goals of excellence.

I am not saying that these are the *only* traits successful specialists share, but these are the traits that have continually emerged in the conversations I have had with other customer service representatives.

Successful Leadership Ingredients

The qualities I have just mentioned are hardly the only ones shared by successful customer service specialists. I have noticed, for instance, that most of the successful specialists I know are positive thinkers. You  rarely hear them complaining about their work or about the pressures they are under. Most of them have a healthy sense of humor: they take what they do seriously, but they can laugh at themselves, too. In short, while they may be single-minded about their careers, they are also well-rounded individuals who give the impression that they would be successful in any field.

There is one more quality that I should stress here, if only because it is one that in some ways transcends everything else: your ability to keep your spirit up in the face of frustrations, rejection, and outright failure. If there is anything you can say about very successful people as a group, it is that they all know what failure tastes like. Most of the successful people I am friendly with, for instance, have been fired from at least one job, and can point to any number of times in their careers when nothing seemed to be going right for them. It is significant, too, that according to a Wall Street Journal survey, a substantial percentage of Americans who had become millionaires by age 35 had also gone bankrupt before they found the financial vehicle that brought them their success.

How are these people different from most people?

Briefly, they see failure as an opportunity for learning. As one highly successful salesman I know likes to put it, "I never fail, but sometimes I simply get negative feedback."

Test Your Business Leadership Quotient

Do you *really* want to be successful?

I have tried to help you answer that question by pointing out some of the qualities that successful business people seem to share.

Below I have put together a self-test that will further help answer the question. The questions are based on statements from a variety of success articles that I keep. I do not claim this test is scientific, but taking it should give you at least some idea of how ambitious you are to be successful.

Chapter 5. Business Leadership

To take this test, gauge the degree to which each of the statements below applies to you. Answer each question on a scale of 1 to 5, with 1 indicating that the statement does not apply at all to you and 5 indicating the statement very much applies to you.

1. I truly enjoy working. _____

2. Given free time, I would rather be out socializing with people than sitting home watching television. _____

3. My first response to a problem is to try to figure out the most practical solution. _____

4. One of the things I like best about work is the challenge of it. _____

5. I believe very strongly in the work ethic. _____

6. I have a strong desire to get things done. _____

7. When there is a difficult situation, I enjoy assuming responsibility for correcting it. _____

8. I frequently come up with ideas—day and night. _____

9. I'm not satisfied with the success I already enjoy. _____

10. I rarely miss a day of work because of illness. _____

11. I enjoy vacations, but after four or five days, I look forward to getting back to work. _____

12. I can usually get along with six hours of sleep. _____

13. I'm interested in meeting people and developing contacts. _____

14. I set high standards for myself in almost everything I do. _____

15. All in all, I consider myself a lucky person. _____

16. I'm not afraid to rely on my instinct when I have to make an important decision. _____

17. I can think of very few situations in my life in which I do not have a great deal of control. _____

18. I recover from setbacks pretty quickly. I don't dwell on them. _____

19. I'm not afraid to admit when I make a big mistake. _____

20. Achieving business leadership and success is important to me. _____

HOW TO RATE YOURSELF

Score yourself as follows:

85 – 100 Very high leadership quotient: with the proper skills, you are almost certain to achieve your goals.

70 – 84 Above average: your chances of achieving your goals are very good, provided, that is, you have the talent and skills to go along with your desire.

55 – 69 Average: if you have achieved your ambition—or are about to achieve it—it will not be because of your attitude or approach.

Below 55 Below average: success, by most people's standards, is not an important goal for you.

In the Second Edition of the Certified Customer Service Specialist Examination Study Guide, Robert Ing, DSc./ CESma, wrote that the Five Primary Objectives of Customer Service are to:

1. EDUCATE. To establish a customer relationship by providing useful and practical information, problem resolution, and support.

2. INFORM. To tell customers what you have to offer and why you are offering it.

3. RELATE. To get to know your present and potential customers: their needs, experiences and concerns.

4. DELIVER. To provide products and services to your customers the way they want them, when they want them.

5. SUPPORT. To leave the customer alone, but never lonely, when it comes to your products and services.

By applying these 5 objectives while maintaining the *desire* of a champion, you will

Chapter 5. Business Leadership

become a customer service specialist who refuses to accept being second best and will possess the traits of a true business leader.

Dr. Ing went on to give us three very effective **Personal Rules for Success in Customer Service**. They are:

1) Always do the best possible job you can. This is accomplished by listening to customers, putting yourself in their position, and providing them with practical options and useful information.

2) Know everything you need to know. This means spending a few hours to read product catalogs, brochures and the owner or user manuals of the most popular products. This also means talking to the sales and technical staff in the office to get an idea of the profiles of customers you will deal with. Of course, reading material on customer service that is specific to your operation helps too.

3) Keep up-to-date. The world of technology is constantly changing, so you have to move with it or be lost in the shuffle. Dedicate at least one hour a week to reading about advancements in your company's area of technology and customer service. For the latest news, check out industry-related specialty magazines, newspapers and suppliers' literature.

Chapter Quiz:

1. **Because customer service is a complex and demanding field, it requires you to have:**

   a. intelligence.
   b. technical skills.
   c. discipline.
   d. all of the above

2. **Commitment to success means to be compulsive in your drive to succeed.**

   a. True
   b. False

3. **Nearly all successful customer service specialists are:**

   a. glad to have a job.
   b. hoping to get into a position to boss others.
   c. success-oriented.
   d. happy to know-it-all.

4. **The part of the brain concerned with success should be:**

   a. ready when it's time to work.
   b. utilized only when you face difficult decisions.
   c. calmed down after you have reached your goal.
   d. on call at all times.

5. **Which of the following is not one of Dr. Ing's Objectives of Customer Service?**

   a. Inquire
   b. Educate
   c. Inform
   d. Relate

6. **The only way to become successful in customer service, or as a business leader, is to actively work 80 hours a week at it.**

   a. True
   b. False

7. **To properly display Business Leadership you need to:**

   a. learn to boss others.
   b. have a "healthy" appetite for success.
   c. stay aloof with coworkers so they always feel you're busy.
   d. never try to learn more because you appear inadequate if you do.

8. **To be a successful customer service specialist, you should:**

   a. have a great desire to be successful.
   b. always be aiming for something.
   c. have your mind concerned with success at all times.
   d. all of the above.

9. **A Personal Rule for Success should include:**

   a. keep up-to-date.
   b. always point out coworker's mistakes to the boss, thereby making you look better.
   c. never do more than a job requires, as it will lead to less mistakes.
   d. none of the above

10. **Patterns for successful customer service workers include:**

   a. getting ahead as a goal unto itself.
   b. working just enough to get the job completed.
   c. never put yourself on the line.
   d. "curiosity killed the cat." Never ask questions.

Answers:

1-d, 2-b, 3-c, 4-d, 5-a, 6-b, 7-b, 8-d, 9-a, 10-a

Chapter 6

Your Legal Responsibilities as a Worker

Dick Glass, CETsr

Dick Glass is an author of previous ETA publications as well as more than a dozen books dealing with electronics technology and business management, published by Howard W. Sams Co, TAB Books, McGraw-Hill and ETA. He has also written hundreds of articles in trade journals and other association publications. Dick is a former Navy Avionics Technician, Industrial Electronics Computer Technician, Technical Writer, FCC Commercial License examination modernization committee chairman, inductee into the Electronics Hall of Fame and currently President of ETA-I. He has a broad background in all phases of work performed by electronics technicians. He oversees ETA's 40-plus certification programs and the training course approval system.

Let the Boss worry about legalities

So you have landed a nice job. Maybe you oversold your abilities and knowledge a little, but from what you see the first few days, you should be able to adapt and handle this new position.

You have concerns. Maybe you need to brush up on your abilities with a computer word processor. Or, you need to quickly learn the geography of your region of the state if you moved in from some other area.

I once took a job in a factory. The job was that of a CNC technician. A day or so into the job someone asked me what the company made. I knew it was an industrial company and in the pre-employment walk-through, I noticed a number of manufacturing machine tools to which the company appeared to be adapting computerized control systems.

So, when asked what the company made, I said: "Well, I believe they make computerized control equipment for drill presses." Well, a drill press does 'look' something like the computerized milling machines the company produced, along with computerized lathes and metal-bending press-brakes.

I had a lot to learn about the machine tool business. I had a lot to learn about CNC electronics. Heck, I had to learn about the company policies, schedules, and a lot of things. A very low priority with me then was concerning myself about how I or my work fit in legally. Let the company worry about that and just let me do my work.

A CSS is Legal

In order to maintain your best attitude and to be able to have a clear mind to do your best work; you need to have the peace of mind that tells you that you are not violating any laws, that you are not working for a company that is violating laws, that your coworkers are not violating laws, and that you are not engaged in immoral, unsafe, discriminatory or wasteful activities.

If you found, after a few days at the new job, that the company was in the business of robbing banks, and that you were to assist in the heists, you might well get the feeling that you had 'struck gold.' This is exactly the kind of a job you have dreamed about. The rewards could be astronomical. The teamwork should be about as good as it can get. The work would be exciting with a certain element of danger.

Most of us would be shocked if we found out that we were working for that kind of company. Most of us would get as far away as possible and we would report the activity to the authorities--even if we needed a job and needed money, very badly!

Elsewhere in this study guide you will note an author telling about another company. This company didn't rob banks. The crime seemed to be that some of the workers, including some middle management people, were engaged in illegal drug trafficking.

So, possibly this drug business would not affect you. Maybe you could just disregard the activity. It could be that upper management would find out about it soon and fire those involved. Or, law enforcement agencies might put those involved in jail. So, maybe this isn't as bad as bank robbery, and you can ignore this illegal activity, since it doesn't seem to be related to the actual business you know the firm is conducting.

Another example: You find that some of the employees are actually conducting a part-time business from their desks or workbenches within the company you work for. This clandestine business may not involve stealing products or supplies from the company or competing with the company for service or sales. Let's use the example of a supplies business like 'Bestline' or 'Amway.'

It could be that this 'side' business really isn't detrimental. If it is merely making contacts at work and the actual deliveries and sales pitches and bookwork are done after hours, that is pretty common. In fact, some people commend these efforts and respect the side-venture entrepreneur for his ambition, drive and legal efforts to make a better life for himself and his family.

But here we are talking about overstepping those boundaries. We are discussing operation of an enterprise which may well use company supplies. Its worst aspect is in the work time that is used.

 A worker is hired to devote a set amount of time to furthering the efforts of the company. To spend time working on your own pet projects, even a private business, using company tools and equipment, phone lines, postage, etc. is cheating your employer. Most companies have policies which address such activities.

So, you happen to be working in a company where you find one or more of these activities going on. Does it affect you or your job?

In most cases the answer is 'yes.' If other employees are draining the company of resources, it may be true that it doesn't affect your compensation. After all, the company seems to still be able to back up your pay check. But in the long run, over time, any activity that reduces your, or other workers' productivity, costs you. It means the company will produce less, sell less, service less, and receive less income. That is a drag on profits. It will be difficult to increase your compensation if profits are not as high as they could be, were everyone pulling in the same direction.

Individual Crime

As an employee you have numerous opportunities to cheat, steal, slack off, intimidate, oppress, bear false witness, cause accidents, waste fuel or paper or other supplies, cause fires, damage equipment, lose tools, raise the ire of customers, waste other workers' time, rally other workers to grouse about management, and so forth.

Theft is a multi-billion dollar crime in business today. If you were hired with the understanding that you would be paid $200 per day, PLUS one ream of copy paper, then it is okay to leave work with a fresh new

ream of 500 sheets of white copy paper for your printer. If you work at your home office part of the time and the company supplies you with office supplies, then that too is okay. Take all of the paper you need to get the job done for your company.

If you have an agreement to work for $200 per day total, then it is a crime to swipe a ream of paper—or anything else.

If you are in charge of changing the oil in the service van, that does not mean you are welcome to change the oil in your own vehicle, since you are in an 'oil changing mode' anyway. If that oil belongs to your employer, either pay for it or replace it. If it takes time to change your own oil, do it after work hours, at home.

Intellectual Property

If you work for a department in your company where authorship, art, software development, inventions and experiments are factors; as an employee, you have the obligation to protect the company's trade secrets. It is a crime to steal trade secrets, graphics drawings, formulas, programs, mailing lists, and other works, just as it is a crime to steal motor oil or a ream of paper. You have to live with yourself. If you are 'living in sin,' it is best to change jobs or get straight with the company. To know that you are cheating your own company brings on other negative actions, just as cheating on your wife starts you on the road to a divorce. Living on the edge of getting caught, or constantly feeling guilty does not make for a pleasant day. To worry that if you get caught your entire career may be tarnished, is something you can do without.

It is the same with unlisted crimes like having a scowl on your face when customers 'bother' you or interrupt some important task. It is the same when you respond to a customer's concern about the size of a service bill, or the lack of help you are giving them as a help-desk worker, by making smart-aleck remarks. I recall not long ago overhearing a conversation in a lawn mower shop. The customer was griping because the problem he was having with his mower had not been corrected. This, after he had paid for the original repair, and then had to return it for a follow-up repair. The son of the mower shop owner responded with: "Look! We haven't been able to stay in business for 28 years by screwing the public."

It is easy, especially in the repair business, to get

frustrated at customers who assume that if things don't work perfectly the first time, then your repair work must be shoddy. It is easy for customers to feel they are being ripped off if they paid for repair work and now things don't work, again. After all, corporate America, with its 'creative marketing' and shortcuts to good service, has pretty well conditioned the public to expect to be cheated or shortchanged.

The only way the world can advance is for each of us to do our part to do the job right. Then, get into the customer's shoes when that customer gets frustrated and has to bring things back for related, or unrelated, further work.

So, it is a crime to treat your employer's customers wrongly.

It is also a crime to leave the door open for customers to find fault. If you track mud on their carpet; scare their kids; kick their dog; scratch their TV cabinet (and not mention it and offer to repair it), or cause a customer to wait around for a half day after your promised appointment time, you are cheating your employer. You should do your work as if you owned the business. If you are just 'putting in your time,' then quit and get a job where you can excel.

Work as if it were your own business if you are a help desk technical support worker. Many companies shortchange this end of their business. They try to save money by hiring too few workers for the number of

> ## Do Your Work as if You Owned the Business!

help phone calls they are receiving. They try to use inexperienced workers who have little or no technical abilities.

You have the same choice in this company as in any other. You can quit and go to work for a decent employer who treats customers with respect, as he/she would want to be treated, or you can try to help your present company improve.

You may not be able to convince management that it is cheating the public by putting people on 'terminal hold.' You may not be able to convince the company that they need more workers to help solve the problems  people have with their products. You may not be able to convince management that many of the tech line calls would not be needed if the technical writers were required to do a better job writing the operator manuals, or if the engineers did a better job of making the product user-friendly. But you can try to do your job to the best of your ability.

That means following the 'fixes card' responses as best you can. It means trying to quickly learn all of the common problems and their solutions. It means trying to find out as much as you can from others about the products and services so that you truly can hold the title of 'tech support,' or 'help' person.

If the company is trying to skimp by, paying you only as a part-time employee in order to not pay benefits, or if the company lets you know they want you only to be there to answer the phone; but they are not particularly concerned whether you actually help the person on the other end, then you have a bad job. Quit. Get a good job.

If the company is doing its best, and all of their competitors are cheating the public, and you know it is trying, then you should be a shining light. Become the best help desk worker in the nation.

Perfect your responses. Try to speak loudly and clearly. Make sure you have all of the trouble symptoms before concluding what the problem is likely to be. If the customer has a legitimate problem with parts or literature or warranty or anything else, make sure that customer knows you are there to help and that you won't quit until the problem is resolved. You will not pass the buck on to a half dozen other people in hopes the caller will just go away. At the point where you can't help further, you will seek advice from those more expert than you. If this bothers someone, quit. You are trying to help both the company and its customers.

There may not be laws that require you to treat the customer right. On the other hand, there are 'Lemon' laws. They do require product makers to refund or replace products which break down an inordinate number of times. There are also fraud laws. If a company advertises that their product is backed up by 800 number help lines, and if their literature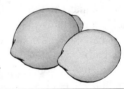

'Lemon' Laws

entices the buyer by claiming to have 24-hour a day help desk workers, and they don't, they are violating fraud laws. Just ask Apple Computer what the fine can be for willful violation of fraud laws.

When one company cheats in the above manner, their competitors are put at a disadvantage. The competitors then see no way out, so they cheat in the same way just to level the playing field. Soon the entire industry is cheating the customers. Then, the entire country sees its product makers cheating the public. Public resentment builds. People quit trusting their previously valued businesses. Commerce suffers. It is a chain reaction that is detrimental to everyone.

Chapter 6. Your Legal Responsibilities as a Worker

Only for a short time does the first cheater company have an advantage. Then no one has any advantage.

So, your job is to help turn that around. You should not be paid so little you have no incentive to do the job to the best of your abilities. You should be encouraged to learn every little detail about the company's products and services and to seek ways to explain them to customers in the most effective way. You should take classes or study books which show you how to communicate better. You should know everything that is in Dale Carnegie's *"How to Win Friends and Influence People"* book.

Realizing that the public is fed up with help desk departments which operate with half staffs, you should try your best to not only treat the customer as an honored guest, but to try to do it in the most efficient manner you can. Time is money. Chatting with a customer has some benefits, but so does convincing the customer that you must not waste time as other people may need assistance quickly too. Everyone can appreciate that, and will.

> **Become the Best Help Desk Worker in the Nation**

Help desks and technical support people aren't all working for large corporations. You are in the same position if you are the only employee in a small service business. The rules are the same. You have an advantage in a small neighborhood business. You can quickly establish a friendly and helpful rapport with the people in the community. People like to know your name. They like to know you are human. Other chapters in this book tell you some of the ways to establish outstanding relations with customers. If you have never had the boss come to you with a letter from a customer who really appreciated your fine service, or who commended you because of your helpful ways on the phone, then you should try to elicit some voluntary responses from customers. It will make your day. On the other hand, hearing that a customer would rather someone other than you handle their problems should put you in a down mood.

If you are the owner of a small business, you usually

have to be the legal expert, the accountant, the technician, the business manager, receptionist and help desk person, all rolled into one. That is one of the drawbacks to being in business for yourself. It is also one of the rewards. There are few jobs that are as rewarding to your soul as operating your own business and providing a needed service for the

public and your neighbors. In doing so, however, you take on some responsibilities which most people never worry about.

You need to be aware that you can't violate copyright laws. Trying to confuse the public by saying things or using marks which are suspiciously similar to those of other companies who have used the intellectual property prior to your use, is a violation of law.

You need to bone up on how to handle credit checks. You need to assure that your company doesn't give out information which can illegally harm a customer's credit rating. If you make a mistake in this area, do all you can to rectify that mistake.

On the other hand, you need to hold customers accountable. Some will try to cheat you. If they do, try your best to collect the bill or resolve the problem. If you have done all you can morally and legally, take that customer to court. Some people go through life cheating everyone they can. It is your duty to recognize these people and to keep them from cheating you and your employees, and to try to alert the community that a predator is around. The

way to do this is to take the non-paying or cheating customer to small claims or a county court. Their names will be published for all to see. Most cheaters build up a record and either quit cheating, or move to another town.

There are other legal aspects to operating a business. The safety of the public and the workers is a concern for local, state and federal agencies. Insurance, taxes, licenses, town ordinances, signage, building and electrical codes, accident prevention and other rules may seem like nuisances, but they did not come about arbitrarily.

So, we are all pretty well-acquainted with personal theft, the evils of company-approved skimming of sales tax income, or of violations of wage-hour laws. But you, as an employee, should be concerned with the legal aspects of your work and that of your company.

An employer can't be watching over you every minute. That is why HR departments in larger firms go to such lengths to qualify each employee, before he or she is hired. Today, drug tests are mandatory. Personality classifying is

> **The Company Can't Watch Over You Every Minute**

performed to try to help the company put an employee in the right place, for his sake as well as for that of the company. Some companies will not hire you if another member of your family is already employed there. Some companies go to great lengths to find out if you were a cooperative worker at previous jobs you have held. The whole idea is to hire workers who can be trusted to do the work correctly, and to safeguard the company.

While you may have, as a worker, few reasons to ever deal with the legal department at your company, each worker is responsible for his own area. That may include frequent decisions which are required to avert any legal problems for the company. We have already discussed averting legal problems for yourself. Now, we take a look at problems you may cause or avert for the business itself.

Which of these events would you consider a problem for the company?

1. While driving the service van, you fall asleep at the wheel and crash into a group of pedestrians.

2. You neglect to put a lockout device on an electrical circuit you are testing. Someone thinks the reason his electricity is off is that the circuit breaker popped for an unknown reason. He turns it back on and someone gets shocked.

3. You tell a customer that some other customer has served time.

4. You burn a hole in a customer's carpet with a drill or soldering iron.

5. You find a fellow worker is very attractive. You make sexually suggestive remarks each time you get near that person.

6. You know a fellow employee is violating safety rules, but you keep your nose out of it. Then he/she gets hurt.

7. You smoke and drink excessively. However, on the company health insurance application forms, you indicate you are a non-smoker and only a casual drinker.

8. While on the job, you drive the company vehicle over to a 'friend's' house for a couple hours of romantic liaison. The spouse comes home and catches you. The police come.

9. You get aggravated at a particularly difficult coworker.

You call him a derogatory name in front of other employees.

10. You 'borrow' a company owned vehicle license tag over the weekend, since the one on your car has expired and you can't get it renewed until Monday.

11. You 'moonlight' frequently, using the company truck and tools without company knowledge.

12. After you were laid off, you began a small service business of your own and found more income than you had at the company. Still, you keep claiming unemployment compensation benefits until they run out.

13. Even though you drive a company vehicle to perform service work, you do not have a chauffeur's license.

14. You install and charge for a used part or product without informing the buyer.

15. You leave a product repair in dangerous condition, such as putting in a 10 amp in place of a frequently blown 2 amp fuse. The product causes a fire.

16. You find you can talk for 'hours' to your friends, while at work. This means other business callers find the lines busy much of the time.

17. While doing a job along a county highway, you figure most people will just drive around your vehicle anyway, so you don't put out safety warning cones, as it is a bother to do so.

18. Since you took 2 hours for lunch break, you are behind. So, realizing this will reflect on your productivity, you take shortcuts in the construction work you are supposed to be doing.

19. Doing warranty work for a chain store, you realize you could, just as easily, claim to have serviced another unit on the floor and no one will be the wiser.

20. The company advertises that they employ only certified workers. You claim to the company that you are certified, but you know that you have no valid credentials.

21. The company had asked you to make a service call after hours, because a certain customer can only be home at that time. You agree. But between the time

you normally get off work and the agreed on time for the service call, you stop off, as usual, at your favorite bar for six or eight beers.

22. A customer claims the computer doesn't work much better than it did before you did the last service job on it. You find the problem is customer inflicted. You purposely erase some important files and claim the unit can't be fixed.

23. A customer asks about the products or services which a competitor offers. You tell him/her the products are outdated and their service is under investigation.

24. You injured yourself over the weekend. In fact, you can't really do your job safely, but you need the money. So you jeopardize your safety and that of coworkers by attempting to do the work anyway.

25. You, as a supervisor, know a potential employee is qualified in every way for a job opening, but you just don't like older workers. So you deny the applicant.

26. A package is lost by a delivery service. Recognizing the package likely will never be found, you claim it at ten times the actual value.

27. As a supervisor, you find an employee is a devout and vocal member of a religious sect you feel is a 'cult.' You start making life hard for that worker.

28. A friend is applying for a job at your company. During the interview and testing, you help the friend with the test questions.

29. When customers bring back a product for warranty repair or replacement, you attempt to find any reason to deny them, such as no signature on warranty cards, or illegible dates, or some other excuse.

Each of the items listed above is a problem for the company. You might be able to add a number of 'sins' to this list. The point is that no company can exist for long if the workers are not responsible for their own actions or inactions. The company will suffer if the employees do not, individually, look out for the interests of the company.

The CSS treats the customer right, as well as coworkers, the community and the employer.

Chapter 6. Your Legal Responsibilities as a Worker

Chapter Quiz:

1. Preparing to unload the service van, you back up to a loading area. Unfortunately, you also back over another worker, who claims you were negligent. Most likely:

   a. the injured worker has no claim as he or she should have been watching out.
   b. the company will have to pay the injury claim.
   c. you, the driver of the van, will be held personally responsible for the accident.
   d. the injured worker will have health and accident insurance and that will cover the costs of the accident.

2. It is unfair for a company to refuse to hire you, just because you have a history of drug abuse.

   a. True
   b. False

3. You know some of the employees are stealing small items from the company you work for. The best thing for you to do is:

   a. ignore these activities. It is none of your concern.
   b. call the police.
   c. bring the activity to the attention of management.
   d. plead with the workers to quit stealing.

4. If the company is paying you less than comparable workers in similar businesses, it is fair to steal a few things or to take care of personal business while on duty.

   a. True
   b. False

5. Wasting time, or taking care of personal business while being paid to take care of company business, is stealing, just as if you were taking a tool or product of the company for yourself.

   a. True
   b. False

6. If you knowingly are working as an employee and the company is treating you as a contract laborer, both you and the company are violating the law.

   a. True
   b. False

7. Not offering to give the customer a receipt, with the intent of not including the income in sales for the day, is a criminal act.

   a. True
   b. False

8. Tech support is an expense for a company. If a company claims to have technical support for the products it sells, but then knowingly hires fewer help desk workers than it needs, it is shifting these costs to the purchaser of its products and is defrauding the customer.

   a. True
   b. False

9. A good way to punish a deadbeat customer who didn't pay his service bill is to:

   a. take him or her to small claims court.
   b. post the unpaid invoice in plain view for future customers to see.
   c. publish a notice naming that customer in the local newspaper.
   d. take several big guys, go back to the home and take your parts back.

10. Help desk workers should make clear to the caller that they have very limited technical knowledge, only what is printed on their 'trouble-symptom' card, and thus cannot help if the problem isn't listed.

    a. True
    b. False

Answers:

1-b, 2-b, 3-c, 4-b, 5-a, 6-a, 7-a, 8-a, 9-a, 10-b

Chapter 7

Employment Rules—Building Trust

Dick Glass, CETsr

Dick Glass is an author of previous ETA publications, as well as more than a dozen books dealing with electronics technology and business management, published by Howard W. Sams Co, TAB Books, McGraw-Hill and ETA. He has also written hundreds of articles in trade journals and other association publications. Dick is a former Navy Avionics Technician, Industrial Electronics Computer Technician, Technical Writer, FCC Commercial License examination modernization committee chairman, inductee into the Electronics Hall of Fame and currently President of ETA-I. He has a broad background in all phases of work performed by electronics technicians. He oversees ETA's 40-plus certification programs and the training course approval system.

Love 'em or Leave 'em

A CSS might be employed in just about every kind of work: Companies like Hewlett Packard, which has over 50,000 employees and has never needed a union. Or companies such as RCA (TCE) whose workers belong to the IBEW. Small companies, such as many of our ETA members have, may be what is commonly called 'Mom and Pop' operations. Or, they may be in companies where the worker is part of an operation that is spread out over the globe. In this last case, it isn't unusual for the worker to rarely, if ever, meet management in person. Some workers now work at home and many, especially in service work, spend a majority of their time away from the shop, perhaps doing field service work where self-supervision is the norm.

The goal of this chapter is to discuss the relationship that should exist between the CSS and the company. The company must establish workable rules. The company should try to build trust in its employees, and the worker should quickly build trust in the company.

Employment Rules

We all dislike a lot of rules. Humans seem to have a certain gene that eventually causes them to seek exodus from the oppressive Pharaoh's lands and find freedom. While we may work as hard as many of history's serfs or indentured people, we feel that we are free. We don't want the employer fooling with our family life, home, car, sports activities, religion or anything else but our work. But, at the same time, we know there must be some rules. For instance, we know that most jobs require our presence during established work hours. A company can't be expected to depend on you, and have you come to work when you decide you feel like it. Other rules might set safety procedures for all employees. These safety rules well might protect you from other employees' unsafe habits or notions.

As companies mature, they establish more and more rules. They do this in reaction to experiences which demand that accidents be headed off, or unprofitable actions be eliminated, or personal conflicts be reduced. Sometimes we see no sense in a rule. Some rules seem to have been made just to have another rule. Some rules seem to beg to be violated.

The idea here is that the CSS needs to do all he or she can to accept the existing company rules. If a rule can't be accepted, then some action needs to be taken to modify the rule, if the company management is open to change, or to cease being an employee of that company.

Good Rules

You should attempt to accept the rules. This isn't difficult in most cases. Clocking in, filling out time cards, keeping a neat work space, abiding by fire regulations, not parking in the company president's space, calling in if sick, dress code, co-worker respect, selecting workable vacation days, abiding by telephone usage protocol and the like are rules we can all easily understand and work with.

Bad Rules

It is the rules that seem illogical, demeaning, wasteful, discriminative or costly to you that are considered bad rules. The satellite provider, DISH Network, has a rule for its dealers which goes like this: The dealer sells and installs a dish system. After 5 months, the customer quits paying the monthly programming charges to DISH. DISH then charges back to the dealer all of the payments made to the dealer for selling the system and turning on the programming, as well as the costs the dealer incurred in doing the physical work of installing the system and running cables, downloading information and so forth. Even if the customer dies or moves away or is going through a divorce, or for any reason, the dealer is socked with ALL of the payments he received which he thought covered his costs and included a profit for making the sale. That is a *Bad Rule*. DISH seems to feel that if you don't like it, quit. They can always find another dealer who will accept the rules they have set.

It is the reverse with rules for an employee where the rule is bad. If the rule can't be accepted, or can't be modified, then the CSS should consider seeking employment elsewhere.

If you can't stomach the rules, you become a disgruntled worker. Disgruntled workers are accepted by some companies. They may figure: "Well, we know Dick doesn't like our rules and we know he is less than 100% efficient because of that, but since we pay him so little anyway, we are willing to accept less efficiency." There are plenty of jobs which are routine or in which a body is needed, but productivity and efficiency are not really required. Some of these jobs go to people who are simply glad to have ANY paying job. Some of these jobs do not require a happy worker. You have met them: workers with scowls on their face, people who act as if you are interrupting their day by asking for service, phone desk people who speak with a scowl in their voice.

What we are after is workers who deal with the public for the most part, or with fellow workers, where a decent attitude is required. Workers who deal with the public, who make service calls to homes and businesses, people who work on parts counters, people who work at the post office counter, or at the license branch — all of these people need to be happy. They need to gladly obey the rules. They need to understand the reason for the rules. Even if a rule is set to prevent pilferage at work, and you don't pilfer, you should easily understand the rule and abide by it. Even if you are only stopping by work for a minute to pick up your check or leave a message, you should understand why you should not park in the president's parking place. Even if checks aren't passed out till 4 PM on Fridays, and you really, really need yours by noon, you should recognize the reason for the company setting that policy or rule.

If you have done your best to understand the 'why' of a rule or policy, yet you know it is wrong, and you have made an effort to have it better explained, and you have thought about it and given it every benefit of your doubts, yet you still abhor it, you need to consider how to cope with it. You can try to ignore it. But some rules can't be ignored. You can let some time pass by to see if you can live with it. You can seek help from management to try to overcome your problem with the rule. Sometimes counting to 10 helps. Sometimes counting to a million leaves you still with a bad taste in your mouth for one or more rules. If you have done everything possible to accept it, and you can't, then you should seek employment at a company that is better fitted to

you. A CSS can't be grouchy all the time. You can't have a chip on your shoulder all the time. You can't just waste away your life feeling bad. You can't do world class service with an outcast feeling and heartache all of the time.

So, you should try to abide by all of the company rules and policies, for your benefit, as well as for the company's. When you find that the company is treating you with respect, that the rules are fair, that no one is being discriminated against, that the policies have been set so that not only does the company survive and even make a profit, but that you profit from the rule too, then everyone wins. This can be profitable to you in getting an advancement and more money or in getting a position change to a more fun job, or in other ways.

When you think the company employment rules are fair, you are happier in your job. If the CSS is happy with the job, he or she will expose that happiness to fellow workers and customers, and to management.

Building Trust

Either the company management, or your straw boss, or the boss' wife trusts you, or they don't. You can't just ask them to trust you. You have to earn that trust. We all think that almost everyone is trustworthy, but after you have been around a group of people for a while, you start noticing that some of them are not as worthy of that trust as others. You have heard of co-workers who are said to be capable of verbally stabbing you in the back, to gain even a small advantage. You may know of coworkers who would 'rat on you' over even a small mistake, in order to make the boss feel you are lower than them. You know of workers who keep company tools or other items that rightfully belong to the company. You know of workers who waste hours each day, whether it be on the Internet, or on the phone six times a day to the kids at home.

To build trust with the company, demonstrate that you are happy with your job and the compensation you have agreed to accept. If the company asks you to do something unethical or against your religion or your morals, don't do it. If you have an opportunity to 'borrow' a battery or a fitting or a ream of paper, or some long distance time on the phone, or a side trip in the company's vehicle, don't take advantage of it. Try to show up back at the shop before you are expected, not a half hour or so later than expected.

It is the same with fellow workers. Treat them as you

Chapter 7. Employment Rules—Building Trust

would want to be treated and show them you do not cheat or skim or waste the company's resources or take sick days when you aren't sick. You will shortly build trust. Once your coworkers recognize you have character and morals and abide by the 'Golden Rule,' they will trust you. Having the trust of your company, your fellow workers, and your customers is about the best kind of a job to have.

The bottom line is that, without a comfortable relationship with the company you work for, and without knowing that you are trusted by the company and coworkers, you will not perform at your best. You will feel you are not part of the team effort. You will feel you are wasting your life away. Both you and the company, as well as your fellow workers, will be worse off. If you don't have the feeling that you just can't wait to go in to work, then you have not achieved that level of relationship which would make your life more enjoyable and productive. The CSS strives for that perfect job environment, knowing that his/her success depends on his/her attitude.

Two books I would recommend that you find and read are: *How to Win Friends and Influence People* and *Stop Worrying and Start Living*. Both of these were written at least 50 years ago by Dale Carnegie. They are easy to read and can put you on the positive track to outstanding relations with your work and all those around you.

Chapter Quiz:

1. **Employers usually add more rules as the company matures.**

   a. True
   b. False

2. **Rules are generally made by a company in order to break the spirit of the workers.**

   a. True
   b. False

3. **Which of these rules might be considered a BAD rule?**

   a. No sexual harassment
   b. No parking in the boss' spot
   c. No pay checks till 4 PM
   d. Only one trip to the water fountain each morning

4. **Which of these rules might be considered a GOOD rule?**

   a. Keep lights off unless absolutely necessary.
   b. Keep food and drink away from your keyboard.
   c. It is mandatory that you attend a certain church.
   d. All employees must wear crew-cuts.

5. **If the company has a rule that no employee can remove products or tools from the premises because they have experienced some theft in the past, but you don't steal, then it is OK for you to take software, tools, products, etc. home if you plan to work on them a bit there.**

   a. True
   b. False

6. **If you don't like an employment rule at your company, you should:**

   a. find ways to evade the rule.
   b. seek help from fellow employees to get around it.
   c. seek ways to have the rule modified.
   d. demand that the rule be eliminated.

7. **One way to build trust with coworkers is to:**

   a. cheat if you find one or more of them cheating.
   b. show them you will report them if you suspect they might be doing something detrimental to the company.
   c. help an employee resist the temptation to cheat.
   d. secretly report all violations to management.

8. **Showing your boss a way to save time or money for the company is a good way to gain trust.**

   a. True
   b. False

9. **The company inadvertently pays you for overtime hours which you did not put in. What should you do to gain trust?**

   a. Go to the payroll department and show them the mistake.
   b. Accept the windfall.
   c. Act as if you didn't notice the mistake.
   d. Explain that you thought you had worked the overtime.

10. **A CSS should seek a job situation in which he enjoys the work and can look forward to advancement.**

    a. True
    b. False

Answers:

1-a, 2-b, 3-d, 4-b, 5-b, 6-c, 7-c, 8-a, 9-a, 10-a

Chapter 8

Company Policies

Randy Glass works as a technology consultant and Executive Director of a national nonprofit organization. He is a faculty member and Sam Walton Free Enterprise Fellow at a private junior college, where he teaches multimedia development and e-commerce; and is a veteran of the U.S. Marine Corps, where he served as an intelligence operator. Randy has also worked as a financial planner, a general manager for several companies, and as an entrepreneur. [ecommerce@Hawaii.rr.com]

Randy Glass
MBA, CST, CIW

Introduction

Company policies are rules within the company that govern how the business and employees are expected to behave. Some policies cover the processes involved in doing business, and others cover the expectations of employees.

The Rules

An example of how policies govern the business process is a typical 'refund policy.' These policies cover under what conditions returns are accepted and any time or other limitations that may be placed on where, when, and how the company will accept refunds or returns.

An example of how policies govern the expectations of employees is a typical 'sexual harassment policy.' These policies cover how employees are expected to interact with other employees within the organization, and could include what the company defines as appropriate or inappropriate behavior.

In either instance of these policies, they are implemented to protect the company and the employee from liability or from making decisions not in line with the company's goals.

Importance of policies

All policies are important. Depending on your business though, they may have more or less effect on your daily routine. Managers must be fully aware of all business policies that apply to their unit and should pay particular attention to their enforcement, while other employees are dedicated to their daily tasks and complying with policies. Managers and company officers also must comply with company policies. These daily tasks are often dependent upon what the business policies are.

Let us look at some examples of how business policies affect the daily tasks for the employees of a business. First,

an airline pilot must be constantly aware of long lists of government regulations, business policies, and working procedures. In this situation, business policies should not interfere with the safety and legal requirements of federal regulations or procedures, but should define what importance is placed on other areas than the safe operation of the aircraft. A business policy may be in effect that they are to arrive within five minutes of their designated arrival time; but at times it may not be safe to do so, and safety takes precedent. On the other hand, if a business policy is in effect that states that the customer's comfort is of greater importance than the fuel consumption, the pilot may fly at a lower altitude to avoid turbulence, but that uses more fuel and costs to the airline. The advantage to the business is that customers would be more willing to repeat the experience if it is more comfortable.

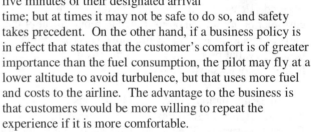

Next, let's look at a manager of a movie theatre. The manager also is subject to regulations, policies, and procedures; and is also responsible for enforcing them within his/her area of responsibility, but may pay more attention directly to the business policies during a day's work. These policies should reflect the regulations and procedures in effect. However, the manager may be exposed to more yes

or no decisions during the course of a day and must consider the policies set forth by the company. At times, even the business policies may conflict with each other in determining the outcome of a decision. If you have been to a movie theatre, you have probably noticed a sign that says 'no outside food or drink allowed' which is a normal business policy for that industry. A manager may be confronted with situations where a one-year-old child is admitted with a bottle of milk, or clinically sick person carrying water. If the business does not offer an acceptable substitute, the manager may make a decision to allow the entry of the outside drink or risk other liabilities. The manager may also choose to make it a unit policy so others may

make the decision in his/her absence. Managers in most industries often make decisions similar to these daily.

Finally, let's consider a support technician making house calls. The technician is primarily responsible for complying with the business policies. Policies may be in effect regarding proper clothing, procedures, warranties, or drug use. As a front-line employee, one that has direct contact with the customer, the technician directly represents the company. In this capacity, the only thing the customer knows about the company is normally how the technician presents him/herself. So a technician who shows up at a customer's house intoxicated would be in violation of several policies and be removed from service. But let's 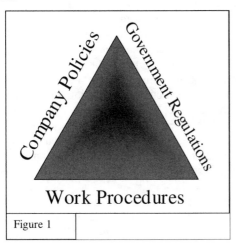 look at a good technician who represents the company properly and is aware of the company's policies toward warranties. He or she knows that the service call is covered, but the unit is old and most parts are not covered under warranty. Let's say the defective source of the problem is not covered. He can use the time allocated to inform the customer of the several options such as replacement of the parts or replacement of the entire unit. This may or may not be a policy, but properly educating the customer can lead to higher customer satisfaction.

In each situation, policies had to be considered along with government regulations and work procedures, as Figure 1 illustrates. They are also the stabilizing factor of these aspects. Compliance to these aspects is equally important in the success of the business. Complying with business policies is as important as complying with driving regulations or tax codes or safety requirements. Noncompliance destroys businesses and could cause irreparable harm.

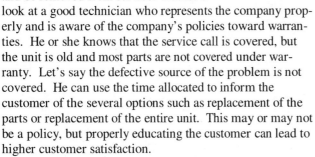

Work Procedures

| Figure 1 | |

Policy Formation

Policies are established so that each person within an organization can be informed as to what is expected of his/her performance in order for the business to run properly. Company executives, with the help of attorneys, create most policies; and great care is taken to ensure that the policies are in accordance with the organizational vision, corporate culture, and the industrial climate (see Figure 2).

Organizational Vision – The strategic goals and mission statement of the organization contribute to the vision. It answers the question, 'Why are we in business, and what are we here to do?'

Corporate Culture – The organization and the employees contribute to the culture. The type of employees, education level, and the overall environment designates the corporate culture.

Industrial Climate – Every industry has a different set of attributes that concern the organization. This includes laws, regulations, competition, and the economics of the industry.

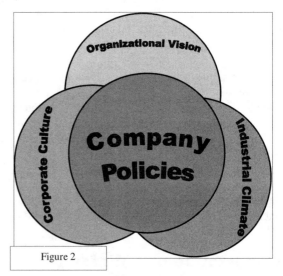

Figure 2

Policy Implementation

Policies are implemented from the top down in a normal organization (see Figure 3). The implementation is similar to a refinery that turns crude oil into several separate forms of fuel. The highest level of the organization sets *corporate business policies* that affect the organization as a whole, such as business unit relationships and accounting procedures. They are based on the corporate vision, i.e.: 'It is our policy to maintain the highest level of customer satisfaction.' At this level, the primary considerations are the mission statement and strategic goals of the organization. At this level, the vision is not implemented, so the policies must trickle down to lower layers of the structure that deal directly with the customer or product.

From the highest level, the policies are distributed and refined within the next level of the structure, the *business unit policies*. Large corporations have different business units that deal with a particular area of the business. One example, Boeing, has business units for making and selling airplanes, helicopters, missiles, and communications equipment. American Express has business units for banking, travel and financial advising. Each unit has its own industrial climate and sets its own policies. Workers in an aircraft factory may not have the same set of policies as the communications unit due to the different climates of the industries. These policies are formed using higher-level policies while considering their industrial climate.

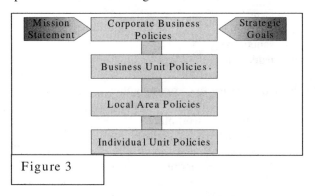

Figure 3

Each business unit may have other departments within themselves serving similar functions, but with different policies. Normally, businesses are structured by geography or by function. Let's call this a local area. Each unit would have similar departments such as customer service and human resources. However, these *local area policies* would be dependent upon the corporate culture and the industrial climate of the region or function. An office in Tokyo would have a different set of employment and ethics policies than an office in Istanbul. The area vice president, taking the geography and industry into consideration, may set these policies.

Each local area may also have individual units such as accounting and customer relations. A general manager who oversees a staff of front-line employees may set the *individual unit policies*. These policies may consist of store policies, code of conduct, or dress code. These policies combine the policies set forth from higher structures and refine them to consider the local environment and individual unit functions.

Most companies publish an employee handbook that contains the business policies that the employee is expected to comply with during his/her time of employment. Some companies also require that the employee sign a statement that the policies have been received and understood during the hiring process. It is important for the employee to understand these policies and comply with them, otherwise find another place of employment.

Policy Framework

We have seen how policies are formed and implemented, now let's look at what makes up a good company policy.

Company policies should be:

Written – Policies must be in writing so they can't be confused with verbal policies, which may or may not be condoned organizationally.

Understandable – Policies must be understandable to anyone they may apply to, including by language and disability.

Available – Policies must be available to any employee who needs to verify their contents.

Without any of the above factors, company policies have little value. Other factors to consider are the relevance of the policy to the work being performed, the legal aspects, and how it will be distributed to the employees.

Policies and Decisions

In the beginning of this chapter, we looked at three jobs where employees had to consider company policies (see Importance of Policies). Policies are made to help with a decision process, protecting the company and employee from liability. Continuously, decisions are being made within an organization. We can use the policies already established to help us make better decisions. However, with an infinite number of business situations to choose from, there are situations where policies don't exist or are not clear, and decisions must be made. Once upon a time, an area manager, whom I was subordinate to, told me, 'when faced with a decision, make a decision and we'll figure out later if it was right or wrong.' This was his policy in absence of any other company policy.

Figure 4 details a decision making process. Using an example, let's say a customer requests a refund on a product after using it for 45 days. Company policy states that there are no refunds to be issued after 30 days of purchase, but exchanges are allowed for 60 days after the purchase date. A policy exists, so the customer should be offered an exchange instead of a refund. If no policy existed, it would be a decision of whether or not to satisfy a customer request and in what manner. This leaves room for interpretation and may or may not yield the best results. This leads to another problem of inconsistency within the company. While one manager may allow a refund on the unit, another may only offer an exchange, therefore confusing the customers.

Conclusion

It is the responsibility of all employees to comply with company policies. It creates consistency within the organization and protects the company and its employees from undue liabilities. Greater risk comes to organizations that do not have well thought-out and implemented company policies.

Policies should not be overused. Too many policies can become burdensome to the employees as well as management and then may become overlooked.

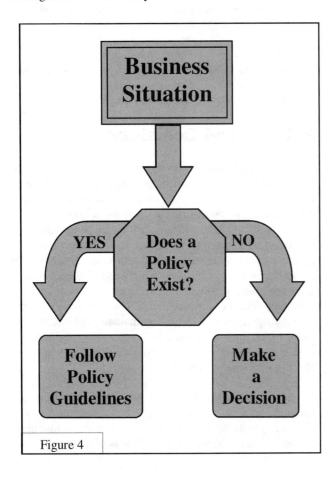

Figure 4

1. **Company policies are rules within the company that govern how the business and employees are expected to behave.**

   a. True
   b. False

2. **The most important company policies are:**

   a. those that affect you.
   b. those that are issued by the corporate office.
   c. those issued by direct supervisors.
   d. all company policies.

3. **Company policies protect the company and employees from:**

   a. fraud.
   b. liability.
   c. sanctions.
   d. bankruptcy.

4. **Noncompliance to company policies does what?**

   a. Creates a fun workplace
   b. Creates a burden on others
   c. Destroys businesses
   d. Makes the day more enjoyable

5. **Who usually creates company policies?**

   a. Corporate executives
   b. Corporate attorneys
   c. Managers
   d. All the above

6. **What factor is considered when forming company policies?**

   a. Organizational Vision
   b. Corporate Culture
   c. Industrial Climate
   d. All above factors

7. **Policies are implemented from the bottom of the organizational structure.**

   a. True
   b. False

Chapter 8. Company Policies

8. Corporate policies are based on what?

   a. Competitor's policies
   b. Mission statement
   c. Strategic goals
   d. B and C

9. Company policies should be:

   a. locked away.
   b. available.
   c. disposed of.
   d. read daily.

10. Who is responsible for complying with company policies?

   a. Everyone
   b. Employees only
   c. Officers and managers
   d. Customers

Answers:

1-a, 2-d, 3-b, 4-c, 5-d, 6-d , 7-b, 8-d, 9-b, 10-a

Chapter 9

Communication in the Workplace

After spending twenty-two years as an avionics technician in the U.S. Navy, Frank has worked for over twenty years as an instructor and administrator at Spartan School of Aeronautics, where he now teaches accounting, business communications, and statistics. He holds an MS in Adult and Occupational Education from Oklahoma State University.

Frank Pendergrass, CETsr

What is business communication?

Business communications may be described in several ways. A business will have both internal and external communications. The most important external communication a business carries on is with its customers. This aspect of communications will be discussed in Chapter 10. Both formal and informal communication networks will exist in most businesses. Communication may have several forms: written, verbal, and non-verbal. Electronic means of communication (telephone, facsimile, and computer) have become so important that they are discussed separately in Chapter 11.

Communicating is a complex task, and it takes training to perfect good communication skills. Employers frequently say that one of the skills new employees often lack is the ability to communicate effectively. Communicating requires the use of symbols (words, gestures, etc.) that do not always mean the same thing to those attempting to communicate. In our multi-cultural society, the job becomes increasingly more difficult.

Customer service relies on good communication. Employees must be able to communicate effectively to be able to understand and assist their customers. Problems may arise when customers become frustrated because of a breakdown in communication between the customer and service personnel. Employees who are well-informed are more likely to be prepared to handle a customer complaint.

Internal communications

Inside a business, workers communicate with each other, with management and with subordinates. Poor internal communications often result in poor morale within the business. Businesses have formal networks for communication. We sometimes call these networks the "chain of command" and draw organizational charts depicting lines of

communication. The larger the business, the more internal communication is necessary. Smaller businesses are more concerned with external communication, such as communicating with their customers.

For a business to operate efficiently, information must flow up and down between workers and management. Business plans, reports, directives, and requests are generated in many forms. Managers use a formal network to communicate written instructions. Meetings between managers and their employees, allow for verbal communication of business information. Workers must keep management informed about the business' operation using reports and other forms of communication. Requests for business needs and personal needs must be communicated to the employee's manager.

In a large business, information may pass through several layers of management. To be sure that meanings are accurately communicated, it may be best to rely on the written word. To reduce confusion, the communication process should use standardized forms and be thoroughly documented. A paper trail may be needed for such things as audits or reports to the stockholders.

Managers at each level should also consider departmental meetings to verbally discuss issues that concern their employees. These meetings can reinforce the management position and allow workers to have a voice in the business. A lack of communication between management and the workers is often listed as the employees' biggest concern.

Employee requests for such things as vacation and sick leave should receive feedback from above to assure the employee that his or her requests have been received. Suggestion boxes are a way to obtain ideas from the employees. When employees see that management values their opinion, they are likely to be more dedicated workers. Open lines of communication, such as management promoting an open door policy, will encourage employees to be a part of the decision-making process in the company.

In addition to formal internal communication, employees will communicate through informal networks. We have all heard of the "grapevine."

Informal networks

When workers talk to each other, they share their knowledge. It is through this informal network that employees can share their ideas, their concerns, and their past experiences. The employees gain the necessary confidence to deal with their problems and with the customers' problems. The employee who takes pride in his or her work and is proud of the company, wants the customer to be satisfied. By sharing past experiences, the older employees instill in new employees the attitude, "The customer may not always be right, but they are still the customer." Without customers, a business cannot exist.

Does the "talk around the water cooler" hurt business? It is important for workers to have someone with whom they can share their concerns. They need to know they are

being treated fairly and respected by management. This informal communication between workers can be very beneficial if channeled properly. Of course, too much time spent in idle chit-chat should be avoided. A good manager must be willing to listen to his or her workers, and encourage the exchange of productive communication among the workers. By helping all of the employees to understand their role in the business, informal communication can boost employee morale and production.

Writing as a communications medium

To write or not to write? That is the question. William Shakespeare is considered by many to be the greatest English writer of all time, but every day people puzzle over the meaning of Shakespeare's words. To be a good communicator, it is necessary to learn to write well. To write well, people must be able to express themselves with words their readers can understand.

There are times in business when things must be written. Manuals, reports and personnel files are some examples of written documents required for business. Written documents provide records for later use.

Most people consider writing safer than verbal communication. The written word is less likely to be misunderstood, and the writer can avoid that face-to-face contact. But writers must choose their words carefully. Consider making a draft before you write anything permanent. Proofread everything you write; don't just rely on spell check if you are using a computer. If a letter is very important, consider having someone else in the office read over it before you send it.

Some external business communications will need to be in writing. Today, many businesses prefer to use electronic mail. While electronic mail is faster, there are concerns about security. If addressees do not check their email frequently, your message may not reach them as quickly as you expect. Other services, such as the U.S. Postal Service, UPS, and Federal Express, provide ways to determine if your mail reached its destination. A good paper trail may help to answer a customer's question later.

Business letters should be professional and to the point. Customers form opinions about a company based partly on the communications they receive. When possible, include the addressee's name in the salutation. Plan your message so that you can be direct and clear, yet friendly. End with a complimentary close (Sincerely) and hand sign your letters. Choose your stationary so that it appears businesslike and it makes your message easy to read.

When writing to suppliers, be direct and be sure to let them know exactly what you are saying. It will save time and money if orders are clear and complete. If you have time constraints, let them be known, but don't constantly ask for special treatment when you do not need it. If it becomes necessary to return items, be courteous and remember that your letters are read by people who have feelings, too.

Verbal communications

President Ronald Reagan was known as "the Great Communicator." His verbal communication skills may have been a result of his career in radio and the movies, but he understood the importance of using the right words. Mr. Reagan was an expert at using the 'you attitude' to make his listeners feel as if he were always concerned about them. In the final paragraph of his farewell address, Mr. Reagan used the word "we" seven times when speaking of his accomplishments. The word "I" appears once.

> *"I never thought it was my style or the words I used that made a difference. It was the content. I was not a great communicator, but I communicated great things...they came from the heart of a great nation."*
>
> *Ronald Reagan*

Chapter 9. Communication in the Workplace

You have heard the saying, "Engage your brain before opening your mouth." This is excellent advice if you are talking with the boss or your fellow workers, and it is certainly true if you are talking with someone outside the business. Think about what you are going to say and about the effect it will have on your audience. Remember to use the 'you attitude.' Consider how you would feel if someone said the same thing to you.

Where and when you have conversations is also important. Remember the saying, "Praise in public, criticize in private." Think about your mental condition before you enter into a discussion. If you are angry or upset, you may let your emotions force you into saying something you will regret. It may be best to walk away from a confrontation and discuss the situation with those involved later.

I never said that!

Non-verbal communication goes hand-in-hand with verbal communication. Body language sometimes can tell a listener more about the speaker than his or her words. Good eye contact is important when talking directly with someone. And don't forget the importance of a good, firm handshake. But be careful. Some people don't want their personal space invaded! We must learn to use non-verbal communication to reinforce our words in verbal communication. Also, as listeners, we must watch for non-verbal communication to help us fully understand the message we are being sent.

When was the last time you were in a store and two salespersons were talking and didn't stop to ask if you needed help? What did you do? If you told the store manager his/her employees told you they didn't want your business, the two employees would say, "We didn't say that." But they did. Non-verbal communication can be as clear as any other form of communication. Attitude, voice inflection, and poor manners can tell someone you aren't interested in what they have to say.

Sometimes our friends or coworkers may say, "I thought you were mad at me." This may result from some simple act, such as your failing to include them in an invitation to lunch. Maybe you haven't had your morning coffee and you fail to return a coworker's "Good morning." If your friends can misunderstand you, think how easy it would be for a stranger to read the wrong message into your

non-verbal communication. "Watch what you say" also should include "and how you say it."

When communicating, it is important to be aware of non-verbal communication. Both as senders and receivers, non-verbal communication adds meaning to the words. How close you are to the other person, certain gestures, and your personal appearance can send messages you sometimes don't intend to send.

"In your face!" You do not have to say it verbally to convey this message. When you invade someone's personal space and wave your finger, you are saying "In your face!" All people have a space they feel is their own. If you get too close, it makes your listeners uncomfortable. They may feel you are trying to intimidate them. Also, many gestures have different meanings in different cultures.

Choose your words carefully

Words are very powerful. Words are capable of creating a wide range of emotions. Some words are more direct and harsh than others. Consider the difference between telling an employee, "You're fired," and "Sorry, we have to let you go." Sometimes it is necessary to use stronger words. As always, think before you speak, and then choose carefully.

Consider who will be hearing or reading your comments. Don't use words that your audience will not understand. Choose short words that have precise meanings and are familiar to those with whom you are communicating. Be careful not to talk down to your audience, but attempt to communicate on a level that is appropriate.

Use technical language only when you are sure the other person understands the meanings of such words and acronyms. Practically every business has a language of its own. Do not assume your contacts outside the business will understand these technical terms. A rose may be a rose, but a mouse is not always a rodent. Again, picture your audience and communicate in words they will know.

Words can make a lasting impression. Everyone in America knows the expression, "I have a dream." Dr. King was eloquent in expressing his viewpoint so that people at all levels would understand. His words were carefully chosen, and his use of metaphors left a picture in the minds of his listeners.

Be careful about using words which may be offensive. Avoid terms that stereotype or which may be racially biased or sexist.

If you are doing business with someone from another culture, take time to learn some of their customs. In the Middle East, for example, discussing female family members is inappropriate. In Japan, you may embarrass persons if you single them out for praise instead of addressing their group.

Avoid references to ethnic groups unless it is absolutely necessary for the understanding of your message. Even in informal conversation at work, avoid the use of words and terms which are unacceptable when writing.

Choose words which are not gender specific. Words such as postman or firemen should not be used. Instead choose words like letter carrier or fire fighters. When writing, avoid using he and she as general terms. One possible way to avoid this is to use plural terms. You may also choose to use he/she. Proofreading your letters can save you a great deal of embarrassment later.

> *Not this:*
> *If an employee is late to work, he may be fired.*
>
> *But this:*
> *If employees are late to work, they may be fired.*

Be careful about culturally biased words. More and more companies are doing business internationally. When communicating with those from other cultures, words may take on different meanings. Use of slang terms can be particularly confusing to someone who is not familiar with the language.

How about those squiggly lines?

Proper punctuation when writing is essential to good communication. It is possible to change the entire meaning of a statement by changing the punctuation. Consider the sentence, "This looks stupid, like no one has done any planning!" But how would you feel reading this in an inter-office memo? "This looks, stupid, like no one has done any planning!"

The overuse of punctuation, such as commas, is a common mistake among many writers. Investing in a good gram-

mar check program can be very beneficial. Try removing a comma from your sentence and see if it changes the meaning; if not, you probably don't need that comma. A good writing manual, such as *The Publication Manual of the American Psychological Association*, is an excellent tool for those who write frequently.

Using short sentences can make it easier for you to write—and easier on your reader. Too many colons or semi-colons probably means your sentences are too long. Try writing the way you talk. Be concise and stick to your point. If you ramble on and on, your reader may get lost and fail to grasp your meaning. Before you take up your pen, do some planning.

Listen, Listen, Listen

A good receiver is essential in every communication. As technicians, we are familiar with the terms *sensitivity* and *selectivity*. To be effective as a communicator, you must develop good listening skills. Someone has said, "We have two ears but only one mouth because God knew that listening was twice as hard as talking."

Be a sensitive listener. Give your speaker your undivided attention. Look and listen with all of your body. Maintain eye contact and let the speaker know that you are listening and interested in what they are saying. Encourage the speaker with signs such as nodding in agreement, or saying things such as, "Yes, I understand," or "Oh, really!"

Be a selective listener. Tune out everything but your speaker. This includes your thoughts about what you will say next. Concentrate on what the speaker is saying and don't be afraid to ask questions. If you don't understand something, ask the speaker to repeat it. Don't try to fake it.

Keep an open mind when listening. Receive all of the information being sent, then form your opinion and prepare your response. Too often we start talking before the speaker is finished. Don't rush to answer; you may miss some critical piece of information.

Listening is hard work and requires an active listener. Practice listening; it will pay dividends when you are communicating with your customers. And don't forget to watch for those non-verbal signs the speaker is sending.

* * *

Chapter 9. Communication in the Workplace

Chapter Quiz:

1. Which of the following types of business communication is known as 'the grapevine'?

   a. External formal
   b. Internal formal
   c. External informal
   d. Internal informal

2. When communicating, we use symbols such as:

   a. words.
   b. gestures.
   c. personal appearance.
   d. all of the above are correct.

3. Which of the following terms would be the most appropriate to use when speaking about your new secretary?

   a. My Girl Friday
   b. My administrative assistant
   c. My male administrative assistant
   d. My female administrative assistant

4. When closing a business letter the complimentary close should be:

   a. Yours truly.
   b. Very truly yours.
   c. Sincerely.
   d. With best regards.

5. Which of the following types of business communications should always be in writing?

   a. Instructions to workers
   b. Suggestions by employees
   c. Personnel files
   d. Gossip

6. A good listener should:

   a. keep an open mind.
   b. be ready to reply.
   c. avoid eye contact.
   d. remain perfectly still.

7. Non-verbal communication includes:

   a. body language.
   b. personal appearance.
   c. the use of gestures.
   d. all of the above.

8. It is always best to use technical language when dealing with a customer.

   a. True
   b. False

9. Which of the following would be an effective way to check for punctuation errors?

   a. Use a writer's manual.
   b. Use grammar-check on your computer.
   c. Have a colleague proofread the letter.
   d. All of the above.

10. It is good to use big words and long sentences when writing because it will impress your reader.

    a. True
    b. False

Answers:

1-d, 2-d, 3-b, 4-c: 5-c, 6-a, 7-d, 8-b, 9-d, 10-b

Chapter 10

Communicating With Customers

Frank Pendergrass, CETsr

After spending twenty-two years as an avionics technician in the U.S. Navy, Frank has worked for over twenty years as an instructor and administrator at Spartan School of Aeronautics, where he now teaches accounting, business communications, and statistics. He holds an MS in Adult and Occupational Education from Oklahoma State University.

Let's talk

Communication requires the use of a communications system. For communication to take place, there must be a sender and receiver. The receiver must be able to filter and interpret what the sender has said and format a reply. Then the sender must be capable of receiving this reply and decoding the meaning. Too often we want to talk and are not willing to listen. Too often we go out to "talk" to the customer instead of being prepared to communicate.

Communication is a necessary part of problem solving. Poor communication can result in poor business relationships just as it can result in many personal problems in our lives. To provide good customer service, we must be prepared to communicate.

Don't hesitate to do more for your customers than what they expect. For instance, if you can't solve their problems, suggest another source they might try. Think about the insurance company that gives you its competitors' rates along with their own. This level of service demonstrates to the customers that you are there to serve them. Sam Walton once said, "There is only one boss. The customer."

Using the 'You Attitude'

James Cash Penney, who became one of America's leading retailers, named his first store 'The Golden Rule Store.' Mr. Penney knew the importance of customer service and understood how people wanted to be treated. Later, Sam Walton built a business empire stressing customer service. These men knew it is essential to treat your customers the way you would like to be treated.

Always attempt to phrase things so that your customers feel they are the center of any conversation. Use "you," and not "I," whenever it is possible. Personalize the communication by using the customers' name. However, it is very easy to slip into that 'I' trap when writing business letters.

You have probably received a business letter filled with I's at one time.

March 15, 2003
Ms. Ura Customer
1111 S. Main St.
Ourtown, IA 44777

Dear Ms. Customer,

I have looked into the problem with your account. I believe your account is in error. I will see that your account is adjusted. I look forward to serving you in the future. I remain,

Very truly yours,

How does a letter like this make you feel about the writer? Is he or she more interested in you, the customer, or in him or herself? Unfortunately, many top business professionals write this way.

Look at your business letters after they are typed. Does each paragraph start with an "I"? Try to rewrite the opening sentences in each paragraph and eliminate the I's. "I have taken your request under consideration." could be written "Your request is being considered." Replace "I believe you are right." with "You are right." Your customers are more likely to carefully read a letter such as this, than one where the I's jump off the page at them.

Some writers believe that the 'You Attitude' is unethical. These individuals believe that you should "tell it like it is," and that the 'You Attitude' is an attempt to deceive the customers. Still, human nature being what it is, the majority of your customers will enjoy it if you know their names, and will be pleased that you put their interests ahead of yours.

Chapter 10. Communicating With Customers

If you are sincere about your desire to provide customer service, the 'You Attitude' is not unethical, it is essential. Just treat all customers with respect and you will find it easier to communicate with them.

Be Direct

When you have good news for a customer, say so. It's much better just to say, "Your account has been corrected." than to ramble on with, "I have studied the problem you reported, and I found your account was in error. Therefore, I have made an adjustment to your account." It is also another chance to use the 'You Attitude.' In addition to making the customer feel better, being direct saves time.

When making a request in a letter, be direct. The reader is more likely to respond favorably to your request if he/she doesn't have to search through your letter to determine what it is you want. If you need a current catalog, ask for it. Don't write a page of reasons why you need a new catalog, and then at the end make your request. The opening sentence of the letter should be, "Please send me a copy of your current catalog." But, don't forget to add "Thank you."

The old style of writing a business letter is no longer used. "I would like to take this opportunity to thank you for being a loyal customer" now becomes, "Thanks for your business." Today we would not end a business letter with the complimentary close, "I remain your devoted servant." but simply say, "Sincerely." Today the trend is to write more like the way you speak.

Don't Be Direct

Sometimes is becomes necessary to deliver bad news to a customer. It is better to use an indirect approach when you must refuse a customer's request. Start with some background material. "Your continued business is very important to us. Your account was examined by our accounting department, and they found your balance to be correct." Then deliver the bad news. "At this time we are unable to adjust your account balance." (It is always good to include some helpful information or an offer of help.) "If you have any further questions, please call me at 555-0000."

This approach requires you to walk a fine line. The employee should refer to company policy and follow the procedures he/she has been trained to use. Being indirect can sometimes seem like you are avoiding the issue. Don't talk down to or belittle the customer. Be honest and sincere and the customer will appreciate your interest in his/her problem even if you cannot grant his/her request.

Avoid emotion when delivering bad news. If you must refuse a request, it is important to keep the customer's goodwill. Angry replies usually are not only ineffective, but they frequently result in more problems. "You should have known that we did not guarantee that product. You have to send it to the manufacturer," is not only too direct; it questions the customer's intelligence. A better reply might have been, "As stated in the sales contract, that product must be returned to the manufacturer for warranty repairs. May I provide you with that address?"

If your company grants credit, credit refusal requires a special touch. Many customers will see credit refusal as a reflection on their character. In addition to being indirect, strive to be positive if you must refuse a customer credit. Thank the customer for buying from you. If you give a discount for cash, show the customer how he/she can save with cash purchases. Assure the customer that you know he/she is working to resolve any credit problems, and that his/her request can be reconsidered at some point in the future.

From Casual to Formal

Writing styles may vary from situation to situation. Conversations may also differ between different parties. While casual language is fine for communicating with friends, most business communications will be more formal. How well you know the person with whom you are communicating will set the tone of the conversation.

With close acquaintances, it is appropriate to use casual words and phrases. This may be in conversation or written communications, such as e-mail memos and letters. Examples of casual communication might include the use of abbreviation in e-mail, technical terms in memos, and contractions in letters. But your reader can't read your mind. Be sure each of you understands the words you choose to use. The further removed you are from a person, the more formal the language should become.

Most business communication is somewhere between casual and formal. When working with customers, it is best not to be too informal. Misunderstandings caused by poor communication can complicate customer relations. Be sure the style of communication fits the situation. Indirect communication, such as the refusal of a request, should be more formal than a direct granting of a request.

"Formal" does not necessarily mean remaining aloof. Remember that non-verbal communication is very important. Customers should feel that customer service personnel are listening and not placing themselves on a level above that of the customer. Remember the importance of listening and give each customer your undivided attention.

At times, a customer service person may have trouble speaking on the telephone with a customer. The employee may sense that the customer is not pleased with what he/she is doing to help them. At times such as these the employee might inquire, "Would you prefer to speak with Ms. Smith (my supervisor, the store manager, the owner)? If you prefer, I can place you on hold, or have her return your call." In most cases the caller will be more satisfied and ask the employee to continue.

Protect Your Customers

Most companies collect a lot of information about their customers. Often, a company will receive a request for some of this information from a third party. It might be a credit check, or it might be a telemarketer wanting to add to his or her call list. Keep in mind that your customers deserve to be protected from unwanted prying.

Do not give out personal information without a written release from your customer. If it is a request from a potential employer, certain information is protected, and you should consider the possibility of civil rights violations. Keeping company records confidential can help keep your company out of unnecessary legal actions.

Protect Your Company

One danger when communicating with customers is allowing information to be passed to the wrong person. When speaking to a customer concerning a problem, you should have a private place available. This prevents your conversation from being overheard by someone who might misuse what you say.

If you are speaking to the customer on the telephone, be careful that side conversations with others in the office are not overheard by the customer. You might say to the customer, "It may take a few minutes to find the answer to your question. Would you prefer to hold, or may I call you back?" Cases of customers overhearing statements such as, "I have that jerk, Mr. Smith, on the phone again griping about his bill." can be devastating.

Check your correspondence before it goes into the mail. Employees have been known to accidentally include confidential materials or unfavorable statements from a customer's file with a business letter. Mistakes like these not only are embarrassing for the employee and the company, they can cost the company customers.

Back Up Your Words With Action

When someone in your company tells a customer something, the company should be prepared to stand behind that communication. I told all of my teachers when they were hired, "Tell the students what you are going to do: then, do what you told them you would do." Customers normally don't know when someone in the company is authorized to promise them something. But they sure know when they don't get what they were promised.

Recently, at a local department store, an employee on the telephone told a customer she could receive a refund for a lost gift certificate. When the customer came to the store, a customer service representative explained that the store policy was to treat gift certificates the same as cash. No refund could be authorized.

Students in my business communications class were asked to write a letter to the customer to resolve this dilemma as if they were store managers. The students were not given a solution, but 100% of the students told the customer she would receive some type of credit for the lost certificate. What would you have done? How much is the customer's goodwill worth to the company?

Often we try to answer questions when we don't really know the answers. When you tell a customer something, it should be like a contract. You should first be sure you can deliver on your promise, and then you should follow up to make sure the customer received what he/she was promised. Fair treatment of the customer will pay big dividends, and besides, it's the right thing to do.

Some Final Reminders

Communicating with customers involves those skills discussed in Chapter 9. The best communicator is the best listener. And to be a good listener, you must use your entire body. Non-verbal communication can be even more important than the spoken or written word.

Choose your words carefully. Be sure they are appropriate for the audience you are addressing. Avoid words which are sexist, racist or infer untrue traits about certain groups, it is the right thing to do, and it is the law.

Chapter Quiz:

1. **When speaking with a disgruntled customer on the telephone, you should consider:**

   a. just hanging up.
   b. telling him or her to calm down.
   c. asking if he/she prefers to speak to a supervisor.
   d. telling the customer what he/she wants to hear so he/she will be happy.

2. **Talking and communicating are the same thing.**

   a. True
   b. False

3. **To be a good communicator, you must be:**

   a. bi-lingual.
   b. a good listener.
   c. well educated.
   d. loud and boisterous.

4. **Using the 'You Attitude' when communicating with customers is:**

   a. unethical.
   b. unnecessary.
   c. dishonest.
   d. building goodwill.

5. **When delivering bad news to a customer it is best to use:**

   a. harsh language.
   b. less background information.
   c. a direct approach.
   d. an indirect approach.

6. **It is okay to provide a prospective employer with personal information about a customer if the employer states he/she has a release.**

   a. True
   b. False

7. **If you cannot help a customer with a request you should:**

   a. suggest where he/she might find help.
   b. tell him or her it is not your department.
   c. never mention a competitor.
   d. call the boss.

8. **Business communications should always be conducted using a strictly formal communication style.**

   a. True
   b. False

9. **When communicating with a customer, you must avoid:**

   a. sexist language.
   b. racist language.
   c. ethnic jokes.
   d. all of the above are correct.

10. **Communication and customer service go hand-in-hand because:**

    a. communicating can help solve problems.
    b. good communication promotes respect.
    c. a company is judged by the ability of its employees to communicate.
    d. all of the above are correct.

Answers:

1 -c, 2-b, 3-b, 4-d, 5-d, 6-b, 7-a, 8-b, 9-d, 10-d

> "People don't want to communicate with an organization or a computer. They want to talk to a real, live, responsive, responsible person who will listen and help them get satisfaction."
>
> -Theo Michelson State Farm Insurance

Chapter 11

Phone, Fax and E-mail Etiquette

Chris Owens, CSS

Chris has spent many years in positions that rely heavily on customer service, specifically in the automotive and insurance industries, working for such names as Cadillac, Acura & Farm Bureau where customer service is at the forefront of corporate strategy. He recently served as Managing Editor of the 'High Tech News', ETA-I's monthly member news publication.

Once upon a time...

If the telephone isn't the most important invention that man has created, then it certainly is one of the most influential. It has become the springboard for so many now vital and necessary forms of communications, that one may fail to remember that the telephone marked the first time that people were able to communicate in 'real time.' Up until that time, every other form of communication had an inherent delay involved, sometimes entailing days, weeks or months, depending on the distance between locales. Couriers transporting written messages could travel only so fast, and updated information had to be sent afterwards, thus giving rise to confusion and inaccuracies.

When Morse Code appeared, the ability to transmit messages in short amounts of time and receive answers back equally as swiftly, was a large leap forward. But this still limited the message to actual words and numbers. Thus no human interaction was available at this point.

The telephone achieved the following: instant communication between two or more points, the ability to update information immediately, and added the element of human voice inflection, which had never before been accomplished. This enabled someone receiving a message to most accurately know what the sender was wishing to communicate without deduction and inference.

Through years of trial, error, invention and triumph, the telephone has given rise to much that we consider rudimentary and basic today. Few households and even fewer businesses operate without e-mail. Facsimile machines are now commonplace in even the smallest ventures, and the telephone has remained the most highly used form of communication to date. Try to remember the last time you saw someone's business card without these three pieces of information on it. These three items--fax number, phone number, and e-mail address--will no doubt continue to be the focus of human business interaction for years to come. For anyone in a customer service forum, using these is an opportunity to set yourself and your business apart from others, and should become tools for understanding, goodwill, and profit.

Can you hear me now?

Besides face-to-face contact, a telephone conversation is normally the most personal communication between any two people in business, whether it is employer to employee, employee to employee, or our focus here: employee to customer. Whether you operate from a storefront where people come in to purchase a product, or they buy your goods from their own home, if and when a problem or question arises, a telephone conversation with a customer service representative is the most likely form it will take. This conversation can become a golden opportunity. What is achieved with this opportunity is up to you.

First impressions are indeed everything they are cracked up to be. There are no second chances, as the cliché goes, and if your preparation for contact with a customer or prospective customer begins the moment you answer the phone, you've already lost your chance to make the best impression you can. Before the first ring of the phone, you must be ready. You have two important tools to get and keep in top order before putting your ear to the receiver.

You, as the voice on the other end of the line with a customer, are the first 'tool' that needs to be prepared. A human voice has the possibility to become either a calming, understanding friend or a provoking, suspicious adversary. Take note of how you sound. To truly get the effect of your voice, record yourself speaking aloud for a few minutes and then play it back. Utilize practicing with a 'script' or a list of 'talking points' to use with a customer. You will be amazed at how you sound to

yourself. You will sound differently from what you expect. Ask another for his/her impressions. Your attitude and state of mind will be read easily through your voice. No one will ever be enthusiastic and carefree 100% of the time, but remember that company time is just that. As much as possible, leave personal business and thought for personal time. This isn't to say that you should come to work without a personality or style—quite the contrary. But always remember to focus on your task at hand…helping others, and in turn, your company and yourself as an employee. Keep your throat clear and well-lubricated. During the winter seasons of cold and flu, take precautions to ensure that you stay easily understood. Lozenges and teas are perfect to soothe tensed and irritated vocal cords. If you sound sick and tired, chances are that your customers will perceive you to be sick and tired of them.

Your knowledge of the phone you use is important as well. Learn its features and where they are before you have to use them. Often overlooked, keep your phone clean. Besides looking better, this can also decrease chances of spreading infectious strains of communicable sickness.

Throwing out the first pitch

Introduce yourself to the customer in the fashion set forth by your company. This may include using the company slogan and a specific conversation-opener such as "May I help you?" or "How may I assist you today?". In most cases, the company is trying to create an atmosphere of uniformity for each call that comes in. This reassures customers that they will be treated similarly by anyone with whom they talk. The company has usually invested considerable money in creating a brand-name image and recognizable greeting. Be sure to use them.

When your customer gets lemons...

Get the Information!
Who?
What?
When?
Where?
Why?

Something has not gone according to a customer's desired wishes, and that is why they are calling you. Gathering as much information as you can to start the process is vital. This way, you can hopefully determine where you can assist the customer in using your product or service to its full potential,

therefore making their chances of becoming a long-term and returning customer even greater. Listening and hearing what the customer is saying is the first step in this process. Every story or event has five basic categories that need to be identified: *who, what, when, where* and *why*. By knowing four out of the five categories, you can increase your probability of finding the fifth: *why*. Solving your customer's problem decreases the chance of a repeat call for further assistance.

...make lemon Pledge!

'Who' is very important, especially to the customer. During a phone call, make certain to remember the focus of the conversation is on the customer and their problem. Write the name down, if need be, to recall the name during the furtherance of the call. Using the customer's name increases confidence that you actually care about the situation and are doing what you can to help. This is not the time to let them know that you know someone by the same name, from the same part of the country, state or city. If their name sounds German, for example, don't bother telling them that you have ancestors from that part of the world. Your customer, more than likely, really doesn't care, and it does nothing to help solve the problem that has arisen.

Knowing exactly the nature of the problem is critical, and can involve the most time. This is generally a very important time to listen, and not talk. Let the customer expound at length, if needed, as to what has or has not occurred that has necessitated this call. By most accounts, customers will not be familiar with using the technical terms that you may be accustomed to using. Write the phrases they use down on paper, so you may look them over later. Don't correct them by telling them the exact phraseology they should use. This isn't a class, but rather a laboratory, if you will. Wait for the entire account to unfold, and then repeat, in a concise version, what they said, and then ask "Is this correct?" or "Do I have the facts in order?" or find your own term to let them know you have been listening and are concerned about getting the facts right.

'When' is also a vital piece of the puzzle. To the best of their knowledge, ascertain during what part of the process an error or malfunction has occurred. The same symptoms during different stages of the process can many times indicate different underlying errors that have taken place. Once again, repeat back to the customer the facts as you have heard them to avoid confusion.

Chapter 11. Phone, Fax and E-mail Etiquette

Depending on the product or service you are helping with, knowing where the problem occurred can shed light on the matter. Most products will come with manufacturer recommendations as to how a product should be used. Humans, however, are notorious for not completely reading instructions and consequently, allowing problems to happen. If you determine that this has occurred, the worst thing you can tell a customer is that it was their fault. Once again, listen to the facts and repeat them back. The solution may become self-evident to the customer as you speak these back. Allow the customer the opportunity to acknowledge this. No one wants to feel stupid. A response on your part of, "Well, there you go, if you had not used it as you did, you wouldn't have had a problem." may solve the immediate problem, but you have created a bigger one. Chances are, the customer will go away from this experience with a feeling of shame, anger, or plain embarrassment. The chances that they will again call for help, or purchase a product from your company in the future, have diminished significantly.

By collecting information in these four areas, determining the 'why' will be easier than it would have been without the data. But sometimes, answers will not be determined during the length of a phone conversation. Model

numbers may need to be researched. Diagnostic tests may need to take place. In events where a second phone call will be needed to let the customer know how to solve a problem, you are responsible for initiating contact to provide the information. Never put the responsibility on the customer to call you back. Phrases such as "Okay, give me 15 minutes to find out some things, and give me a call back then." should never find their way into your vocabulary. You represent the company. The company's product has failed, at least in the eyes of the customer, which is the perception you are interested in. Take down the phone number, any other information you might need to solve this problem, and then tell them you will call back. Tell them your name again, and when they should expect a return call. Give a realistic time. Most reasonable people don't mind waiting, as long as you return the call when you say you will. If you know it will take 30 minutes to find an answer, don't say you'll call back in 15 minutes. That's not doing anyone any good. Then, you should do something contrary to human nature: apologize. You are sorry that they had to call in the first place. Every product will not work 100% of the time, and you should let them know you and your company are sorry for the inconvenience. Then thank them for assisting you in fixing this problem. This gives a feeling of being helpful

and a vital part of the solution. Even if they haven't been that helpful, they will feel better, and also will be more open to answering any other questions that might need to be asked during the next phone conversation.

The Famous Final Scene

The last thing that needs to occur sounds simple, but can prevent great problems: hang up the phone. That's right, hang up the phone. End the call. Don't slam it down out of frustration over the customer's ineptitude or lack of assistance, and don't start another conversation with someone else in your office until the handset is securely in the cradle. The last thing a customer needs to hear over the phone is a voice talking to a coworker saying "Wow, you should hear how dumb this guy was!" or even "Let's break for lunch." Give customers your respect from start to finish, and they will return.

Just the facts, err...fax!

Facsimile transmissions have been known for years by their abbreviated name: fax. The ability to send a piece or pieces of paper, documents and pictures from one machine to another anywhere else in the world has now taken on the role of necessary office equipment rather than a high-brow novelty. Knowledge of proper fax etiquette is vital. Since no human voice is involved, it is incumbent upon the sender to properly convey the message using words only. However limited, the fax is a great tool for an opportunity to achieve superior customer service.

Fax transmissions are made up of two important parts: the actual body of what needs to be sent and the introduction of said work. A cover sheet should accompany all fax documents in a business-type setting, especially if the document is being sent to a customer. A document may entail 40 pages of schematics or instructions and a cover sheet is usually only one page, but don't let the relevance of size diminish the importance of the cover sheet, for this is where many misunderstandings, miscommunications and mistakes can be avoided or rectified.

ETA-I Cover Sheet
To:
From:
Subject:

Just as a letter delivered through a courier service comes in an envelope to notify all who it is supposed to be

Chapter 11. Phone, Fax and E-mail Etiquette

delivered to and where it has come from, a fax needs an 'envelope,' in this case—the cover sheet. When conducting company business, use the company cover sheet. This will identify to anyone receiving it exactly from where it has come. Conversely, don't utilize the company sheets for personal faxing. It just isn't professional.

Most cover sheets will have prearranged fields of information that simply need to be filled in by you. It is important to properly mark all areas. Not that you don't know, but the receiver may need it. If it is being sent to a fax machine where many users have access, the only way to determine where your fax is intended is to have all the informational fields filled out.

The receiver's name should include both first and last names, and the contact phone number needs to include an area code, even if it is toll-free. Don't just assume that the customer knows where you are located. Accurately tabulate the number of pages you are sending. If you put down 12, and the receiver gets 10, they will know to contact you and let you know that information is missing.

The way you send information is also a valuable technique to master. If you are sending copies of documents, make certain they are clear—not smudged, or dark. Fax machines will usually magnify any blemishes in what you have sent, so avoid carbon copy receipts, memos written in red ink, or anything that is a copy of a copy of a copy. Also, if your cover sheet information is hand-written rather than produced from a computer template, use a thin to medium point ink marker (such as a Sharpie). This eliminates problems with small ink pens or worse yet, pencils that can lose their imaging during faxing.

The documents can also cause problems. Staples will need to be removed and paper clips detached as to not jam the machine. If a batch of papers has been folded or otherwise bent, attempt to straighten them out as much as possible. Fan out the stack of papers, maybe blowing softly between them. If they have been sitting in a file pressed together for an extended period of time, they may not feed correctly through the fax machine.

Drawings, diagrams, and pictures that contain either small or detailed information may not always keep their integrity during faxing. Most fax machines can also make copies. Test the image by sending it through the machine and make a copy of it. This will give you an idea of how it might look to the receiver. If it is too light, too dark or unclear in any other way, contact the receiver and arrange to send them via courier or through some other method.

Follow through

During the actual sending of the fax, physically stay at the machine for the duration of the process. This accomplishes three purposes. The first ensures not wasting time.

If you walk off immediately after inserting the documents and dialing the number, you may not see that the fax machine you are trying to dial had a busy signal, therefore delaying the fax and the information your customer needs. The second is to see that all pages were transmitted, rather than becoming the subject of a feeding error where the fax machine took two or three pages at a time. The third concerns security. You may find yourself in an environment where you fax documents that aren't for general consumption. Problems may arise when the wrong people see things they aren't supposed to, through no fault of their own, but from your attempt not to 'waste' a few minutes babysitting the fax machine.

Facsimile transmissions were designed to save the time and money sending documents that were normally relegated to delivery. It has indeed accomplished that purpose, but without tending to these few, but important, matters concerning etiquette, you can't maximize the potential it can realize as a tool for providing superior customer service.

E-mail doesn't stand for Evil Mail

Electronic mail, or e-mail, as it has commonly come to be known, has become one of the most used, if not misunderstood and therefore misused, forms of communication in the world today. It should, however, be one of the easiest and most uncomplicated tools you have at your disposal.

E-mails have either two or three parts that need to be addressed, depending on your need. The first involves the 'introduction' type information that starts all e-mail messages. 'Who' and 'what' are of major importance in starting an e-mail. E-mail addresses are very specific, and since a computer cannot decipher and determine what you 'meant' to type, make certain you have the recipient's address in correct form. It will always have three parts. Let's look at an example of an e-mail address.

yourname@domain.suffix

'Your name' is the specific recipient's address, and will be different for each person. Many times people within the same company have very similar addresses. They may use the initial of their first name and last name in their address. Therefore, Mark Smith and Matt Smith may have almost identical addresses. Get the proper name from the recipient, and read it back to them to ensure that you won't send information to either a different person or a nonexistent address altogether.

All addresses will contain the 'at' symbol @. This routes the address even further along the line, giving you directions on where Mark Smith is located.

Domain is the name of the internet service provider (ISP) where mail is collected. Many times the names will be business-related, if the company has its own ISP.

The suffix can be one of a number of two or three letter names. It is the last part of the address, and it is vital to get it correct. Two people can share the same 'name' and 'domain' but use different suffixes, *.com* and *.org*, for instance. With the seemingly infinite number of people using e-mail, it is not uncommon for this to happen.

Most e-mail programs have a space provided to enter a topic that is the subject of the e-mail. This needs to be directly to-the-point. Use either an order number you have given the customer or the topic of any previous conversation. You may also want to state your company name in this area, as sometimes your e-mail address may not be specific, and some people don't open e-mail from unfamiliar addresses.

The second part of an e-mail message comprises the actual information you want to get across. Keep any text to a minimum without sacrificing clarity. Utilize the tools your e-mail program might be equipped with, such as spelling and grammar correction programs. Whether you are unsure of a spelling or just accidentally keystroke the wrong letter, cleaning up your message eliminates mistakes and instills confidence in your customers. Re-read your message at least twice before sending. Listen for flow and a logical thought process, many times what sounds good in your mind doesn't translate as well on paper.

This last part may or may not be applicable in all cases, but is equally important. Attachments could sometimes be needed. An attachment is something the customer may want to reference later and not keep in their mailbox. An attachment could be an owner's manual, brochure, schematic or an order form, among others. Before sending an attachment to a customer, make certain to ask whether their e-mail program will accept and read attachments. Some types will not recognize picture formats, while some will not open any attachments altogether. Let the customer know what form the attachment takes. It may be a document made with Microsoft Word or a graphic program created with Adobe Acrobat, for instance. The file type will tell you and your customers if they have the proper program to read your attachment. The file type is the suffix following the dot (.) in your file name. Be sure of compatibility before sending attachments to avoid both confusion and the need for additional phone conversations or e-mail messages.

Generally, remember that e-mail messages should be clear, concise, and limited to company business, specifically meeting the needs of the customer. Common sense, more than anything else, should be used to determine the acceptability of your e-mail.

Don't Become a "Cell"-Out

Remember when mobile phones were larger than a camper's backpack? In the late 1970's and early 1980's, these mammoth beasts were reserved for only the wealthiest, most important people in the country. In retrospect, it looks rather funny to see a picture of a Fortune 500 CEO lugging around a first-generation dinosaur from that era. Today, however, as technology has driven convenience and pricing, cellular phones are as numerous as the traditional 'home' phone, with seemingly everyone having one clipped to a belt, stuffed in a pocket, hung around a neck or more commonly seen: attached to an ear.

In real estate, the three maxims of success have always been 'location, location, location,' implying that it is so important that it needs to be named more than once. To make the parallel to cell phones, it's all about remembering safety, safety, safety. As customer service situations sometimes require on-site service, a cell phone can help eliminate wasted 'downtime' where, for example, the technician has been traditionally out of the communications loop during the time it takes to get from the office to the customers home. The rise and proliferation of hands-free devices equipped with microphones, speed-dialers and earphones gives the frequent cell phone user a myriad of options to avoid potentially dangerous situations, which should be used. Also, check your local and/or state ordinances concerning cell phone usage on the road. There are a number of laws on the books, and under debate, that limit or prohibit cell phone usage in particular situations.

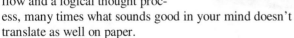

Chapter 11. Phone, Fax and E-mail Etiquette

As either a customer service representative or a technician, there are some simple, common sense guidelines to follow in order to use your wireless communicator as a tool for productivity:

1) *When at work, keep it all about work.* Cell phones are not supposed to be your private 'hot-line,' as to circumvent the office phones for incoming phone calls. As always, emergent situations are different, but if you are supposed to be answering a phone and listening to a customer, it can be rather hard to do that to the best of your ability with another phone attached to your other ear.

2) *It's a cell phone, not a megaphone or a jukebox.* Today's phone models feature 'gadgets', for lack of a better term, that many times distract all in the workplace. Ringer volumes need to be set at appropriate levels so as to not startle or disturb your coworkers. Even better would be to use the discreet vibrate feature that virtually all phones have. Speaking of ringers, none of us really need to hear Beethoven's *Fur Elise* or any other song to notify us you are receiving a phone call. Companies market these phones to show your personality, but remember...although an important part of your life outside of the customer service setting, personality shown through a cell phone can be unnerving, unsettling and downright annoying.

3) *Don't buy the hatchback, get the Cadillac.* The only thing worse than not being able to reach someone is not being able to understand him or her once you are having a conversation. Cell phone providers usually will give away a phone with a service plan. This is generally because they can't sell them! Obviously, they want you to buy a better quality handset, and many times they are worth it. Do some research: consumer advocacy magazines, websites, and simple word-of-mouth testimony should give you a feel for what will work and what will make you sound like the voice coming from the dilapidated drive-thru speaker at the Greasy Burger next to the busy highway at rush hour. Mistaken messages, descriptions of problems and customer needs can and will cost more than the price of a quality phone in the long run.

***

Chapter 11. Phone, Fax and E-mail Etiquette

Chapter Quiz:

1. Telephone conversations give the participants a greater understanding of the intended message because they give the listener a feeling of the caller's:

   a. mood.
   b. height.
   c. weight.
   d. marital status.

2. Your opportunity for success in dealing with a customer's problem begins:

   a. when the problem is presented to you.
   b. when you come across a solution.
   c. when you answer the phone.
   d. before the phone rings.

3. Keep something to munch on during a phone conversation. This will keep you from having to take extra breaks later on.

   a. True
   b. False

4. Find your own style and phrasing in answering the phone. This allows the customer to identify with you instead of the company.

   a. True
   b. False

5. Before you can solve a customer's problem, you need to find out:

   a. who he/she is.
   b. what the nature of his/her situation is.
   c. when the problem occurred.
   d. all of the above.

6. Letting the customer know that he or she has made a mistake is good because:

   a. it shows that you know more than he/she does.
   b. it makes you feel better about your own knowledge.
   c. it keeps the customer in his/her rightful place.
   d. none of the above.

7. The following information needs to be included in all faxes.

   a. The company's quarterly report
   b. A cover sheet
   c. A notation of how much time you spent on this fax
   d. Your lunch order

8. The best way to make certain a fax was transmitted properly is to:

   a. come back later and see if the machine has produced any error code messages.
   b. wait for the customer to call and let you know if it was received.
   c. 'baby-sit' your fax until the machine has confirmed it transmitted.
   d. allow another coworker who is already at the fax machine to send it after his/her fax is done.

9. Which of the following could be a valid e-mail address?

   a. richardnixon@sneaky
   b. bobknighttemper.com
   c. jeffgordon@racing.net
   d. frank.sinatra.com

10. E-mail attachments will automatically be converted to a format where the receiver can open them and read the information.

   a. True
   b. False

Answers:

1-a, 2-d, 3-b, 4-b, 5-d, 6-d, 7-b, 8-c, 9-c, 10-b

Chapter 12

Techno-literacy and the Successful Employee

Alex Lorentson

Alex Lorentson is in his twentieth year as an Instructor at Renton Technical College in Renton, Washington, teaching Analog and Digital Electronics. He has a BS in Education from Southern Illinois University and was previously a Field Engineer for Hewlett Packard working with HP3000 Systems and Digital Computers. Alex also served as an ET1(SS) in the U.S. Navy.

After completion of this chapter you will be able to:

- Identify the three most essential personal characteristics of a successful CUSTOMER SERVICE employee.
- Distinguish several characteristics of fuses, wire, AC characteristics and basic electronic components.
- Identify several methods of obtaining new information concerning service and new products.

In any business that is successful today, individual employees may be required to provide technical support to customers or other fellow employees in everyday activities. To provide an acceptable level of support, it is essential that the successful employee become literate as to their company's products and services and be able to communicate this information to others efficiently and effectively.

New employees or non-technical customer service personnel must possess a positive attitude and be willing to advance their technical and product knowledge to a competent level. This creates an environment that is productive to customer's needs, as well as the company. The purpose of this chapter is not to present an extensive technical education, but to present an overview of some of the basic information and attitudes CUSTOMER SERVICE personnel need to be aware of. This content includes technical concepts, background information, and how to obtain technical and other information that may be required in everyday situations.

Background:

Occasionally an individual working in the customer service field believes that once they begin a new job it will go on forever, no matter what the quality of their work and  ethics. The truth is that an employer's only reason to hire an individual is **To Make The Company Money!** There

are some exceptions to this rule, but this is the basic truth. Each employer expects to receive a profit return on the dollars invested in each one of their employees. When the quantity of sales and/or services that create this profit decline, non-essential or non-profitable employees will be trimmed or laid-off. The decision of who is to be released will be based on the economic times and the individual performance of each employee. How management views the profitability and attitude of each employee will be the only basis for his or her decision of whom to let go.

Positive attitude is the *number one* characteristic that an employer will be looking for when considering a new hire. Responses from human resource departments, or from people who do the hiring and firing, have almost unanimously indicated that the ability of an individual to get along with other employees is the most important skill or ability that a candidate can possess. No matter what academic skill level is attained by an individual, the reality is: **Attitude is Everything**.

Everyday attendance is the *number two* important characteristic that a successful employee must possess. Will you be there every work day, on time, and ready to work? Employers notice if employees are working with customers at opening time, heading for the coffee pot, or just talking to other employees about personal matters. Being professional in your work ethics includes the concept that you are there during normal work hours, working for your employer, and not just for a paycheck. Managers and company owners notice professionalism. Demonstrated professionalism leads to higher paid positions.

Trainability is another important ability that is looked for in an individual. Today's changing workplace requirements concerning products and other high-tech knowledge insists that a person be able to learn new concepts and information. Growing with the company requires education regarding new products and technology.

Chapter 12. Techno-literacy and the Successful Employee

Training and education of employees is usually presented in two basic ways. The first is formal education. Formal education is your employer arranging to have training presented to you while you are away from your usual work location. This allows an experienced instructor to present the information in an organized manner, without interruptions. The obvious disadvantage is that you are not performing your normal job. The decision to send employees to formal education is based on the idea that your new knowledge will create new and higher profits, and the cost of your training must be offset by these profits. After completing training, you may be the "resident expert" and expected to train others on the basics learned. Another method of training is informal training. This could be a short one or two hour instructional seminar, getting together at lunch hour with "pizza on the boss," or just short discussions from employees that have already been trained.

Employers agree that a prospective candidate is acceptable for hire if they have the correct attitude and arrive on time for work each day groomed and ready. If candidates are basically trained and knowledgeable, they are willing to further train employees concerning new products and company methods. A long-term employment with growth potential is the intent of most employers when interviewing candidates for jobs. The successful candidate must become an asset to the company, and therefore can expect fair pay, benefits, training, and promotions as he/she qualifies for new positions.

Basic technical concepts:

Electricity:

There are very few high tech items in today's world that operate without electricity. A few of the sources we see today include power provided to your home by the "electric company," batteries of various sizes and voltages, alternators such as in our automobiles, generators for backup, solar arrays, wind generators, and in the near future, fuel cells for personal transportation.

The two most important terms or characteristics used to describe electricity are "Voltage" and "Current." Voltage, or Electro-Motive Force (EMF), can be thought of as simple water pressure in a garden hose. The "Current" of electricity is similar to the water flowing in the same garden hose. An Ampere of electrical current can be thought of as "gallons per second" of water flow. Increasing the Voltage in a circuit will cause an increase in the Ampere flow of a

circuit. V for volts, or E for EMF, are the common letters used in electrical calculations. A or I is used for calculations containing ampere calculations.

Resistance is a characteristic of materials, liquids, and gasses to resist the flow of an electric current. An "Ohm" is the unit of electrical resistance. One ohm will limit electrical current flow to one ampere, if one volt of "electrical pressure" is applied. Low resistance substances are called conductors, and large amounts of current will flow with low voltages applied. Non-conductors will only allow small amounts of current to flow, even though very high voltages are placed across the object. An insulated wire is an example of a metallic conductor, surrounded by an insulating, (non-conductive) material. Electricity will flow more easily through the wire, and not through the insulation.

Fuses:

Fuses are safety devices that are found in many electronic devices, especially when higher voltages are used to power the device, medium to high currents are present, or if the AC outlet is used as a power source. Fuses are basically devices that will typically melt if excessive current flows, therefore opening the current path. It is very important that CSS personnel and technicians replace defective fuses with exact replacements. Replacing a "blown" fuse with one of a different value or operating characteristic could lead to further equipment damage or injury to personnel.

Blown Fuse

Many electronic equipment and consumer electronic devices contain the common cartridge fuse. This type fuse comes in two basic types, fast blow and slow blow. Fast blow fuses are designed to blow immediately when the current flowing through it is in excess of its designed current. You can most easily recognize this type of fuse by its element, which will appear to be a straight wire within the cartridge. If the element appears to be a straight wire in series with what appears to be a coil or spring, it probably is a "slo-blo" type. This slow-blow type fuse is used in equipment where the initial start up or turn-on current is considerably higher than the normal current draw. This time delay allows the device to settle to its normal current draw before the fuse will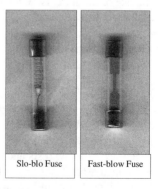

Slo-blo Fuse   Fast-blow Fuse

blow. Do not place a slow-blow fuse into equipment that normally requires a fast blow fuse.

Warning Labels, Interlocks, and Warranty Seals:

A warning label on a product is the manufacturer's way of telling you that there is the potential of damaging the equipment by certain action or the possibility of receiving electrical shock. Read these labels carefully and follow their directions.

Warranty seals are usually placed over case gaps, alignment holes, or any point that will indicate that the equipment has been opened by the end user. Factory warranties are based on the idea that the customer will not "fool around" with
the equipment. Repair or alignment is for trained personnel. Do not break these seals, or the customer will not be able to obtain warranty repairs or alignments under the normal warranty terms.

The basic purpose of equipment interlocks is to eliminate the possibility of electrical shock when a piece of equipment is opened. Television receivers are the best example of items that use very high voltages and require some form of safety interlock. Removing the back cover disconnects the AC power cord from the chassis. A customer who removes this cover would be protected from the high voltages present during normal operation, except for residual high voltage on the picture tube. Only trained technicians should remove interlocked covers to perform maintenance or alignments. CSS personnel should discourage customers from opening up equipment to "take a look."

Electrical Wire:

Electrical wires are the normal means to allow electron flow from one point, usually designated the Voltage Source, to another point usually described as the load, and return back to the source. In simple terms, a power source is used to supply power for a device. Technically, electrical wire is visualized as a low resistance conductor, normally covered by an insulator. Wires come in many sizes, ranging from large cables that would be difficult for a person to lift, to very small ones that would be very difficult to see without magnification. The larger the wire, the lower the resistance per foot, and therefore it is able to carry larger currents without excessive voltage loss.

The American Wire Gauge (AWG) charts are the normal source of information concerning the size, resis-

tance, and current-carrying capabilities of copper wire. The smaller the AWG number, the larger diameter of the wire, therefore the lower the resistance per foot, allowing a higher continuous current-carrying capability. It should be noted that if two wire sizes are compared that have an AWG size **difference** of ten, then the current-carrying capability of the **smaller** sized wire is approximately ten times larger than the other. (AWG size 24 to 12, 18 to 8, etc.) The size of common extension cords is usually AWG 16, 14, 12, or 10. The number 10 AWG size is best for higher current devices or longer extension cord lengths. Smaller diameter wires in portable electronic devices are in the AWG range of 26 to 30+.

The numbering system defined in the basic resistor color code is also extensively used to identify wires by number, which would be typically bundled in cables, as to individual number. Sometimes it is difficult to place a written number on a wire. If identification of wire numbers between one and ninety-nine is suitable, a two-color scheme can be used. The basic color, or body color of the wire, is the first digit, and a color stripe is the second. Example: Brown=1 Red=2

A brown wire with a red stripe = wire #12
A red wire with a brown stripe = wire #21

Capacitors:

Capacitors are defined as two conductors separated by an insulator, or dielectric. They can be visualized by imagining two metal plates, separated by a piece of non-conductive glass. They are also electrically described as blocking DC voltages, and
passing AC voltages at higher frequencies. The high resistance of the glass will basically not allow DC current to flow. However, with the idea of "like charges repel, and unlike charges attract" they appear to pass these higher frequency AC voltages as the capacitor charges, discharges, and then repeats the cycle with the opposite voltage polarity. This characteristic is extremely useful when coupling an AC voltage from one point to another while the two points are operating at different DC potentials.

Although capacitors, sometimes called condensers, come in many sizes and shapes, there are two basic types: polarized and non-polarized. Capacitors have two main characteristics: their capacity, and their working voltage. Always try to replace a capacitor with an exact replacement. Never replace a defective capacitor with another of a lower voltage rating because it will probably fail. In some cases,

Chapter 12. Techno-literacy and the Successful Employee

you can replace a capacitor with another capacitor with a higher capacity, however, an exact replacement is always recommended.

Polarized capacitors, commonly called Electrolytic, can be installed only one way in a circuit. These capacitors are used because of their high capacity, compared to non-polarized ones. Polarized capacitors will have a polarity mark showing which is the positive or negative lead. The marking on smaller electrolytic capacitors that are commonly mounted directly to a printed circuit board is normally a minus sign, (-), indicating the negative lead. Small Tantalum capacitors may show a plus symbol indicating the positive lead. Larger electrolytic capacitors, which are usually clamp mounted, will be marked with a plus "+" symbol indicating the positive screw terminal. Make sure to look for these polarity marks before installing the capacitor. Also, check for polarity markings on the printed circuit board before you install a replacement. You cannot install an electrolytic capacitor in any circuit that reverses the actual voltage polarity across the capacitor. Reversed voltage on these capacitors will quickly destroy them. They may explode and cause damage to the PC board, other board parts, or cause personal injury.

Non-polarized capacitors normally have less capacity for their size, but can be manufactured to withstand higher voltages than electrolytic capacitor types. You will not find a polarity mark on them, therefore, they can be installed either way on a circuit board.

Batteries supply the required energy to most of our portable electronics devices used today. They may also be used as power back-up for devices that must function during AC power losses, such as telephone systems, critical computers, or medical life support systems. The manufactured size and voltage of each battery is  determined by its intended use. Very small batteries in physical size are used where only very low current drains are required, while larger ones are used to provide large amounts of power. The most common characteristic of batteries, besides the actual voltage of the battery, is the amp/hour rating. This rating tells us the total work capacity, or amount of power the battery will provide before it is discharged. A larger size battery of identical voltage will typically have a higher capacity or amp/hour rating.

NiCad batteries that are rechargeable are sometimes substituted for alkaline batteries in different devices. Some devices will not function properly because of the difference in the output voltage of the two types of cells.

Alkaline batteries produce approximately 1.5 Volts each, while NiCad batteries produce approximately 1.2 Volts each. This is the possible cause of some electronic devices not working properly with freshly charged NiCad batteries installed that are designed to have alkaline power source batteries installed.

How much techno-literacy is appropriate?

A new employee who is just beginning to work with customers and others as a technical support person will probably be over-whelmed by the multitude of new questions concerning existing and new products. Most customers wishing to purchase products, or who are new to products, probably will have similar questions each wishes to have answered. In reality, many of these answers can be found in the *Owners Manual*. CSS personnel will usually be prepared to answer most customer questions after becoming familiar with these manuals. More in-depth questions might require the use of service information or by asking trained technicians. Sales persons rarely have to answer questions that are not contained in the technical description section of each manual.

The best method of becoming Techno-Literate is to learn something new each day. It is not the time to stop learning when you can answer most of the questions you are asked each day. Continue to learn. Your next step upward might be to become a product specialist, technical guru, or to continue your education into the area of electronics and repair. Other knowledge necessary to succeed would also include information on other company products, services, and procedures. Progression upward within your company also has a prerequisite of understanding an additional broad base of knowledge about whom you work for.

Where to find technical information

Before the extensive use of the Internet, most user manuals and service manuals were in printed form. The disadvantage of keeping large amounts of information in book or manual form is the large storage area required. In the past, it would not be uncommon to find a radio and TV repair shop having as many as twenty file cabinets full of service and product information. Sams Photofact® electronics repair manuals were probably the most popular source of service information utilized by repair shops in the past. Another popular technology for storing large quantities of information on small microfilm cards is called Microfiche®. This film method has been used for many years, but required a Microfiche® Card Reader to enlarge or project the images to a screen. Both Sams Photofact® and Microfiche® are still used today.

Before the mid-eighties, large businesses, companies, schools and government facilities were the only owners of computers. The costs involved prohibited most individuals from owning one. Today it is commonplace for individuals to have a PC (personal computer) and to have access to the Internet. With the rising costs of paper, printing, transportation, and mailing costs, many manufacturers have decided to turn to CD's or the Internet for product and service information. Many manufacturers offer operator's manuals and product information that can be downloaded at no cost by an individual by visiting their website. Typically, most service manuals supplied over the Internet must be purchased, but there is a new trend within a few companies of consumer electronics

to make this service information available to bona-fide repair shops at no charge. Other information concerning discrete repair parts, integrated circuits, circuit modifications, hardware and software upgrades can also be found by visiting the manufacturer's website.

General parts information that, in the past, had to be obtained in book or manual form can now frequently be ordered directly from the factory in CD format. Typically this is done by anyone filling out an order form online. Still another method of locating miscellaneous information on almost any subject or product is to use an Internet search engine. These search engines will find all types of websites that contain part numbers, words, or phrases asked for.

Conclusion:

There is a formula or attitude for success. Be one of the individuals who possess the motivation to "Make it Happen," and "Do it Today." Keep up-to-date on new products, how your company does business, and develop new skills in working successfully with people. Professional performance and being a team player are essential qualities to have in order to gain respect from your coworkers and be highly regarded by your employer.

BE SUCCESSFUL!

Chapter 12. Techno-literacy and the Successful Employee

Chapter Quiz:

1. During an interview, which of the following would probably be LEAST considered?

   a. Your attitude
   b. Night school electronics classes
   c. Your personal appearance
   d. You're "always on the job."

2. Three customers today have asked about a new product that you were unaware of. It would be best to:

   a. ask your friend in the service department about it.
   b. call the manufacturer long distance and ask for a brochure.
   c. look in the current information files for a service manual.
   d. go to the manufacturer's web site.

3. Which of the following fuses can be substituted for a 3.5A slo-blo fuse?

   a. A 3.5 A fast blow
   b. A 4.0 A slo-blo
   c. A 3.0 A slo-blo
   d. None of the above

4. Electrolytic capacitors:

   a. can be substituted for non-polarized types.
   b. are of the axial type.
   c. are polarized.
   d. must be discharged before installation.

5. A disadvantage of formal training of employees is:

   a. the employee is away from his job place.
   b. the costs involved for training are usually high.
   c. most employees do not like homework.
   d. all of the above.

6. Bill got a good raise in pay, and Bob received a smaller one. Bill probably:

   a. complained about his low pay, considering his ability.
   b. had satisfied customers asking for Bill by name.
   c. asked his immediate supervisor for the large raise.
   d. all of the above.

7. Warning stickers, interlocks, and warranty seals are placed on electronic devices to:

   a. insure that customers do not come into contact with high voltages.
   b. identify adjustments that can only be performed by the factory or service personnel.
   c. to detect if a device has been opened by the customer.
   d. all of the above.

8. Voltage can be thought of as:

   a. a pressure that moves electrons from one point to another.
   b. the amount of electrons per second that pass through a point.
   c. current flow from an AC source.
   d. a and b above.

9. A store display is a good distance from the wall receptacle that is to be used. The best extension cord to use would be:

   a. a 50 foot #14 cord.
   b. two 25 foot #16 cords.
   c. one 50 foot #12 cord.
   d. one 50 foot #10 cord.

Answers:

1-b, 2-d, 3-d, 4-c, 5-a,b, 6-b, 7-d, 8-a, 9-d

Chapter 13

Safety

Bob Ing of Toronto, Canada served as Chairman of ETA-I in 1998 and developed much of the material in the first CSS Study Guide. He is Director of King's Markham Forensic Services in Toronto, a project management contractor specializing in the validation and examination of digital technology. Bob has been a prolific author of professional publications. He lectures and gives workshops in both Canada and the United States. ETA President Dick Glass is another prolific author of books and other publications. He has a broad background in all phases of work performed by electronics technicians, having started as a Navy avionics technician. Dick is also an inductee into the Electronics Hall of Fame.

**By Bob Ing, CESma
and Dick Glass, CETsr**

General Safety

The majority of on-the-job accidents are the result of human error. Through common sense, proper knowledge, hazard awareness and preventive action, people can avoid these accidents.

Use what you know. You know that sparks, open flame, or lit cigarettes can ignite flammable gases. Avoid any use of these items in areas where there are known, potential, or suspected flammable vapors.

You also know that you cannot defeat gravity. Don't climb on, hang from, or jump off equipment, stacked products, or any other height. Use your common sense in all situations.

Beyond common sense, there are federal, state, and company regulations you must follow while on the job. These cover the safe handling of toxic or flammable chemicals, including but not limited to paints, fuels, cleaners, and propellants. These chemicals cannot always be seen or smelled. If you suspect there is a chemical leak or spill, alert others who may be in danger, and go to a safe location.

Company regulations also cover the proper use of machinery, safety equipment and warning signs. Whether your job is one where injury is historically low, or whether you work in a hazardous job, it is your responsibility as an employee and a Customer Service Specialist to know these regulations and follow them.

There are also company regulations concerning emergency evacuation and fire procedures. You are responsible for knowing these procedures, as well as those that cover hazardous chemical handling, biohazard care, and accident reporting. You must also know the locations of emergency exits and safety equipment and who to notify in case of an accident.

Most jobs within a company have specific safety requirements. For instance, people working at heights are now required to be attached to a full body harness that can withstand excessive weight loads and which limits a fall to less than six feet. Hard hats are required for many jobs. Most employers notify you of company policies and your responsibilities when you accept employment.

Personal Safety

Many customer service specialists work at jobs in which they are at higher risk than general office workers. But even receptionists, parts, help-desk people, and sales and management workers can be injured on the job. A CSS should be on the lookout for potential hazards. These may include ragged carpet, loose objects, ice, moisture, oil, or even a simple scrap of paper on the floor which may cause slips or falls. Then there are more complex problems, such as: desks, counters, doors, benches or chairs that are in need of preventive maintenance and repair.

In offices, workers occasionally find they need to hang something on a wall, replace a fluorescent bulb, run a new coax or phone wire, etc., and thus have reason to climb. Because these extra chores are most often not routine, the tendency is to simply get the job done. Standing on desks, building a platform out of available boxes,  shelves, tables, etc., can be a recipe for disaster. Treat these tasks with the same concern you might if you were professionally climbing a roof or working at any construction job. Efficiency and expediency are worthy attributes, but your company and your family put your safety above those two words.

If you are not comfortable, or capable enough to do the task, contact your supervisor or a coworker to assist you. Do not be afraid to call in a professional if the job is beyond

Chapter 13. Safety

your knowledge or comfort level. Your bruised ego heals easier than do broken bones or electrical burns.

"Now children, stop that before someone gets hurt!" Your mother said it. Your high school teacher said it. Don't make your supervisor say it. Careless rough-housing is one of the top causes of personal injury and property damage at the workplace. It is also one of the easiest to avoid. You must understand that the workplace is not a playground.

Don't let it be "all fun and games until someone gets hurt!" Enjoy your job, safely.

Don't neglect personal safety while off the job. You may break your leg while learning to ski or racing motorcycles. When that happens, your company suffers too. Someone must perform your duties. Provisions must be made for limited physical efforts during recuperation. Nobody wins except the doctors. Accident-prone workers usually find they are not favored employees and may be the last to see compensation increases.

Customer Concerns

Occasions arise when the customer may be put into a compromising position on company property. Customers may be at risk when moving heavy or unwieldy products, walking into work areas, or demonstrating equipment problems. Whenever possible, take control of the situation. Assist the customer by carrying their purchases. Walk with the customer through any restricted areas (this is a good time for them to see your clean, neat work area). Handle all equipment during problem demonstrations--just have the customer stand by to walk you through the normal steps he or she takes. Customers will appreciate the extra personal care, and it *will* help protect you in case of an accident. If an accident does happen to a customer while on company property, notify the appropriate personnel, no matter how minor the incident may seem.

Sometimes products themselves pose potential safety threats to customers. Usually these are covered in the manufacturer's literature, owner's manuals, or on safety stickers attached to the item. If you are aware of common safety concerns that may or may not be mentioned in the literature, take the time to cover these with the customer. Not only will this show customers that you are concerned with their safety, it will lower the possibility for any potential personal injury lawsuits.

Mentioning little helpful hints, safety procedures and the "do's" and "don'ts" to the customers (as well as seemingly obvious suggestions) will leave the customer with a well-cared-for feeling.

Let's look at microwave ovens for an example. These useful appliances are normally quite safe to work with. Control panels, transformers, magnetrons, power cords, fans and lamps are the most commonly replaced components. The technicians who service these will use a radiation checker to assure that the door seal, and the unit in general, emits no microwave radiation before and after the repair is made. Some of them are heavy, so care must be used in transporting them and in removing their shields and covers. These units produce high voltages and should only be serviced by trained technicians. The users are warned against placing metal inside the oven, and not to cook sealed foods that might explode, such as an egg.

Packaging

The safety of the product itself is also important. People go to college to learn packaging. Thus, it is not always simple to do the shipping work that many customer service people find is part of their job.

Your first encounter with a damaged product - damaged in shipping - may end in a dispute with UPS or FedEx or the USPS. The best plan, if you are the shipper, is to become an expert at packaging things correctly. You can't put a chicken egg in a flimsy UPS 'overnight' envelope and expect it to get anywhere unsmashed. Unless they have internal support such as packing 'peanuts' or foam forms, the sides of a corrugated carton will buckle and products will get bent or broken. Parts, pieces, and other loose items must be secured, or they will bounce around and damage themselves and other items. Even if you think your package is 100% secure, put another layer of fiber packing tape (not cellophane tape) on it or fill up the internal space with just a little more packing.

Keep records of each shipment, even though you have a purchase order or a return authorization number and expect the recipient to know everything about your shipment. Include full details on the inside and use outside packing slips. Where possible, use the original packing foam forms and double wrap. If there is any doubt about the

Chapter 13. Safety

recipient's address being secure against theft, use return receipts or other secure delivery verifications.

Shipping isn't the only area of the workplace where safety of the product is a concern. Desks, workbenches and the service floor are all areas where safety concerns apply to persons, as well as products and equipment. As a general rule, keeping work areas clean and clear of clutter is an easy accident prevention practice.

Product Safety

A Customer Service Specialist must have respect for items that must be shipped, serviced, or otherwise handled. Lose respect for someone else's goods, and they will lose respect for you and your company. Clean work areas help insure the careful handling of products. Scratches, dents and scrapes are small but costly mishaps that can easily be avoided. It is much easier than explaining to a customer why he or she must wait while you order a replacement part or call in a specialist because you were clumsy or sloppy. You will lose your customer, your reputation, and the money to mend your unnecessary mistake.

Take care. Shops that take extra care in presenting the customer with clean, undamaged goods, including a professionally prepared bill of charges, leave the customer with a good feeling for the transaction. Your customers will be more likely to continue to do business with you, as well as to suggest your services to a friend.

It isn't up to the boss or the receptionist to take these extra steps to ensure product safety. It is up to the CSS - YOU! It is up to the entire customer service crew to maintain a 'tight ship' and to treat customers' goods with extreme care.

Equipment Safety

Equipment must be handled carefully as well. This includes anything from heavy machinery and service vehicles to box knives and office equipment.

In the field, many Customer Service Specialists drive and work from utility vehicles, vans, and delivery vehicles. There are a number of resources for regulations that apply to construction, utility and service workers and linemen. Depending on the type of work, each CSS should seek out the company and industry rules for safety. Hard hats, traffic cones, warning signs, safety harnesses, ladder accessories, and so forth, serve a purpose and should be used appropriately.

Special rules apply to digging, trenching and underground equipment and workers. You may think that taking the time to have a 'locate' made for possible gas, electric, phone, or water lines, dog fences, and lawn sprinkler systems may take a few moments of your valuable time. However, it actually saves time, money, and customer relations if it keeps you from being the one who cuts off a service that causes an expensive repair job.

Office work holds its own hazards. Box knives, paper cutters, office machines, and other small equipment must be handled carefully. Common sense can prevent most incidents with these items. Though you may find it amusing, it isn't funny when people do something careless like running a staple into their fingers. Pay attention to your work to prevent foolish mishaps.

Customer Premises

Since the customer's property is his business, safety might seem to be of little concern to you. Even if you are the victim of a dog attack, the customer will find an excuse to blame you. If unruly children bother you in your job, it is up to you to explain any safety hazards to the parent before the child gets into trouble. If a customer has some hazardous conditions that he wants you to overlook, be aware that after you fall through the rotten porch, or after the rail breaks or after the ladder slips on a makeshift footing, it is you who will get hurt and you who will have to explain to the boss how your ladder crashed through a wall or window and fell on the Cadillac.

Power Cords

Power cords take a lot of abuse. They are frequently plugged and unplugged, and many people do not handle them carefully. Thus, the male plugs may become cracked or broken. More frequently, the zip-cord loses its insulation at the point where it is attached to the plug or to the product, due to the frequent strain. Once the copper wires touch, a spark or arcing will occur. If this short does not cause the house fuse to blow on that circuit, the arcing can persist, generating heat and catching nearby materials on fire.

I once was called by my wife to the kitchen where an old toaster cord was sputtering at the point where the heavy cord is molded into the power plug. Flames about the size of a large candle had appeared at the back of the plug. As the wire melted and thus the arcing started traveling up the wire towards the toaster body, the flames gradually worked their way up the cord. What if I had not been home? What if my wife had not caught the event as it happened? That flame was plenty strong enough to catch the kitchen cabinets on fire. In most cases you don't get the chance to see just what a frayed, work-hardened, damaged old AC cord can do. Usually, by the time you know what has happened, the house has already burned down.

A CSS can spot faulty power cords, polarity-defeating adapters and overloaded outlets. This is a good opportunity to advise the customer about safety and dangerous conditions.

Batteries

Batteries store electricity as a result of chemical reactions. As with most chemical based products, the disposal of batteries must be done within health, safety, and environmental considerations and regulations. The chemical compounds in batteries are poisonous and

For serious chemical burns from batteries, apply baking soda until medical attention is received. Keep a box of baking soda handy if you work with batteries often.

acidic. Should a battery become damaged and leak, its chemical compounds could burn or irritate the skin. Skin that comes into contact with battery chemicals should be flushed with cold water as soon as possible, and depending on the amount of exposure, medical attention may be required. Batteries should be kept out of the reach of small children.

Batteries provide a supply of direct current (DC) and have two terminals: positive or red (+) and negative or black (-). For the battery to power an electronic device, both of these terminals must be connected to the corresponding terminals on the device to be powered (positive to positive and negative to negative). Care must be taken never to accidentally short circuit or attach the positive terminal of a battery to its negative

terminal as the battery will get hot due to excessive current generation and conduction, and it can explode. Customers should be advised when carrying spare batteries in their pockets that the batteries should be placed in a plastic bag or case. This will prevent any injury due to the batteries "shorting" on loose change or keys in the pocket or purse.

Contrary to popular belief, batteries should never be stored in the freezer or frozen as this will shorten the life of the battery or destroy it. Batteries should be stored in a cool (40 to 55 degrees F), dry environment if they are not going to be used within a 60 day period. For non-rechargeable batteries, this storage method will prolong the chemical and charge life of the battery.

Rechargeable batteries, depending on their chemical composition, will lose from 1% to 10% each day whether used or not, and will have to be recharged regardless of how they are stored. However, this storage method will prolong the chemical life of the rechargeable batteries.

Static Electricity

It only takes a small, sometimes undetectable, amount of static electricity to cause irreparable damage to an entire electronic circuit. On most electronic equipment, technicians need to be grounded, using a grounding strap, and keep replacement components in static-free packages until the time arrives to install them. Likewise, when connecting cables or wires, the operator should touch an exposed metal part of the frame or chassis, to remove any static on his body, before touching the connection points.

Damage from static might not be immediately noticeable. It can cause a problem that shows up only under certain circumstances or it can result in a deterioration of a component that can get worse over time.

Surge and Spike Protection

When electrical devices are turned on, and during times of transition between high and low power usage, variations appear on the power lines. These may be

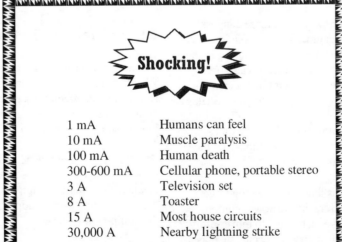

Shocking!

1 mA	Humans can feel
10 mA	Muscle paralysis
100 mA	Human death
300-600 mA	Cellular phone, portable stereo
3 A	Television set
8 A	Toaster
15 A	Most house circuits
30,000 A	Nearby lightning strike

surges or spikes. Spikes and surges might be observed on an oscilloscope.

"Brownouts" occur when the source can't keep up with demand, so voltage drops slightly. "Blackouts" occur when power is lost completely for any period of time.

Brown-outs result in reduced performance by some devices, but rarely cause damage. If damage occurs, it is usually in motors and overworked power regulators. Black-outs, of course, result in equipment shutting off. But the real damage they cause is in the equipment coming on all at one time, turning off and on several times in quick succession, or coming on too soon after being powered off.

Spikes and surges are usually caused by lightning hits or large devices, such as elevators, motors and copiers being turned off and on. Because of lightning, there is virtually no limit to the size of surges.

Protection against damage from all the various sources is possible, but often the cost is prohibitive. It ranges from a fuse to an inexpensive surge protector to the best surge protectors to battery back-up devices, to diesel-powered back-up power sources.

Electrical Fire

In the event of an electrical fire, the first consideration should be to remove the power source, but this is not always possible. The proper extinguisher is either halon or dry chemical. Never use a water or foam type.

Computer Monitors and Picture Tubes

Kinescope display tubes have at least three dangers. They are made with a total vacuum. When broken, there is danger of an implosion and thus flying glass. During manu-facturing, a steel band encircles the face of modern tubes. This compresses the glass face to the point that it cannot collapse or detach pieces from the face of the glass. Striking the face of a modern picture tube or monitor will only put a hole in the glass. Even with improved safety, the tubes should be handled with extreme care. Also, tubes that have a crack or chip in the glass should be replaced.

A second problem today is that we are seeing larger size display devices. 35" TV screens are now common. These are too heavy for a single technician to move safely by himself. If dropped, serious injury can occur, such as a broken foot. Voltages near 40,000V may be used on these large screen TVs or monitors. While the 'pigtail' that

Caution!

Shock Hazard

connects the high voltage button to the side of the kinescope has a rubber insulating boot, and the cable from the high voltage source may be specified to 60 KV, there is always the possibility of a crack in the insulation and possible shock to the worker. After the monitor or TV is turned off, the voltage may be retained, bleeding off very slowly. Servic-ing of these tubes should be done by a qualified technician, who will safely discharge residual voltage, using an insu-lated tool to discharge it to a safe ground.

Lastly, the other elements in the system typically use several hundred volts and can represent a shock hazard to the technician. Handle with care!

Cleaning a picture tube can subject the customer or the technician to a static charge. The dust that accumulates on the bell of the tube may become moist on rainy or muggy days. This can result in the high voltage attached to the side of the tube finding other paths to ground, which creates a hazard to users and CSS's. While these paths are poor conductors, a person spraying liquid cleaners unknowingly provides paths for that voltage to arc. Thus several thousand volts can snap at you as you attempt to clean the surface. If it is deemed worthwhile to clean the screen while power is on, it should be done only by applying cleaning fluid to a clean cloth and wiping it clean with the cloth. Don't allow the cleaning fluid to drip around the edges of the monitor or tube!

Fresh out of Windex? For cleaning purposes, a little distilled white vinegar and water solution will do the trick.

Other Electronic Equipment

Some electronics equipment requires special care. Whether cleaning, maintaining or repairing this equipment, follow the manufacturer's guidelines for the action. If you do not have access to manufacturer information, the follow-ing are some basic rules to work by.

When cleaning plastic and rubber parts, especially if they are cleaned often, use a non-alcohol, non-wax based cleaner. Ammonia, as in most window cleaners, is usually the best choice. Again, apply all cleaners to a cloth, not to the equipment surface.

Make sure all cables and power cords are tied back or threaded through wall conduit to prevent the possibility of someone tripping over the cords, or plugs being yanked from the equipment or wall outlet.

All electrical and electronic components require safety considerations. Some are designed for safety; others present potential safety concerns. Others require that we protect them from exposure to damage.

Radio Transmitters, Walkie-Talkies, Cellular & Cordless Telephones

The debate goes on as to whether or not long term exposure to transmitter radio frequencies that emanate from the antennas of these UHF units can cause cancer. Some experts say "Yes;" others say "No." Some common precautions are:

1. Fully extend the antenna before using.

2. Never touch the antenna while transmitting.

3. Never place the antenna directly in line with the eyes, or in the mouth while transmitting.

4. Try to use your auto's external antenna when possible.

The tissue in the eyes and mouth are more susceptible to damage by radiation. In addition, using the unit as outlined above, permits optimum performance.

Privacy

Any device that has an antenna and is capable of transmitting information is susceptible to having its transmission monitored by unknown parties. This means a cellular or cordless telephone call, a two-way radio transmission, and even a baby room monitor may be monitored by anyone who has what is known as a scanning receiver or scanner. Scanners are readily available at many specialty consumer electronics stores. Although there are laws governing the monitoring of such communications, the privacy concern is a real one. Many cellular and cordless telephone manufacturers have devised various security schemes to thwart scanning enthusiasts. However, most of these are easily overcome by technically competent monitors. Users of all wireless devices should be made aware of this issue and advised never to give the following information over these devices:

1. Credit card or account number information
2. Confidential business or personal information
3. Detailed vacation plans

This information is more securely conveyed via a conventional "wired" telephone, or in person.

Connecting and Disconnecting Things

It is inevitable that most users of electronic devices will find themselves plugging and unplugging a myriad of accessory devices. Whether these devices are computer printers, stereo speakers, cable-TV splitters or whatever, one simple rule applies: Always turn off the power to the main and accessory device before plugging or unplugging it. By following this simple rule, the user can avoid costly repairs and even extend the life of all devices concerned.

Magnets

Magnets are used in speakers, headphones, electric motors, door and window alarm switches, and many other devices. What you should be aware of is that certain items, if exposed to magnets (or more properly, the magnetic field of the magnet), may be damaged or destroyed. Some common items affected by magnets are:

1. Computer hard and floppy disks
2. Audio, video and computer back-up tapes
3. Credit, bank machine, and access cards
4. Television and computer screens
5. VCR and audio tape record and play heads
6. Photographic film
7. Some navigational instruments

Consumers should be aware that the device they are using is susceptible to, or generates a magnetic field.

Chapter 13. Safety

Chapter Quiz:

1. **Which of the following packing scenarios is cause for concern that the job is not satisfactory?**

    a. Corrugated box sides are bowed out.
    b. Shaking the box lets inside objects move back and forth and rattle.
    c. The masking tape used to secure the box flaps appears to be tearing.
    d. All of the above.

2. **Who is responsible for reporting or, if possible, removing potential hazards at the workplace?**

    a. You
    b. Your supervisor
    c. Fellow employees
    d. Your customers

3. **If you need to reach a product stored on an overhead shelf that you can almost reach, and you cannot find a ladder, you should:**

    a. just use a nearby chair to stand on as you reach for the product.
    b. quickly climb on a lower shelf to reach that extra inch or two.
    c. tell the customer that you cannot sell them the item.
    d. contact your supervisor or someone to assist you.

4. **Which of these is most susceptible to damage from permanent magnets?**

    a. Credit cards
    b. Cellular telephone antennas
    c. Polarized power connectors
    d. AA batteries

5. **What is the greatest aid to a Customer Service Specialist in preventing accidents?**

    a. Government safety manuals
    b. Fellow employees
    c. Common sense
    d. Customer suggestions

6. **In which of the following situations should you contact your supervisor for assistance?**

    a. You find a small spill that you are fairly sure is water.
    b. You encounter small debris on the floor of your work area.
    c. A customer falls, resulting in apparently minor bruises and abrasions.
    d. A coworker lightly pinches a finger in the clasp of a 3-ring binder.

7. **Voltages of as much as 40,000V would be expected:**

    a. on NiCad batteries.
    b. from diesel power back-up sources.
    c. at cellular telephone antennas.
    d. on TV or monitor display devices.

8. **If you are having computer hardware problems that you are not sure how to repair, you should:**

    a. unplug the equipment and attempt the service yourself.
    b. since you aren't trained in such repair, contact a computer repair specialist.
    c. leave the problem to be found by someone who might know more.
    d. while wearing safety goggles, use a fairly large sledge hammer to beat the computer into very small pieces, sweep them into the waste basket, then call the supply room and ask for a new system.

9. **You, as a CSS, are responsible for knowing each of the following except:**

    a. location of sprinkler shut-off valves.
    b. safe handling procedures for frequently used equipment.
    c. emergency evacuation procedures.
    d. company safety policies.

Answers:

1-d, 2-a, 3-d, 4-a, 5-c, 6-c, 7-d, 8-b, 9-a

Chapter 14

Independent Contractor Status

Dick Glass, CETsr

Dick Glass is an author of previous ETA publications, as well as more than a dozen books dealing with electronics technology and business management, published by Howard W. Sams Co, TAB Books, McGraw-Hill and ETA. He has also written hundreds of articles in trade journals and other association publications. Dick is a former Navy Avionics Technician, Industrial Electronics Computer Technician, Technical Writer, FCC Commercial License examination modernization committee chairman, inductee into the Electronics Hall of Fame and currently President of ETA-I. He has a broad background in all phases of work performed by electronics technicians. He oversees ETA's 40-plus certification programs and the training course approval system.

The Independent Contractor

Most businesses have a need to hire people or firms for specialized tasks. These are not employees. They are individuals or firms which provide specialized services. Examples are:

A. Plumbers
B. Roofers
C. Window washers
D. Appliance or electronics repair persons
E. Accountants
F. Snow removal or lawn care firms
G. Odd jobs workers
H. Trainers
I. Equipment operators
J. Cleaning firms
K. Blacktop sealers

Nearly everyone needs a little help now and then. Sometimes we need help because we do not have the time to do some task. We may be incapacitated temporarily. More often we need help because we do not have the expertise to do the job right.

If we need more employees because the business is growing, or we are working the present employees too hard, we have to decide whether we need another full-time worker, or if, perhaps, we can hire someone temporarily until the work load is brought back down to normal.

Why Worry About the Difference Between Employees and Contract Workers?

There might be little difference between the work performed by a regular employee and the worker employed as 'Contract Labor.' Either may work part or full time. Either may have the same expertise and skills. So, since there is very little difference in who they are or what they do, why be concerned with defining the differences between the two?

The answer is that there are legal concerns which can affect the business if the employee is not given correct status. There are tax consequences. There are Wage-Hour law requirements.

If the worker is not hired as a bona fide employee, he or she may not receive the benefits and wages he or she expects. Worker Social Security may be affected. The Wage-Hour state employment service agency may penalize the company if the worker rules are violated.

No Benefits!

The reason we include this discussion in our study for CSS—Customer Service Specialist—is that contract labor is an area of small business that is often violated. If the business manager tries to 'bend' the rules or requirements, he might do so for an extended period of time and get away with it. If so, the company may save a few bucks. The loser may be the State, or the employee. If he/she gets caught, it will be the company that loses. If you have a situation where everyone may lose, it sets up a concern in the minds of the worker, his/her boss, or the company. If they are operating in a 'cloudy' area, the employee may have a feeling of being treated unfairly, or that he/she has been pressured into working in a less-than-legal manner. If this causes tension, bad feelings about management, a sense of being cheated, or a worry that 'some day I might get caught,' then the whole concept of Customer Service will suffer.

This isn't always a black and white issue. There are times when the dividing line between 'contract labor' and 'employee' is not absolutely clear. Because of that possibility, the right attitude is to try to assure that the worker is treated as one or the other and that you are following the rules to the best of your ability. If it still isn't clear which the employee is, then seek guidance, either from your accountant, lawyer, or the wage-hour department of your state workforce agency.

Chapter 14. Independent Contract Status

Sometimes it is the worker who requests that he or she be treated as 'contract labor.' If you know that this is wrong, don't do it. Advise the potential employee that you cannot violate the law or bend the rules, both for the well-being of the company and for the worker.

Reasons Companies Bend the Rules:

Few larger companies will attempt to cheat on this topic. However, many newer and less experienced firms are tempted. Small operators, perhaps with only one or a few employees, may see a benefit to classifying a worker as 'contract.' Here are the reasons:

1. The CL (contract laborer) pays his own Social Security and other employee taxes. This may be a savings of 15% or more for the employer.

Pay your own taxes!

2. It is easier to fire a 'contract' worker, thus keeping the unemployment penalty rate lower for the employer.

3. The employer does not pay insurance fees for contract workers, such as health and accident.

4. Less than perfect service can be excused by blaming it on 'outside' workers rather than the official crew.

5. Workers who would rather be 'employees' may try harder to excel in order to keep their job.

Reasons Companies Should Not Bend the Rules:

1. If you, in fact, are knowingly cheating by hiring workers and then treating them as 'contract' labor, you likely will get caught by state investigators. You will then pay all Social Security and other costs you would have paid, plus sizable penalties.

2. If you do not carry insurance on the worker and he or she is injured or killed on the job, you are in a heap of trouble. Your business may have to pay all costs, and this could put you out of business. My son was injured when an inexperienced 'cherry picker' hoist operator broke the connecting cable and dropped him 28' onto a concrete pad. The only

reason he wasn't killed was that his ankles and vertebra crunched and softened the crash. The costs went to a million+ dollars. The insurance company would not have paid that had he been working as a temporary employee, or part-time, as contract labor. The company would have been saddled with all of the costs.

3. The worker does not gain the sense of teamwork which he/she would have as an official member of the work force at the company. Loyalties are less. He/she may tend to look for other part-time jobs in order to pay for insurance, and the added Social Security costs he/she will now incur. The employee may also realize that he/she is being short changed (even though the job may have been taken under the 'contract' conditions, because of desperation).

Reasons a Worker Should Not Agree to Work as a 'Contract' Worker When He Should be Classified as an Employee:

1. The hourly pay rate may seem sufficient, but when you calculate the loss of Social Security funds going into your account and other employer-paid benefits, the hourly pay is usually lower than comparable workers are receiving.

2. You do not receive vacation and sick day benefits in many cases. You get paid only for the hours you work.

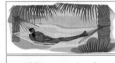

No vacation!

3. Unemployment compensation does not apply to business owners, as you are classified when you work as 'contract labor.'

4. You can't become part of any joint action by employee groups, unions, etc.

5. If you happen to be using one of the company's vehicles, you had better have a state chauffeur's license.

6. Chances for advancement, seniority and other benefits which usually occur with continued employment are often non-existent.

7. Fellowship, bonding, acquiring pride (in the company, the management or products) is usually less than if you were an official employee.

The Rules

Just what are the rules?

Chapter 14. Independent Contract Status

1. Contract labor persons are 'temporary' employees or workers.

2. They do not use company vehicles, service trucks or machinery. They own or rent their own equipment.

3. They do not work by the hour. (Although, their compensation may be based on expected hours worked to complete the tasks they are contracted to do.)

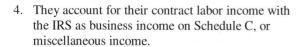

The Rules!

4. They account for their contract labor income with the IRS as business income on Schedule C, or miscellaneous income.

5. They pay their own Social Security reserve, including the portion an employer normally pays for them.

6. They provide their own accident, liability, vehicle and health insurance.

7. They establish their own hours. They do not punch a clock or fill out a time sheet.

8. They use their own tools.

9. They usually belong to associations rather than unions.

10. If their work is good, the company may decide to hire them full-time after a trial period as 'contract labor.'

Why Have Rules?

Isn't this a free country? Why do we need to be burdened by silly rules? Isn't it hard enough to be successful in business without being hampered by nuisance regulations?

Given human nature, the above is true. The wage-hour laws implemented by federal and state laws are a nuisance. They hamper your style if you are trying to beat the competition and keep your head above water in your own small business.

But it is also true that human nature is such that most of us aren't able to go into business for ourselves, because we do not have the capital to do so, or because we simply aren't business types.

So, most of us look to work for others--to provide services by using our brains or brawn to accomplish tasks for which other people or firms do not have enough help.

Throughout history, people with money or power have hired others to do work. Throughout history, employers have tried to get workers to work for low wages while they work for high compensation. To do this, the worker is sometimes pressured into working long hours; doing dangerous jobs; spending extra time preparing for actual unpaid work hours; not taking rest periods; working in hot or cold conditions; spending days away from home, etc.

So, it is natural that an employer, seeing he can gain by bypassing the tax and worker laws, attempts to do so. If the competition pays twenty percent or more in employee benefits and you can get by with none of these costs, you have a big advantage. For instance, you could lower your service call or labor rates, making your competitor seem to be the greedy one.

So while we may all voice our opinion that the state should stay out of our lives and that businessmen should be able to do as they please, eventually civilized people come to the conclusion that there should be some rules to protect the worker.

Some feel that if a company agrees to hire you, at any wage, you should be thankful, pledge your allegiance to the company and its products, work as hard as you can (no matter how oppressive the job may be) and never complain.

Some might say that, if the boss is making $200,000.00 per year and you are being paid $20,000.00 per year, you should realize the difference is: "Intelligence." When the company first hired a worker, the worker had no investment in the business and should have been properly grateful that he was hired.

On the other hand, some feel that there are few companies that are successful merely because the founder had a good idea or invention.

After the workers have participated in the production, invention, delivery, repair, marketing, sales, quality control, safety, packaging, upkeep, cleanliness, and other aspects of the business, the employees now have an investment in the business. Without the employees, the company could not exist. With good employees, the company can out-compete other similar businesses. So, the employee deserves a portion of the profits of the company. This doesn't mean that each worker is entitled to an equal share. It does mean he or she should be compensated fairly. It is history that this happens in few businesses, if employers are left to their own devices.

Thus, most of the civilized world has concluded that workers need some protection. Some towns have only one or two manufacturing businesses or large employers. If there are only a few possible places to get your first job, the business has the advantage. It can dictate how much it will pay you and whether it will give you any benefits at all.

 In a competitive market, where companies are seeking technical workers (or any workers) where there are too few unemployed people, the companies may bid for workers. They may pay a premium wage or offer lavish perks just to get the needed and experienced employee. Between the two extremes is a balanced work market where workers are offered decent compensation for their time and expertise, but this doesn't always happen.

So, there is some protection for workers all over the country and in most of the world. The state tries to enforce that protection, knowing that if workers receive decent compensation, the worker can purchase products which his company (as well as others) make. When sweat shops prevailed (and slave labor and child labor were used), and women were paid far less than their male counterparts for the same job, the economy invariably slumped. True, a few businessmen made millions. They built large and impressive edifices in honor of themselves. I can't remember any building monuments to the employees of the company.

Intimidation

When first on the job, things may not seem fair or the work may be overwhelming. A new employee needs to find out what is going on and attempt to fit into the program.

Sometimes the company's operations have been running okay for months and years. The new employee sees that others are doing their jobs, and that the straw bosses and supervisors are doing their best to obtain maximum production from the workers. Soon the rules of conduct are learned and the policies set up by management are explained. In most cases, these are safety and productivity rules: parking, clocking in or out, harassment of other employees, security and the like. If the rules are fair, they should be adhered to. If they are unfair, the worker should attempt to

help modify them and, if not successful, he/she should consider working elsewhere.

Contract Labor

Contract labor rules are clear. These are pointed out on the previous page. So the first rule is to make sure you understand the rules. If you know the company is intimidating you into agreeing to work 'Contract Labor' when you know you are really working as a regular employee, you should take action. The simplest action is to tell the human relations official, supervisor or boss that you feel you do not meet the contract labor definitions. If this is clear, ask to be put on as a permanent employee.

It may be that the employer does not yet know your qualifications. It is not a simple thing to hire someone in today's business world. The moment you are hired, the company has an obligation.

We don't all fit in!

Insurance, employee forms and reports, licenses, retirement, safety, education and many other factors come into play. It may take several weeks before the company feels they can fit you in. Some companies dictate a 'probationary' period of perhaps a month to ninety days before you are considered a permanent employee.

Smaller companies may also want to hire you on a 'probationary' status. The easiest way to do this is to just let you come to work as 'contract labor' for a few days or a few weeks, until they see that you work safely or that you can do the job. This may not be sticking to the letter of the law, but it may be what seems to be an overwhelmingly proper thing to do. It may be what you would do if you were the owner of a company.

So, if you find you are working as 'contract labor,' you will want to determine first whether you are either an employee or actually doing 'contract labor' work. Do you set your own hours and use your own vehicle, test equipment and tools? Do you account for your pay for tax purposes as miscellaneous income or business income? Or do you get a W2 from the employer? If you get a W2, you are an employee. If you get a form 1099, you are not an employee. The employer must provide you and the IRS with an annual report of any compensation paid to you by the company.

If it is clear that you are being used as contract labor rather than as an employee, find out if this is really a

Chapter 14. Independent Contract Status

temporary 'trial' or an intentional violation of the law. The company may be the owner's first. The owner may have other worries and may not know the law. You may have to point it out to him or her.

The Problem

You might wonder how this fits into the CSS, Customer Service Program. Isn't it more of a legal thing?

The reason we include it here is that if your position at work is unclear or even illegal, it will affect you, as well as

 the company. Most of us have run into people who seem unhappy all of the time. You have encountered those who have a scowl on their face most of the time. We have all been confounded by coworkers, neighbors or others who seem mad all of the time, for seemingly no reason. For some, the reason is that they are doing something wrong. They may be unhappy with themselves. They take this unhappiness out on others. They may want to show others that they made a mistake, did something wrong, or violated a rule, just to see that they aren't the only one whose conscience is not clear. If the company is cheating you, and knows it, it will not treat you with respect either. If you are not treated with respect, you will find you end up violating many of the principles of this book. If you have willingly let yourself work illegally, that will hang over your head. You may excuse your own agreement to work illegally as an opportunity to perhaps actually, later, work on your own, in your own business as a contractor. Or, you may feel it is the best you can do and thus, you had better go along with management rather than risk getting terminated. Surely the need to provide for your family, or to get some work experience may be a factor in your decision.

Peace of mind is what you will not have if you are classified improperly at your work place. The company may not want to do things right. Making it clear that you know the law and that you expect the company to properly classify you is doing the company a favor as well as yourself. Continuing to flaunt the law and the reasons for the law leads to trouble, for the company and for you.

You can't have pride in your job, your company, its products, your fellow workers, your education and your status in life if things aren't 'right' at work. You may not be able to do anything about it, short of reporting the violation

 to the state authorities. That is the last resort. Most companies will not argue the case once you point out the violation in your status. Some companies may believe that you don't know the rules. So long as they believe that, they may be too busy to make any changes. If you are working in a large company, it is your immediate supervisor who has the obligation to see that you are correctly classified. If you work for a small service firm, it is up to you to have a face-to-face talk about it with your boss.

So, in the end, this chapter is not entirely about 'contract labor.' It is about any circumstances at your work which are illegal or just wrong. Ferret out the problem if you can. Don't keep a wrong situation 'simmering.' It affects your ability to do your best. It reduces your worth to the company. Use all of the tactics in this book to make your work life (and your personal life) fair, legal and profitable to your employer and to you and your family.

Good Luck!

Chapter 14. Independent Contract Status

Chapter Quiz:

1. Technically, if a company classifies a worker as 'contract labor' for a few weeks while checking out the employee to see if he or she is going to 'work out,' it is a violation of state and federal law.

   a. True
   b. False

2. So long as a worker sets his own work hours at a company, he can be classified as 'contract labor' even if he does operate out of a company truck.

   a. True
   b. False

3. So long as a worker uses company-owned test equipment and tools and the company vehicles to perform his work, he is not allowed to also use some of his own private test equipment or tools.

   a. True
   b. False

4. Which of the following would a worker receive if he is working as a 'contact laborer'?

   a. Workman's compensation insurance
   b. Social Security insurance
   c. Unemployment benefits
   d. Monetary compensation

5. It is a violation of the wage-hour law to require a worker to accept 'contract labor' status when he or she is actually working as an ordinary employee.

   a. True
   b. False

6. It is illegal to hire a person as 'contract labor,' then later hire him/her full or part-time as a regular employee.

   a. True
   b. False

7. A person who works as a 'contract labor' worker must account for any income received either as Schedule C business income or on a 1099 MISC income.

   a. True
   b. False

8. An employer who illegally intimidates a worker into accepting 'contract labor' status can not expect to save money in which of the following ways?

   a. Not paying employer share of FICA
   b. Not paying unemployment insurance premiums
   c. By avoiding worker compensation insurance
   d. By finding it more difficult to fire the worker

9. One positive result of an employer hiring a worker, but treating him or her as 'contract labor' might be:

   a. the employee resents not being an employee, knowing he legally should be.
   b. the employee doesn't trust management in its other activities since it is cheating on him.
   c. a work-related accident can bring on additional legal problems for the employer.
   d. the employer would save the 15% FICA tax.

10. Which of the following are reasons the employee might choose to work as a contract worker?

    a. He may not be covered by accident insurance.
    b. He doesn't participate in retirement plans.
    c. He is not accruing Social Security credits.
    d. He wants the flexibility of setting his own hours.

Answers:

1-a, 2-b, 3-b, 4-d, 5-a, 6-b, 7-a, 8-d, 9-d, 10-d

Chapter 15

Record Keeping

Randy Glass works as a technology consultant, Executive Director of a national nonprofit organization, and faculty member and Sam Walton Free Enterprise Fellow at a private junior college where he teaches multimedia development and e-commerce. A veteran of the U.S. Marine Corps, where he served as an intelligence operator; he has done work as a financial planner, general manager for several companies, and an entrepreneur. [ecommerce@Hawaii.rr.com]

**Randy Glass,
MBA, CST, CIW**

Record keeping is a fundamental part of the customer service experience. Without good record keeping a company would have little way of validating whether or not they are successful at providing solutions for the customer. Records management, more than just keeping records, is the planning, controlling, directing, organizing, training, promoting, and otherwise managing activities regarding the administration of records. This chapter will cover the fundamentals of record keeping, including formulating policies, managing and using the records, and the ultimate destruction of the records themselves.

Good and Bad Records

The difference between keeping good and bad records is dependent on the purpose of keeping those records. If the

overall purpose is fulfilled, presumably they are good records. If the overall purpose is not fulfilled, presumably they are bad records. The most important factor is whether the records are useful to the organization's goals. Some organizations may be using records to provide customer service; others may be simply collecting information. Keys for determining if you are keeping good records are legibility, proper format, and proper distribution. Conversely, if you are keeping bad records, they are probably illegible, improperly formatted, and/or improperly distributed.

Reasons for Records

Companies use records to track performance, perform quantitative analysis, and for maintaining accountability. Customer Service Specialists keep records to track their own performance and perform quantitative analysis as well as track customer data. You can track your performance by measuring how many customers have been serviced in a certain period of time and the results of each call, leading to further quantitative analysis. Using quantitative analysis, one can assign numbers based on successes and failures, calculate them, and find better ways for improving the service provided.

As an example, a Customer Service Specialist may be assigned to a support center that assists in first-level (the initial call) software support. Their job is to find out the problem from the customer and either handle a small problem (like plugging in the power cable), or forward the call to a higher level support center. Normally, the customer is issued a 'ticket,' which follows that particular problem through its life cycle until it is solved. Sometimes called a 'trouble ticket,' it contains all the information that should be required for proper handling of the client. This information may include the ticket number, customer name, name of all specialists who have approached the problem, the contact information, dates, times, assumed problems, and solutions. There are three primary reasons for keeping records in this instance: 1) to pass information to higher level support specialists; 2) so the company can quantify how much support is needed for the software, along with other accounting matters; and 3) so the specialist can track patterns arising from customers using the software. If we can track patterns, we can remedy some future trouble calls by providing updates, or by changing the procedures for handling trouble calls.

In the example above, we pass information to higher levels of support to save time and to divide work into areas of specialty. Rarely does any one person know enough to handle every trouble call to enter the system. The next specialist to receive the ticket then knows the symptoms of the problem and could find a solution before either contacting the customer again or asking further questions. They also may need to contact the lower level specialist to confirm assumptions left by inadequate communication. The specialist also may have seen the symptoms before and will have a quick diagnosis, the third reason for record keeping, tracking patterns. Patterns arise from customers using the software, the same problems occurring with different people. This could signify a flaw in the software or in the accompanying manuals, which can subsequently be fixed. It is also much easier to fix a problem you have seen before and have solved, than to start fresh every time. For this reason, over-documentation is rarely a problem in customer service, but it can quickly become overwhelming. The company then will need the tickets to account for hours spent, to track software problems for future updates, to account for the overall cost of the software package (that includes your wages), and to verify that the customer has been properly serviced. The company may also send a questionnaire to the customer to ask about their satisfaction with their experience. A customer who has not been serviced properly will probably not continue to be a customer.

Policies

Companies create policies in order to have standardized practices throughout the organization. They maintain policies for employee conduct, administrative procedures, sales guidelines, as well as for record keeping. Policies should be adopted relating to what records are used, the records management life cycle, storage, legal requirements, and the destruction of records.

Most companies determine their policies based on their company's values. The main things to ask when setting these policies are: a) What are the organizational goals? b) Who will be collecting these records? c) What will they be used for? d) How long must they be kept? e) How and where will they be stored? and f) Who must have access to the records?

Even in small companies, all policies should be in writing and available to those with questions about the policies. They do no good if they are hidden. Good policies would reflect the usability of the records: how they are collected, stored, analyzed, and discarded. Bad policies reflect poor communication between levels of the company structure and are of little real value. An example of a good policy is to write down a customer's name and phone number before collecting further information because they could get disconnected and you can call them back. An example of a bad policy is asking for the customer's mother's maiden name before assisting them with a routine software problem. The last example is a waste of time, invasive, and is of no true value to solving the problem. Remember that records should add value to the customer's experience as well as the

company's effectiveness.

Life Cycle

Everything impermanent has a life cycle. A record keeping life cycle is illustrated in Figure 1. Any type of record will go through each of the 7 stages listed below. Notice that the stages can loop back into previous stages, as it should if the records are being used properly. Once the record reaches the storage stage, it could be called upon again for a later purpose.

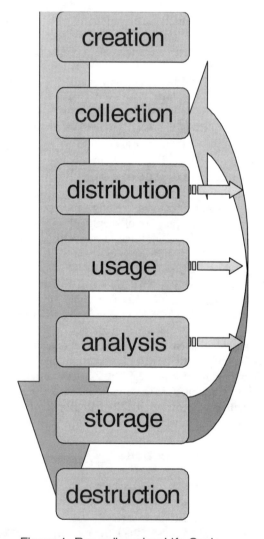

Figure 1. Recordkeeping Life Cycle

Creation: The physical production of the record itself deals with the development of fields to supply information from the customer and determine what information is needed or required.

Chapter 15. Record Keeping

Collection: Collection entails supplying the record with raw data like name and phone number, case number, and so on. This data could be supplied by either the specialist using the data, the customer, or a third party. Simply collecting data involves asking questions and listening to the customer. There should be no reason to react to any data input at this point, unless there is an underlying reason, like dealing with an irrational customer.

Distribution: The data will then be distributed to the user. Some data in a given record may be used in one situation yet have little or no use for other users, so it could be left out for some channels of distribution. Some records may be bad and unusable, and having used them, you would not have accurate data. Some records may be  distributed in their entirety to another user. In any case, some type of data should be retained for future use. In some situations, one person collects and uses the data before it is further distributed. The distribution and usage stages can be interchanged, depending on the environment.

Usage: How the data will be used should already have been determined during the creation stage. A different life cycle may develop at this point, depending on the organization. In technical shops the data may be used to diagnose a problem and solve it for the customer, going through several processes. Similarly, a travel agent would use the data to search for and to book a vacation.

Analysis: Data is only data unless it is used. Intelligence or structure added to the data makes it into information. During the usage stage, many hours of analysis could  have been used before arriving at a solution. However, in this stage, an analysis should be taken of the overall records situation. The analyst could find common trends among the data collected and how it was used. The storage and distribution should be analyzed to ensure that it fits the proper needs. Many times, poor record keeping stems from the processes involved throughout these several stages, and redefining them makes it better. A common situation is to begin using a database and find out that the files are too large to store or transport digitally. Microsoft Access users can quickly run out of storage space on smaller hard drives. Many people can still relate to having filing cabinets overflowing with paper, which is a similar situation; too much paper, too little space to store it. My father used to tell me

about stuff called paper but I still don't 'get it.'

The analysis phase should be able to feed back into all other phases. A good analysis should include other sources of data as well as new methods of data collection. Sometimes, during the analysis phase, you may find that you could improve the collection process, policies, and marketing procedures.

Storage: Records must be stored in some type of physical medium, whether it's magnetic, optical, vinyl, or paper. Some companies today have a double problem of storing everything on two mediums, such as paper and magnetic.  There has to be a tradeoff between importance and available space. Again, some database users quickly find that any type of storage on a large scale, meaning many customers or large amounts of data, costs money. During the storage stage, and all stages preceding it, there may be some need to go back to prior stages to collect more data, use the data, engage in distribution, and to do more analysis.

Destruction: When the storage space or importance of the data runs out, it is time to destruct. This stage leads on to another concern of information security, or InfoSec. Simply throwing away records in the garbage can is not considered a responsible way to care for your customer's personal information. If it's paper, it can be shredded, but how much of your customer's information is on a digital format? Even the delete key leaves data on the hard drive. Every time I see a person at the post office going through trashcans at midnight, I wonder how safe any information really is. To complicate matters, each type of media presents its own problems when it comes to destruction. Optical media, like compact disks, need to be melted before the data is completely destroyed. Please don't forget to consider that customer data that is no longer being used by you may be of great use to someone else. Don't contribute to identity theft by not taking proper security precautions when destructing records.

Legal Considerations

In most situations, the law doesn't require specific record keeping activities for the normal business. However, common law does require keeping records on employees and certain financial records. Employee records must be kept for two years in most states. Tax records must be maintained for several years before being destroyed.

Chapter 15. Record Keeping

Administrative agencies also require keeping records, depending on the industry that the agency oversees. An example of this may be an automotive shop that is required to keep records of the disposal of hazardous waste such as batteries and oil. In some circumstances, the shop may be required to report this disposal at given intervals, in others the records may be required to be kept in case the agency asks to verify their compliance with regulations.

Companies may keep records on file as protection from liability. If a customer accuses the company of wrongdoing, and the company has records to prove otherwise, it could save many thousands of dollars in legal defense. Conversely, records could be used to prove a company's wrongdoing. Many companies have fallen victim to legal disputes and have had their records used against them. Microsoft had their internal emails used against them to charge them with using monopolistic practices. In any case, records can be used to prove negligence or innocence. This is why good record keeping is vitally important.

Records Management

Records management entails managing the life cycle of the record. Proper and effective management of the records makes them useful to the company and the customer. The International Organization for Standardization (ISO)

published a standard for managing business records. ISO 15489 "focuses on the business principles behind records management and how organizations can establish a framework to enable a comprehensive records management program." (ISO Public Relations). This standard is targeted to everyone in contact with the record's life cycle. It identifies the key issues involved with record keeping, how to make the record useful, and how to properly dispose of the information when the record is no longer being used.

By using standards that are published by an international organization such as the ISO, you are optimizing the effectiveness of your process. Similar to becoming certified to add value to the organization, it also lets both the employees and the customer know that your record keeping complies with a set of standards. While these standards are not mandatory for most organizations, some organizations adopt these standards and require employees to strictly adhere to them. Some contracts and governments may require this adherence to ensure that proper records management principles are in effect within an organization.

Database Records

A collection of records is a database. We refer to databases as being digital in nature, and not paper. These digital records are referred to as files. The problem with paper is that you can't easily manipulate or mine the data. Microfiche was created to help combat this problem, but now with a digital environment, we can have much greater control over how records are used. Two common examples of database software are Microsoft's Excel and Access programs. Excel is on one side of the fence, a simple interface and a collection of cells that can be easily manipulated. On the other side is Access, a relatively robust program that allows you to design an interface, reports, and some level of automation into the record keeping process. Many companies will choose to design their own database software, or buy one from a manufacturer that specializes in their industry. The most important factor for the organization is finding a database that matches the needs of the organization.

The design of the database and its proper use are the most important factors of its success. Clear analysis of how data will transition through its life cycle, well-thought-out process specifications, quality programming, and thorough training are all parts of the design process. Having a poorly designed or implemented database is just as bad as having none. A large organization that intensively uses the data they collect could have many versions and series of databases, all being used for different functions.

Imagine the database of a credit card company. They may have millions of customers. Some employees may use the data to send statements, approve transactions, or help with customer service. The company certainly wouldn't want everyone in the company to be able to share all of the information in the records for security reasons, so it would be dissected into several series of records with different permissions for each  field for different users. Similarly, the customer may need access to change, update, or otherwise manage the data relating to their record at any time. In this instance, the proper design and use are very important to the success of the database, and ultimately the success of the organization.

Disposing of Records

Disposing of records means the complete destruction or otherwise retirement of a record or series of records: the seventh stage of the life cycle. The destruction of records becomes necessary when the storage space or its importance

Chapter 15. Record Keeping

runs out. This process depends on the type of medium the records are stored on and the data it contains. Shredding is a standard disposal method of paper records, but complete disposal would entail the burning of records. Most commer- cial shredders still leave traces of records that can be reconstructed, leading then to improper use of the records, such as identity theft.

Magnetic media storage is more difficult to dispose of. Magnetic media consists of tapes, floppy disks, and hard drives. Some non-sensitive records can simply be deleted from the hard drive, but traces of this file are still remaining on the disk. Complete destruction requires degaussing the disk surface. For some records with security concerns, a simple reformatting of the disk is not sufficient and the disk must be degaussed. Degaussing involves removing a magnetic field and realigning the polarity of the electrons. The reason for this is that on a disk or tape, simply deleting the record only removes the reference to the data, and not the data itself.

Optical media storage is still more difficult. Optical media consists of Compact Disks (CD), Digital Video Disks (DVD), and other media still in development. Again, to completely dispose of the record we must resort to a burning process. Disposing of the waste from burned plastic and metal becomes a bigger problem, let alone the pollution and expense of the burning process. Both of these problems can result in an organization not choosing optical storage as its storage medium.

The easiest medium to store and dispose of records is volatile media. This consists of Random Access Memory (RAM) and other temporary storage that is subject to a continuous supply of power. This type loses all contents of a record as power is turned off from the unit. The drawback to this form of medium is its inability to store large records for an extended period of time, and it is typically only used when the records are actively being used.

Conclusion

In this chapter, we have covered many aspects of record keeping from formulating policies, managing and using the records, to the ultimate destruction of the records themselves. Throughout an organization, good record keeping and proper procedures ultimately reflect the organizational goals, and its view toward quality customer service.

Remember that proper record keeping adds value to the customer, as well as quality to the customer service.

Chapter 15. Record Keeping

Chapter Quiz:

1. **Records management involves:**

   a. planning record keeping activities.
   b. training users of records.
   c. controlling records.
   d. all the above.

2. **Responsible companies use records for:**

   a. selling data to other companies.
   b. performing quantitative and qualitative analysis.
   c. spying on the customer.
   d. identifying competitors.

3. **Why would you issue the customer a ticket?**

   a. To show them the right way to use the equipment
   b. They are going too fast
   c. To track the problem
   d. All the above

4. **We pass information to higher levels to:**

   a. let the boss know we are working.
   b. divide areas of specialty.
   c. answer the next call.
   d. pass the responsibility.

5. **Record keeping is fundamental to the customer service experience.**

   a. True
   b. False

6. **Asking questions and listening to the customer begins at which stage of a record keeping life cycle?**

   a. One
   b. Two
   c. Three
   d. None of above

7. **The first step in the development of the record keeping life cycle involves:**

   a. listening to the customer.
   b. analyzing the problem.
   c. developing fields for the record.
   d. all the above.

8. **The record is no longer used once it is stored.**

   a. True
   b. False

9. **An organization may be required by law to keep what kind of data?**

   a. Employee records
   b. Hazardous waste disposal
   c. Customer income levels
   d. a and b

10. **Complete destruction of records stored on magnetic media involves:**

    a. shredding.
    b. emptying the recycle bin.
    c. throwing it away.
    d. degaussing.

Answers:

1-d, 2-b, 3-c, 4-b, 5-a, 6-a, 7-c, 8-b, 9-d, 10-d

Chapter 16

CSS—Evaluating Your Performance

Randal Reusser has been involved with the ETA-I since 1990. He has served as Chairman, Vice-Chairman, Secretary, Shop Owners Division Chairman, Certified Technicians Division Chairman, Certified Technicians Division Secretary/ Treasurer and Certification Administrator. Randal received the "Pete" outstanding national officer award in 1996. He is a senior CET in Consumer Electronics, Communication, and is also a CFOI and CSM. Randal holds an MBA from Marquette University, a BA from Carthage College, an AA from Gateway Technical College and many other honors and technical certifications.

Randal R. Reusser, CETsr, CSM, MBA

Job Evaluation

It is likely that your job performance will be evaluated on a regular basis. How often you are evaluated will depend on the size of the organization where you work. Most companies evaluate and review employee performance annually. This information is used to determine raises, bonuses, additional training requirements, employee strengths and weaknesses, and provide feedback to the employee.

In addition to evaluating individual employees, most companies also evaluate departments. Different departments are evaluated by different measures. For example, a Human Relations or Personnel Department would generally be evaluated in the areas of recruitment, selection, and employee retention. The scope of this book will limit our discussion to customer service departments and the individual customer service employees.

Many companies are realizing that what separates them from their competitors is the quality of their customer service. Customer Service departments should strive to provide quality service and work towards continuous improvement. Here is where the problems start. What is quality service? Who decides and how do you measure it? Quality service is meeting or exceeding customer expectations with the service you provide. Therefore, your customers will ultimately determine what is quality service. This is often called Customer Driven Quality, which can apply to products and services.

Quality service doesn't happen by accident and is not easy to achieve, but it is well worth your effort. There are many components to quality service including store/shop appearance, wait time, employee appearance/attitude, accuracy and many others. What is important to the customer will depend on your type of business. For example, to deliver quality service in a grocery store, the speed and accuracy of the checkout lanes is very important. If a

grocery store has a good selection and low prices, but keeps you waiting in line for an hour, they are not providing quality service.

How do you evaluate the performance of your customer service department and measure your own quality of service? It all depends on the type of service you are providing. In the cable TV industry, some key indicators used to measure the quality of service are: signal level, phone answer time, hold wait time, billing accuracy and speed of installation and repair. All of these items are directly or indirectly linked to what customers expect from a cable company. For a cable company to continuously improve its level of customer service, it would have to fine-tune its systems and procedures to reduce the number of billing errors, answer calls quicker, reduce customer hold time and improve other areas that are important to customers. It is common for a company to benchmark or compare itself to its competitors and other industries, in addition to its own historical records to evaluate its customer service performance.

It is now time to turn our attention to measuring or evaluating individual employees. As a professional certified Customer Service Specialist you should be continually evaluating your own performance. Every day is an opportunity to expand your customer skills and improve the quality of service that you provide. When a situation with a customer goes very well or very badly, you should take a step back and analyze what happened.

When you finish serving the customer (on the phone or in person) and they were obviously satisfied with the service, ask yourself some questions. The questions to ask are: What did I do right to satisfy that customer? Was I pleasant? Did I appear confident and professional? What systems are in place at my company that contributed to that customer's satisfaction? Replay in your mind the entire transaction and make notes to help you focus on the key things that satisfied the customer. For example, if you worked for a computer service center, some key things that might satisfy a customer are: the repair was done when promised, the cost of repair was lower than the estimate, the staff was pleasant/attentive, and the people at the service center seemed to care. Discuss your findings with other employees and your supervisor. Try to duplicate the situation with every customer if possible.

When things go wrong and a customer is unhappy or dissatisfied, use it as an opportunity to learn. When you finish serving the dissatisfied customer, ask yourself some questions. The questions you should ask are: How could I have reduced or eliminated that customer's dissatisfaction? Was I unpleasant? Did I appear disinterested or unprofessional? What systems are in place at my company that contributed to that customer's dissatisfaction? Apply what you learn to future situations to prevent, reduce or eliminate what went wrong. Again, discuss your findings with other employees and your supervisor.

Too many companies spend all of their time "putting out fires" (solving problems after they happen) instead of "fire prevention" (preventing problems from happening). In reality you will always have to deal with both, but quality service should strive for more fire prevention and less fire fighting. Self-evaluation and system evaluation are valuable tools that you should use.

Evaluation by your supervisor or boss can be a stressful experience. If you do a little record keeping about your strengths and weaknesses, it will be less stressful. When people compliment you on your work and are satisfied with your company, ask them to tell your boss or supervisor. As a manager, I know that it is not often that I get to talk to a satisfied customer. Make a note of the customer's name, the date, other relevant data, and why they were satisfied. Save this in a file folder and use the folder at your evaluation. Also use it when customers write letters to express their happiness with your service. Give a copy to your supervisor and keep the original in your file folder. Customers will write letters only when they are exceptionally pleased or extremely dissatisfied. I used to get many letters when I was an electronic technician and I still have them.

You should also give letters from dissatisfied customers to your boss and keep a copy in your file folder. Make notes about the situation that led to the letter and also suggest possible solutions when bringing the letter to your supervisor. It is extremely important that these letters receive immediate attention. Even if the customer is wrong,

he or she deserves a response that addresses the concerns. Some people are unhappy even when they receive the highest level of quality service. In other cases, you or your company made a mistake and now have a chance to correct the error.

Complaints should never be taken personally and always used to discover shortcomings in your service and systems. Good managers will not use the complaint against you. Instead, they will look at what you did to resolve the complaint and prevent future complaints.

There are a few other things that you should include in your review file folder. Keep a record of any in-house training and any external training that you received since your last evaluation. If you have taken any classes or attended any conventions, include this information. Finally, keep notes on any suggestions that you have made and any other improvements that you have contributed to the quality of service that your company provides. Managers are very busy and cannot be expected to remember all of these things.

There are many areas that are of general importance to all employers in the area of employee evaluation. They include but are not limited to:

| Appearance |
| Attitude |
| Computer Skills |
| Growth |
| Honesty |
| People Skills |
| Punctuality |
| Reliability |
| Work Ethic |

Appearance

Earlier I mentioned appearance when discussing shops and stores. Your appearance may be of greater importance to the customer. If your clothes are dirty and your hair is uncombed, then it will reflect badly on your company. You must wear proper attire at work, especially when dealing with customers in person.

Chapter 16. CSS - Evaluating Your Performance

While working as a Service Manager, I discovered that it was easier to deal with upset customers when I was better dressed than they were. My appearance conveyed authority and professionalism, and they responded. Your customer service counter, shop, office, or desk can also convey positive or negative messages.

For example, if you took your new car to a garage for an oil change, saw beer cans littered on the floor and the mechanic smelled like beer, would you let him work on your car? Probably not. My example is a little extreme, but I am trying to emphasize that you are an ambassador of your company and should pay careful attention to your appearance.

Attitude

Attitude is everything. Being positive will always put you at an advantage over your coworkers and competitors. I have heard many executives say that they would hire a less skilled person with a good attitude over a highly skilled person with a bad attitude. They know that a person with a good attitude can be trained to do almost anything. People with bad attitudes can be highly contagious and infect a company. One person with a bad attitude can pull down an entire company.

Over the years I have known many people (including myself) who would blame their bad attitude on a company or life situation. Changing companies will not change you. If you constantly have a negative attitude, it will follow you.

We are personally responsible for our attitude and even in the worst of situations (I have been there), a positive attitude can help you succeed. There are many methods to start your day with a positive attitude, including getting a good nights sleep, not watching the morning news or reading the newspaper before you go to work. I pray and read the Bible each morning to start my day off right. Exercising or taking a short walk before work can help start your day with a positive attitude. Getting to work early and having time to relax before you start will help your attitude. Building a positive attitude each day is your personal responsibility and well worth the effort.

Computer Skills

Having the right computer skills is essential in today's highly computerized world. Each of us needs to continually improve our computer skills by learning and using new

features, programs, hardware and websites. Even people who have used the same program for years can benefit from a one or two-day seminar.

Nearly all companies rely heavily on computers, and you can never have too many computer skills. It is in your best interest to learn all of the programs in use at your company (when practical). This will allow you to help with other projects and move into other opportunities as they become available.

Ask to go to seminars, sit in on new software training, watch videos, use interactive training resources and actively pursue other training opportunities. We should all strive to become experts with the programs and hardware that we use daily. It is also important to become literate and familiar with the other software and hardware in use at your company.

Growth

Growth is another important area in which employees are evaluated. As an employee, you should be striving to grow in both knowledge and skills. Your job will become easier and you will enjoy it more when you have mastered all the necessary skills that your job requires. Many people stop at this point but, if you want to be successful, mastering your current job is only the beginning. Your current job may be changing and it is necessary to keep up with technology. I firmly believe that continuing education and the learning of new skills is fundamental to a successful career and personal job satisfaction. The day we stop learning and growing is the day that we die.

Where and how do you get new skills and increase your knowledge? You can learn new skills from your boss and coworkers right at work. Try attending a one-day seminar on computers, customer service or anything else that may enhance your career or that you find interesting. Many employers are willing to let you have the day off and will pay for your additional training. Even if they do not, there is no better investment than the investment we make in ourselves.

There are plenty of opportunities for free training and seminars at colleges, public libraries and other places. Many suppliers offer training free to customers, and this type of training is often the best available. Knowledge and new skills can be obtained from reading trade journals, books, watching videos, the Internet, your local trade school or college and many other sources.

Today many companies develop career paths for employees that lay out a training plan to chart a course for the employee to follow in order to prepare them for their next promotion. If your company doesn't offer this service, talk to your manager or mentor and start developing your own career path. Typical career paths can include earning degrees, certifications, learning new job skills, taking a class, and other things to strengthen weaknesses or build new competencies. Think of it as a plan and map that can take you where you want to go.

As a Customer Service Specialist, you may occasionally train others and should always encourage your employees and coworkers to grow both personally and professionally. I believe that our personal growth flourishes when we help others to grow.

Honesty

Remember the old saying "Honesty is the best policy?" It is true. Over the years I have had to terminate employees, and the number one reason is dishonesty. A dark cloud follows those who lose their job for lying or stealing from their employer. Excessive debt or drug use has led many employees to make bad decisions. It is not worth losing your job. If you are having personal problems that interfere or might interfere with your work, discuss them with your supervisor or human resources department (if you work at a larger company).

Never lie to your customers or employer. The lies always grow and usually get out of control. At a company where I used to work, they told customers that we would work on their equipment in a week to ten days. In reality, we were three weeks behind. Customers would call in to see if their equipment was repaired before it had even been touched. Lying to the customers sets them up to be dissatisfied with the service. Do not lie to the customer. If your employer wants you to lie, find a different employer.

People Skills

Having good people skills is important to be successful in any job. This is especially true for the customer service specialist. The majority of your workday is spent dealing with internal and external customers.

Developing good communication skills is essential for success as a customer service specialist. Good listening skills can reduce or eliminate misunderstandings. While listening, take notes, do not interrupt, and don't formulate your answer until the other person is finished speaking. Repeat the information back to the person in your own words to make sure you understand. When speaking to others, always be clear and concise. Look into their eyes when possible and never use slang or profanities. Do not hold back important information, but do not give too much information either.

Empathy is also important when dealing with people. Try to put yourself in their position and experience what it feels like. The golden rule of "do unto others as you would have them do unto you" should always be followed. People skills are something that must be cultivated and polished throughout your entire career.

Punctuality

Being late has always bothered me as an employer. I expect people to be on time or early. If you get to work a few minutes early, your whole day will generally be better. Being late for work sends the wrong message to your employer. Too many people put unnecessary stress on themselves by barely making it to work on time each day. People are counting on you. Be on time!

Reliability

From my experience, people who are on time are much more reliable than those who are not. Reliability means showing up for work on time, not missing days, and not calling in sick at the last minute or on a regular basis. I once had a coworker who was consistently late fifteen minutes every day. My reasoning was that if he got up fifteen minutes earlier he could be on time. There were times when customers were waiting for him. Many people use their car or children as excuses to miss work frequently and/or come and go as they please. A good, organized employee will make alternative arrangements to solve these problems. If your car is unreliable, use a car pool. Always have a back-up plan for your transportation and childcare.

Work Ethic

Work ethic is one of the most important areas in which employees are evaluated. Giving your employer a day's work for a day's pay is my definition of work ethic. This is

Chapter 16. CSS - Evaluating Your Performance

a very simple definition, but it should be sufficient to build upon.

Many people find themselves doing extra work because their coworkers have a poor work ethic. This causes friction at work and resentment towards coworkers and even the boss, for allowing or not noticing the substandard performance of coworkers.

You will be a much happier person if you don't worry about other people's work ethic. Doing a little more than your fair share has never hurt anybody, and it will make you a more valuable employee and a better person in the long run.

When you have employees who report to you, their work ethic becomes your concern. Then it is your responsibility, and you must find ways to improve your employees' work ethic or find new employees.

There are other areas in which you may be evaluated. Good managers will make them clear to you when you are hired, or if any of the evaluation criteria changes. It is important to remember that even the worst evaluation is a useful tool to expose areas where you need improvement. Without both positive and negative feedback it is impossible to improve your job performance and achieve customer service excellence.

Chapter Quiz:

1. Quality Service is defined by the:

a. industry.
b. customer.
c. service company.
d. service employee.

2. How often do companies usually evaluate employees?

a. Monthly
b. Bi-annually
c. Annually
d. Semi-annually

3. What is it called when a company compares itself to its competitors?

a. Customer driven quality
b. Leveraging
c. Reflection
d. Benchmarking

4. Which of the following is not part of an employee evaluation?

a. Work Ethic
b. Appearance
c. Personal Issues
d. Attitude

5. Putting out fires is best described as:

a. solving problems after they happen.
b. conflict resolution.
c. fire fighting.
d. management's job.

6. What best determines your attitude?

a. Your circumstances
b. Your lifestyle
c. Your outlook on life
d. Genetics

7. What is a Career Path?

a. A plan and map for your career
b. The progression of jobs you have held
c. A training plan
d. A company hierarchy

8. Lying to customers:

a. is essential in today's business world.
b. sets you up for failure.
c. makes your job easier.
d. solves many problems.

9. Which of the following would not improve your reliability?

a. A backup transportation plan
b. A backup child care plan
c. A career path training plan
d. A car pool

10. What is work ethic?

a. Situational Ethics
b. Doing as little as possible
c. There is no such thing
d. A day's work for a day's pay

Answers:

1-b, 2-c, 3-d, 4-c, 5-a, 6-c, 7-a, 8-b, 9-c, 10-d

Chapter 17

Employee Career Plans

Randal Reusser has been involved with ETA-I since 1990. He has served as Chairman, Vice-Chairman, Secretary, Shop Owners Division Chairman, Certified Technicians Division Chairman, Certified Technicians Division Secretary/ Treasurer and Certification Administrator. Randal received the "Pete" outstanding national officer award in 1996. He is a senior CET in Consumer Electronics, Communication, and is also a CFOI and CSM. Randal holds an MBA from Marquette University, a BA from Carthage College, an AA from Gateway Technical College and many other honors and technical certifications.

Randal R. Reusser, CETsr, CSM, MBA

Career Planning

When we were children, adults would ask us, "What do you want to be when you grow up?" No one answers this question with drug dealer, burglar, or white collar criminal. As children, more common answers are doctor, policeman, or model. I doubt that most children take their future very seriously, and many don't realize their childhood career goal.

In India, the caste system is still prevalent in rural areas. How you will earn a living is decided when you are born. For example, if your family members are silversmiths, that will be your occupation. America has informal family traditions where children follow in the footsteps of their father or mother. There are many third-generation firefighters, policeman, and doctors.

Recently I was in a job interview and the person asked me, "What kind of a job do you want when you grow up?" My answer was, "The job for which I am applying." To begin career planning, a person must answer this question.

High schools and colleges have career counselors to help you decide what career to choose. When I worked for Carthage College, I saw many students change their major two or more times before deciding on a career. This was wasteful in the sense that some classes they had already taken would not count towards their degree. However, changing your mind early about your career plans is usually less painful than changing careers later in life.

A recent study found that "working people are making on average 5-7 career changes in a working lifetime."[1] The days when a person worked at the same company for his or her entire career are gone. Most won't even work at the same occupation or in the same field during his or her working career. This is not necessarily a bad thing.

Career planning is essential if you want a career and not just a job. Jobs tend to be more static and unchanging when compared to the dynamic and progressive nature of a career. Two people can be doing the same work and, for one person, it is a job, while it is a career for the other. For the purposes of this chapter, I will define a job as something you do to earn a living, or for purely financial gain. A job is something that you wouldn't do if you didn't need the money.

A career provides much more than an income. For many, a career fulfills emotional and spiritual needs along with providing a paycheck. A person with a career normally has a much deeper involvement and dedication to his or her work than a person with just a job.

Many times in my life I have wondered why people choose a job over a career. I also find it interesting how some turn a job into a successful career. I personally believe that a career is more than the general field of work in which one earns a living. It is an integral part of what defines a person and is a reflection of his or her skills and abilities.

Career Paths

When driving across country, using a road map or some other form of navigation is highly recommended. Without something to guide you, you could get lost or at least go out of your way. In much the same way that a road map helps us to find a destination, a career path maps out a route to a desired career or specific position within an existing career.

On the following page I have illustrated a simple career path that a person might follow to become a licensed electrician. It is only an example and does not contain the details found in a typical career path. Becoming a licensed electrician is complicated and also varies with union requirements and local laws.

Chapter 17. Employee Career Plans

Electrician Career Path	
High School	Take electric shop Graduate
Apprenticeship	Start an apprenticeship Take college classes Work for four years
Journeyman	Pass state licensing test Become a Journeyman

The electrician career path looks pretty easy, but realistically, it is tough working as an apprentice. You will work hard and do every dirty job. Also, apprentices earn much less money than journeymen. Typically, apprentices will work with an experienced electrician and learn by doing. They will need to pass the state test, after completing their apprenticeship, to become journeyman electricians.

Career paths are usually directly tied to a training plan. In the previous example of an electrician's career path, working four years as an apprentice and taking college classes were the training plan.

Getting Started

Today many companies develop career paths for employees and lay out a training plan to chart a course for the employee to follow in order to prepare him or her for the next promotion. If your company doesn't offer this service, it is time to start developing your own career path. Your career path may include earning degrees, certifications, learning new job skills, taking a class, and other things to strengthen weaknesses or build new competencies. Think of it as a plan and a map that can take you where you want to go.

Getting started on your career path and training plan is easier than you think. Most people already have an informal career path or desire to achieve a certain career goal. To start a career path, I suggest writing out your desired career goal or goals. Place it in a prominent place where you will see it every day.

Suppose that you want to become president of a large corporation. That is your career goal. Before you can develop or design a career path and training plan to reach this goal, you must first examine your current skills, level of education, and work experience. We tend to see ourselves with  rose-colored glasses and need external input during this evaluation stage. Talking with a mentor, career counselor, coworker, supervisor, or close friend can help bridge the gap between our own perceptions and others' views of our strengths and weaknesses.

Obviously, the career path and training plan to become president is much shorter and less complex for a current vice-president than for a high school student. The vice-president may already have paid his or her dues within the corporation and have the skills, training, and education required to become president. For that person, taking on some of the president's responsibilities or even just waiting for him or her to retire, may be all that is needed to achieve the goal of becoming president.

Career Path Contents

A career path should contain steps or goals that you need to complete in order to pursue your desired career. It should at least answer the 'what,' 'where,' 'when,' 'how long,' and 'how much' questions. The career you are seeking answers the 'what' question. It does not have to be specific, but needs to address your career interests. For example, a specific career is veterinarian, a more generic answer may be 'working with animals.' Being less specific allows a person to work towards a goal and still have flexibility in his or her career choices.

Answering the 'where'  question is often as hard as the 'what' question. Each year in fall or early spring, millions of high school seniors start applying to colleges. Many have not yet decided on the career they want, and some haven't even narrowed it down within the major academic disciplines. This makes choosing a college much more difficult. If you already have a career in mind, you can limit your college search to places that specialize or have a good reputation in that field.

The road to a career for a high school student can be paved with a lot of rejections from colleges. Some may have several colleges that want them, and they may even be offered attractive scholarships. For people who are furthering their career or working on a career change, there are fewer options. As we get older and gain responsibilities, it becomes more difficult to attend school full-time. Many need to work to make ends meet while attending college part-time. This situation will limit your choice of schools to ones that are close and offer convenient hours. There are other options like Distance Learning, but many employers remain skeptical about these schools.

Chapter 17. Employee Career Plans

The 'when' question needs to be answered in your career path. If you do not have a start and a target completion date for your goals, it is less likely that you will ever achieve them. For most high school students, starting college in the fall after their graduation is ideal. There is an even better time to start college—while you are still in high school. In some states, including Wisconsin, the state will pay for high school juniors and seniors to take college classes. These classes count for high school and college credit! When my friend's son graduated from high school, he had already completed his first semester of college.

The completion date is nearly as important as the start date. For students going on to graduate school, they need to finish on time or possibly have to wait a semester before starting. Many college students do not complete their program in four years. This is because they need additional remedial classes, or they change majors and need to take additional classes. For a person taking college classes for career advancement, not finishing on time could be disastrous. For example, your career path has you taking classes to prepare for your boss's position when he or she retires. If you don't have the degree or other required credentials at that time, you could be passed up or not considered for the promotion.

The 'how long' question will be answered as, "the time period between the start and projected completion date." For some goals on a career path, it can be days or weeks, while other goals require years. Don't lose heart because some goals take a long time to achieve; just keeping working toward your goals. Regardless of what career you choose or at what stage of your career you are in, you should have, and be working on, goals. There is a great feeling of accomplishment when you complete an educational or training goal. It is well worth the time and effort that it takes to build your future.

 The cost of completing your goal is very important. This answers the 'how much' question. Some one-day seminars can cost over $1,000, and a four-year degree can easily cost $100,000. First, don't let the cost deter you from attempting college or any other worthwhile training. Think of it as an investment in your future with a tangible return of personal satisfaction and financial gain.

Those already in the work force have an advantage over full-time students. Many companies offer tuition reimbursement that will pay for some or all of your training or education expenses. It is amazingly sad how few people use these benefits. Check with your human resources office to find out what your company has to offer. Normally, you will have to agree to stay at the sponsoring employer for a period of time after completing classes or a degree. This is typically six months to two years. During this time, the company hopes to benefit from its investment in you.

For students who do well in their undergraduate classes, chances are good that your first employer will be willing to pay for part-time graduate school. Even if you need to pay for your own training or education, it is a great investment. I don't recommend going into debt for graduate school, or any training or education, after you are working full-time. Instead, save for that special seminar or pay as you go, taking one class at a time. It will take longer, but unless you have a compelling reason to hurry, take your time.

It may take a while to recoup an investment in your education or training. If the bill is already paid, the wait is easier. For many, the new skills learned can be used immediately and may help in your current position. How your training plan fits within your career path will determine your next step.

Sample Career Paths

Let's now look at two different sample career paths. The first one is for Joe, who is in high school and wants to focus on building a new career in the field of electronics.

Joe's Electronics Technician Career Path 2003

Requirements	Training/ Education	Start Date	Completion Date
Electronic Shop Class	Greencastle High School	1/10/03	5/24/03
High School Diploma	Greencastle High School	8/29/99	5/24/03
A.A Degree Electronics	Gateway Technical College	8/23/03	5/21/06 (expected)
Experience	Part-time job in electronics	05/20/04	Open
CET	ETAI	1/28/06	5/28/06 (expected)

After discussing his career plans with Bill, his high school counselor, and Pat, an electronics instructor at Gateway Technical College, Joe developed the above career path. Bill suggested that Joe take the Electronics Shop class during his last semester at Greencastle High School. This will introduce Joe to basic electronics theory and practices.

Chapter 17. Employee Career Plans

Pat told Joe about Gateway Technical College's electronics program, and the ETA Certified Electronics Technician certification. He also suggested that Joe find a part-time job in electronics after completing his first year of college. If Joe follows this career path, he is well on his way to becoming an Electronics Technician.

The second career path is for Sally, who wants to advance within management at her current company. Sally is a site manager for Technology Corporation (T-Corp) with three people working for her. Sally's goal is to be promoted to area manager. She met with her supervisor to develop the career path below:

Sally's Area Manager Career Path 2003

Requirements	Training/Education	Start Date	Completion Date
B.A. Degree Business	Carthage College	8/26/02	5/26/05
Management Certificate	Technology Corporation	4/29/03	5/30/03
3 Years Experience as Site Manager	Technology Corporation	2/15/00	2/15/03
Certification Administrator	ETA-I	10/28/02	11/28/02 (expected)
Open Position	Technology Corporation	?	?

Sally currently has an Associate Degree in Business and a Customer Service Specialist certification from the ETA. There are five requirements to become an area manager for T-Corp. They are: a Bachelors Degree in business, a Management Certificate, 3 years experience as a site manager for T-Corp, Certification Administrator authorization, and there must be an open position for an area manager.

Sally talked to an advisor at Carthage College and found that she could earn a B.A. degree in business by going nights for two and a half years on a part-time basis. She also learned that her company would pay all costs, including books. Sally's supervisor, Patty, enrolled her in the company's Management Certificate Program. It is a one-month intensive class in management held at T-Corp.

Sally has worked for T-Corp as a site manager for

nearly three years and will meet that requirement before completing most of the other requirements. At T-Corp, area managers administer the ETA CSS test to their employees and must be Certification Administrators (CA) for the ETA. Sally will need to contact the ETA and fill out an application to become a CA. It could take up to a month to become approved.

Finally there must be an open position before Sally can be promoted to area manager. Patty, Sally's area manager, is working on her own career path to become a regional manager for T-Corp. If Sally is ready, and there is no one more qualified when Patty becomes regional manager, she will become area manager.

Sample Training Plans

I have provided the training plans that work in conjunction with the sample career paths. First let's take a look at Joe's training plan. As you will recall, Joe's career goal is to work in the field of electronics. Specifically he wants to work in home automation.

Joe's Training Plan	
Electronic Shop Class	1/10/03 - 5/24/03
Generic Classes for A.A. Degree	8/23/03 - 5/21/06
Home Automation Electronics Classes	8/20/05 - 5/21/06
Find a Part-Time Job in Home Automation	5/24/04 - ?
Study for Associate CET Test	1/28/06 - 5/28/06

In Joe's real training plan, each class would be listed and he could use it as a check list as he completes each class. For illustrative purposes, I lumped together all of the classes required to earn an associate degree. For elective classes, Joe will take classes in his chosen specialty of home automation.

Joe will look for a job in home automation after completing his first year in college. If he can't find this type of job, he will find another job in electronics. Gaining hands-on experience while working towards his degree will help to prepare Joe for his career. It will also help when the time comes for him to take his CET Test.

Chapter 17. Employee Career Plans

Sally's training plan is illustrated below. Again, for space considerations, I did not list each class required for her to earn a bachelor's degree in business. Also, she would list specific elective management classes that fit her work situation.

Sally's Training Plan	
Generic Classes for B.A. Degree	8/26/02 - 5/26/05
Elective Management Classes	8/24/03 - 5/26/05
T-Corp Management Certificate	4/29/03 - 5/30/03
Certification Administrator Certification	10/28/02 - 11/28/02
Wait for open Area Manager Position	?

A rigid part of Sally's training plan is the Technology Corporation Management Certificate Class. It is offered only once a year and has a waiting list. Fortunately, Sally's manager enrolled her some time ago for this class. This class is offered during the day, but Sally will be also be taking night school classes. It would be wise for her to schedule less demanding college classes during that semester.

Becoming a Certification Administrator for the ETA is really a clerical task, but will allow her to serve and represent her professional association in her local area, assuming Sally meets the ethical requirements. Finally, before Sally can achieve her career goal to become an area manager, there must be an open position. Even if it is some time before there is an opening for Sally, she will be ready. In the meantime, she can work on her next career path and training plan.

End Notes

[1] Best of Biz. "Radical Career Change." Retrieved September 25, 2002, from http://www.bestofbiz.com/briefings/default.asp?p=133

Chapter Quiz:

1. **What is the name for the system in India in which a person is born into his or her career?**

   a. Career path
   b. Family tradition
   c. Caste
   d. Socialism

2. **How many career changes will the average person in the United States make during his or her work life?**

   a. 1-3
   b. 5-7
   c. 8-10
   d. Over 10

3. **Which of the following is directly tied to a Career Path?**

   a. Social status
   b. Apprenticeship program
   c. Training plan
   d. Personal goals

4. **Who is responsible for your career path and goals?**

   a. Employer
   b. You
   c. Career Counselor
   d. Human Resources

5. **One advantage of being a full-time student is:**

   a. more homework.
   b. tuition reimbursement.
   c. less free time.
   d. more college choices.

6. **One disadvantage of being a part-time student is:**

   a. a longer completion time.
   b. tuition reimbursement.
   c. less homework.
   d. more homework.

Answers:

1-c, 2-b, 3-bc, 4-b, 5-d, 6-a

Chapter 18

Ethics

Tom Janca is actively working in the communications field as an engineer in the development of secure wireless products for Bell Labs Global Communications Lab most recently being on the development team for the conceptually new Base Station Router. He has 20 years of experience with electronics, optical and radiometric systems beginning as a component level engineering technician. He has written an ACCET approved telecommunications curriculum for an adult education program and taught semiconductor electronics as an adjunct professor at Pueblo Community College. He has presented seminars in CDMA wireless technology and taught RF principles and techniques in a corporate environment and presently is a DCIC instructor who recently officiated at the US Skill Olympics Telecommunication Cabling competition. He has been a member of the ETA since 1998 winning the Presidents Award and serving in various positions within the ETA. An excellent teacher, writer and speaker on technical subjects who brings the human element and understanding into his communication style and delivery.

Tom R. Janca, CETsr

Ethics is the fulcrum point of my choices and the character of my actions. The character of my actions is the measure by which I am separated from the beast. Let my choices be made that my actions might show the human I have become and not the animal I was born or the wolves amongst whom I was raised.

Ethical Dilemma

Your company has just received notice of a product failure from the manufacturer. This failure is being covered outside of normal warranty. The notice is only being circulated among authorized service agents for the product through service bulletin channels. Your manager has decided this would be a good way to boost his numbers for the quarter because the average customer isn't aware of the extended coverage on this product; and more revenue could be gained from billing the customer and submitting a claim under warranty. He has asked you not to inform the customer of this if any repairs related to the known product failure are brought in.

When a customer arrives at your counter with a product that is experiencing the warranted failure, what should you do?

Your personal dilemma is that your job is on the line. The customer is looking to you to correct the problem. Your next action affects not only the customer and the company, but also the future perception of your company and the manufacturer's company (along with how well you sleep at night). How do you handle this situation?

In this situation, as in many, it is a challenge to your individual ethics, the business' ethics, and the customer's ethics. Should you just explain it away even though it isn't something you would want someone to do to you? Should you risk your job to stand up for what you feel and know is right and risk everything for this complete stranger?

This is a question of ethics. The premise of what you value as right or wrong is the ethical basis that will

determine your personal choice in the situation. Is your conviction in the value of honesty and fairness important enough to defend and suffer possibly painful consequences?

Ethics is often filled with more questions than answers, and unfortunately you have a very limited time to respond. If you are conflicted about the choice because your course of action is muddled, your customer can often read your physical response and can sense when something is making you anxious, creating a sense of mistrust. As a customer service specialist, your actions will affect how your employer's ethics and the customer's ethics merge for the benefit or demise of the relationship. Having a clear sense of ethics for yourself and knowing the company's ethical guidelines in advance helps you respond quickly as dilemmas are created and resolved.

Ethics is the organization of beliefs and values that determine, for an individual or group, the morality of an action's perceived appropriateness to an encounter or event that occurs in the scope of the individual or group environment. It is the intellectual and emotional discernment of right and wrong, coupled with an emotional valuation that carries a reward or punishment for appropriate and inappropriate actions. Your difficulty lies in the reality that, while some moral values may be inherent; often you may be challenged by group and cultural morality that is different than your own. This may cast doubt upon your internal ethical values and challenge the validity of your moral assumptions.

Today, many would argue that the relativism of what is right and wrong is based upon who is affected. If the choice injures me or causes me to make sacrifices, then it is better for the other to suffer rather than myself. Survival of the fittest has this as the basis of its premise. If I am stronger and can take from the weak, then I should take all that I want. This reasoning is that if they could take it from me, they would, or that they don't deserve the same benefits for

Chapter 18. Ethics

their labors. Farmers who rotate the crops on their fields know the soil can only give so much and, if it is to be fertile, it must be given to as much as it is taken from. History has shown the world turmoil caused when a king or government has continually exploited the citizens to the crown's or government's own benefit with no concern for the people's welfare or suffering. Intellectually, it is easy to rationalize ethical relativism to avoid making the hard decisions that are for the benefit of one's relationship to the whole and the whole's relationship to the one.

Relativism, though intellectually arguable, is wrong in reality, for life is partnered with death, just as actions are partnered with their result of good or harm. Relativism's fault is in arguing the definition given ethics, which is based on intellectual discernment of language and not the natural emotional response when you do something positive or negative. The description and definition (by language of what ethics is) is the child of the living response existing before the first stone was cut with a letter or symbol. The weakness of good ethical choices, as well as the strength of the bad choices, is the reasoning away of what is harmful and what is beneficial. Bearing a child into the world and raising it is a huge sacrifice on the health of the mother and a great burden to the parents. Women today still can die during childbirth. It could be argued that because parenting is so harmful and causes so much suffering, it should be avoided at all costs; but each of us knows by living that the sacrifice required to bring life into the world has rewards beyond expression, for life would not exist without its sacrifices. How many times does a child try to reason with a parent that something the child wants to do is okay because everyone else is doing it? The parent knows the action could be harmful or dangerous to the child or other children and must do what is right for the child, not what everyone else is doing. So why do we, as adults, justify our actions by the group? If I just follow the group without question or pause, where is my freedom of conscious choice?

Types of Ethics

In business, three different systems of ethics can be identified in one customer-relations encounter: individual (as employee or customer), company, and organizational ethics. This chapter will primarily focus on these ethical arenas and their interrelation. Individual ethics will examine, in brief, the value system an individual carries as either a customer or as an employee and how these ethics interact with both

Ethics Types
Individual
Business
Organizational

business and organizational ethics. Business ethics is concerned with the collective group behavior of a private industry. Finally, organizational ethics will examine the influence that trade organizations and professional fraternities can exert, both on individual and corporate ethics, for better or worse. As a customer service specialist, you need to be prepared to make a conscious choice of action rather than an emotional or instinctual reaction to a challenge.

Individual Ethics

Individual ethics are the values and beliefs you hold true to the conduct of your life, whether it be in an interaction with individuals, groups or objects in your environment.

Where do these ethics come from? Some would argue that the immediate family and the culture you are brought up in teach these ethics to you. This viewpoint can be validated in our global world by examining different cultures where individuals are guided in their personal choices by completely different ethical ideas and values learned through parenting. Another argument believes that many of our personal ethics are classic ideas of right and wrong present at birth as a more developed system of conscious guidance. Evidence of this is typically the emergence of a radically different ethical standard generated by an individual, apart from the culture's ethical values he or she was taught. Complexity arises because we  are each raised in different cultural groups whose ethical values may clash with another's. Ethical conflicts often arise because two individuals are operating under different ethical premises or theories. These learned or inherited individual ethics become each individual's guidance points for carrying out interactions in life's variety of circumstances. This set of values helps determine individuals' responses to one another.

What are your ethics?

Does the good guy always win, even if he or she dies?
Is winning more important than losing honorably?
Is "might" always right?
What qualities define a leader you would follow?
What qualities define an individual's character you would model?

Knowing your ethics and following a code of internal beliefs you know to be valid, through experience or belief, gives you a consistent course of action to define your

Chapter 18. Ethics

character and develop the dream of yourself, as you are yet to become. A friend of Thomas Merton once told him that the first step to being a saint was the desire to be one. What type of person do you want to be known as? If only your worst enemy was able to attend your funeral, what would he or she say about you? When you die, only the life you have led, the relations you foster and the actions you have chosen will be there to define you and tell your story. It is important for you to define your ethics, for they shape the meaning and focus of your life. While you may have inherited or learned ethics, it might be necessary to question the validity to your life of these assumptions. It is also important to know your ethics because you should know the walls of the castle you are seeking to defend and the lands you have inherited. If you do not know what you defend, then how can you defend it when the storms of life that surely come with any good adventure attack your battlements?

How does this relate to customer service? You have a career that gives you satisfaction and that provides your life with the sustenance for survival and hopefully a little enjoyment. A customer comes to you with a set of needs, desires and wants much like your own and with his or her own set of expectations. The ethics you operate from will determine how the exchange occurs and whether both your needs are met, establishing a positive relationship.

Your perception of the encounter defines and shapes the ethics of the encounter.

Do you see the customer as someone you are able to control and have more power over in the situation?

Ethical premise: It is important that the customer know I am in charge and accept my judgment. I am right and in control, regardless.

Do you see the customer as an enemy coming to harm you and bring you conflict?

Ethical premise: The customer is coming to take advantage of my employer and me, and he/she doesn't care if I lose my position. The customer isn't trustworthy and must be deceived, or I will be harmed.

Do you see yourself in the customer, trying to find someone to trust who will assist him or her and not take advantage of him or her?

Ethical premise: I am here because the customer has a need, and the position I have is dependent on that customer whose needs are dependent on me. This customer is valuable to me and I am valuable to him/her. When I am done

with work, I become a customer of goods and services as well, thanks to him or her being my customer.

The individual morality or ethics of what is right is how I perceive the situation within myself, but not always is it beneficial to the encounter or myself, because the perceptions that I have may be incorrect. If the customer arrives with the expectation that you are concerned with his or her needs, but the premise of your decisions is based solely on your needs and not your customer's, a conflict of ethics exists. Ethically, your actions are wrong in the customer's eyes because the character of your actions has no concern for the other in the interaction. Conflicting standards can result in a feeling of anxiety and injury that will cause the customer to avoid doing business with you in the future. When you encounter a conflict of ethical ideals with a customer, realize that the conflict arises because different ethical assumptions exist on how the situation needs to be resolved.

Your first step is being aware of your own perceptions of the encounter and the ethical assumptions of what is right and wrong or a good and bad resolution. Second is identifying the customer's assumptions and expectations. When you ask, "How can I help you?" listen to what the customer expects out of the encounter. Clarify with him/her what you understand his/her needs to be by repeating it to him/her. Then identify any limitations in what you can or cannot do for him/her and convey them to the customer. Once you have identified what the needs are of each party, the work can begin on negotiating a result with a classic "win-win result." A good ethic is one that takes both the customer's needs and yours into consideration and looks for a mutually beneficial solution.

As an employee of a business, individual ethics and company ethics need to merge to an agreeable position for both the company and the individual. Ideally, no one wants to work in a place that creates a constant sense of anxiety because actions performed have a questionable morality. Companies also don't want to have employees who conflict with their business ethics and expose them to unnecessary risk and promote an undesirable image to the customer. "Sir, if you would like a refund for this product we need a receipt, but if you wish to exchange it the company will allow that without a receipt."

Ethically, you are not arguing the worth or value of the product. You are defending your needs by supporting your employer's position on refunds and defending your customer's needs by offering a solution. If the customer still has a problem, it is possible he/she is trying to exploit you and does not hold to the same ethical system. (i.e., I can get something for nothing, or he/she is out to get me.)

As a leader of a company or business, the individual ethic becomes the ethic of the company. It is important that the company's ethical policy is evident in both its statement and its adherence to an ethical ideal. The conflict arises when the practiced ethics of an individual or business contradict the professed and printed image of the business. Using a common expression, there is a failure to "walk your talk," and deception is not as rare as honesty. The first ethical dilemma gives an example of leadership failure in adhering to good ethics. The employee in the first dilemma should be aware of his or her own ethics and the ethics of his or her employer. If the manager's ethics are in disagreement with company ethics, the employee should follow company ethics and defend his/her action accordingly. If the company ethics are in disagreement with individual ethics, the employee has an obligation prior to accepting an offer of employment or continuing employment to determine the agreement of the two ethical systems or the flexibility of the company to an ethical change in operation.

"And the dead will come to a scale where Maat will weigh their hearts and only those lighter than a feather shall pass to eternal life." This is a paraphrase from the Egyptian book of the dead. What weighs on your heart and mind is the burden of your soul; release it and make amends, for soon the day comes to an end and who can guarantee themselves the gift of dawn?

Business Ethics

Business ethics are concerned primarily with how a business carries out transactions of goods and services between individuals and groups. A secondary focus of business ethics is the morality of how it treats its employees. Business ethics usually flow from leadership and create the public reputation and personality of a company in its dealings with individuals and other companies. If profit is the main focus of business ethics at the cost of human dignity, mutual respect and the environment, the character of your actions will speak volumes over your marketed image. Negative images of companies, such as "cut-throat" or "sharks," come from ethical premises based on survival of the fittest, and not from mutually beneficial ethical premises. These images serve as a warning to those who would choose to do business with them to be on guard. A good business ethic is one that treats each encounter as unique and seeks the benefit of both parties while protecting its own interest from exploitation and abuse in the process.

This type of ethic approaches the interactions with customers as a long-term relationship that needs to be earned and maintained. The benefit of this type of ethic over the prior, is that it is sustainable longer into the future, and neither party in the business interaction needs to be harmed in the encounter for both to succeed. Think of it as harvesting the fruit of the tree and not the tree itself.

Business ethics also affect the employee and employer relationship and the ensuing community relationship that exists with large employers. Kant's *Categorical Imperative*, **"A person should never be treated as a means to an end, but only as an end in itself,"** lends itself to application here. Employees are more than just tools of production, but integral members of a business' success. An employer who looks after its employees' welfare and the community's welfare (of which it is a member), is a respected and honored member of the community. Treating all members of your operation ethically and with equal respect creates a sense of belonging and respect that creates loyalty in the business workforce and aids in recruitment of the needed talent to succeed.

A culture that is not agricultural-based relies heavily on its prosperity and health from the industrial and technical industries that call its cities and states home. The prosperity of these industries requires a population whose standard of living and income is at a level where they can afford the goods and services created. Constantly moving operations to areas of less environmental and labor regulations, where the wages are pennies a day, appears to momentarily excuse the action by increasing profits; but the long-term effect is the decline of profitable jobs and consumers who can afford the production of industry. Is this ethical, and is it beneficial to a long-term sustainable relationship?

Trade Organization and Professional Fraternity Ethics

Trade organizations and professional fraternities can support and foster a higher standard of individual professional ethics in the workplace. Offering the strength of a large group, these organizations can allow the individual professional to stand for higher work ethics and create a better professional image for his or her trade or profession. Working with individuals to raise ethical standards, trade organizations can often provide mentors and role models to encourage correct ethical behavior among professionals. ETA performs ethical guidance where members agree to a code of conduct.

These organizations can also provide a platform for

Chapter 18. Ethics

resolving ethical conflicts between businesses. Often, businesses in an industry have put their interest at the forefront of their ethical considerations, and this causes many conflicts in the day-to-day interrelations with other businesses. Trade and professional organizations can create a platform for ethical debates among businesses where two companies can attempt to reach an agreement on appropriate and inappropriate behavior. These organizations can also help companies realize the interdependence they each have on one another and define ethical guidelines for the industry. Due to professional organizations working with industry, product incompatibility has become less of an issue. By working with professional trade associations, manufacturers were brought to a more beneficial ethical practice of product development, since industry looked to independent organizations to develop standards that benefited the industry as a whole.

Chapter Quiz:

1. **Ethical values are the same for everyone.**

   a. True
   b. False

2. **One consequence for breaking an individual ethical value would be:**

   a. imprisonment.
   b. a fine.
   c. guilt.
   d. a disciplinary warning.

3. **Ethical values of right and wrong can be influenced by reason and changed.**

   a. True
   b. False

4. **A consequence for breaking a business ethic with your employer might be:**

   a. imprisonment.
   b. a fine.
   c. guilt.
   d. a disciplinary warning.

5. **In a confrontation who should "come out on top?"**

   a. Customer service representative
   b. Employer
   c. Customer
   d. Everyone

6. **A good ethical choice is one that respects the dignity and needs of yourself and the other person in a conflict and reaches a mutually beneficial compromise.**

   a. True
   b. False

7. **Trade organizations are beneficial because they foster:**

   a. communications among professionals.
   b. common solutions among competitors.
   c. practices and standards that benefit everyone.
   d. all the above.

8. **The character of who you are perceived to be is influenced by:**

   a. your ethical choices.
   b. your ethical actions.
   c. the relations you foster.
   d. all the above

9. **How can a multiple choice test measure your understanding and application of good ethics?**

   It can't! But a peaceful nights rest, a content heart and a clear conscience are good road signs to experience.

   You are tomorrow's change, today!

Answers:

1-b, 2-c, 3-a, 4-d, 5-d, 6-a, 7-d, 8-d

Chapter 19

Teams and Teamwork

Randy Glass works primarily as a technology consultant. He also serves a private foundation helping to bridge the digital divide, and is a policy adviser for AmericaAtLarge - an ICANN At-Large Structure providing input into general Internet policies. He is a faculty member and Sam Walton Free Enterprise Fellow at a private junior college, where he teaches business, multimedia development and e-commerce, and is a veteran of the U.S. Marine Corps. Randy has experience in working as a financial planner, a general manager for several companies, and as an entrepreneur. [eta@rjglass.com]

**Randy Glass,
MBA, CST, CIW**

Overview

Teams and teamwork are integral parts of the business environment. In this text, some points are noted as a difference between academics and actual methods, or how to be good or successful. We can read about teamwork through academics, but it should be practiced and analyzed in a working environment for one to develop as a good team member and then a successful team leader.

The reason teams exist is to successfully accomplish an overall goal (the end result of the team effort), set either by the team or outside entities, often referred to as a client or a sponsor. This goal is normally much loftier than one person could accomplish alone, so many members of the team exist to perform in their specialty area. A sports team's goal is to win the competition; a development team's goal may be to analyze a product's market viability; or a project team's goal could be to build a bridge. The project team's life cycle would be finite, meaning after the goal is completed, the team then dissolves. However, the sports team would continue to operate and achieve their goals continually over a period of many years, sometimes succeeding and sometimes not. The development team, on the other hand, may have a time constraint, or deadline, in which to complete their task.

The success of the team is directly related to the performance of every team member. This is the reason why understanding how successful teams operate is as important as the professional skills each team member possesses.

Team Structures

Team structures will differ depending on the goals of the team and the structure and environment of the organization. A typical team has a hierarchical structure, with a team leader, support staff, and various team members, as shown in Figure 1. It is important that each member's roles and responsibilities be designated prior to the journey toward the goal. The purpose of the team must also be

designated and understood by each team member prior to that journey. In order for a team to successfully complete its purpose, everyone on the team must understand (1) the goal; (2) their roles and responsibilities; and (3) the structure of the team.

The structure of the team exists for two primary purposes: (a) Reporting; and (b) Goal Orientation. Reporting involves both dealing with issues and communicating within the team, and reporting the team's status to the organization. Goal orientation is a term that deals primarily with leadership. It is the responsibility of the team leader to keep the team oriented toward the overall goal, and the responsibility of each team member to orient with his or her individual area of responsibility.

Let's look at an example of a team structure. As a Certified Customer Service Specialist (CSS), you have been assigned as team leader for a customer support software system being developed by the organization to automate 80% of the organization's customer support process. The organization has assigned people to you (one each from the finance, operations, and customer service departments), and has given you funds to hire three additional team members from outside the organization. In this scenario, you would probably want to hire two programmers and a network or Internet technician. Each team member has his or her area of specialty. The finance team member would probably be responsible for tracking the budget and analyzing cost and

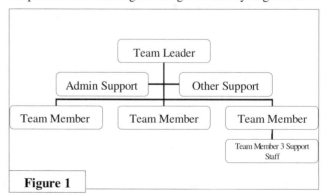

Figure 1

Chapter 19. Teams and Teamwork

profit projections; whereas the programmers would be responsible for coding, testing, and presenting for review the product being developed. Their tasks would not normally overlap. You, as the team leader, would be responsible for orchestrating the team and ensuring the successful completion of the project in a timely manner and within a designated budget.

Team Environment

An organizational team is bound by three constraints: time, budget, and resources, none of which are infinite. We can represent this as a triangle as in Figure 2, where these three constraints are the tips of the triangle. The team operates in the middle somewhere, depending on the level of these constraints available.

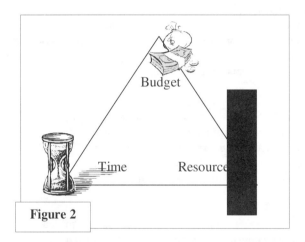

Figure 2

In the example, your team is constrained by the budget that has been assigned to the team by the organization. You would also have a time schedule for implementing or closing the project, known as a 'delivery date.' Your resources would include the seven members of your team (including yourself), any equipment that has been assigned to you, such as computers and desks, and the intellect that each member has accumulated over his or her career.

The budget deals with the financial aspects, such as how much the team can spend toward completing the goal and any other capital resources that are to be utilized. Time constraints deal with how long the team is scheduled to operate and when results are to be presented. Resources are human and asset-related, such as intellectual assets, team members, or other equipment that otherwise would not be specified in the budget constraint.

As with any organization of any size, none of these constraints is infinite, thus we designate them as constraints. An effective team can work within the given constraints and

complete a successful goal. An ineffective team either will have constraints that are too limited or exceed reasonable limitations, which is also known as 'waste.' They will not be able to successfully complete the goal.

Group Dynamics

Group dynamics, as defined by *Webster,* are the interacting forces within a small human group; or the sociological study of these forces. Group dynamics involve personalities, influence, conflict, human nature, beliefs, and culture; and how these relate among certain people within a group. It is vitally important that the team leader understand group dynamics and how his or her team's own dynamic operates.

Everyone has his or her own personality; this makes us different from each other. Each person is influenced by certain things, such as religion, politics, family, friends, and media. Each person has his or her set of beliefs, meaning what is right and what is wrong. However, human nature is one thing people have in common, as people tend to have similar actions and reactions to events, based on simply being human. Culture is usually shared through a large number of people from a similar society. We could justly say that individuals in a group operate differently in Japan than in Cuba. Humans also tend to have conflict in the factors listed above—different views of what reality is. Conflict is not a bad thing—many times it is necessary in order to complete a goal; and normally, it is a sign that members of a team truly care about the outcome and their level of participation. Some conflicts, though, should be immediately rectified and a conclusion sought before the goal becomes unreachable.

Communication

Effective communication is the cornerstone to the success of a team. Each member of a team should have the knowledge and opportunity to communicate within the team.

Communication involves speech, listening, facial expressions, and gestures. Good communication involves not just speaking, but listening as well. If something is said but not understood clearly, it is just as bad (and sometimes worse) as not saying anything at all. Similarly, the right expressions and gestures greatly define the subject of conversation, and add clarity to the subject of discussion.

Chapter 19. Teams and Teamwork

Many methods of communication exist, whether interpersonal (person-to-person), through mail, email, the Internet, telephones, or any other medium. But through any of these methods, there are barriers. Barriers are the hindrance of effective communication.

There are four barriers to communication: the sender, the receiver, the communication medium, and communication static. The sender of the message may be a barrier because he or she is not willing or able to transmit a clear message. The receiver may be a barrier because he or she is not willing or able to receive a clear message. If one tries to send a message of distress, the postal service may not be the appropriate medium of communication because of timeliness, and the fact that there is a limited amount of information that can be transmitted. Some recipients may not understand the true intent of the message. Static is an ever-present variable to any communication, and it depends on the other factors as well. Static can be decreased by increasing the clarity of the message. The importance of clear communications cannot be overstated.

Teamwork

Teamwork involves combining the subject matter already discussed in this chapter with the human element, or the members of the team. Teamwork is the direct interaction of the people on the team, to accomplish the overall goal. The team must interact, using each member's special skills as his or her strengths, to carry out any matters that may evolve during the course of the project to make the outcome successful.

Like rolling a log uphill, each team member must contribute his or her share, or the log will not roll straight up the hill. One side may move faster than the other, which turns the log, making it go sideways. If one member does not push as hard as the others, the extra burden is shared by the rest. If one member pushes harder than the others, it also creates a burden on the others to push harder. The team leader's role would be to judge the level of contribution by each member and place him or her at the appropriate place, like placing the hardest-pushing member in the middle of the log, so it can still go straight up the hill and lessen the burden on the others.

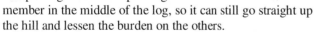

Leadership

Leadership is the most important aspect of a team. Without direction and guidance, a team would be left unguided and rarely accomplish its goals. The trend of today, from an academic perspective, is to shy away from leadership roles, having the team operate as a loosely-led group, with everyone sharing the leadership role equally. However, successful teams that accomplish their goals are more likely than not to have a strong team leader who can make rational decisions and take action.

There are three types of leaders: democratic, autocratic, and laissez-faire. Democratic leaders are normally well-organized and will take the input from all team members before making decisions or taking action. Autocratic leaders are strong decision makers and do so without the input from team members. Laissez-faire leaders use the art of self-direction, meaning that the team members operate with little regulation or input from the leadership, who fills primarily a reporting or analysis role.

The roles of a successful leader are to coordinate the team's activities, assign roles and responsibilities, make decisions, analyze team performance, motivate team and individual actions, and provide a medium for communication. All of these roles are equally important, and how the leader performs these roles is directly related to the success of the team.

The team leader has a dual fiduciary (confidence or trust) responsibility. One responsibility is to the team, making sure that all relevant matters are properly addressed, and nurturing the team through to the project goals. The other responsibility is to the organization, ensuring the organization's interests are addressed, and providing the direct communication link between the organization and the members of the team.

There are common expressions that say "good leaders are made," and other expressions that say "good leaders are just born that way." Good leaders are made. Through learning and experience, good leaders are able to make appropriate decisions at the appropriate time and drive the team toward the goal until it is achieved. Good leaders are born. There are inherent characteristics or traits that good leaders possess, like determination, self-confidence, drive, and a strong will. Therefore, leaders are born with certain traits, and through experience and education, they then become good leaders.

Chapter 19. Teams and Teamwork

Problem Solving

Problems arise continuously in most group scenarios. They stem from customers and clients, the internal organization, suppliers, other team members, and ourselves. Assigning blame to a problem should never be a primary issue, but finding a quick and rational solution to it is. Thus, I have heard, if we point our finger at someone or something, we point three back at ourselves.

Solving problems is not just the responsibility of the team leader, but the responsibility of everyone on the team. Solving problems as they arise helps the team operate more efficiently. But, there are times when a member of a team is not able to solve a problem, and he or she must rely on the input from other team members or the team leader.

There are logical steps to follow in the problem solving process:

Step 1) Collect and analyze data relating to the assumed problem. Gather any relevant information and begin to digest it for further steps.

Step 2) Identify the problem. It seems that it would be easy to identify a problem, but this is why they call them "problems." Many times, the problem that presents itself is not the real problem, but a development of the real problem.

Step 3) Identify the cause. There may be many potential causes to a problem, so never assume that you have properly identified the cause at this point. Simply make a list of potential causes in order of probability.

Step 4) Formulate alternatives. If you have identified more than one potential cause, each one may have different alternatives for a solution. A decision tree would be used for complex matters of this nature, that would map out potential causes and potential alternatives.

Step 5) Evaluate alternatives. Evaluate what may and may not work, based on probability. At this point the team member has not taken direct action for a solution, but has done only his or her homework to ensure better results.

Step 6) Solve for a solution. Now take action. Try each alternative, the most probable first, until something works to alleviate the problem.

Step 7) Evaluate the solution. Did it really work? If not, return to step 6. Many times, a solution works for a defined problem, and another problem arises in its place. If this is the case, it is time to go back to step 2. This is the time to ensure that the solution to the problem is the correct one and that the appropriate action has been taken.

Step 8) Report the problem and solution. Some organizations may require that you keep a database of known problems; others may request you keep a log of lessons learned; others may not be concerned with reporting at all. Whichever way, it is important that everyone involved know that the problem has been adequately solved. Chances are that you will run into a similar problem in the future. If one has recorded the procedure, he or she can skip several of the steps listed and look like a true expert.

Problem avoidance is a method where problems are anticipated and measures taken to avoid having the problem arise at all. Sometimes, this can be done as a result of properly using the eight problem solving steps listed above. Other times, they may be part of company or team policy, or dictated by a team leader or others involved. In any event, problem avoidance is much cheaper and more productive than continually solving similar problems. Standards are developed and agreed upon by organizations to prevent problems. Problem avoidance is similar to taking a flu shot before flu season; you realize the flu has occurred in the past and is about to hinder you again, so you get a shot before you have to deal with the problem arising.

Conclusion

Teamwork, leadership, and communication are integral to the success of any team. By working in team environments, one may learn to become a better team member, better leader, and better communicator. Remember that everyone has his or her individual strengths and

Chapter 19. Teams and Teamwork

weaknesses. It is a practiced art to recognize where those strengths and weaknesses can be used in organizational projects. By practicing these measures, a team can increase its probability of success, where successful completion of the project goals is the primary purpose of combining these resources.

Chapter Quiz:

1. **Teams exist to:**

   a. make life easier for us and others.
   b. combine the efforts of several people.
   c. let others do our work.
   d. report the actions of workers.

2. **Team goals are normally:**

   a. loftier than one can accomplish alone.
   b. used to motivate the team members.
   c. set by the team leader.
   d. designated by the team.

3. **Who is responsible for the success of the team?**

   a. Only the team leader
   b. The entire team
   c. The project leader
   d. The C.E.O.

4. **The structure of the team exists for reporting and disciplinary functions.**

   a. True
   b. False

5. **Each team member has his or her specific roles and responsibilities.**

   a. True
   b. False

6. **Organizational constraints are:**

   a. finite.
   b. infinite.
   c. poly-finite.
   d. rasta-finite.

7. **An effective team leader would deal with conflict by:**

   a. immediately disciplining those involved.
   b. making a report and filing it with Human Resources.
   c. yelling and screaming.
   d. immediately rectifying it.

8. **Gestures are as important as speech in interpersonal communications.**

   a. True
   b. False

9. **What is the first step in the problem-solving process?**

   a. Report the problem
   b. Solve the problem
   c. Collect and analyze data
   d. Identify the cause

10. **Decrease static by:**

    a. tuning the attenuator.
    b. sending clear messages.
    c. speaking louder.
    d. simplifying the message.

Answers:

1-b, 2-a, 3-b, 4-b, 5-a, 6-a, 7-d, 8-a, 9-c, 10-b

Chapter 20

Pride and Company Loyalty

Edward Bell, MBA, AAMS, CMFC, CSS is from Columbus, Ohio and graduated with honors in a course, "Writing for Children," from the Institute of Children's Literature. He has served as Contributing Editor of the Autograph Times. Ed won the 1999 award for best screenplay from the PEN American Center in New York and garnered the runner-up award for non-fiction writing in 2000. He earned his Masters in Business Administration from Hamilton University, and his Accredited Asset Management Specialist and Chartered Mutual Fund Counselor from the College for Financial Planning. He earned the ETA Certified Customer Service Specialist in August 2001.

Edward Bell, MBA, AAMS, CMFC, CSS

Pride is a strange, yet powerful, word and emotion. It can generate ridicule or high regard, depending on the circumstances. For example, pride in one's appearance can easily lead to feelings of conceit, whereas proudly cheering your children on as they excel in sports can lead to greater feelings of bonding and parental success.

Pride in the workplace can have equally varied meanings: from the company "yes man" proudly gloating over another raise, to the Customer Service Specialist (CSS), who has just received praise from a satisfied customer concerning the wonderful service the company provided.

Loyalty, on the other hand, is synonymous with everything right in an employee. A loyal employee will be devoted to a company mission, reliable when given an assignment, and dependable in displaying a good overall company image.

Loyalty doesn't stop there. While we should be loyal to our employer, our customers deserve no less than the highest standards of loyalty as well.

When we display traits of honesty and integrity, we exude loyalty to our employer and customer. Throughout our lifetimes, we have all displayed pride and loyalty. But how do we mesh the two and distribute them fairly between our employer and customer?

As a customer service specialist, you occupy a middle ground between your employer and the customer. Certain loyalties are owed to each. As a middle-of-the-road entity, the CSS has a fiduciary duty to both. According to *Webster's New World Dictionary* (Third Edition), a fiduciary relationship exists whenever a person holds something in trust or relies on another.

The fiduciary duty to look first at the customer's best interest is the fundamental duty owed to the customer and requires the customer's interest be put ahead of one's own or the employer's, and that all actions be made solely for the benefit of the customer.

It would be unfair to our employers, however, if every decision we make is geared toward making our customer happy and not holding firm and steady on our employer's behalf. This balancing act can be difficult at times, but if we follow a few easy concepts, we can display loyalty to both customer and employer, while maintaining a sense of company pride.

- **Concept #1 INTEGRITY -** Integrity demands honesty and candor, which must not be subordinated to company gain and advantage. Any CSS who offers advice must possess integrity and use it as the ultimate arbiter of right and wrong behavior with respect to customers. Displays of integrity toward the customer reflect loyalty to the company by advertising the ideal employee the employer chooses to hire.

- **Concept #2 COMPETENCE –** A CSS is competent only when he/she has attained and maintained an adequate level of knowledge and skills, and applies that knowledge effectively in providing services or advice to customers. Competence also includes the wisdom to recognize the limitations of that knowledge and when additional consultation or a customer referral is appropriate. A CSS is obliged to strive to maintain and improve his/her competence and the competence of others within the profession.

- **Concept #3 FAIRNESS –** In ETA, fairness is associated with treating others in the same fashion as you would wish to be treated, with a subordination of one's own feelings, prejudices and desires in the important balancing of conflicting interests between the company and the customer.

Chapter 20. Pride and Company Loyalty

- **Concept #4 PROFESSIONALISM** – A Customer Service Specialist owes to fellow professionals an obligation to cooperate with fellow designees to enhance and maintain the profession's public image and to work jointly with them to improve the quality of services.

A profession that renders service advice can justify its existence as value-added only to the extent that it can demonstrate to customers that it can do something that customers cannot do as well for themselves. Further, it must be done in a manner that inspires trust and respect.

A CSS is required to practice, and encourage others to practice, in a professional and ethical manner that will reflect credit on members and their profession. While the concept of professionalism may be vague, all recognize its presence – or absence – in the behavior of those encountered in the workplace.

- **Concept #5 DILIGENCE** – Diligence is the provision of service in a reasonably prompt and thorough manner. Diligence also includes proper planning for, and supervision of, the rendering of a professional service.

To implement these five concepts is to show you have a lot of pride in your employer, workplace and personal ability. To practice these concepts daily within your workplace will quickly have you displaying loyalty to your employer, coworkers and customers.

Pride in your work should be established immediately upon being hired. Consider that, as of this writing, unemployment rates in the United States are around 6%. Now, that may not seem like such a bad figure when you realize that for every 100 people looking for work, 94 are successful. For the six who did not find employment, they undoubtedly envy you and your good luck in finding a job.

Was it really good luck though, or did you possess traits and skills that your employer could use? Did you go the extra mile after high school by seeking out and successfully completing additional training? Is it by the fact that you are reading this CSS Examination Study Guide, and have expressed pride in yourself to go the additional step in becoming that valuable asset to your employer?

The desire to give 100% of yourself is derived by the drive to succeed -- to be better than average. Going further than being just "a good worker," and gravitating to becoming a well-respected, highly thought of company asset is your goal.

A person with positive pride also carries another valuable trait -- the desire to be a professional and to search for professionalism in others. Rarely, if ever, will you find the person who gives 100% hanging around with someone who gives only 50% of themselves. The positive pride in us will not allow us to gravitate to that which we recognize as failure.

Others recognize positive pride as well. From employers to customers, positive pride beams through like a beacon, in the way we dress, speak and carry ourselves. Pride radiates confidence and professionalism.

Group Pride

Positive pride can be contagious. Think back to any team you were on, or of which you were a fan. Can you remember an instance when your team was behind by what seemed like insurmountable odds, only to have a single team member with positive pride take a "can-do" attitude and rally the team to come from behind? It may sound corny, but it happens every day, on a football field, in a corporate boardroom, or a customer service office. Positive pride can be a contagion that turns losers into winners.

Loyalty

Companies exist and flourish through the hiring of employees from every ilk and stature of life; and while a company can function without employee loyalty, the truly successful firm will need to have loyal employees in order to surpass competitors.

Loyalty is more than cheerleading from the sideline. True loyalty takes effort and is an ongoing process as the employee learns to stay on the same page with shifting company goals. To assist companies in their growth, employers strive for loyalty through the understanding and implementing of obligations. While there may certainly be others, the following are some obligations loyal employees can perform to assist their company's success:

- **Obligation #1 – DISCLOSURE**
  The duty to disclose all facts and conflicts of interest are covered by all professional codes of conduct. Full disclosure on new products, services and procedures is required even if it may result in the short-term loss of profit for the company. (Example: A customer needs a replacement o-ring, and the one your company normally sells generates a substantial profit with its sale. Your company also offers a secondary o-ring that

Chapter 20. Pride and Company Loyalty

DISCLOSURE

DIAGNOSE

KEEP CURRENT

is just as effective but cheaper for the customer to purchase yet generates less profit to the company).

In the example given, while the company may lose some profit in the short-term, the added customer value from the disclosure will result in long-term success as word spreads of the company's disclosure policy.

- **Obligation #2 – DIAGNOSE**
  The obligation to know your customer, and to investigate the suitability of any product and/or service recommended, is complementary and falls within the ethical obligation to diagnose. This obligation is supported by the importance of learning all the essential facts about a customer and his/her situation.

  When a CSS makes a suggestion to a customer, he/she does so in light of the customer's stated circumstances, which usually includes an ultimate goal. The duty to diagnose is important in all stages of the customer-to-CSS process. When a CSS gathers and analyzes customer information, he/she must strive to learn everything necessary for making suitable suggestions.

- **Obligation #3 – KEEP CURRENT**
  Because the manufacturing and retail arenas are constantly experiencing changes, all individuals serving as professionals in the customer service field have an obligation to keep current with new development and changes that affect their customers.

  Recognizing the importance of keeping current, the Customer Service Specialist, through the Electronics Technicians Association, Int'l (ETA-I), as well as various trade organizations and publications, can adequately keep abreast of advances within the industry.

  Any individual who plans to maintain a career in the Customer Service field should take advantage of any added training. Indeed, any individual who holds him or herself out to the public as a professional in the customer service field, has the duty to keep reasonably abreast of current products, services and information in his or her field.

Career success in customer service depends on qualities that go beyond technical expertise. The further you advance in your profession, the more important these qualities become. What exactly, *are* these other qualities—the qualities that, when combined with technical competence, differentiate successful customer service specialists from the customer service clerk struggling to hold his/her own in a lower-level position?

I put this question to people I work with and, as you might expect, I received a variety of answers. All of our customer service personnel have earned the coveted CSS designation, yet, each has his/her own opinion on this subject. For instance, one talked in terms of feeling a sense of responsibility "to your customers, to your profession, and to the public." Another stated learning how to view problems through the eyes of the customer, while still another stressed motivation, noting that almost all the customer service clerks he knows who have failed to achieve career potential were insufficiently motivated. Loida Ramos, Industry Manager, emphasized dedication and the ability to communicate. "We look for people," she says, "who can dedicate themselves and who can communicate not only with customers, but within the organization as well. You need competence, compassion and understanding, but at the same time you need a level of professional independence."

I can do little more than echo the views expressed by the professionals I have just mentioned. Motivation, dedication to the profession, clear thinking, a sense of responsibility to the people you work with, or for, integrity, good judgment—these and others are crucial qualities for customer service specialists seeking success. But *having* these qualities is not enough. You have to be able to demonstrate these qualities day after day on your job.

Be A Team Player

I know of no firm or any company (of any size) that does not put a high premium on company loyalty. It's a very positive attribute. The fact that you're proud of your organization can't help but show itself in everything you do, particularly in your dealings with customers.
Loida Ramos

You demonstrate company loyalty in any number of different ways. The easiest (and the most important) way is to support your company policies. But there are other, subtler things that can demonstrate loyalty and pride: little things that you might not think about, like being punctual and putting in a *full* day's work; being willing, when the need arises, to work extra hours; and being pleasant and

Chapter 20. Pride and Company Loyalty

courteous to all the people you work with, from the janitor to the head of the firm.

These are little things, but do not underestimate their importance. Many times these qualities alone—punctuality, caring, the willingness to work hard—have induced companies to keep, and eventually promote, people they might otherwise have terminated.

By the same token, you need to develop good working relationships with the people who work both *for* you and *with* you. It is important that you treat with respect everyone with whom you come into contact on your job.

I am talking more about a matter of mindset than anything else. If you recognize that, by being nice to people and by showing your appreciation in tangible ways, you are benefiting *yourself*; it will be that much easier for you to develop the rapport and gain the support you need to get ahead in organizations. I am not suggesting that you flatter people you would not normally be nice to, but something as simple as saying "Good morning" to the people you see when you arrive at work each morning can go a long way to smooth out your working relationships. The point, let me emphasize, is not to make everyone you work with think you are the greatest human being in the world. The point is to make sure that when you need help, the people you need it from will be there to offer it.

One of the most difficult things about being a team player, not only in customer service, but in any job, is getting along with a boss who may not be the easiest person to deal with. Many customer service clerks who want to make a change are looking for this very reason: they do not get along with their supervisors. But, I have noticed that many customer service clerks who leave jobs because they do not get along with their bosses run into the same problems in their new jobs. On the other hand, when I asked a successful customer service clerk I spoke with to explain her rapid rise in one of the large distributorships, she said to me, "I always made my boss look good."

It is part of your job responsibility not only to get along with your supervisors, but to make their lives easier. One way to do this is to make up your mind to do more than follow orders. In other words, do your best to *anticipate* your boss's needs. You should know, for instance, the communication style your boss prefers: whether he/she likes you to spell things out in detail or simply give the rough outline of a project. You should be able to sense when your boss is under pressure and pitch in to ease the pressure. You should also know as much as you can about the person your boss reports to and the kinds of pressure this person puts on your boss. The better you can understand these stresses, the better you will be able to anticipate them. I repeat: *whatever you can do to make your boss's life easier and to make your boss look better will generally enhance your own career progress.*

Know Where The Power Is

I have never seen a company (or any organization, for that matter) that was not "political" to some degree — political in the sense that certain people in the organization hold power disproportionate to their position. All things considered, customer service is probably a little *less* political than other areas. But to say that, as a specialist, you do not have to concern yourself with company politics would be naive.

One of the best, if not one of the easiest, ways of gaining recognition is to take on those jobs that no one else wants to do—providing, that is, that you are doing them for the right person and providing it is the right kind of job.

Yet another way to gain recognition is to anticipate your firm's needs, which you can do by analyzing where your firm's weaknesses may lie and making it your business to develop strengths in these areas.

> *There's no such thing as not having enough time if you're doing what you want to do.*

Just imagine, for example, if years ago you could have foreseen the role of computers in customer service and you had learned about computers before anybody else in the organization knew anything about them. You would not necessarily have to know how to program the computer. Simply knowing what is available and what is suitable for your company might have been enough to give you additional stature.

As I mentioned earlier, doing your job well is not enough to show pride and company loyalty, nor to assure you of rapid progress in your firm. Equally important is making sure that management perceives you as a valuable member of the company. We have covered some of the ways in which you can do this.

Chapter 20. Pride and Company Loyalty

Summary of the key points in Chapter 20:

1. *Show loyalty to your firm.*

2. *See the totality of your job.*

3. *Understand and anticipate your boss's needs.*

4. *Take credit (modestly) for your work.*

5. *Give co-workers and subordinates the same respect you give your supervisors.*

6. *Get recognition by taking on certain assignments nobody else will take.*

Chapter Quiz:

1. **Which of the following are <u>not</u> concepts?**

   a. Integrity
   b. Diagnoses
   c. Competence
   d. Fairness

2. **Integrity demands honesty and candor.**

   a. True
   b. False

3. **Which of the following are Obligations?**

   a. Having low prices
   b. Having concepts
   c. Being fashionable
   d. Keeping current

4. **A "fiduciary" relationship involves:**

   a. a desire to get divorced.
   b. the act of getting as much out of a customer as possible.
   c. providing the latest gossip to the customer.
   d. a person holding something in trust or relying on another.

5. **Positive pride cannot become a contagion within a group experience.**

   a. True
   b. False

6. **You demonstrate company loyalty by:**

   a. supporting company policies.
   b. constantly looking to change company policies.
   c. checking to see how your company ranks with competitors.
   d. all of the above.

7. **A CSS is displaying competence when:**

   a. he/she has taken useless courses for credit and advancement.
   b. he/she sticks close to the boss, agreeing with every word.
   c. he/she passes off customers to better-qualified clerks.
   d. he/she attains and maintains adequate knowledge and skills.

8. **The concept of "fairness" means to:**

   a. anticipate the customer's needs and take away any opportunity for argument.
   b. insist your company is always right and point to the company's record as proof.
   c. treat others in the same fashion as you wish to be treated.
   d. continue to interrupt customers so they have no chance to complain.

9. **As part of professionalism, the CSS is required to:**

   a. practice and encourage others in the industry to practice ethical manners.
   b. act better than others because of his/her designation.
   c. not share knowledge with others so he/she maintains professional superiority.
   d. none of the above.

10. **Your industry is experiencing rapid growth through innovation. To keep abreast of constant changes, the CSS is expected to practice what obligation?**

    a. Disclosure
    b. Keep abreast
    c. Diagnose
    d. Fairness

Answers:

1-b, 2-a, 3-d, 4-d, 5-b, 6-a, 7-d, 8-c, 9-a, 10-b

Chapter 21

Handling Emotions

Logic out the Window, Reducing Stress, Personalities

Carolyn Carson

Carolyn Carson first joined ETA's staff in 1994, just one week after retiring from the U. S. Department of Agriculture. She later left ETA to become a mortgage loan officer, then retired again, but has been back with ETA for five years. Carolyn and her husband John have owned a successful marketing business for many years, and she has had numerous hours of training in motivation and handling emotions. She believes that you can learn to make your emotions work FOR you rather than against you. Carolyn has three daughters and eight grandchildren.

Handling Emotions

Unless you are a lighthouse keeper or spend your working day in a fire tower in a national forest, you've probably had the experience of having to put up with someone else's emotions in the course of your workday. If you've "been there, done that," you know how miserable it is to be on the receiving end of someone's "out of control" emotions.

Understanding Personalities

Dealing with people becomes a whole lot easier when you have a basic understanding of personalities. There are basically four different personality types; and while most people will have traits of more than one personality type, one will usually be dominant. Various authors give different names to the personality groups, but the ones that seem to be used most are Sanguine, also called Popular Sanguine; Choleric, or Powerful Choleric; Melancholy, or Perfect Melancholy; and Phlegmatic, also known as Peaceful Phlegmatic. Once you learn the traits of these personality types, you can easily put the people you work and live with daily into their proper categories, and it helps you to know how to deal with them. I think it's useful to know why a person does things in a certain way, and to realize that it's not that this person is trying to drive you crazy by not doing things your way.

For example, the Perfect Melancholy needs a sense of order. He or she needs to be organized, and to plan ahead. If you try to force these people to "fly by the seat of their pants" as the Popular Sanguine would, or to chair the meet-

Personality Types
Popular Sanguine
Powerful Choleric
Perfect Melancholy
Peaceful Phlegmatic

ing without a totally planned-out agenda, you'll probably be looking for someone to fill their position. They NEED the plan. They can't operate without one. Spontaneity scares them. But, if you need someone to handle your money and keep your books and get your reports out on time, you want a Melancholy.

The Choleric is the "take charge" person. If you want something to be done, the Powerful Choleric will get it done. He or she may step on a few toes getting it done, but it will be finished….and on time. He or she has opinions and doesn't mind sharing them with you. You have to walk fast to keep up with Cholerics, but they will perform. They don't mean to hurt your feelings. They just don't spend any time thinking about your feelings being involved.

When you hear laughter, you can probably follow your ears to the Popular Sanguine. The Sanguine meets people well, sometimes said to "never have met a stranger." When you are with a Sanguine, you don't have to worry about carrying the conversation, as he or she is very interesting and wants to be entertaining, as well. It's even possible that he or she might "enhance" a story just a little, to make it more interesting. Sanguines are a good choice for sales, but you'll have to watch to be sure that the paperwork gets done. Details bore them. Time flies when you're visiting with a Sanguine.

Find the person in your workplace who never makes anyone mad, and you've found your Phlegmatic. The Peaceful Phlegmatic hates strife and will work hard to make peace between any warring factions. This is another personality who definitely does not want to chair the meeting. Ask him or her to take the minutes, help with arranging the room, anything else, but don't expect him/her to get up front without enduring pure pain. He or she is very happy to work in the background.

Usually, it takes just a short period of time to figure out the personality types of both the people you work with and the external customers that you encounter. Just knowing the type people you're dealing with can make it easier for you to choose the right way to proceed with them. If you're trying to sell a car to a Popular Sanguine, you'll probably want to emphasize what a pretty color it is and demonstrate all the "bells and whistles." Don't expect to get by with that with the Melancholy. You'd better be prepared to explain the size of the motor, how much air to keep in the tires, the complete details of the warranty, etc. The Choleric will probably take over the sales presentation and ask you the questions. Just have the answers ready and don't stammer. You really won't know whether you've hit the Phlegmatic's hot button or not, until he/she tells you he/she is ready to buy. Just give a Phlegmatic the facts.

It's also helpful to know your own personality, to enable you to place yourself in a position where you can do the best job. More than likely, you'll find that you have the traits of two or more personality types, with one being more predominant than the others. For instance, I can do the detail work that is required to keep the books, and can even organize a system. But, I'd probably be bored if I did only that, day after day. If I'm sitting in a meeting that isn't accomplishing the job at hand, my predominant Choleric side wants to jump up and take over. But, since I've also got a little Sanguine and want everybody to like me, I have to stifle myself at times. I definitely have more of my Choleric dad in me than my Phlegmatic mother.

I would recommend that you read some of the books on the four personality types and learn what you can to help you in your everyday dealings with people. It's a fascinating subject. You'll be amazed how the people in your life fall into these four categories. Use this knowledge to your advantage. I'll list some books that I have read on the subject at the end of this chapter.

Emotions among coworkers

You've probably heard the old saying "One bad apple spoils the whole barrel." Nowhere is this more true than the one employee whose daily emotional ups and downs make life miserable for all the unfortunate people who have to work with him or her. It's unlikely that any of you have totally escaped this. I've had the misfortune to work with such a person more than once, and believe me, I didn't get out of bed in the morning eager to go to work. No business needs the mercurial person whose tantrums are just plain embarrassing—not to mention painful for the object of the tantrum. If you're the tantrum-thrower, GROW UP! If you are the employer of the tantrum-thrower, it's time for a little heart-to-heart talk. You cannot allow that in your workplace if you want anything to be accomplished during the workday.

It's not just the bad-tempered employee who causes problems, either. The complainer can get everyone down. Pretty soon the whole business can be in a deep blue funk if you have an employee singing a "woe is me" tune all day long. Of course, there are sometimes legitimate reasons why a person is feeling down.

If you learn that there is major problem, such as a serious illness in a coworker's family, you certainly will want to be sympathetic. Don't, however, allow that subject to take over your place of business. If you need to do something extra to take up the slack when your coworker has to be off work or is distracted, do so. But, changing the subject back to the work at hand may be the very best thing for him or her. A sense of normalcy may be the very best medicine for a person whose personal life is out of control. Your basic human nature will probably cause you to want to do whatever you can for this coworker, both in and out of the workplace. You can always offer to babysit, bring in a meal, drive a patient for treatments, etc.—things you would want someone to do for you. This is a good place to practice the Golden Rule.

In other words, there is a professional and a non-professional way to conduct yourself during the working day. It's nice to be friendly with the people you work with, but anything beyond just friendliness needs to be kept outside the workplace. If the person at the next desk is your very best friend in all the world, don't make that obvious to the others in the workplace. It will make them feel at a disadvantage, especially if a promotion is on the line.

Problem Areas

There are almost as many problem areas with emotions in the workplace as there are employees. You can't turn off your humanness while you're at work, and it's impossible for most people to adopt an aloof, "above-the-fray" attitude for any extended period of time. Try your best to keep your personal life private. Not only is it taboo to air your personal problems to everyone in the workplace, it can work against you in the long run. Don't put yourself in the position of losing out on a promotion because someone in authority thinks you have too many personal problems to handle the job.

Chapter 21. Handling Emotions

Jealousy sometimes rears its ugly head in the workplace, too. There are many reasons this happens, but the more discreet you are about your personal life and your pay rate, the fewer problems you'll have with jealousy. Another problem is an employee's coming in late and leaving early. It may be that no one will say a word about it, but you can be sure that it is noticed. Also, there is no excuse for rudeness. No matter how irritated you are with someone, you can express yourself politely. Think of two U.S. Senators on the exact opposite sides of a question. You don't see them speaking rudely of each other. In fact, they refer to the other person as "my dear friend, the distinguished Senator from….…… ." Politeness is required in the workplace. Period!

Love affairs and flirting in the workplace also cause problems. You can't totally rule out dating someone that you work with—a large percentage of married couples met their spouse at work. You can, however, use some discretion. It doesn't have to be obvious to someone walking in off the street that you have a special attachment to another person on the job. And…..you're there to work. Give your employer an hour's work every hour for which you're being paid. Save the sweet nothings for after work.

Gossip and back-stabbing can quickly ruin the atmosphere in the workplace. Neither belongs there, and be aware that these actions can boomerang right back at you. Stay away from these petty actions that make you look bad, rather than the person you're belittling.

Be very, very careful if you're ever considering just a wee bit of deception or sneakiness. It will come back to haunt you. I, personally, never ever believe a person who has lied to me even once in the past. Don't pad your time or your travel expenses or pretend that you have done something that you haven't. The long-term results just aren't worth whatever it may get you at the time. Your reputation is the most important thing you own. Don't be known as a cheat!

The bully who threatens you or lords it over you is no better than his or her counterpart on the playground. That technique may work in the short-term, but it will eventually catch up with him or her. If you've never had the pleasure of working for a bully, you're lucky. Usually, bullies are coming from a position of feeling incompetent, but understanding this doesn't make it any easier to work

with one of them. If you see yourself in the bully category, do something about it. Become competent in your job or leave it and find something you can do. Don't make others suffer by working with you.

Most of all, don't let any of these emotions take over your own good common sense. Don't become so emotional that you let logic fly out the window. You cannot allow emotions to make your decisions. If you feel that you are yielding to emotions rather than logic, sit down and put it on paper. This exercise is older than dirt, but it works. Get a piece of paper and draw a line down the middle. On one side, title the column "Assets." On the other, title it "Liabilities." Then, just do a little brainstorming. Write down every itsy, bitsy thing you can think of that would be an asset to this decision. Then, think of what can go wrong, and what the liabilities could be if you make the opposite decision. Once you've gone through this exercise, the paper should speak for itself. You may find that something that seemed "nice to do" could have disastrous results. Always leave out the emotions and let logic make the decisions. You'll be glad you did.

For Instance,

Let's say that your boss has called your coworker Joe into the office and really berated him over something that was questionable as to whether it was right or wrong. When Joe returns to his work station, you can see that he is totally devastated. You're well aware that any work that he is able to do right now is not going to be of the best quality.

We'll assume here that you are on good terms with the boss, and that he or she probably didn't intend to get carried away enough to cause problems with Joe. If I were in that situation, I'd tell the boss that I'm going to take Joe out for a cup of coffee. A good employer will appreciate this. Now the key here is that—when you get Joe out, you don't join him in beating up on the boss. Just let Joe have his say, contribute what positive input you can—maybe a suggestion on how to avoid such a problem in the future—and help him to get calmed down and see the situation in a better light. You've given Joe some time to get control of his emotions—away from the eyes of other employees, and maybe helped him to see the other side of the picture.
Everyone is better off for your intervention. Joe didn't have to stomp out mad, and he didn't have to be concerned about other employees seeing him lose control.

110

Chapter 21. Handling Emotions

Sadly, another situation we sometimes see is when a coworker has a devastating personal tragedy, like Mary's losing a child in an auto accident. You certainly can't "make it better" for Mary, but you can surely try to help. Even if you're not a close personal friend of hers, now is the time to act like a friend. By this, I mean that you do what you can to make the workplace a pleasant place to come to for her. Work is probably good therapy—to have some part of her life seem normal. But, this is a time to be watchful to see if your lending a hand now and then can make things easier. Every person handles grief differently. Some people need to talk it out, and some can't talk about it at all. Whichever it is, understand that it's going to take a long time for her to feel back to normal again, if ever. Play this one by ear, but if you see tears, don't be alarmed. Let her know that you understand. Hand her a tissue, give her a pat on the back or a hug. You may need a tissue, too, but just "being there" will help her to cope.

Maybe you're the one on the receiving end of the boss' outrage. And, maybe it's for good reason. Let's say that you screwed up a repair job not once, but twice, in the same week. The boss is going berserk, and you don't really have a good explanation of why it happened. It's time now for you to stay in control of your emotions. No one likes to be yelled at, and it's almost worse when you have to admit that he's right and you're in the wrong. But, now's the time to do just that. It's also time to take some of the heat out of the situation. I've always found it's best to just own up to the mistake, suggest how you can "fix" the situation and promise to be a lot more careful in the future. If it's really your error, and there's really no good excuse for it, admit it and move on. There's something absolutely disarming about your accepting the blame and suggesting ways to prevent it from happening again. What else is there to yell about? Hopefully, this will end the tirade.

You Can't Avoid Emotions

You can't avoid experiencing emotions, but you can learn how to live with them. You will need to figure out just what works for you when your emotions threaten to take control of your brain. Work at it. It's definitely worth your while to learn the techniques needed to remain calm, cool and collected when the world is whirling around you, out of your control. There are lots of books and seminars on stress management. Take advantage of them. It just might add years to your life.

Similarly, you might be able to help your coworkers when emotions erupt. Maybe it's just a bad day or an exceptionally difficult project, and a little help from you can

turn the tide. Or, maybe a few minutes conversation on a light subject will distract them enough so that they can gain control again. Sometimes just the thought that someone else is sharing your load makes all the difference.

The Irate Customer

The good news is that there are ways to handle the situation if the out-of-control person is an irate customer. First of all, it's important that you remain calm and in control of the situation. If the person is in front of you—not on the phone—look directly at the person with a serious, but pleasant, look on your face. Ask what the problem is with an attitude of "I'm here to help you." You need to talk slowly and quietly. It's just possible that your pleasant expression and soft, slow speech will convince the person that he or she can also stop shouting and get serious. Then, try your best to explain the situation. If it is a valid complaint, slowly explain in detail what the options are to resolve the situation. If the complaint isn't really valid, try to explain why it isn't valid in simple, easy-to-understand terms.

Sometimes, when the matter is something that isn't within your control, you can use the following with success: "I know how you feel; I felt the same way myself, until I realized that…… ." It's surprising how many times that particular phrase will work. By approaching the problem in this manner, you are agreeing that he/she is not being unreasonable and that while you can understand the point, you are still unable to do what he/she is asking. This helps to defuse the situation a little and may keep the situation from escalating.

The important thing is that you cannot allow yourself to join the customer in being out of control. We're all different personalities, and the type of personality we are will affect how we react to a situation. The laid-back, phlegmatic personality will usually have no problem reacting calmly to an attack by a customer. Phlegs always want to keep the peace, so they will naturally react as described above. It's the Choleric, like me, who has to hold himself or herself back to keep from coming back with an "Oh, yeah?" It's important, though, that you use your brains and not your emotions when the other person is clearly in an emotional state. The payoff is that you may retain a profitable customer who might even send more business your way. At the very worst, he or she might badmouth you to a friend who is in the market for your goods or services if the situation is not handled correctly.

Chapter 21. Handling Emotions

Reducing Stress

There are some methods to reduce your stress even in the middle of a busy, stress-filled day. For a quick pick-me-up, just sit back for one minute, close your eyes and imagine yourself in a place that's very relaxing to you—maybe a white sand beach with palm trees blowing in the breeze, or maybe in a boat on your favorite fishing lake. Just pick the one that's the most appealing to you. That may bring your blood pressure down a few points. If it's possible at your workplace, some soothing background music might help you to relax.

 If you feel that you're ready to explode, get up and MOVE. Go to the restroom, take a drink, walk around the perimeter of the office, chat with another worker for a minute. Then, when you get home after work, do some calisthenics or walk around the block. Take time to read the paper or play with your children for 15 or 20 minutes before plunging into your evening's work.

Much as we couch potatoes hate to admit it, exercise is just about the best thing available to combat stress. And, it isn't necessary to pay the cost of joining a gym. Walking is an excellent exercise, and the only expense is the price of a good pair of walking shoes.

If all else fails, and the stress on your job is making you sick, maybe you need to consider changing jobs. Perhaps there is another position in the same workplace that offers less stress. Constant, ongoing stress can make you sick, and it's not worth it.

Additional Reading:

Littauer, Florence, *Personality Plus: How to Understand Others by Understanding Yourself*, Fleming H. Revell, ISBN: 0-8007-5445-X, 1983-1992

Littauer, Florence and Littauer, Marita, *Personality Puzzle: Piecing together the personalities in your workplace*, Fleming H. Revell, ISBN: 0-8007-1676-0, 1992

Several other books by Florence Littauer address this subject.

Chapter 21. Handling Emotions

Chapter Quiz:

1. **There are five different personality types into which you can categorize yourself and the people you meet.**

   a. True
   b. False

2. **A good way to deal with an irate customer is to:**

   a. pass him/her on to another employee.
   b. duplicate the customer's tone when answering.
   c. speak softly and slowly while looking at him/her with a sincere expression.
   d. ask him/her to leave.

3. **A person with a Phlegmatic personality is the most likely to be a troublemaker at the workplace.**

   a. True
   b. False

4. **The stress is getting to be too much for you. One good way to handle stress is to:**

   a. let it all hang out. Throw a tantrum so that every one will know just how tough your job is.
   b. quit. You can find a job with no stress.
   c. ask for a raise if you're going to have to put up with this much stress.
   d. meditate or get up and walk away for a while.

5. **A Choleric coworker may hurt your feelings without realizing it.**

   a. True
   b. False

6. **A person who acts as a bully in the workplace is often that way because of:**

   a. his or her superior ability of the job at hand.
   b. his or her feeling of incompetence.
   c. that's the only way to get subordinates to work.
   d. management will notice his or her ability to work with people.

7. **There is usually no problem with dating someone at work if you:**

   a. are discreet and continue to do your job well.
   b. tell everyone that you are dating and spend a lot of time together on the job.
   c. ask someone else to do part of your work so you can spend more time together.
   d. rearrange the workplace so you can be together.

8. **The person with a Sanguine personality is very shy.**

   a. True
   b. False

9. **If you need someone to fill a position that requires a lot of planning, meeting deadlines, and attention to detail, your best bet is a:**

   a. Sanguine.
   b. Phlegmatic.
   c. Melancholy.
   d. Choleric.

10. **A little white lie on the job now and then is no cause for concern.**

    a. True
    b. False

Answers:

1-b, 2-c, 3-b, 4-d, 5-a, 6-b, 7-a, 8-b, 9-c, 10-b

Chapter 22

Protecting Customer Values and Property

Dick Glass is an author of previous ETA publications as well as more than a dozen books dealing with electronics technology and business management, published by Howard W. Sams Co, TAB Books, McGraw-Hill and ETA. He has also written hundreds of articles in trade journals and other association publications. Dick is a former Navy Avionics Technician, Industrial Electronics Computer Technician, Technical Writer, FCC Commercial License examination modernization committee chairman, inductee into the Electronics Hall of Fame and currently President of ETA-I. He has a broad background in all phases of work performed by electronics technicians. He oversees ETA's 40+ certification programs and the Training Course Approval system.

Dick Glass, CETsr

Primordial Etiquette

In the beginning.............well, according to human scientific evidence, early man lived by the principle of anarchy, pretty much taking what he wanted if he happened to be larger than his neighbor, or if he had a gang to help him overcome his neighbor, grabbing any tools, food, wives and kids, and making off with them. Eventually, this was found to not work out well, since a man might be able to overcome his neighbor, maybe even multiple neighbors, but eventually, unless he had a big gang, he became the victim, rather than the winner.

So, for some reason, even early man decided that for the good of the species, some rules for survival should be established. Some of these rules weren't much better than the anarchy before, since most early civilizations generally were led by a big dictator who was nearly as oppressive as the marauders under the 'no-law-at-all' condition. However, since the ruler or king (later) offered the protection of his warriors or the larger community, man was willing to submit to the tyranny of the king.

While living under the king, a lot of people in the same small area found, after a while, that others offended them. Sometimes people stole from their next door neighbor; some kicked their kid; some kept vicious dogs who threatened everyone's safety; and some ridiculed another's animal skin loin cloth or dress, kid's ugliness, relatives, cooking, and so forth.

So, fights broke out. Some were maimed or killed, kids left homeless, others banished from the tribe. In other words, things weren't working out well.

Personal Relations

So, to again try to preserve the species, to keep from killing each other (in order to have enough neighbors to fight off saber tooth tigers or marauding evil clans), people decided they should attempt to live together more amicably.

They quit grabbing food away from others; they worked together to grow food or to capture it and they found that by treating each other as he or she would like to be treated, they all began to prosper. Less of them were killed needlessly, fewer kids were mauled by dogs, and some semblance of real civilization began.

Change Takes Time

You would think that once humans saw all of the benefits of cooperation and treating others with respect and caring about the well-being of the entire clan that man would, in a very few, perhaps only a score of years, progress to a utopian world. In this world everyone would share, and do his part of the work. He would use reason and logic to convince others to do things his way. He would have respect for his neighbor's property, values and kids. Utopia would be reached. You would think the benefits were so huge that anyone not treating others with respect would be ostracized, kicked out of the cave, and given a very bad job recommendation.

But like most things, as they evolve, they do not do so in a linear fashion. Instead, they take a small step up, get complacent and fall back a half step or more, then take another step up, surpassing the first step up, get complacent again, fall back or become extinct, then some other clan takes steps even higher than the first, and eventually civilization progresses to a higher level. Eventually.

Roadblocks

In the 5,000 or so years in which, most agree, man has been around in some form of civilized groups, we find that there are too many sidetracks to reaching the human relations utopia we all verbally agree that we want. The kings, cops, soldiers, land owners, ogres, trolls, pharaohs, high priests and others in authority most often took advantage of their power. This led to sacrifices of those whom the powerful didn't like, or were envious of, to making drudges of those too unorganized to protect themselves; to becoming servants to those who somehow had acquired most of the wealth or property. In some countries, it led to a caste system where some could never advance to a better life, simply because of who they were born to.

This worked out well for those who had the power over the common people. And in fact, the upper class developed some fine human relations customs: The kings invited the rest of the upper class to formal dinners and dances, pleased their ears with lute music, pleased their eyes with dancing girls and pretty fabrics and gold furnishings. Even running water made life so much better .....for the upper class or royalty.

A Step Up

At least it seemed like a step up when some of the people decided to get rid of the rulers and form democratic societies. Individuals were recognized. The Magna Carta was a step. An even more important step was the United States' Bill of Rights. It was an attempt to recognize the human being as special—to recognize that there should be no arbitrary classes based on birth rights, royal background, color of skin, sex or other false reasons to oppress people.

Etiquette

Somewhere along the way, Emily Post and others decided that there were right and wrong ways to act around other humans. People at license branches and post offices work so hard that they have never had the time to read these books about etiquette, but many others have.

It is not easy learning all of the rules, and all of the rules don't always apply in every situation. We allow youngsters to get by with things we would abhor in adults, or even teenagers.

Manners Aren't Easy

In the first place, most of us don't see a lot of use in supercilious manners. In fact if no one is watching, we likely will skip quite a few of them. We open the car door for our wives or secretaries when we are in public. We let them open it themselves at other times. After all, isn't 'women's lib' still in vogue?

But still, just because we don't want to be mannerly, and really don't need to in many circumstances, it isn't a fact that everyone automatically knows what is appropriate and what is unsociable. For instance, Helen Keller was afflicted, after 19 months of life, with no hearing or sight. It was difficult for her parents as Helen grabbed food off of others' plates and dumped the gravy on the floor. Think of it: her parents could not even fathom any way to change Helen from a rude, pushy, vulgar being, most unpleasant to be around, to someone resembling a lovable daughter.

But her teacher took on the task. Slowly, and with great opposition from the parents, who understandably could not bear to see Helen treated in any way that she didn't like, Anne Sullivan taught Helen Keller to communicate and understand and even later to be a part of the movie about her life named *Deliverance* (not the backwoods banjo movie of the same name).

Helen Keller learned manners and how to interact with people.

It's Easy

If Helen, being blind and deaf, could learn how to speak and act around people, should it not be much easier for the rest of us to quickly acquire the discipline to keep from offending others? If we were of another tongue, for instance, and we spoke only one of the Indian languages, would it not be a hundred times harder to be able to communicate and to keep from making blunders or offending people? Surely, our job of acquiring these 'soft skills' should be simple. We are able to remember the names of all of our favorite sports heroes. We know the winning speed of the latest NASCAR or INDY 500 race. We can tell you the actors in the latest movies we watched. We can rattle off computer jargon that impresses many of our friends. Politics, religion, history, automobile models, hip hop record artists, the list is endless. We have learned more facts and statistics than almost any society the world has ever known.

The Time Has Come

So, for you and I to become experts in only one small aspect of Customer Service, manners should be 'duck soup.' It should be so easy for us to become experts at Protecting Customer Values and Property that the world will be amazed at how suave we appear to customers and co-workers, church members, poker club friends, and so forth.

Chapter 22. Protecting Customer Values and Property

Just as we don't run red lights, yell 'fire' in crowded rooms, drag potential mates home by the hair, 'jump' the chow line, throw things at the referees, ask the bride if she is pregnant, and so forth, there are certain niceties that a CSS candidate should be aware of when interacting with customers. There are certain things that should not be said or done and, likewise, certain things that should be.

That is the purpose of this chapter: To get you to think about how best to interact with customers you may be acquainted with, and those who may be entirely unknown until now.

Values

I'm not much on dogs. Yes, I have a beagle—Sort of like Charlie Brown's—but mine is old and fat. He 'walks' rabbits. He quit 'guarding' the house and yard a long time ago when he found out nearly all of the neighbor dogs and other varmints in the area could either beat up on him or outrun him. His main attribute is his ability to beg food. He never wastes any free hand-outs, although he very often turns up his nose at dry dog food like Kibbles and Bits. He won't bathe and if you wash him, he immediately heads for the nearest dead animal or some other smell that might convince other dogs that he, in fact, killed something. Thus the bath does little good and it keeps him from enjoying a visit into the house now and then.

Oh, I might miss Henry, should he pass away, but I'm not so sure how long, since a new skinny beagle that smells better and can run rabbits and bark at intruders might be an improvement around our place.

However, most people with dogs have very different attitudes. Virtually every week you read about a vicious dog that mauled and/or killed a baby or even a grown person. Why would anyone keep such a dangerous animal? Maybe it is for protection, like the pioneers needed to do. Maybe it's because the dog establishes some sort of understanding or knows a few tricks that amuse a person. Or maybe because the owner gets a sense of authority or control that he may not have in any other aspect of his life.

Still others keep dogs or cats, especially in their old age, because they get lonely and may not want any more troubles with human companions on a live-in basis. But they do like the animal and may pay thousands of dollars to have one which people notice or on which they can devote their affections, possibly to show their acquaintances how 'caring' they really are at heart.

There are probably hundreds of other reasons why people keep dogs, cats, snakes, mice, birds, monkeys, horses, fish, rabbits, mountain lions, and other pets. Still others have animals which they raise as a business, such as emus, buffaloes, sheep, rats, and so forth.

The object here is to convince you that whatever strange reasons people have for harboring disease-carrying, smelly, time-consuming, dangerous, costly, obnoxious animals/pets, and no matter how much money some poor family that can't afford shoes for the kids is willing to spend on the original price of a pet, or the continuing vet bills, the CSS cannot make judgments about it. The customer values these non-humans, sometimes much higher than they may have, or might still, value their offspring.

Rather than passing judgment, then, we need to over-come our much higher sense of values in this world, and try, instead, to fit into the customer's shoes to see if we can recognize how much that pet, or anything else the customer has an interest in, really means to that person.

This is not always easy. I have always been interested in painting. Some of my paintings have received top awards at our area art shows. This being the case, I, naturally, find it easy to compliment a customer, in his home, on any art-work that adorns the walls. Making a service call, one day, to our college art professor's home, I did praise some of the art works. About to leave, and being accompanied by the professor to the door, I noticed in the hallway an oil paint-ing. I thought it was pretty atrocious, but the main thing that caught my eyes was that the oils had actually dripped in some places down the face of the scene. Fortunately I wasn't very vocal in asking about the drips, so no harm may have been done, even though the professor assured me the drips were part of the finished product. But nothing would be gained by my criticizing that ugly painting.

So, the CSS would do well to recognize the customer's values on the furnishings in the home. More people have Wal-Mart prints hanging on their walls than actual paint-ings. Why not compliment them if the scene is pretty, or the colors are vivid? The customer may feel that print is about the most beautiful wall hanging in the home.

More Than Keeping Up Appearances

The looks of the house or yard or the quality of the customer's electronics or furniture may be nothing to pass a compliment on, but the least we can do is to keep quiet. Surely there is something in the house that shows good

Chapter 22. Protecting Customer Values and Property

quality, or is pretty, or shows a good choice. If you see a copy of *WAR AND PEACE* on the bookshelf, surely complimenting the owner on reading an 1800-page classic would show your recognition of the customer's knowledge and value of history.

The brat messing with your tools or test equipment is a problem that may take some tact to overcome. But the child might well be a blessing that makes him or her the joy of that family's life. That dirty-faced, wet-diapered, smelly, screaming nuisance might well be, under most circumstances, a treasure to that family. Things just aren't going well today. If things are really bad, you might find you can offer some sort of help, like asking if the mother would like for you to move the test equipment to a table or another room where the door can be shut. Or, just maybe the mother or dad is on the verge of breaking down because life today has become unbearable. While a service person should be extremely careful about becoming involved in anything other than making the repair, if someone is desperately ill, has broken a bone, is bleeding, or an emergency is at hand, who better than you should do the humanitarian thing and help out, if requested?

So, we have intellectual values and the 'things' the customer owns that may be valued very highly by the customer. Dale Carnegie always preached: Never Criticize, Condemn, or Complain. The other side of this is: Always compliment the customer on those things which you see as worthy, and try to understand the customer may place a very high value on something you consider junk. I remember another customer. His wife had died a year or so ago. In his home were a dozen or so paint-by-the-numbers wall hangings. These weren't pretty. The colors had faded. They looked cheap. You would not buy one for a nickel at a garage sale. But this customer valued them highly and pointed them out to us on more than one occasion. Why? Because his wife had put her time and effort into making those pictures to adorn their walls. Who cares if they are award winners? Who cares if they are PBTN works? The walls looked more like a home with those paintings hanging there, reminding the widower of the most important person in his life. The least you could do was choose one as your favorite of the bunch. Or you could note that one of the frames was expensive looking. Why not?

If the customer has an outdated 8-track player or is trying to get his 1950's phonograph to pay an old Hank Williams 78 RPM record, you may not feel this equipment is worthy of the effort to take it to the dump. Or, you could compliment the customer on his valuing these heirlooms and keeping them in operation and being able to get the exact reproduction of Hank's 'I Saw the Light' which your father, or his father listened to when those sounds were 'just about as perfect as anyone could ever want.'

When you are a CSS, you are trying to make every customer a hero. Just as the things you value cause you to like others who compliment you and your values, so do all customers. By being an expert at making heroes, you will also find you make lasting customers who sometimes tell the boss about what excellent employees he has. Besides, you will find out that some of these people rarely ever have anyone say anything good about anything they have or do or say. You may find you make a friend for life. Why not?

Property

The same rules apply for the customer's property. If that TV set has a shine on it and a clean face plate after you worked on it, that shows respect for the property. If you ask if you should take off your shoes before entering that trashy house, the customer feels better about having called your company. If you explain things in detail, always looking to impress the customer that you recognize his choice of brands, or model, or style, you and your company win. The customer is less likely to be picky about something else. He assumes your caring flows over into the details of the repair.

Why not? The Golden Rule applies to service work too.

Chapter 22. Protecting Customer Values and Property

Chapter Quiz:

1. Never Criticize, Condemn or _____.

   a. Castigate
   b. Compliment
   c. Cauterize
   d. Complain

2. If the customer has an outdated unit, you should explain what a piece of junk it is and send him to Wal-Mart for a new one.

   a. True
   b. False

3. The customer's daughter has just run off and gotten married to the slimiest no-gooder in town. The parents are distraught, but mention the problem to you. Of the four choices below which should be your response?

   a. What a tragedy! Disown her.
   b. Gosh, that must be a disappointment to you. But, you know? Sometimes things work out better than you expect.
   c. I always thought your daughter had loose morals anyway.
   d. I agree. That guy is a jerk and will never be a success.

4. If a customer asks you to spend a few minutes as he brags about his expensive duck hunting dog, you should explain that you are too busy to play with dumb animals.

   a. True
   b. False

5. Practicing etiquette while performing service work or talking to people on the help-line may be nice, but it is a wasteful use of time.

   a. True
   b. False

6. Teaching a "Helen Keller" the rules of living should be how many times harder than teaching the same rules to a person with hearing and sight?

   a. Twice
   b. 10 times
   c. 50 times
   d. 100 or more times

7. A small scratch you implanted on the top finish of a TV probably won't be noticed by the customer.

   a. True
   b. False

8. The customer tells you about his/her daughter being in her first recital, playing the piano. What would be a good response from you?

   a. So what?
   b. I played the piano in grade school. Let me tell you about my experiences
   c. Being able to play the piano is a blessing. When is the recital?
   d. I never liked the piano. Now, give me a guitar.

9. The customer has what appears to be a vicious dog which seems determined to attack you as you approach the house, what might you do?

   a. Spray the dog with Mace and warn the customer that your firm will not make further service calls until the dog is killed.
   b. Yell at the customer and tell them to get that *$#%@*& animal restrained or face a !&%$#@ lawsuit.
   c. Call from your vehicle and ask that the dog be tied or penned up.
   d. Call the dog catcher.

10. The customer has a statue of a Buddha or a picture of some religious personality representing a faith you don't think much of, because it isn't the one you believe in. What might be a good comment to show your interest in the customer's values?

    a. Wow! That is a beautiful statue (or picture).
    b. Hasn't that religion been shown to be false?
    c. Do all Hindu's keep these icons in their homes?
    d. I hope my kids never get exposed to that religion.

Answers:

1-d; 2-b; 3-b; 4-b; 5-b; 6-d; 7-b; 8-c; 9-c; 10-a

Chapter 23

Customer-Coworker Problems: Prevention & Solutions

Randal Reusser has been involved with ETA-I since 1990. He has served as Chairman, Vice-Chairman, Secretary, Shop Owners Division Chairman, Certified Technicians Division Chairman, Certified Technicians Division Secretary/Treasurer and Certification Administrator. Randal received the "Pete" outstanding national officer award in 1996. He is a senior CET in Consumer Electronics, Communication, and is also a CFOI and CSM. Randal holds an MBA from Marquette University, a BA from Carthage College, an AA from Gateway Technical College and many other honors and technical certifications.

Randal R. Reusser
CETsr, CSM, MBA

Conflict

Conflict is part of our everyday lives, and dealing with conflict will certainly be a part of your job as a professional certified customer service specialist. Don't make the mistake of assuming that conflict is always bad. Conflict can expose problems or weaknesses in a plan, policy or procedure.

In the book, *Making the Team,* by Leigh Thompson, two types of conflict are discussed. They are *emotional* and *cognitive* conflict. Emotional conflict is described as "personal, defensive, and resentful...rooted in anger, personal friction, personality clashes, ego, and tension."[10] This is destructive conflict, and it hurts people and organizations.

Cognitive conflict, on the other hand, tends to separate the people from the problem and "consists of argumentation about the merits of ideas, plans, and projects...it forces people to rethink problems and arrive at outcomes that everyone can live with."[11] For example, the unfair administration of company policies can cause conflict. When a manager allows some employees to come to work late, while holding others to a higher standard, it can cause conflict. In this case, it is weak management that is causing the conflict. One solution would be offering "flex-time" to all employees.

When conflict does occur, it is important that we deal with it on a mature and professional level. Some customers have a gift for causing conflict. We must work to provide them with a win/win solution. This is not always possible, but arguing with a customer is never the correct response. Even if you win the argument, you will probably lose the customer.

Often company policies or procedures, which are

beyond your control, are the underlying cause of employee/customer conflict. These issues must be addressed to managers and company leaders, and they should change these policies to minimize this type of conflict.

We each must do our part to reduce and resolve conflict as it arises in our work lives. Using empathy and putting yourself in the other person's shoes can help. If conflict is not resolved, it can escalate to workplace violence.

Workplace Violence

Workplace violence is a very serious problem. According to the Bureau of Labor Statistics, there were "645 homicides in workplaces in the United States" in 1999.[8] It is estimated that "Two million American workers are victims of workplace violence each year."[7]

Those who study workplace violence have developed four categories to investigate and seek solutions that will reduce workplace violence. They are Criminal Intent (Type I), Customer/Client (Type II), Worker-on-Worker (Type III), and Personal Relationship (Type IV).

In the Type I criminal intent cases, the violence is related to another crime like robbery or theft. The criminal has no "relationship to the business or its employees."[8]

In the Customer/Client (Type II) incidents, the customer becomes violent and attacks the person who is serving him or her. These are the irate customers who take their frustration to the next level. These attacks occur in schools, doctor's offices, stores, and prisons and can happen anywhere that customer service is provided. Incidents where a service provider attacks the customer, which are more rare, also fall into this category.

Type III, Worker-on-Worker violence, is self explanatory and is probably the most preventable, if the worker conflict is addressed before it can escalate to violence. A disgruntled former employee is a likely perpetrator of this type of violence, and every threat must be taken seriously.

Personal Relationship (Type IV) violence is associated with someone who has a personal relationship with an employee, but no relationship with the business. Husbands, ex-husbands, wives, girlfriends and boyfriends are the ones who can bring their problems to their companion's workplace.

Now that we have identified the types of workplace violence, we need to discuss what a company and its employees can do to reduce or prevent violence. Businesses have an obligation to protect their employees, and employees have an obligation to inform their managers of possible threats or problems.

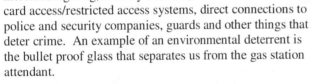

The Workplace Violence Report identified three "general approaches to preventing workplace violence."[9] They are Environmental, Organizational/Administrative, and Behavioral/Interpersonal. Some successful environmental tools are increased lighting, security cameras, card access/restricted access systems, direct connections to police and security companies, guards and other things that deter crime. An example of an environmental deterrent is the bullet proof glass that separates us from the gas station attendant.

Organizational/Administrative tools include zero tolerance policies against Worker-on-Worker violence. Many companies have security practices that require two people to do bank deposits or close the store at the end of the day. Companies need to have an open channel of communications between employees and management to address employee safety and vulnerability to violence. If you are threatened by someone at work or from outside of work, you should tell your manager.

Training is used to help prevent violence on a Behavioral/Interpersonal level. Teaching employees to look for, identify and react to workplace violence can be effective. For example, if a person seems to be getting increasingly abusive or irate over time, seeking Human Resources involvement may prevent him or her from escalating to violence. In my experience, people occasionally lash out at work in response to personal problems at home. As an employee, you have a duty to your employer and coworkers to report incidents that involve anger, inappropriate responses, or sudden and pronounced changes in someone's behavior. I believe that the old adage, "a stitch in time

saves nine" applies.

In one company where I worked, a man threatened his girlfriend and beat her up outside of work. The company increased security to prevent the man from entering company property and the girl, who was a temp, was moved to another location. Wherever you work, you should know and follow your company's workplace violence policies or procedures.

Customer/Client Relations

Good customer/client relations start with happy, well-paid, and well-trained employees. If you don't feel good about the company you work for, it is hard to treat customers well. Company policies, procedures and employee training are also key to good customer/client relations.

Many of us work in places where the customer is already upset before we talk to them. For example, when I worked in a TV repair shop, most of the customers came in because something they spent good money on was broken. It was important for the customer service people to understand the customer's emotions. Often I would relate my own experience with broken electronic products to empathize with and relax the customer in order to provide them the service they required.

I have seen poorly trained customer service people blame the customer for buying a "cheap product" when often that product was purchased from the very same company. This is like pouring gasoline onto a small fire.

Management has a large responsibility in how well a company does in the area of customer/client relations. As I mentioned earlier, most of it will depend on employee training and company policies and procedures. Going back to the TV repair example, when customers leave their TV for repair, they need to know what to expect. How much will it cost? How long will it take? Is it worth fixing? Is this a common problem?

These and other questions must be answered correctly and truthfully to set the customer's expectations. If this is done properly, much customer dissatisfaction and unhappiness can be avoided. Employee empowerment, giving your employees the power to make decisions on the spot to solve customer problems, is very helpful. For example, Mr. Jones' TV is one month out of warranty. An empowered employee at the customer service desk could reduce the repair charges, get special authorization to repair the set under warranty, and/or expedite the repair. Mr. Jones could

Chapter 23. Customer and Coworker Problems

feel very special instead of feeling like he got a lemon.

All employees need to be concerned with providing superior customer service. It is a lot easier said than done. Managers must find ways to measure client satisfaction using surveys, time measurements, profitability, and employee and customer feedback, along with other tools. This information should be used to shape policies, procedures and training to continuously improve the service your company provides and enhance customer/client relations.

Employee Dating

Many companies prohibit managers from dating employees. This is a good policy. There are many problems that can occur when a subordinate dates the boss or vice versa. There is the possibility of a lawsuit when the relationship ends. If the employee is later terminated with cause, he or she can allege that it is related to the previous relationship. Also, if the subordinate is later denied a raise, promotion, or given additional work assignments, the question of discrimination can arise.

Today lawyers make a great deal of money in sexual harassment law suits that hurt companies. In June of 1998 the Supreme Court ruled that "the employer is responsible for the actions of the supervisor, even when the employer is unaware of the supervisor's behavior."[5] According to a recent study "at least 40% of all women report being sexually harassed at some point in their career."[5] The same study indicates that men file over 11% of sexual harassment cases reported to the Equal Employment Opportunity Commission (EEOC).

The Mayor of Milwaukee, John O. Norquist, a married man, had a sexual relationship with his aide, Marilyn Figueroa. According to the Milwaukee Journal Sentinel, "Norquist has said the relationship was consensual."[1] Ms. Figueroa later filed a sexual harassment suit that was settled "for $375,000, a sum Norquist will repay the city through a mix of campaign funds and his own money."[2] The taxpayers would have had to pay this bill if Norquist had not agreed to pay. The city still "spent more than $33,000 for court reporters, expert witnesses and other outside costs"[3] associated with the case.

Strong personal emotions can cloud the employee/employer relationship, cause bad decisions, and impair the judgment of both parties. The two parties involved in the dating are not in a vacuum, and their relationship affects others at the workplace. The other employees can feel at a disadvantage and can seek legal remedies if they feel they are being discriminated against in the areas of workload, raises, and promotions. The legal term for treating some employees differently from others is disparate treatment. A manager must treat employees fairly and not show favoritism to any for reasons other than job performance.

Every company must decide how to handle these situations. Having a policy in place that prohibits managers and supervisors from dating employees protects the company and helps prevent other employees from receiving disparate treatment. The best advice I can give on this subject is not to date your boss or any of your employees, even if your company is silent on the subject.

Coworker Relations

Companies must be careful not to do anything to hurt coworker relations. At one place where I worked, there was a bonus plan that caused unhealthy competition among the technicians. It was intended to increase productivity, but unfortunately it caused some customers to be overcharged and technicians to "cherry pick." Cherry picking is when a person picks the easier or more profitable work for themselves. A bonus plan that strains coworker relationships and cheats customers is bad for everybody.

Managers are the people who should design fair bonus plans and distribute work so cherry picking does not occur. A better bonus plan for the example above would have been one tied to overall shop productivity with a smaller additional amount for individual piece or dollar count. This would have promoted technician cooperation and unity.

The best thing a company can do to promote positive coworker relations is to treat each employee equitably and fairly. The relationships between employees will be much better if no disparate treatment exists. When one employee is promoted over another, it is the manager's job to make sure everyone knows why that person was chosen. For example: he or she continually got the highest reviews of the candidates, missed less work, achieved a higher education, or other credible reason for his or her promotion.

There are many things that a company can do to promote good coworker relations. Providing regular team meetings where employees are kept informed and can voice their concerns is a good start. Sponsoring outside social events like company outings to baseball games, picnics, and parties can build coworker cohesion and strengthen employee relationships. Many companies also sponsor baseball, bowling, soccer and other teams. These teams can be beneficial in several ways, including encouraging teamwork and physical fitness—both of which can benefit the company when they return to work.

Coworker Dating

Many hardworking people let their job dominate their lives, leaving little time to meet new people. Finding romance at work may seem natural and is certainly convenient. Some office romances have led to successful marriages. A recent study found that as many as "six to eight million Americans enter into a workplace dating relationship every year."[6]

However, there is a danger when you mix your work life with your personal life. When dating someone from work, it is likely that work will be the primary topic of discussion. People who like to separate their work life from their personal time are better off not dating coworkers.

You need to know if your company has an office romance policy or any rules against coworker dating. From a company perspective, "a well-drafted policy can provide considerable legal protection and provide clear guidelines for employees without destroying the workplace environment."[4] If your company has such a policy on dating, forget about it! If there are no rules against inter-company dating, you should still proceed with caution.

If you decide to ask someone from work out on a date and they decline, do not continue to pursue them. Continually trying to date a person who declined could be considered sexual harassment and lead to your dismissal or worse. Building a good working relationship before trying to develop a personal relationship is important. If you can't get along at work and don't have mutual respect for each other, the relationship is doomed.

Remember that people talk. Your workplace relationship is likely to be the topic of many water cooler discussions. Also, your professionalism is key to your success as a certified Customer Service Specialist. Do not openly express your feelings towards your workplace boyfriend/ girlfriend. It is very unprofessional to be kissing, hugging

or expressing your affection for your coworker at work or any company event.

The worst part of a coworker dating scenario is when it ends. Most people don't ever want to see their old flame again. However, in workplace dating, that is not possible. The perceived injured party can go out of his or her way to make your workplace a hostile environment. This is illegal and could jeopardize both of your jobs. In the best case, where the break-up is by mutual agreement, it is still difficult to deal with the feelings you once had for the other person.

I have worked at companies where fist fights have occurred between new and previous boyfriends over an ex-girlfriend. These almost always result in disciplinary action against one or both of the parties. Situations like these can also cause other employees to take sides, similar to what happens when two people get divorced.

My final thoughts on the subject are that a person should think long and hard before dating a coworker. It should never be taken lightly, especially if you love your job. If things go wrong, you may find it necessary to find a new job.

Employee Discipline

Why, when, where, and how a manager disciplines an employee are all important considerations. Depending on what the employee does, discipline may or may not be the appropriate action. For example: If a manager observes an employee being rude to a customer, a simple discussion on why this is wrong may be all that is required. On the other hand, if this employee has been talked to previously about this behavior, some form of discipline may be necessary.

In most cases the best time to discipline an employee is at the time the undesired event or action occurs. This is not always possible. The matter should be addressed as closely as possible to the incident. Generally speaking the old rule of "praise in public, punish in private" is recommended. I hope that you work for a professional manager who understands that people make mistakes and doesn't yell at you in public or private. If your action deserves discipline, accept it and move on.

Employee discipline can take many shapes and is usually spelled out in the employee handbook, if the company has one.

Chapter 23. Customer and Coworker Problems

Many companies use the formal write-up to discipline an employee. This is a written record of the incident or behavior that led to the disciplinary action including the time, date, and names of any witnesses. The manager sits down with the employee, discusses the problem and usually requires the employee to sign the document. The write-up would also specify any action that the employee must take and also a follow-up date, for example—30 days to improve. This document then becomes a part of the employee's permanent record.

Due to our ever-increasing litigious society, many companies are documenting employee disciplinary actions in anticipation of a lawsuit, in the event that employee is later demoted or fired. Some offenses that typically lead to immediate termination are stealing, or bringing a weapon into work.

Theft

Shoplifting and employee theft cost companies millions of dollars annually and increase the costs of goods and services that we all buy. This and other types of stealing impact us all. Companies need to have open and honest relationships with their employees. They must put security measures in place to prevent customer and employee theft.

 I once worked for a company where nearly one-third of the managers were stealing cash from their stores to support their drug habits! This almost caused the company to go bankrupt. If the upper management had been more in touch with these managers, much of this theft could have been prevented. There were many warning signs of these individuals' drug problems, and the company later initiated pre-employment and random drug testing. They also offered treatment to employees willing to admit their problem.

I have always believed in doing an honest day's work for an honest day's pay. Many people justify their stealing because the store charges too much for their products or the company doesn't pay them enough. This is "stinking thinking." If you feel you are being exploited by your company, find another company to treat you fairly. Don't let that somehow justify your dishonesty.

This chapter is not on ethics and I don't want to tell you what to do if you observe another employee or manager stealing at work. Once, I almost lost my job for reporting a theft. The manager had an informal agreement with the owner to steal expensive merchandise. For a while I was considered a "squealer," but the owner later ended his relationship with the manager.

Honesty is always the best policy. Don't steal from your employer or anybody else. If you observe someone at work behaving dishonestly, "let your conscience be your guide."

Chapter 23. Customer and Coworker Problems

End Notes

[1] Borowski, Greg J. "Depositions give details in Figueroa case." The Milwaukee Journal Sentinel 12 June 2002. Retrieved August 16, 2002, from http://www.jsonline.com/news/Metro/jun02/50478.asp

[2] Borowski, Greg J. "Figueroa, mayor told of deposition release." The Milwaukee Journal Sentinel 29 June 2002. Retrieved August 16, 2002, from http://www.jsonline.com/news/Metro/jun02/55295.asp

[3] Borowski, Greg J. "City will pay $33,000 in Figueroa case bills." The Milwaukee Journal Sentinel 18 May 2002. Retrieved August 16, 2002, from http://www.jsonline.com/news/Metro/may02/44159.asp

[4] D' Anocona & Pflaum, LLC. (1999, November 22) "Dating in the Workplace". HR Watch, no page numbers. Retrieved from http://hr.monster.com/hrwatch/1999/11/22/from http://hr.monster.com/hrwatch/1999/11/22/

[5] Employer-Employee.com. "Sexual Harassment in the Workplace". Retrieved August 26, 2002, from http://www.employer-employee.com/sexhar1.htm

[6] Inc.com. "Acknowledgement and Waiver Regarding Employee Dating". Retrieved August 9, 2002, from http://www2.inc.com/leadership_and-strategy/freetools/22161.html

[7] Merchant, James A., et al. Workplace Violence: A Report to the Nation. Proc. of The University of Iowa Injury Prevention Center. Washington, 2000. Iowa City: University of Iowa, February 2001. Page 2

[8] Merchant, James A., et al. Workplace Violence: A Report to the Nation. Page 4.

[9] Merchant, James A., et al. Workplace Violence: A Report to the Nation. Page 6.

[10] Thompson, Leigh, Making the Team: A Guide for Managers. Upper Saddle River: Prentice Hall, 2000 Page 132

[11] Thompson, Leigh, Making the Team: A Guide for Managers. Page 133

Chapter 23. Customer and Coworker Problems

Chapter Quiz

1. **What are the two types of conflict?**

   a. Personal and Cognitive
   b. Emotional and Cognitive
   c. Emotional and Physical
   d. Positive and Negative

2. **What is Disparate Treatment?**

   a. Disciplinary action
   b. A fair reward system
   c. Treating some employees differently
   d. A legal loophole

3. **How many Americans are the victims of workplace violence each year?**

   a. 100,000
   b. 200,000
   c. 1 million
   d. 2 million

4. **What can be done to help prevent customer dissatisfaction?**

   a. Raise customer expectations
   b. Limit employee dating
   c. Set the customers expectations
   d. Lower your prices

5. **What is Employee Empowerment?**

   a. When employees form a union
   b. Restricting employees from making decisions
   c. Giving employee's decision-making authority
   d. Providing electrical power to an employee's cube

6. **Who can prevent Cherry Picking?**

   a. The Labor Relations Board
   b. Government
   c. Employees
   d. Management

7. **How many Americans enter into a workplace dating relationship every year?**

   a. 6 - 8 million
   b. 800,000
   c. 1 million
   d. 2 - 4 million

8. **Asking a coworker for a date after they have previously declined can be considered:**

   a. disparate treatment.
   b. cognitive conflict.
   c. cherry picking.
   d. sexual harassment.

9. **What type of offense typically leads to immediate termination?**

   a. Employee theft
   b. Sexual harassment
   c. Employee dating
   d. Excessive absences

10. **Who ultimately pays for shoplifting and employee theft?**

    a. Government
    b. Consumers
    c. Insurance Companies
    d. Store Owners

Answers:

1-b; 2-c; 3-d; 4-c; 5-c; 6-d; 7-a; 8-d; 9-a; 10-b

Chapter 24

Customer Service Techniques - Do's and Don'ts

Tom Marler, who recently died of cancer, was a retired US Navy Aviation Electrician Mate Chief Petty Officer. After the Navy, he worked as a Logistics Maintenance Specialist, Researcher, for NAVAIR on Reliability and Maintainability (R&M) program of the Electronic Warfare (EW) F/A18 E/F and conducted lab and flight testing of the Avionics Upgrade of F-14 A/B and F-14D aircraft. Tom held the following licenses and certifications: FAA Airframe and Powerplant, FCC GROL w/ships radar, CETsr, and he was also a Certification Administrator for ETA-I.

Tom Marler, CETsr

ETA Solution?

Four easy steps to customer satisfaction:

E = Evaluate the problem
T = Troubleshoot/Test the problem
A = Authenticate/Answer question
Solution = Solve the problem

Evaluate the problem

Evaluate the specific customer problem. Ask questions to determine what the basic problem is, then probe for the specific problem. Listen to the customer all the way through, without interruption, then ask open-ended questions. Without knowing the details, you won't be able to solve the problem.

Troubleshoot/Test the problem

Make sure you know how to use your company's product, then test it. Many products aren't actually defective at all. The customer might have programmed it incorrectly or possibly put the batteries in backwards. A full check will determine if problems exist.

Authenticate/Answer question

Authenticate. Is this the problem that the customer is having?

Answer, educating the customer on the correct use of the equipment or service capabilities, yet allowing him or her the opportunity to have a hands-on experience. This will benefit both you and your customer.

Solve the problem

Once you've determined the actual problem, it's time to solve it. Work with your customer to come up with the best possible solution. When you have an idea of the real problem, make suggestions for resolution, and get your customer's input. When you are listening to the customer's alternatives, remember your goal in customer service is to build positive relationships with your customers. Once you feel you've reached an acceptable conclusion, get the customer's agreement that the problem is resolved. Thank the customer for letting you help and tell him/her to call you if any other problems arise.

Who are You?

At the very least, you are the *Customer Service Specialist*. To the customer, you are *the Company*.

You are the most important person in the shop/store when dealing with the customer. As a frontline representative, your interaction with the customer is what forms the customer's impressions of the company you work for. You become the frontline link between management, merchandisers and the repair shop. Your *Manners, Dress, Personal Hygiene, Body Language, and Communication Skills* also play a very important part in dealing with a customer.

What is Customer Satisfaction?

When do we consider a customer satisfied?

The truth of the matter is that customer satisfaction is a perception issue. And as we all know, perception is reality. If a customer believes that he or she has had a situation resolved to his/her satisfaction... or if a customer believes that he or she has received satisfactory service, the customer is satisfied.

Use that golden rule: **"Treat your customers as you**

Chapter 24. Customer Service Techniques - Do's and Don'ts

would want to be treated." Keeping that in mind will help you make certain that you are giving your customers exemplary service.

It would be great if customers always bought the right products at the right times and were always totally satisfied. Unfortunately, that's not always the case. Sometimes the customer can't make a product work the way he/she intended it to work. Sometimes, products just don't work at all.

Manufacturers maintain the high quality of their products by maintaining stringent Quality Assurance Programs, but failures do happen. Even BMW and Rolls Royce have service departments. Although their names, by themselves, stand for high quality, when they fail, it gets expensive.

With the *Angry Customer*, you have to get beyond the emotion before you can solve the problem. Remember, an angry customer is really a customer who is screaming for help.

Customers sometimes develop attitudes that they feel will get them what they want. Angry customers feel that the "squeaky wheel gets the grease" mentality will assure them a quick solution to their problem.

When confronted by angry customers, remember that the customer's anger is not aimed at you. **Don't take it personally!** It can be tough to keep your thoughts in control of your emotions, but you must keep your reactions in check.

Be a Good Sounding Board

Be *Attentive* and *Understanding*. Some customers are irritated or upset when they have a problem. From the customer's perspective, the product stopped working just when they needed it most. (After all, if they hadn't tried to use it, they wouldn't have discovered that it needed repair.) It's an inconvenience to have to bring the product back into the store or shop.

Let your customers express their feelings and supply you with the information that they think is important first. Listen all the way through without interruption. Many times, the customer has a desire to be heard and to have his/her feelings appreciated even more than the desire to have the item repaired. Let your customers say what they have to say. Very often, you will pick up some vital information.

Ask open-ended questions, those which cannot be answered with a simple "YES and NO". Instead, open questions encourage conversation and are essential to determining specific customer needs. Your attitude can help turn this inconvenience into a positive experience for you and the customer.

However, you may have an angry customer who refuses to discuss the situation calmly and just wants to get a refund or exchange and leave. These occasionally unpleasant encounters are, unfortunately, unavoidable when dealing with the public. Your best tactic would be to complete the transaction as professionally and as quickly as possible so you can proceed to the next customer.

Remember, other customers are watching how you handle yourself .

Be Professional and Do Business

Remember that the customer's anger is not aimed at you. Don't take it personally.

Anger is not the only difficult behavior

An *Evasive Customer* dislikes confrontation and will offer little help in solving the problem. Take an active role in determining the actual problem with helpless customers. You won't have much to work with, but remember to probe for more information. As with the angry customer, you have to get beyond the emotion before you can solve the problem.

The *Victim Customer* tries to motivate with guilt. The situation is clearly not the customer's fault! This situation is something that has been done to them. Listen and respond with understanding, not sympathy. Don't apologize for the customer's situation and don't feel sorry for that situation. Assure the customer you wish to help, but avoid getting emotionally involved in any discussion. Once you've moved past the emotion and the customer explains the situation, you'll be in a better position to negotiate a solution. There is a difference between being "more than fair" and giving away the store.

Chapter 24. Customer Service Techniques - Do's and Don'ts

Service - an Inconvenience to the Customer

When a customer brings in an item for service, it's an inconvenience for him or her and rarely a pleasant experience. Your professionalism both during the transaction and after the customer leaves the store/shop can make a huge difference.

Remember:

"Do"

Use the *ETA Solution.* The four easy steps help to ensure that you are giving the customer exemplary services. We can't tell a customer to be satisfied, nor can we second-guess what a customer might need. That's why we ask pertinent questions. We need to know if the customer is satisfied, because it's in our best interest. Think about it... satisfied customers will return again and again and buy more from you and your store/shop.

The ETA Solution	
E	Evaluate the Problem
T	Trouble-shoot/Test the Problem
A	Authenticate/ Answer the Question
Solution	Solve the Problem

"Do"

Ask questions that guide the customer in the right direction, then give the customer the floor. Listen to the problem closely. Many customers, in fact, just want someone to listen to their problem or complaint. Try to see the situation from the customer's point of view.

"Do"

Stay calm. By fighting the urge to respond defiantly, you show that you are truly a professional. Don't help to create a scene. You'll find that by reacting calmly to angry customers, you can often diffuse a great deal of their anger. Customers sometimes just need to vent. Let them vent!

"Do"

Keep up-to-date. The world of technology is constantly changing, so you have to move with it or be lost in the shuffle. Dedicate at least one hour a week to reading about advancements in your company's area of electronics and customer service. For the latest news, check out industry-related specialty magazines, newspapers and suppliers' literature.

"Do"

Admit that *Mistakes happen*. None of us are perfect, and we certainly don't expect you to be. It's never pleasant to have to admit to a customer, "I made a mistake..." However, honesty is indeed the best policy in these types of situations. It's always best just to be honest and admit that you made a mistake... and then solve the problem. Don't just point the finger at someone else.

"Do"

When sending items for service/repair, the single biggest cause of delay in getting items returned to the customer in repair situations is failure to properly complete the repair tag information. NEVER put vague statements like "Doesn't work" or "DOA" on a repair tag. You must become the eyes and ears for a repair technician who may be hundreds of miles away from the customer—a technician who has just as great a desire to satisfy the customer as you. Type a short, but complete, description of the problem. Get complete customer information, such as name, address, and work and home telephone numbers.

"Don't"

Do not insult your customer's choices. Saying, "Why did you buy that piece of JUNK?" is not a good way to gain a customer's confidence. **Be professional** and give an honest "rough estimate," using the appropriate rate for labor and additional percentage for parts (the rule of thumb is labor less than $50.00, parts 25%; for labor over $50.00, parts 50% of labor cost). For example: labor $65.00, parts $31.00—total estimated repair $96.00. Remember, this is an **ESTIMATE** (it could be more or less). This might exceed the economical cost of the unit. Make sure the customer understands this. Ask the customer if he or she would like to proceed with the repair, or would he/she like more information on a replacement.

"Don't"

Don't play games like **"You and Me against the Company."** Resist the temptation to play hero by giving the impression that you are giving more than the company allows. **Remember, you are the company.** Make your suggestions and offer the solutions on behalf of the company.

Chapter 24. Customer Service Techniques - Do's and Don'ts

"Don't"

The customer is there to solve his/her problem, not to listen to you complain about the company, a supervisor or coworker. I cannot overemphasize how important it is to be professional at all times. Remember, there are avenues for you to resolve your complaint.

You, the Customer, and the Telephone

The telephone is a critical business link between your company and the customer. The telephone *and how you use it* can play a vital role as a Customer Service Specialist. The telephone is a medium where the customer is not physically present. But, the same techniques are used that would be used if the customer were standing in front of you. Remember, use the *ETA Solution*—the four easy steps to help ensure that you are giving the customer exemplary services.

Remember:

"Do"

Answer the telephone by the third ring. Your telephone customer will appreciate your prompt service. If you don't answer on or by the third ring, the customer might assume that you are not available and that he or she may be connected to an answering machine or voice mail system. This likely will cause them to just hang up.

"Do"

Take a moment and put a smile on your face before you speak (remember the customer cannot see you). Your voice will sound different when you smile—**"a difference your customer can sense."**

"Do"

Speak at a moderate pace, clearly and distinctly. When you are rushed, it is easy to sound like a auctioneer.

"Do"

Get the caller's name and use it frequently. Treat the customer as though he/she is in the room with you. Personalize the call as much as possible.

"Don't"

Don't take it personally. Remember that the customer's anger is not aimed at you. Well, that was before you put the customer on hold. No one likes to be left in *"CYBER SPACE."* Have you ever called a company and as soon as they answer they say "Please Hold," and you didn't get a chance to say anything? The hold button should only be used to let you change phones… **and ALWAYS** *ask your customer for permission before placing them on hold.*

"Don't"

DON'T transfer a customer from one associate or department to another. Customers HATE explaining the same thing over and over to a seemingly endless chain of individuals. When you don't know the answer, find the answer or the person who can provide it and put them in touch with the customer.

"Don't"

DON'T take incomplete phone messages. When customers say "He has my number," remind them that the call can be returned much faster if the number is on the message. If a customer says, "Oh, he knows me!" after giving you a common first name like "Bob" or "Sue," simply explain that the person they called INSISTS on a complete message so they can give the best possible service.

The Dread "Menu" Telephone System

It was designed, I believe, as a cruel joke to be played on the Customer Service Specialist. You thought the customer was angry when you put them on hold. Well, just wait, the customer has already waded through multi-layers of menus to get to you. He or she was then put "ON HOLD" with a recording telling your customer that the Customer Service Specialists are all assisting other customers and there will be a wait of " XX minutes". (The equation is Anger level = Layer of Menus x Number of Minutes.) As the customer rips the telephone from the wall, "Remember that the customer's anger is not aimed at you. Don't take it personally." Be professional. Do smile, talk slowly, and personalize the call, as if the customer is right in front of you. As with the angry customer, you have to get beyond the emotion before you can solve the problem, using the *ETA Solution.*

Chapter 24. Customer Service Techniques - Do's and Don'ts

You are the Company's Frontline Representative

You are the most important person in the shop/store when dealing with the customer as long as you keep the customers' wants and needs at the forefront, by reacting calmly to angry customers. Asking the customer questions and listening to the answers, using the ETA Solution, will ensure that the customer will be satisfied. Satisfied customers will return again and again and buy more from you and your store/shop. This is truly the key to being a true Professional Customer Service Specialist.

Remember, Without the Customer, the Company Wouldn't Exist, and Neither Would Your Job.....

Chapter Quiz:

1. **What is the ETA Solution?**

   a. Evaluate the problem, Troubleshoot/Test the problem, Authenticate/Answer question, Ignore the problem
   b. Evade the problem, Troubleshoot/Test the problem, Authenticate/Answer question, Solve the problem
   c. Evaluate the problem, Troubleshoot/Test the problem, Authenticate/Answer question, Solve the problem
   d. Evaluate the problem, Troubleshoot/Test the problem, Authenticate/Answer question, What is the problem?

2. **What type of an Angry Customer will not be able to help resolve his or her problem?**

   a. Customers who are irritated or upset when they have a problem
   b. Customers who feel the "squeaky wheel gets the grease" mentality will assure them a quick solution to their problem
   c. Customers who feel it's an inconvenience to have to bring the product back into the store or shop
   d. Customers who refuse to discuss the situation calmly and just want to get a refund or exchange and leave

3. **To ensure that you are giving the customer exemplary services you should:**

   a. play "You and Me" against the company.
   b. be "more than fair" and give away the store.
   c. use the ETA Solution.
   d. both a and b are correct.

4. **How should you answer the telephone?**

   a. The telephone should be ignored, and treated as an interruption.
   b. Answer the telephone by the third ring.
   c. Take incomplete phone messages.
   d. As soon as the phone rings, answer and say **"Please Hold."**

5. **To get repaired items returned to the customer in an expeditious manner you should:**

   a. NEVER put statements like "Doesn't work" or "DOA" on a Repair tag.
   b. become the eyes and ears for a repair technician.
   c. type a short, but complete description of the problem. Get complete customer information, such as name, address, and work and home telephone numbers.
   d. all of the above.

Answers:

1-c, 2-b, 3-c, 4-b, 5-d

Chapter 25

Time Management

Bob Ing of Toronto, Canada served as Chairman of ETA-I in 1998 and developed much of the material in the first CSS Study Guide. He is Director of King's Markham Forensic Services in Toronto, a project management contractor specializing in the validation and examination of digital technology. Bob has been a prolific author of professional publications. He lectures and gives workshops in both Canada and the United States.

Robert (Bob) Ing, DSc, CESma

"What you do today is important because you are exchanging a day of your life for it. When tomorrow comes, this day will be gone forever; in its place is something you have left behind ... let it be something good."

Whether it is in our personal or business life, we often find ourselves faced with options as to what we should be doing, could be doing and are actually doing. It all comes down to choices and then putting in the time to accomplish them.

Wasted Time

If you work five days a week, and were to waste just five minutes each day, that would add up to 21 hours a year that you have wasted. Although five minutes goes by quickly, it does add up. Can you imagine how many hours a year you really waste?

The best way to reduce wasted time is to plan ahead and do things when they can be done in the least amount of time. Here's a list of things that, with a little planning, could take less time:

♦ Waiting in line at the bank, grocery store, gas station, etc. (go when it's less busy during off hours)

♦ Being put on hold or trying to get through to customer service or the help desk by telephone. (best times to call: Tuesdays to Thursdays 8:00 am to 10:30 am, 2:00 pm to 3:00 pm and after 9:30 pm if they are still open)

The next time waster is being interrupted when trying to complete a tough project, so what can you do? Here are some ideas:

♦ Readjust your schedule, if possible, to work on the project before 8:00 am or one hour after normal

business hours.

♦ If before or after normal business hours, avoid the temptation to answer your telephone. Let your answering machine or voice mail pick it up.

♦ Organize your workspace, with all the tools and equipment you will need for the project, hours before you will begin.

♦ Put a "DO NOT DISTURB – WORK IN PROGRESS" sign on your door if people have a tendency to "barge" into your workspace. Lock your door if possible.

Avoid wasting time during your day by:

♦ Organizing your workspace with only the items you need to get the job done.

♦ Keeping telephone calls to not more than 3-6 minutes and not engaging in non-business-related chat.

♦ Purchasing items you use a lot of in bulk, so that you will make fewer trips to the store.

♦ Creating forms, form letters and lists on your computer that you can use time and again by just making simple edits.

♦ Organize and schedule errands and deliveries so that they are done geographically (in the same neighborhood) and not during rush hour.

♦ Whenever possible, get the audio cassette tape version of the book you want to read; this way you can listen to it while you are driving or doing another task.

◆ Reduce the amount of time you spend cleaning up, by taking care of things as you use / mess them up. (dishes, wastebasket, dusting desk, etc.)

◆ Always keep a mug or glass full of pens, pencils and markers on your desk and by the telephone.

Remember if you can save just five minutes a day, you will have gotten back the equivalent of an extra day in your life each year!

Task Prioritization

Before you can manage or make the most out of the time you have, you must first decide to what you will

 commit your time. What you commit your time to will dictate how you manage your time. As an employee, your supervisor or manager will assign you routine and one-time tasks, and if you are like most employees, you may receive task assignments from more than one super-

visor or manager. The ability to prioritize the tasks you are given will help you build the framework required to manage your time.

A common occurrence whenever an employee is assigned multiple tasks is that they go to their manager or supervisor and ask, "… which one should I do first?" or "… which one do you want me to do first?" This should be a clear indicator that the employee has no real grasp of task prioritization, and needs to learn this skill. As well, this also indicates that the manager or supervisor is not providing a specific timeline, due date or objective for the task assigned. Unless a task can have a specific timeline or due date, it is more of a wish or "nice-to-have" item but not an actionable task.

In order to prioritize each task you are given, you should ask yourself these questions:

1. Which tasks, if not completed, will cause the greatest upheaval?

2. Who will be affected and what will be the impact if these tasks are not completed?

3. Which tasks will provide the highest Return On Investment (ROI)?

4. Which tasks do my manager / supervisor consider most vital?

5. How much preparation or staging is required prior to actually beginning the task?

6. Can the task be completed solely on my own efforts, or will support be required from others?

Being able to answer these questions will allow you to make a preliminary list of the tasks you have been assigned in order of importance from highest to lowest. After doing this exercise a few times, it will soon become second nature and you will find that you will no longer have to write your preliminary task list but simply organize these tasks mentally. Now you are ready for the next step in prioritizing your tasks.

The Priority Matrix

A Priority Matrix is used to determine the order in which tasks are to be done. The Matrix consists of four levels, with Level 1 being the highest priority and Level 4 being the lowest. A Priority Matrix determines the order in which tasks are to be executed based on three criteria, in descending order: Priority Level as determined by a manager or supervisor, Deadline or Due Date, and the Customer or Client Type.

The criteria and specifications of the Priority Matrix must be established by all the stakeholders (management, employees and customer concerns/needs) as it relates to the specific environment in which it will be used. For instance, a Deadline or Due Date of 0 to 36 hours for a Level 1 Priority may be suitable for a business, but may not be suitable for a technical support operation servicing bio-medical life support systems.

Figure 1 is an actual Priority Matrix that has been implemented in the business development unit of a computer internetworking firm. Let's discuss how it works.

To use the Priority Matrix a task is selected and its Priority Level is compared against the Priority Levels listed in the Matrix: Level 1 – High/Urgent, Level 2 – High/ Important, Level 3 – Medium/Necessary, and Level 4 – Low/Routine. If the task has a matching priority level on the matrix, it is assigned a position on your task list or "to-do list" based on this.

If the task does not have an assigned Priority Level, it is then compared against the Deadline or Due Date periods listed in the Matrix; Level 1 – 0 to 36 hours/0 to 1.5 days, Level 2 – 37 to 72 hours/1.5 to 3 days, Level 3 - 73 to 120 hours/3 to 5 days, and Level 4 – more than 120 hours/more than 5 days. If there is a match, it is placed on your task or "to-do list."

Priority Matrix

U **R** **G** **E** **N** **T** **N** **E** **C** **E** **S** **S** **A** **R** **Y**	Priority Level: HIGH Code: RED **I** Deadlines 0 - 36 Hours / 0 - 1.5 Days Customer Type: Existing Customers Business Development Tasks: *Customer Service & Customer Support Project Tasks: *Tasks required to start project Meeting Type: Kick-off & Planning Meetings	Priority Level: HIGH Code: YELLOW **II** Deadlines: 37 - 72 Hours / 1.5 - 3 Days Customer Type: Internal Customers Prospects at First Appointment Business Development Tasks: *Prospect relationship building and sales Prospect Tasks: *Tasks required to move project to next step Meeting Type: Strategy Meetings	**I** **M** **P** **O** **R** **T** **A** **N** **T** **R** **O** **U** **T** **I** **N** **E**
	Priority Level: MEDIUM Code: GREEN **III** Deadlines: 73 - 120 Hours / 3 - 5 Days Customer Type: General Prospects Referred Leads Business Development Tasks: *Lead Qualification, Lead Intelligence Project Tasks: *Project Administration Meeting Type: Reporting & Informational Meetings	Priority Level: LOW Code: WHITE **IV** Deadlines: > 120 Hours / > 5 Days Customer Type: Cold Leads Business Development Tasks: *New Lead Generation Project Tasks: *Non-Critical Project Tasks, "Nice, but Not Necessary To Have" Meeting Type: General Meetings	

If the task does not have an assigned Deadline or Due Date, it is then compared against the Customer or Client Type listed in the Matrix; Level 1 – Existing Customers, Level 2 – Internal Customers or Prospects at the First Appointment Stage, Level 3 – General Prospects or Referred Leads and Level 4 – Cold Leads. If there is a match, it is placed on your task or "to-do list."

If the task cannot be classified by comparing it against the three categories above, it should by default be categorized as a Level 4 Priority and placed at the bottom of the list in relation to other Level 4 items that have matched that level's criteria.

As mentioned earlier, it is important to note that each Priority Matrix is custom created specifically for each work environment, department or operation. Therefore, "one-size does not fit all" and the content or criteria used in a matrix must be established through input and feedback from all the stakeholders on whom it will have an impact. So, don't just photocopy our example and adopt it!

After deciding where tasks are within the Priority Matrix, classify the tasks into two categories; those you can do on your own, and those where you require the support of others.

The total number of Level 1 and Level 2 priorities combined must not exceed 3 tasks per day for one individual. If they do, you will need help to complete them on time, or you must ask for a deadline extension that will downgrade the additional tasks to a Level 3 or Level 4 priority.

The Task List

The Task List, or as it is informally called a "To-Do List," is a schedule that sets down the tasks you must do in priority order with Level 1 tasks at the top of the list to Level 4 tasks at the bottom. A Task List for business purposes must go beyond the traditional or informal "To-Do List" as it must include the following details:

1. Day, Week or Month the Task List is for

2. Name and Description of Task

3. Priority Level

4. Special Notes or Comments

5. Estimated or Desired Completion Date or Time

6. Actual Completion Date or Time (as opposed to a check box).

Task Lists should be made for each day and, if applicable, for a week or month.

At the end of each day, a Daily Task List is reviewed and the tasks that are not completed must be carried over to the next day's list, unless they have been cancelled or have been changed in priority level. When making a task list, be sure to include routine or repetitive tasks.

Chapter 25. Time Management

Always schedule a 10% block of your total daily and weekly working time as a Level 4 priority contingency task. This time is reserved for new daily ad hoc tasking and will change in priority relative to the task. For instance, if you work an 8-hour day with an hour off for lunch, you should allow 70 minutes for ad hoc emergencies or tasking in your daily schedule.

A task list need not be complicated. If you use a diary or agenda system, then you already have the beginnings of a very effective task list. Simply write the tasks next to the time slots in your agenda, allowing for a reasonable amount of time for completion. Details regarding the task may be made in the notes section of the agenda.

 When assigned a task, ALWAYS get a Due Date or Deadline! As Soon As Possible (ASAP) is NOT a due date. If no due date is provided, assign the task a Level 3 Priority and advise that the task will be completed in 5 days. In most cases this will cause the person who gave you the task to provide you with the due date they really want.

The Multi-Tasking Myth

The concept of multi-tasking originated with the birth of the computer where the original single processor computer with its blinking lights gave the impression that it could do several tasks at once, hence multi-tasking. In reality, it wasn't really multi-tasking but simply doing each task in turn much faster than a human, giving the impression that it was doing several tasks concurrently.

In reality, there is no such thing as multi-tasking when it comes to individuals, as we can really only concentrate on one task at one time. Now this is not to say that one person cannot do several tasks in one hour, but they will simply switch between tasks devoting a few minutes at a time, and their attention to each 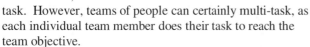 task. However, teams of people can certainly multi-task, as each individual team member does their task to reach the team objective.

So perhaps the idea behind multi-tasking really is to do your assigned tasks as efficiently as possible, reducing wasted time in between tasks, so that it will look as if you are doing several tasks at once.

The Secret of Managing Your Time

Despite all the time management systems from agendas and diaries edged in gold and bound in the finest leather to electronic organizers that are just as powerful as a desktop computer, the real secret of time management lies in what you decide to put in these systems.

Most people fail at managing their time because all they think they have to do is just fill-up their daily calendar and just roll with whatever else might come up.

To manage your time, you have to:

- Prioritize your tasks.

- Schedule your tasks into your day (and agenda).

- Commit yourself to effectively managing your time until it becomes a habit.

- Ask for help or a deadline extension if you get "swamped."

- Leave time in your business day for emergencies or the unexpected.

- Schedule time after work to be with your family.

So, the real secret in managing your time lies in knowing how to prioritize your tasks: in essence … what to do and when to do it.

Chapter 25. Time Management

Chapter Quiz:

1. **In order to manage your time, you must first:**

   a. prioritize your tasks.
   b. use an agenda or diary.
   c. make a "to-do" list.
   d. none of the above.

2. **A Priority Matrix is used to:**

   a. manage your time.
   b. prioritize tasks.
   c. replace a task list.
   d. schedule appointments.

3. **By saving just 5 minutes a day for 5 days per week you would:**

   a. not make much difference in managing your time.
   b. be able to finish a tough project.
   c. have saved and gained 21 hours in a years time.
   d. none of the above.

4. **The best time to call customer service or the help desk is when they are least busy, which could be:**

   a. 9 am to 5 pm Monday to Friday.
   b. 10 am to 2 pm Tuesday to Thursday.
   c. 8 am to 10:30 am Tuesday to Thursday.
   d. 8 am to 4:30 pm Monday to Friday.

5. **Audio books are better than printed books because:**

   a. you can save time by listening and doing something else.
   b. they are less expensive.
   c. there are more of them on time management.
   d. you can play them in your computer or CD player.

6. **ROI means:**

   a. Reduce Our Inventory.
   b. Return On Investment.
   c. Returned On Invoice.
   d. Reduced Overtime Income.

7. **One Priority Matrix designed for one department:**

   a. can be used by other departments.
   b. cannot be used by any other department.
   c. is all that is needed for one company.
   d. needs to list all appointments and schedules.

8. **Real multi-tasking is only possible:**

   a. with one person.
   b. with the first computer.
   c. with a team.
   d. none of the above.

9. **The total number of Level 1 and 2 priorities combined for one individual must not exceed:**

   a. 9.
   b. 6.
   c. 3.
   d. 2.

10. **A 'To-Do" List is also called a/an:**

   a. task list.
   b. priority matrix.
   c. agenda.
   d. schedule.

Answers:

1-a, 2-b, 3-c, 4-c, 5-a, 6-b, 7-b, 8-c, 9-c, 10-a

Chapter 26

Avoiding Crooks

Dick Glass, CETsr

Dick Glass is an author of previous ETA publications as well as more than a dozen books dealing with electronics technology and business management, published by Howard W. Sams Co, TAB Books, McGraw-Hill and ETA. He has also written hundreds of articles in trade journals and other association publications. Dick is a former Navy Avionics Technician, Industrial Electronics Computer Technician, Technical Writer, FCC Commercial License examination modernization committee chairman, inductee into the Electronics Hall of Fame and currently President of ETA-I. He has a broad background in all phases of work performed by electronics technicians. He oversees ETA's 40-plus certification programs and the Training Course Approval system.

Why Avoid Crooks?

If your company is to be as efficient as we humans can make it, we need to look for ways to conserve expenses and to maximize income and profits. It does no good to maximize income if you are maximizing expenses at the same time. Only salesmen who work strictly on commission look at maximizing income with no regard for any expenses they may occur.

We are all aware of expenses. We try to keep the overhead costs down. We look for ways to conserve paper, cleaning materials, automobile repairs, tools, electricity and so forth. We also look at major expenses such as wages and benefits to attempt to conserve where possible. We try to hire people who will work and not just put in their time. We try to hire people who will be concerned about small, but necessary, costs such as printer cartridges, solder, snowmelt, anti-freeze and similar expense items.

We also try to find ways to sell products or services which maximize the profit to be realized from the sales. It is important that we don't just sell a computer, antenna, hamburger or house, with no concern for any costs associated with the sale. For instance, we should not sell a hamburger, then when the customer asks for catsup or other condiments, give him or her a sack full, just because the restaurant has not established a price for these minimal-cost items. Somebody has to pay for the catsup packs, even if they are only one cent each.

So there are other ways to maximize profits. For instance, making sure all of the employees are aware of any potential liability mistakes they might make might prevent a lawsuit. Sure, you have insurance to reduce the potential costs and the insurance company (if they insure you for these mistakes) will

Maximize Income and Minimize Costs

probably pay the damages. But then, you might expect to pay a higher premium next year. So you attempt to reduce any claims and any injuries and as many problems as you can. By doing this, you and the other workers are attempting to make the business as efficient and profitable as you can.

That doesn't mean cutting expenses to where you never have the windows washed or get your signs repainted because your workers might fall off a ladder. It doesn't mean you must spend outlandish amounts to protect your company against insignificant possible damage. For instance, building a handicapped ramp in the back of your business, where no one ever is allowed to enter, might be taking the handicapped access rules a bit far. On the other hand, not obtaining workman's compensation insurance for your workers (in order to save a hundred bucks a year) is not cost effective, since the state is going to find out and fine you a lot more than that. If an employee pokes his eye out while on the job, you are liable for the injury also, and the hundred bucks savings will not be a significant part of the medical bills.

Okay, you have maximized income and minimized expenses and looked for every possible way to conserve, within reason. You have hired workers who are paid well, and being on the 'team,' do far more to protect profits than anyone you could have hoped to hire. After all of this, there are still areas where the business can be hurt. One of these is by falling prey to crooks.

Crooks come in many sizes and styles. Here are some types:

1. Burglars
2. Stick-up Artists
3. Armed Robbers
4. Confidence Men (or women)
5. Petty Thieves
6. Shoplifters
7. Swindlers
8. Embezzlers

Crooks. They're Out There!

Chapter 26. Avoiding Crooks

9.   Muggers
10.   Pickpockets
11.   Shysters
12.   Looters
13.   Counterfeiters
14.   Purloiners
15.   Racketeers
16.   Cheaters
17.   Cheating Customers
18.   Cheating Suppliers
19.   Sales Tricks
20.   Government Schemes

Beware!
Beware!
Beware!
Beware!

Twenty Types of Crooks?

I expect that is not the complete list. If you concentrate, and if you include any examples of crookedness you know of outside of your employment, and in your personal life, or the life of your friends, neighbors and townspeople, you can probably double the list to 40 examples of crookedness and violations of the ten commandments or the civil law.

The idea here is that a segment of the population is evil. Some are desperate and have survival as the motive for taking from others. Some have not been brought up to respect anyone else, or the property of others. Surely you know some who have always been given 'everything' and thus (in their adult lives) expect this to continue. If they wanted a pacifier, they got it. If they wanted a soft drink every hour, they got it. If they wanted to discard the bread crust, they were allowed to do so. If they never made their bed, they were not made to get into that habit. When they were in primary school, if they wanted to stay home and play hooky, that was okay. The parent would write the excuse note.

In high school they found they could bully the immature or slow or shy kids and get away with it. When they got a summer job, they found they could goof off a lot of the time and no one would catch them, or they could have a handy excuse and get by with it. They found they could copy lessons in school, or get the test answers from another clever member of their gang.

At work, they quickly found ways to circumvent the attendance, sick days, or other rules. Some found they could get ahead by telling a few falsehoods or claiming skills that they didn't have. Their parents gave them a nice car when they quit school, so they have no understanding of the sacrifice someone had to make to be able to buy that car. So, they wrecked it shortly. But that didn't matter much. It was an inconvenience, but heck, their friends have nice cars. They just financed them and they haven't had much trouble paying the monthly bills, they say.

Some get caught by the law and start a criminal record for themselves. They resent this and sometimes feel that since they have been mistreated, that they have every right to mistreat others.......including those 'rich' people who run service businesses.

To think that we live in a world of nice people, then, is to leave ourselves open to be taken advantage of by those with less than honorable intentions. If you deal with others, you should be alert to potential people problems.

The List

Okay, let's check out the list: Burglars may choose to break into the business any of the 365 days this year, but they likely will choose only one of those. Because you don't know which one, you are at a disadvantage: You have to prevent them 365 days. They need to plan to break in on only one day. Well, most of us in business or working at a business know the rules for security, and most businesses have alarm systems. Most also have insurance. All that the CSS need be concerned with is that his/her work day duties include assuring that doors and vehicles are locked, alarm systems turned on, keys not distributed to unauthorized persons, and that everyone keeps his eyes open for possible ways a burglar might defeat the system.

Armed robbers, pickpockets, shoplifters, petty thieves, looters and so forth may not be easily defeated, but every business worker must concern himself with them. Being aware that they are real threats is the first step. Most companies have policies for reducing the possibilities, but for most retail businesses they can only be reduced, not eliminated.

Some of the listed 20 crimes are usually handled by management. Embezzlers, counterfeiters, purloiners and racketeers too, would not usually be as much of a concern for employees as for management. However, each worker needs to be aware of the problems. Workers who see crime being committed against the company will suffer because the company will be less profitable and chances for advancement or higher compensation will be infrequent. In fact, it may be the worker who is in the best position to uncover fraud, theft, or anything else detrimental to the company. To continue to work in an environment where you know this is going on causes one of two things: Either

Chapter 26. Avoiding Crooks

you decide to join in the larceny, etc., or you become depressed because it is happening and that no one is putting a stop to it. You may be cautious about reporting it as most of us like to 'keep our noses out of it,' especially if we are new on the job.

There are always schemes to filch money from a small business. It is difficult to determine what causes should be supported. The local band booster candy sale is probably a good cause where you could donate a few bucks. But these causes generally range from good community programs to gimmicks which play on your good nature and only *seem* like good community causes. Some that seem like good causes are not. Every year businesses and individuals are hit up to donate to the disadvantaged kids fund, or to the retired fireman's fund, or to help with the drug prevention campaign of the local police department. Some of these are worthy causes and can be of value in cementing the company image in the community. My friend Leon, for scores of years, donated to the Catholic church for their various fund raisers, bingo project and other events. He was Baptist. However, since he had six kids, and his name was on a lot of things at the church, many people assumed he was Catholic and a strong supporter of the church. Many of these people favored his TV business for scores of years.

> ## Did they *raise* the money?
>
> ## Or did you *donate* it?

Parents of school age children usually favor a business that they notice has advertised on the school football schedule poster, or the music program guide. Nowadays, businesses can even buy space to advertise in the gymnasium or on the football field fence.

But while many of these are causes a business would not want to be left out of, there are many solicitations that are simply promotions for clever opportunists. Some of these are outright fraud. How many times this past year have you read in the newspaper that the current solicitation in the name of the Police Dog Benevolent Society, the Anti-Drug Crusade, Alzheimer's Prevention Fund, or some other seemingly good cause has been denied by the real organizations, or the police, the postal authorities, etc. Some are scams which prey on small businesses, as well as private individuals.

If you are in business, you can find yourself advertising in, not one, but several telephone book advertising sections. Since they all seem to be

allowed to use the hand graphic that walks through the yellow pages, they all claim to be legitimate. Usually people in a community find only one of these books is the best. That is the one people use. Being in the others isn't a total waste. Some people may use them. It is just good business to be careful about how and where you spend your advertising dollar.

There are always schemes that claim to be new marketing efforts that you just *must* get into. The ads at the check-out counter at the grocery store, the ads they started attaching to the grocery carts, ads on hand-out sheets that customers play games on with the possibility of winning prizes, placemat ads in local restaurants, billboard ads, ads on county maps or directories, and sponsoring of race cars, little league uniforms, or any of a hundred other types of donation schemes.

The tricky part is knowing which of these are worthy causes and for which you would like to foot an expense. Of course, most of those who make money selling these programs will be quick to tell you that your donation is 'tax deductible,' and therefore, it is hardly an expense at all! The problem is that it *is* an expense. It is money directly off of the bottom line. If you donate $100.00, chances are your business had to do over a thousand dollars worth of business to net that $100.00. Our concern in this chapter isn't whether to support worthy causes or not. It is to be concerned about spending profits money on unworthy causes, rip-off schemes and fraudulent activities which may be aimed at filching money from you and your firm. How do you keep from losing money to these crooks? Simply learn how to say "No." They all play on a small business' fear that if they don't donate, the police will be watching every time they get in their car; the fire department will take its time getting to your house should it catch on fire; the 'word' will get out that you don't support the schools, the churches, the civic organizations, the zoo, the kindergarten or the poor people. No one wants to be considered a Scrooge or to have a negative reputation in the community. Faced with that possibility, it is difficult to turn down the telemarketer who claims to be working for the police retirement pension old age benevolent fund and states, "We are counting on you again this year."

'Shyster' means a dishonest lawyer. However, it has come to mean nearly any dishonest business type of person. We call them loan 'sharks' when we are talking about a person who charges usurious interest and loan fees. We use

Chapter 26. Avoiding Crooks

the term when we have some repair done and find we paid ten times the normal price to some opportunist. Workers have to be aware of these operators. If you are in charge of having some work done for the company or purchasing goods, you should be as careful about getting good value as if you were buying it for your own family. One of my

companies in the past occasionally had need for an item called an 'attenuator,' used with antenna and cable distribution systems. These might have been normally priced at 50 cents each. Once we ordered some from a distributor that we favored, but who wasn't in the signal distribution end of things in a big way. When we got the attenuators from that distributor, the price was $9.00 each.

Had we not been aware of the price, we would have gone on in our ignorance, assuming the higher price was correct. In this case, it may not have been a shyster distributor. Maybe they just made a mistake. Or maybe they were used to selling small parts at what seems like exorbitant markups, thinking no one would be the wiser. But, it pays to know the value of the product and services you use.

Muggers and Stick-up artists are around. The CSS is no more able to defeat them than anyone else, other than by being alert. Mace, stun guns, iron bars, firearms and other deterrents are illegal in many towns. Some forms of protection against direct criminal acts are allowed, and many service truck drivers have used them over the years.

So the last group of criminals are made up of these:

Cheaters
Cheating Customers
Cheating Suppliers
Defrauders

It is this group with which the CSS is most often faced. It is these who need special attention in this book. While much of this book is aimed at helping us win friends and influence people, to spend some time in the other person's moccasins, to see the other person's point of view, to turn the other cheek, to practice the golden rule, and so forth, the fact is that we must deal with those who intentionally try to cheat the business.

Encounters with cheaters might be cases where a person borrows money from you and has no intention of repaying it. Or stocking up his tool belt with company tools, then taking *his* tools with him upon leaving the firm. I remember renting a car once, down in Jacksonville and driving less than 100 miles round trip, then paying for a full tank of gas in the rental car at check-in. I remember buying

$9.99 or $49.99?

some flowers at Kroger's which were sitting on the $9.99 shelf, but with no price tag on the pot. At the checkout, they turned out to be $49.99. I remember an acquaintance having a couple shingles blown off his roof and then demanding and getting the insurance company to pay for an entire $4,000 roof job. I remember a plumber's son coming over to replace a faucet and walking in with a pair of channel locks to attempt to do the job. The faucet never did work right and the plumber's son chipped the sink. I remember paying $3.50 for a beer at the fieldhouse.

You can probably name a dozen instances where you were cheated, intentionally, by someone. So, we all need to keep on our toes, ever vigilant.

Cheating Suppliers

Back in the old days, parts and product distributors, in a lot of cases, were just small business owners trying to make a buck, just like retailers and service shop owners. In order to build their businesses they placed a lot of emphasis on building a relationship between their company and the retailers they depended on for their existence.

Those suppliers didn't hire delivery services. They had their own employees to do that. You got acquainted with the delivery guys and usually formed a trusting relationship. You got to know the receptionist who did her best to quickly route your call or help you out. The firm conducted sales or service seminars to  help each of its family of retailers and servicers become more capable. The service department always had an expert whose job it was to help you. If you had a problem with a product or a customer who had purchased that product, the supplier worked with the retailer or service technician to resolve it.

Today, very little of the above relationships remain. Today, the supplier is likely to have a classy phone system that prevents you from talking to anyone. If phone traffic is heavy, callers are allowed to wait "until the next available associate gets to you, *in the order in which your call was received.*" That's fair, except that what would solve the problem is having sufficient people, rather than shifting the time burden to the customer. That is cheating you. You should find suppliers who have sufficient workers.

You also find suppliers who shift the costs from themselves to your company. Their defective product was

Chapter 26. Avoiding Crooks

shipped to you and you paid the shipping cost. When it must be returned as defective, you likely will get to pay the freight. A defective product should not cost you further money. You probably already had a customer problem to deal with. Then you had a service call to verify that the product was bad, and that neither the installation or customer was at fault. Now you get to pay for the privilege of attempting to save the customer--for your firm's sake, for the distributor's sake, and for the product maker's sake. You got cheated.

You also find companies who survive by selling you products. They have a toll-free line to serve your product ordering needs. But if the product they shipped you is dead-on-arrival, that is different. Now you likely must use their *not*-toll-free number to attempt to solve the problems their products caused. You got cheated.

A product is delivered to your company. It gets moved to your storage area for a few days or weeks. When you  open the box, you discover something is broken. It might have been broken when the part was packaged and shipped from the product maker. It might have been dropped at the distributorship. It might have been damaged when delivered to your company. In fact, it could have been damaged after it was delivered to you. But you are first asked to sign a delivery bill which confirms that the product was delivered in good condition. You may not be able to ascertain that for days or weeks. You can't unpack everything you get before the delivery truck leaves.

There is no 'always-right' answer to this type of problem. If there are no crooks involved with any of those involved in getting the product to you, reasonable people will determine where any fault might lie. If there is no clear picture as to where the unit was damaged, then more than one entity may need to share the blame, and the most economical solution should be found. If the fault turns out to be within your company, you, as a CSS, should not join in any cheating by your company which tries to get the supplier or delivery people to foot the bill. If the company cheats the supplier in this way, it is likely they would not hesitate to cheat you. Quit. The point here is that businesses should not cheat. If you work for a cheating company, you will not be happy. You will not enjoy your work. You will not see advancement at that company as a part of your success story. You will find life not much fun, whether it is because your company was cheated, or because it or you cheated. It is like continuing to live in a dirty, smelly house: Life can be better than that.

Defrauders are people who sell you something that is different than what it was touted to be. You are defrauded if you pay for a service which was less than advertised or commonly expected. If you contract to have a sign painted and mounted on your company property and the paint starts peeling in a month, you did not receive what a reasonable person would expect. If the sign falls down because it wasn't waterproofed, or because the post holes were only six inches deep, you were defrauded, unless the company comes back and does the job right with no questions asked. If you purchase a truckload of new satellite dish systems and a week later the supplier lowers the price to half what you paid, and now you can't sell them for as much as you paid, you were defrauded. On the other hand, if the supplier/product maker alerts you to a potential price cut, weeks or months before it goes into effect, this allows you time to adjust. In that case, you weren't defrauded.

Cheating Customers

Most states have Attorney Generals and Consumer Protection agencies. Their job: Take the customer's side in any disputes between retailers or service providers. Their job is not to *arbitrate* a dispute. It is to take the side of the consumer. No one is more likely to keep customers from cheating a firm than a CSS. Treating customers with respect; giving fair value, searching for solutions to misunderstandings, resolving every complaint, following up on sales or service jobs--these are ways to reduce customer complaints.

The problem is that some customers are like vultures. They are waiting for an opportunity to take advantage of you or your firm.

It is obvious to everyone that a certain segment of the population intentionally writes bad checks. Collection bureaus make money because some people just won't pay their bills. There are also those who take advantage of the good nature or policies of a business. They use a product for a few weeks or months, then claim it is defective as they return it. Some people jump at the opportunity to get cable free for the first month, then never pay for succeeding months. The satellite industry has tried every scheme in the world to keep these types from defeating their subsidized 'free dish' deals, yet still, people find ways to cheat.

Many who work in retail or service businesses are under some pressure to make a sale. Small businesses, especially, are under that pressure as they try to compete with mass merchandisers who may have been awarded unfair purchase deals or other benefits. So, when there is a possibility of making a sale, the pressure is on to actually

Chapter 26. Avoiding Crooks

get the job done and get the customer's signature on the sales ticket.

Each worker in a position to help increase sales of products or services should do his/her best to nail down the sale. But there are 'red flags' which customers present to you that could alert you to the possibility that the customer may not be the kind you want to do business with.

One 'red flag' might be to find out the customer does not have a valid credit card. Another would be that the customer has no telephone. Either of these items on its own might be no cause for concern, but when you begin to see a negative pattern develop, you may want to check further. Another is liquor strongly on his/her breath. Most companies, of course, do a credit check. Finding a bad credit rating may exempt you from continuing the sale or service.

No credit card?

Many of the above will come to a small business after they know they have worn out their welcome at the larger ones. They are looking for businesses which are 'hungry' to make a sale. Most small businesses have erratic income experiences. It is either 'feast' or 'famine.' When it is 'feast' time and you have made some welcomed sales of products or some profitable-looking installs or repairs are lined up, it is easy to conclude that your hard work is finally paying off. Days or weeks later, business drops off, usually through no fault of your own. It is normal to conclude that you are

doing something wrong and customers are going elsewhere. So when any potential customer enters the business, or calls for service on the phone, you are likely to disregard one or more 'red flags' and try to nail down the business. The pressure is on. Bills and employees must be paid; floor plans are coming due; stock is getting old; the overhead keeps going on. So, you hope the customer will purchase something and you hope the final results will be a good job with a paid bill and a happy customer. Maybe you will get lucky and that good customer will tell his friends and relatives and you will get even more business from that single well-done job. Don't disregard the red flags.

So, the CSS should be as alert to possible cheating customers as he might be towards armed robbers. That means total concern that it is important to make a good sale, not just a sale. Here are some samples of ways customers of an antenna/satellite business might cheat:

A. Bad checks
B. Stolen credit cards
C. Claims that what they thought they were buying was not what they received
D. Damaging the product or installation, then claiming it is defective
E. Defaulting on financial terms arrangements
F. Moving so that you can't find them to pursue payment
G. Lying (such as 'first-time-satellite buyer' misrepresentation)
H. Blaming you when their dog chews or digs up wiring
I. Killing the sale or work because another piece of equipment is bad and doesn't work well with the new one
J. Wanting their money back because your repair service had to be called twice, and both were the result of lightning or power company surges
K. Bringing in a unit for repair for some small defect, then claiming they now have a much more expensive problem *that they didn't have any symptoms of before*
L. Spilling liquids in keyboard or remote hand units and then demanding a new one for free
M. Shoplifting when they catch you manning the store by yourself and you have to locate something that is out of their sight
N. Claiming they paid a bill when they didn't
O. Claiming you damaged the cabinet, etc. when they either weren't aware, or were aware it was damaged long before you were called
P. Demanding money back because their equipment was out of service for two weeks through no fault of yours
Q. Finding out that some elusive and intermittent fault in their connected system units was actually caused by one of their components, rather than by the one you sold them or performed a repair on, and then refusing to be responsible for any part of the expenses incurred in rooting out the problem
R. Having defective and dangerous house wiring which damages some unit you sold to them, then disclaiming any responsibility
S. Blaming your antenna or satellite installers for their roof leaking when it had been leaking for months prior to your work
T. Digging up your cables, then claiming they should have been buried deeper and refusing to pay for the work
U. Cutting a 300 foot piece of underground cable and demanding that it be spliced, but not paying for the expensive multiple waterproofing components required
V. Claiming they shouldn't have to pay for your SMATV or cable service, since they were gone for a month and didn't actually view it
W. Tapping into your cable service illegally
X. Claiming you mounted the dish, or installed an outlet or routed the wiring someplace other than where they really wanted it
Y. Claiming you cut their invisible dog fence, even though

Chapter 26. Avoiding Crooks

they didn't mention it to your crew

Z. Asking you to do a job, but not being willing to buy the proper components, even though you thoroughly explained how things were bound to work, then not paying because it didn't work perfectly

That is a long list. But it is only a fraction of the problems customers can and will cause, intentionally. Here is a classic:

Our company was called to service an existing early model big dish system. It happened to be located some 300 feet down a steep embankment at lakeside. Since the equipment was old and the owner had a crazy A-B switch setup for multiple room operation, we were asked to put in a modern receiver, drive arm, and switchbox distribution system.

We did. Everything worked okay until the son started reprogramming the receiver. After a couple of free calls we cautioned them that the only answer was for the son to quit reprogramming. Things worked okay until the owner cut the  cable with a backhoe. He was perturbed because his fairly new (now) system was having entirely too much trouble. However we put in new cable and things worked okay. A few weeks later, it was out again. Again, the problem was a cut cable as some other work was going on around the place. A month or so later a lightning storm blew through and knocked out the unit, along with other equipment at his home. We repaired the receiver and got everything back in operation. A few weeks later some other event occurred which we could not determine exactly what the cause was. But the receiver appeared to be losing memory, now and then. The customer was furious since he had experienced multiple problems ever since he purchased the equipment. While none of these seemed to be related to poor service or installation, or to the product, the owner felt differently.

To resolve the problem, we thought it best to replace the receiver, thus removing any concerns that he had a 'lemon.'

Whether the identical replacement unit ever had a problem or not, we never knew. What we did know was that the customer then contacted his attorney who demanded that our firm now give the customer a brand new (not comparable or reconditioned) unit and one that was more expensive. Because, in our efforts to resolve the case by replacing the receiver with a comparable unit that looked and was the exact same model receiver, we legally had 'taken' the customer's original receiver, we were legally at fault— never mind the practicality and honesty of our solution. The result: We gave the customer a new upgraded receiver, and never heard from him again.

Did the customer cheat us? You be the judge. Did he take advantage of our good nature?

Cases of customers cheating retailers or service technicians are many. It is just part of being in business. It is a problem for everyone. The CSS can be alert for potential problems, and once there appears to be a 'red flag' popping up, attempt to prevent the problem, to be sure that the customer has no legitimate beef, and to assure that any misunderstandings are completely addressed.

To do all of the other things this book suggests is the first step towards prevention of customer cheating. If the paperwork is exact and complete; if the service job has been done better than expectations; if the customer has been involved; if any explanations have been detailed; if any hints that the customer is trying to pull a 'fast one' have been addressed; if the financial arrangements are perfectly clear and the customer has signed for the work and also that the work was completed in a satisfactory manner; if the customer is kept informed of any delays or changes in plans or products or prices, then that is all you can do. But at that point, you should have a pretty good case built up. If the customer does cheat by making false claims, or by not paying, you should have a good case for the courts.

By going to court, you are not admitting that your customer relations efforts failed. If you are in business with the public, you will have cheating customers. Going to court is something many of these cheaters do not think you will want to do. They play on that fact. They know it is a nuisance and that you will never make a profit on them if you take them to small claims court. You, as an employee, need to always work with the thought in mind that this job  could turn sour. Have you done everything you can to provide the evidence that will be needed in court? Can you produce the service order, the service ticket, the invoice billings, notes about attempted phone calls to the customer, details of the job, serial numbers and models, dates of any follow-up service or re-service? To come to court with a small feed-store service ticket as your only evidence, and only some approximate dates of when events happened, no record of phone calls or any sort of sequence of events, will not impress the judge. To have all of this in detail and to be able to explain who, what, why, when and where, will impress the judge, and you will win in most cases. The good part about cheaters being taken to small claims or county courts is that most cheaters won't even show up for a court hearing. They know they will lose, so they don't bother. If you, too, don't show up, they will win. The worst they can do is have a judgment against them. They won't be asked to pay triple damages or to compensate your company for the time wasted. But it is important that you do not let a cheating customer get by with it. When each customer knows that retailers and service firms do have rights and that they will pay a penalty, even if it is only the $35 court fee tacked onto the claim your company has, they will quit cheating you and possibly be less prone to cheat others.

Chapter Quiz

1. **The best thing to do if you observe a fellow employee pocketing money that rightfully belongs to the business is:**

    a. file a court case against the employee.
    b. report the crime to management.
    c. tell the other employees so that word gets around.
    d. ask the criminal to share.

2. **Consumer Protection Agencies work to arbitrate disputes between businesses and customers.**

    a. True
    b. False

3. **It is usually good practice to just write off debts incurred by deadbeat customers, as the cost of taking them to court outweighs the possible amount recovered.**

    a. True
    b. False

4. **It is not the responsibility of workers to prevent or reduce incidents of cheating. That is management's job and a reason they get paid more.**

    a. True
    b. False

5. **Since larger businesses usually have good crime prevention, video surveillance and other deterrents, small businesses are more likely to be targeted by shoplifters and opportunists.**

    a. True
    b. False

6. **Running a credit check on a customer is usually illegal.**

    a. True
    b. False

7. **People who have no telephone are more likely to have bad credit than those who do.**

    a. True
    b. False

8. **Because of business agreements, a distributor or product maker who lowers the price of a product at retail, without giving the retailer a chance to clear his stock out, is cheating the retailer.**

    a. True
    b. False

9. **A business which offers a help-desk service for buyers of its products, then reduces the help-desk pool so that callers must be on hold for long periods of time is:**

    a. more efficient than others.
    b. cheating the public and their customers.
    c. not legally liable for fraud.
    d. simply taking advantage of the fact that their employee's time is much more valuable than that of a servicer or the public.

10. **An auto dealership which advertises 0% financing, knowing full well that only 6% of the public can qualify for its narrow rules to get 0% is:**

    a. violating truth in advertising laws.
    b. using innovative marketing techniques.
    c. unfairly competing with truthful businesses.
    d. cheating the public.

Answers:

1-b, 2-b, 3-b, 4-b, 5-a, 6-b, 7-a, 8-a, 9-b, 10-a, c, d

Chapter 27

Membership and Certification

Jason Hopkins currently works as an electrical engineer with Underwriters Laboratories Inc. in Camas, Washington. In addition to performing product safety evaluations around the world, he is a state approved continuing education instructor in Alaska, Oregon, and Washington. Jason provides National Electrical Code continuing education training to hundreds of electrical license holders in the Pacific Northwest as well as Canada and overseas. He holds several electrical licenses in the State of Washington, a Professional Engineer's license in California, and is an ETA Certified Fiber Optics Installer. He functions as UL's Certified Exam Administrator and mentor for the CET and FCC examinations. Jason holds a Bachelor of Science degree in Electrical Engineering from Montana State University.

Jason D. Hopkins
PE, CFOI

The first thing many people mention when entering my office for the first time is the number of certifications and professional association memberships hanging on my wall. I have frames containing everything from my Eagle Scout certificate to my Professional Engineer License and many things in between.

"How in the world did you get this certification? I did not know you were a member of this organization. Why do you have this? What is a Certified Fiber Optics Installer?" These are the most common questions asked, and all are valid.

If you examine the top professionals in your industry, you will invariably notice they are associated with numerous organizations outside their company of employment. By association, I mean they are a part of an organization, *associated* with the organization.

Association

There are many ways to become associated with a particular organization or group. We can break all of these associations into two groups: those that require some form of certification or credentials to join, and those whose membership is open to virtually anyone.

The more difficult it is to join an organization, the more prestige and value individuals place on their membership. For example, membership in the Mensa Society is viewed quite differently than a membership at your local video rental store! This does not mean that *all* valued associations are of this type.

Many volunteer groups, industry associations and the like are more than willing to have you join them. Countless individuals derive endless pleasure and value with these types of organizations. In the end, the value you extract from any organization will be correlated to the value of your contribution.

What is Your Time Worth?

Time is money. Each of us has only 24 hours in a day. We spend approximately eight at work and eight in bed. That leaves only eight hours for all of the important activities that make us who we are: time with our family, relaxing, household chores, shopping, reading, and everything else that must be done.

With so many demands of our time, how can we possibly justify spending time contributing to an organization, or even becoming certified so that membership is even an option? Many have foolishly entered into certification or membership in professional organizations with the expectation of direct financial reward.

Various studies and surveys have attempted to place a quantitative dollar value on a specific certification, license or association. The most aggressive will provide a calculator that enables the user to start with a base salary and add a certain amount of money for specific credentials or memberships. If you are seeking certification or professional association with the expectation that your salary will instantly increase by seven percent as soon as you succeed, you are likely in for a large disappointment.

The fact remains that the vast majority of companies, large or small, do not provide instant gratification for virtually any certification or membership. Although some might, we must dig deeper to find the true value of these activities.

Most employers are justifiably unwilling to pay for a piece of paper hanging on your wall. However, the best companies are more than willing to pay more for an employee who is better able and willing to perform at a

Chapter 27. Membership and Certification

level higher than the average employee.

So, how can professional association be valuable?

Credibility

When you are handed a business card and "PhD" follows the person's name, how does your view of this person change? Most people would agree that they instantly place higher credibility on what a PhD has to say. This is largely true because the average person knows that to become a doctor, one must complete a very difficult program and prove to a board of other doctors that he or she has the knowledge to carry the title. Anyone who completes this type of program has a *minimum* level of knowledge and ability, or he or she would not have earned the title. This person may not be the smartest or best doctor in the world, but has demonstrated, at least, the minimum level to call himself or herself a doctor.

Although few reading this book will end up as doctors, the same holds true for certifications in the electronics field, or any other field, for that matter. Once you achieve certification, you will have demonstrated mastery of a certain level of knowledge and performance.

This can be of vital importance if you happen to be looking for a new job. For example, let us look at Sally who wishes to become a test technician. When the recruiter glances through her résumé, they notice she is a Certified Electronics Technician (CET).

The next day, the recruiter receives a résumé from Harry, another technician who is not a CET. The recruiter has never heard of the company where Harry claimed to have a few year's experience.

Although it is unwise to make such an important decision without further investigation, the recruiter already has a pretty good idea of Sally's capabilities. Instantly, our recruiter knows that she has a minimum level of technical knowledge useful to the company. The recruiter also knows she can use Ohm's Law and is familiar with the operation of an oscilloscope. However, the recruiter knows nothing about Harry. Although Harry may make many claims about his knowledge and ability, Sally has backed it up with proof.

When Sally is interviewed, the recruiter will likely ask her questions trying to figure out how high her level of knowledge is. When Harry is interviewed, the recruiter must first verify that he has the basic skills we already know Sally has. Obviously, Sally enters the interview with a distinct advantage. Although this will not guarantee her the job, the odds are distinctly in her favor.

Differentiation

Constantly in life, we are compared against others. Our supervisors compare us with our coworkers to determine who receives a promotion or a raise and who does not. Our clients compare us with our competitors to determine with whom they should do business. Obviously, coming out on top is vitally important!

I frequently hear criticism from coworkers who claim that "I will never use that certification," or that it is "just a piece of paper." The truth remains that while they were watching television or surfing the internet, I was learning, studying, and proving my worth to a certification organization. Going the extra mile is valuable to both you and your employer. Please do not be discouraged by these comments: remember, jealousy is ugly!

Certification is a double-edged sword. While it can help those who do complete the requirements, it also may hurt those who fall short. Unfortunately, in order for certification to be beneficial and helpful to those who make it, the certification process must limit the number of people who are certified. After all, if everyone who applied for a certification were accepted, how valuable would that certification be? Along with differentiating you from those who do not try, those who succeed are further differentiated from those who try but do not succeed.

Professional Education

From the moment of birth, human beings begin learning. They learn about their surroundings, their parents, and eventually how to speak.

Then, they progress into school. They learn math, science, writing, even woodshop and sewing.

Upon graduating high school, some progress on to a technical school, apprenticeship, or college. Those who graduate college have spent a minimum of seventeen years in school, or about 77 percent of their life.

Chapter 27. Membership and Certification

After college, technical school, the military, or high school, most people find a job, but an interesting thing happens. The seventeen-year streak of learning large amounts of new information is broken! Although we continue to learn throughout or lives, the *rate* at which we learn typically decreases quite dramatically.

Why is this? Have we learned everything there is to learn? Absolutely not. Have we learned everything we *need* to know? Most likely not.

"Our best engineers and technicians will not only want to get the work done and out, but to really understand and increase their knowledge. This is, for the most part, what separates great engineers from good ones." Although this is directed specifically at engineers, I believe my CEO truly understood the power of learning when he made this statement. Those who display the desire to improve themselves are also more likely to display the desire to improve their company.

In nearly every company in the world, there exists a large percentage of people who learn their job and do it well. The world would not continue to progress without them.

There also exists a minority that continue to challenge their minds. They take every opportunity to learn new skills, perfect existing skills, and absorb all available knowledge. They attend college or trade classes, participate in industry groups, ask questions, and learn.

A good outlet for this thirst for knowledge is through professional organizations and the often accompanying certification. While at work, you are limited by the scope of your particular job or industry. Professional organizations merge industries, blend professions, and enable you direct access to the "big picture" we so often hear about. Where else can you associate and learn from not only your competitors, but your clients, potential clients, and those who do business with you?

Additionally, if you go through the process of becoming certified within an organization, you invariably learn many new things. In addition to this, the act of studying and performing well under pressure during the examination is good practice for honing your mind and increasing your performance elsewhere. The best part is that after you are finished, you have something of substance to show for your efforts!

Networking

"It is not what you know, but who you know." While most will agree that this famous quotation is at least partially true, many do not know how to make the important professional contacts that could help you achieve your goals.

A professional association is, by nature, comprised of members such as yourself, typically in similar fields. Membership in these associations provides an excellent opportunity to rub elbows with some of the best people in virtually any industry.

Since professional associations typically contain members from numerous companies throughout the United States and sometimes the world, they afford you the opportunity to keep abreast of the latest knowledge and news in your industry. This could help you with your work, allow you to help someone else, or be a great place to find talented staff to join your company.

Keep the Doors Open

In the 1940's and the early 1950's, most professionals signed on to a company for life. They provided labor and expected lifetime employment in return. Well, this is not the 1950's! Most statistics indicate the average professional changes jobs at least six times in their lifetime.

Although many change jobs for more pay, shorter commutes, or increased responsibilities, some job changes are not planned. Layoffs, downsizing, restructuring, acquisitions, mergers, bankruptcies, and site closures surprise far too many people each year.

Once you are in the unfortunate position of not having a job, it is too late to improve your résumé or contact list! Now is the time to think about the future. What do you want to do five years from now? What field do you want to be in? How can you get there? How can you ensure that you are as employable as possible in case you need to be, or how can you progress in your current company?

All of these questions can be better answered through professional associations. The fact is that you never know what the future will hold, and it is always better to be safe than sorry. Association is an important part of a strong résumé, and a strong résumé is vitally important for your

Chapter 27. Membership and Certification

professional well-being.

Have you ever thought about changing professions? A great way to learn about a new field is to learn about what they do by interacting with them. I know of several people who have reluctantly accompanied me to a meeting or helped on a project only to find out that they enjoy something other than what they are currently doing. I have seen technical people enter non-technical fields as well as administrative people move to the test bench. Associations can be a great way to "test the waters" without the danger of changing jobs.

"Do a Good Deed Daily"

During my extensive participation in the Boy Scouts of America, this philosophy was reinforced constantly. I feel strongly that human beings are not placed on this earth for self-satisfaction and the pursuit of personal gains.

Sometimes, association with an organization should be sought for nothing more than to advance mankind. These activities bring things into perspective, balance our busy lives, and renew our spirits.

This can be through volunteering your technical expertise to advance progress through research projects, or lending a helping hand building low-income housing.

Thousands of organizations exist only with the selfless support of their members.

Choose your Association Carefully

Although we learned the potential value of a professional association, all associations should not be considered equal! Since you are going to invest substantial amounts of time and effort, you must ensure you are seeking to be associated with the best possible organization.

Ideally, the organization should be very well known in the industry. Look at leaders in your company or industry and see with what groups they are associated. This should give you a good idea where to start. Remember, there are technical and non-technical organizations, so consider both options.

Organizations may be certified, just like individuals.

The organization you choose should be certified, sponsored, or otherwise accredited! For example, Electronics Technicians Association International (ETA-I) is certified by the International Certification Accreditation Council, which assures recognition of its certifications. If you really want to cover all bases, investigate the accreditation agency!

Before you choose a specific certification, you should pay attention to several important factors.

Do you qualify for membership? Many times, a certain certification, education, experience, or training is required to apply.

How much will the membership cost? Figure out how much any applications, examinations, study materials, certifications, and annual fees will cost. This could be a small amount, or a very large amount, but you should be aware. Also, consider how much it will cost to retake any examinations if you happen to have trouble the  first time. Sometimes your company will help you with the expenses. Also, some of the expenses may be tax deductible. The GI Bill will reimburse military personnel for certification expenses.

Finally, the logistics are important. Is the association located within a reasonable driving distance from your home? Where are the meetings held? Are there local chapters, and if so, where are they?

The above factors should be considered so that you choose the right organization.

It will not be Easy

By now, you should realize that membership in a professional association is more than paying annual dues and reading a monthly newsletter.

In order to receive, you must first give. In order to learn, you must also teach. By contributing to the success of the association, you are also elevating yourself.

The more you contribute, the more your efforts will be recognized. This potentially opens doors to leadership positions within the association such as president, editor, or treasurer. By elevating your efforts to the next level, you can help shape and guide the organization as well as benefit by the additional exposure these positions provide.

Chapter 27. Membership and Certification

Persistence

Since some associations require certification, perhaps the most important thing to keep in mind is that not every person achieves certification on his or her first try. Actually, this is part of what makes the association valuable! Once you decide to seek association which requires certification, do not quit until you achieve your goal.

My experience with the CET program suggests that less than ten percent of those who have trouble the first time ever take the examination a second time. However, almost 80 percent of those who take it a second time pass!

The moral of this story is that if you have trouble the first time, make sure you carefully remember and write down the areas of the examination you had trouble with. Studying the second time should be a shorter and easier process since you know exactly what to study. Although you will likely take a different examination, the concepts should be very similar.

Several years ago, an engineer decided to achieve a state electrical license. When he showed up for the examination, he realized that he had forgotten his calculator. Despite his best efforts, his performance was below the minimum allowed for certification.

Persistent as he was, he immediately scheduled himself for the next available examination. There was no doubt that armed with the calculator, victory would be his. Things were proceeding as planned when the calculator's batteries abruptly died. Luckily, he had a spare calculator. The only problem was the spare did not have many of the functions, such as square root. Two weeks later, he filed the notification letter next to the first one and again scheduled himself for the next available examination.

The third examination began at 8:00 a.m. At 10:30 a.m., he remembered that he was supposed to be at the examination.

The fourth examination was nearly a success; he only missed passing by two percent.

He arrived two hours early for the fifth examination armed with three calculators, two sets of spare batteries, ten pencils, and several hours of careful studying under his belt. Today, he proudly displays the certificate on his wall.

This person, of course, was me.

Remember, things do not always go according to plan, but if you are determined, persistent, and hard-working, you can elevate yourself by being associated with the best and brightest in your industry. In the end, it is up to you.

Chapter 27. Membership and Certification

Chapter Quiz:

1. **Professional networking is:**

   a. connecting computers together to share information.
   b. working and associating with desired people.
   c. earning a difficult certification.
   d. joining an organization to help out.

2. **Professional organizations are:**

   a. technical only.
   b. non-technical only.
   c. technical or non-technical.
   d. tax-exempt.

3. **Membership in an organization really means:**

   a. paying membership dues in a timely manner.
   b. joining because it looks good on your résumé.
   c. making a valuable contribution.
   d. having a wall certificate.

4. **Some good sources for membership ideas are:**

   a. private certification organizations such as ETA.
   b. professionals you admire.
   c. the company you work for.
   d. all of the above.

5. **Achieving membership in important organizations usually results in a pay raise or promotion.**

   a. True
   b. False

6. **All organizations are equal, so it does not matter which one you choose to be join.**

   a. True
   b. False

7. **The best companies are willing to pay more for:**

   a. someone with twelve certifications.
   b. someone who brings credibility to their organization.
   c. a highly qualified top performer.
   d. b and c.

8. **You may have the opportunity for a leadership position in an organization if:**

   a. you are the most important member.
   b. you are a CEO or Vice-president in your day job.
   c. you make a generous donation.
   d. you make an important and valuable contribution.

9. **Membership in a professional organization may be absolutely required for some jobs.**

   a. True
   b. False

10. **Professional associations help "keep the doors open" by:**

    a. building a network of contacts.
    b. keeping you updated on industry trends.
    c. exposing you to many different companies.
    d. all of the above.

Answers:

1-b, 2-c, 3-c, 4-d, 5-b, 6-b, 7-d, 8-d, 9-a, 10-d

Chapter 28

Handling Resistance to Change

Jeanette Stroud is the CET Division Director for ETA, having joined the staff in August of 1998. She holds the Customer Service Specialist and Fiber Optic Installer certifications. Jay has also written technical and human interest articles for ETA-I's High-Tech News journal and is active in exam research development. She attended Indiana University-Purdue University at Indianapolis. Past employment with state government has allowed her to have working contact in computer, legal, and medical fields.

By Jeanette Stroud, CFOI, CSS

Change--What Change?

We are constantly subjected to change. Usually, little notice is made of the daily changes that take place until we are confronted with the need to make even the smallest adjustments to our daily routine. Now, you're probably thinking, "Daily changes? What's so hard about dealing with change? This is not a problem for me. Anyone can cope with simple modification." But it is simply human nature to resist even minor, and often unexpected, change.

We've all had to make adjustments to daily schedules and routines due to unexpected change. However, the manner in which we handle these, as well as many other types of change, will set the stage for how we handle resistance to change in other areas of our lives, including the workplace. On a personal level, for example, how do you react (be honest!) when someone takes your parking place, or when the store closes just five minutes before you get there? Take a moment to think about how you reacted the last time you misplaced your car keys (chances are you were also running late for work). When confronted with changes of inconvenience, how do you respond? In retrospect, you'll probably find that these slight alterations to your daily routine didn't result in minor reactions.

It's not easy to respond in a positive manner when dealing with a situation of *seemingly* negative dimensions. However, many times a negative change can have a positive outcome. Have you ever had an appointment cancellation, only to find that this opened up a much needed time-slot in your day? It's always more beneficial to approach change constructively by considering the positive aspects to be gained from change.

> Do you have a *major problem* with *minor change*?

Another major benefit of implementing and maintaining a positive attitude toward change is *stress reduction*. How much of your stress can be contributed to coping with daily changes? According to NIOSH reports on work-related stress alone, 53% of those surveyed felt that "daily hassles" were a leading cause of this particular type of stress, rating only below the top two stress-related concerns regarding money (80%) and family (74%). It's

much easier on your nerves (and on all those around you) when you maintain a positive attitude and apply it, not only to situations of change, but to all areas of your life, rather than bemoaning the adversity of a situation.

Are you *emotionally* prepared to deal with unexpected change? Do you readily adapt to the situation by making the necessary and appropriate change(s), or do you emphatically resist, making sure that your complaints and whining are heard by all? Do you go out kicking and screaming, shouting promises of, "Over my dead body!"?

More importantly, are your Customer Service skills up to the task of helping the CUSTOMER deal with "change resistance" when it rears its ugly head?

Let's Define It...

When confronted with sudden change, we may not even think about the manner in which we react, how we are affected emotionally, or the chain reaction of how those emotions affect others. Oftentimes, we simply react without knowing *why*.

> FEAR OF CHANGE—usually the **biggest** obstacle with the **least** validity.

Basically, resistance is a fearful response to change and is a natural component of any change process. Resistance will frequently occur in response to any type of change, whether organizational or interpersonal, that appears to have the capacity for personal impact. The best way to deal with resistance to change is to be prepared for it. Recognize and come to terms with the *fear* of change—understand that *this fear is usually the biggest obstacle with the least validity.* How many times has fear been the needless cause of worry about an impending change in your life, only to find that all your worries were without foundation and completely unnecessary? Do you brace yourself for the worst because your emotional habits lead you to assume that nothing good can come from change? We usually tend to associate imminent and adverse developments in conjunction with common statements such as "We need to talk," or "I need to see you in my office."

Chapter 28. Handling Resistance to Change

When the boss proclaims that "we're going to make some changes around here," a comment such as this will usually strike a note of fear in most employees. Aside from the obvious fear of unemployment, why do we otherwise automatically interpret this as a 'negative' statement? This recently happened when the ETA staff was informed that we were in for some major changes. For many, this announcement automatically translated into "changes of an unfavorable nature"—until it was discovered that the organization was only planning to move its headquarters to a larger facility. This particular transition ultimately resulted in several positive alterations. In addition to larger offices (and additional parking space), it allowed for improved departmental organization and room for the association's future growth.

As you can see, when a negative attitude toward change is already in place, fear compounds the situation by causing us to assume the worst case scenario. Imaginations begin to work overtime and things get blown out of proportion. So it's easy to understand why resistance to change is so prevalent. Has anyone

> *"Fear is not created by the world around us, but in the mind, by what we think is going to happen."*
> Elizabeth Gawain

ever accused you of making a mountain out of a mole hill? If so, maybe it's time to make some adjustments and turn your attitude in a more positive direction. In doing so, you can expose your fears of change for what they really are: self-imposed smokescreens of reason; those gremlins of the imagination, whose only weapon is the false impression of fear used to paralyze us into inaction.

Recognizing the Face of Resistance

Let's take a look at some common types of responses to imposed change. The following examples illustrate four basic reactions:

Aggressive Resistance

- You break out in a cold sweat at the mere mention of change...it brings to mind an image of a sudden turn of events of gut-wrenching proportion...you automatically feel the need to defend your position against an onslaught of unreasonable requests to make changes to your

present position of security. Under no circumstances will you conform to change—nothing will convince you to alter your present belief system by adopting another one. Statements such as, "I'm afraid this just won't work," "Things are fine the way they are," "We'll be wasting our time," and "What's wrong with the old way?" are your mantras. The *aggressive* makes no effort to disguise an obvious refusal to adapt to change, making him/her the easiest type to identify.

Passive-Aggressive Resistance

- Even though the mention of "change" automatically evokes a negative reaction, you may agree to follow suit to suggested changes by family, friends, or coworkers. Unfortunately, these promises to change never materialize; he/she can always find an excuse for his/her inaction. You'll often hear the *passive-aggressive* say, "I'll be happy to cooperate, just as soon as I finish..." No need to hear the rest, once you've heard the qualifier in this statement.

Passive Resistance

- Disguised as complete and enthusiastic acceptance, the *passive* type will wholeheartedly agree to change in a heartbeat. "You have my vote," "Sounds like a great plan," and "I absolutely agree," are comments that imply enthusiasm and compliance to suggested changes; however, complete failure to take any action will always be the end result of these vows. This type of resistance is the most difficult to identify because of the false impressions of support and agreement.

Apathetic/Denial

- Your reaction to the idea of change results in a seemingly neutral response. Complete denial may appear as though this concept is simply not within your realm of comprehension. "I don't know what you're talking about," or "That doesn't make any sense to me—I just don't understand," are remarks often made by the *apathetic* type. This individual presents total ignorance of a situation. Complete and unmasked denial is their way out of having to deal with change or modification.

However, if the prospect of change leaves you with a feeling of excitement, of looking forward to a new challenge or opportunity for personal growth; if you welcome change and treat/view it as a positive avenue that will allow you to apply your talents in a creative and constructive manner; if you embrace change because you believe it will have a positive impact and will profit others, then you are one of the "flexible few."

CHANGE DEFINITIONS

POSITIVE	NEGATIVE
Modify	Convert
Advance	Reverse
Evolve	Separate
Alter	Disturb
Move	Displace

Establish your definition of *change* to help determine the reason(s) for your own personal resistance. Do you find yourself using positive words such as "rearrange" and "advance" to define change? Or is your definition of change dotted with negative words, such as "displace" and "disturb?"

We all follow an established pattern of behavior. But the choice is ours to make—to either remain stuck -in-a-rut by maintaining the same pattern of inflexibility, or to willingly (and, yes, enthusiastically!) make a conscious effort to change direction and adapt by looking for the positive aspects that change can offer in our lives.

Understanding Emotional

"The only thing we have to fear is fear itself..."
Franklin Delano Roosevelt

Resistance

Before we can learn to manage our resistance to change, we must first have a basic understanding of emotional resistance and the psychology of change. After all, we are only human, and it is in our unique and inherent nature to resist changes and the resultant psychological pressures of trying to handle them. The initial urge to dig in with both heels and 'stand your ground' when confronted with change is an instinctive reaction to the most basic of human emotions: FEAR.

When change is introduced, we feel threatened, or *fearful of being changed.* Resistance is the natural emotional reaction a person exhibits when it is felt

that they are being forced into a situation that may require personal transformation. Change feels more like an intrusion, as though our "space," our personal sphere of safety, is being challenged. Everyone has experienced this unpleasant emotion. It is the feeling of being pushed into unfamiliar territory, toward some unknown destination not of our making. This is why the automatic reaction is to take a resistant, *defensive* position when change is imposed. We'd like to feel that we're in the driver's seat and in charge of deciding which paths to take in our own lives. No one enjoys the prospect of losing control of a situation.

Fear of the unknown is usually a learned emotion, based solely on a *generalization* of past experiences; and although the *fearful emotion* that arises in reaction to change is real enough, the reality of any actual imminent personal danger is not.

Remember your first day of school as a child? This was literally a whole new ballgame that required adaptation, not only to a new physical and social climate, but it also introduced an entirely new set of rules to be learned (and followed) in order to properly interact in this new and unfamiliar environment.

"When men are ruled by fear, they strive to prevent the very changes that will abate it."
Alan Paton

While there may be many others, this singular childhood event serves as one of the most important introductions to the world of imposed personal modification. Its influence has a substantial impact in the development of our behavioral patterns and established attitudes toward change and adaptation.

Although fear plays a major role in our resistance to change, there are many other factors to consider. Resistance may also be due to the following:

Peer group pressure
Lack of skills needed to implement the change
Lack of information/Poor communication
Lack of participation
Threat to economic finances

Existing habits and belief systems, based on past experiences, may direct some to cling to old practices that don't work anymore. These tend to hinder any progress toward positive change. People who base their opinions solely on established belief

Chapter 28. Handling Resistance to Change

systems will often comment that, "This is the way it's always been done. It has always worked before—why should I change now?" You've probably encountered, and even know, a few of these people. These are the types who are 'set in their ways' and are adverse to anything labeled 'new' or 'different.'

I remember an elderly gentleman who would only shop from one well-known department store. Purchases made from any other establishment were, in his opinion, foolish and a waste of hard-earned money. He explained that only this particular store, and no other, could offer items of quality, and was often heard to say that "I've always done my shopping here—I can't believe that anyone would go elsewhere!" This man's existing belief system was based solely on *his* past purchasing experiences. He was convinced that only one retailer was able to offer quality merchandise (to the exclusion of all others), thereby greatly limiting himself to the vast marketplace of choices available.

> *"The man who never alters his opinion is like standing water, and breeds reptiles of the mind."*
> William Blake

Many people succumb to this habitual fear of all things new and different. And, when change is rarely permitted, they subsequently allow themselves to become mired in a monotonous, unvaried and stagnant lifestyle, with a strict and unyielding belief system as their foundation for reason.

A few other popular 'fears' that may inhibit our ability to accept change are:

Fear of inconvenience

Fear of extra work

Fear of failure/rejection

Fear of personal loss

Fear of complications/drawbacks

Fear of having to apply yourself mentally

The *fear of **learning*** *something new* will prevent a majority of those opposed to change from trying a different product, considering a new approach, or from having an open mind to novel and unique ideas other than their own.

The conservative individual has a tendency to resist change, based on a *fear of the unknown*, because "there's no need to upset the apple cart." "Leave well enough alone" is his/her motto.

> *"If in the last few years you haven't discarded a major opinion or acquired a new one, check your pulse. You may be dead."*—Gelett Burgess

When confronted with informational data that goes against his/her beliefs, the dogmatic personality is unwavering in his/her convictions and will be the hardest to convince that change is needed in order to progress. His or her *beliefs tend to be based on biased opinion*, coupled with an attitude toward authority.

It's All About Attitude

While watching a documentary about American entrepreneurship, I noticed a small plaque sitting on a bookshelf behind the desk of the very successful businesswoman being interviewed. It read:

"Attitude Is Everything."

You've probably heard this phrase before. And you may or may not have been impressed by its simple message. However, I was pleasantly surprised to see that it was now being proudly displayed not in a grade school classroom (or as a refrigerator magnet), but in the office of someone whose success was obviously impacted by this basic concept.

> *"Nothing can stop the man with the right mental attitude from achieving his goal; nothing on earth can help the man with the wrong mental attitude."*
> W.W. Ziege

Simply put, attitude **is** everything when approaching the decision to deal with change. In order to create positive change, you must have a *positive attitude*. Despite this elementary logic, it's always amazing to witness the determination of those who insist on meeting any type of change with all the negativity they can muster. Here, again, fear plays

> *"The pessimist sees the difficulty in every opportunity; the optimist sees the opportunity in every difficulty."*—L.P.Jacks

an important role and will always fuel an existing negative attitude. But it's also much easier to resist and say 'no' to any idea for change for another reason: This "safe" solution requires absolutely no thought or effort.

Chapter 28. Handling Resistance to Change

Negativity and cynicism are non-productive attitudes. Really useless and inept negativity will always equal **RUIN**.

> R EALLY
> U SELESS &
> I NEPT
> N EGATIVITY

Our expectations that the worst will happen will only invite the same—if you expect the worst, that's probably what you will get. You're more likely to blow things out of proportion with this type of mind-set, thus losing any real perspective on the true nature of change.

Remember, you can sit back and let change happen to you, or you can take control by adapting to change. Allowing yourself the flexibility to "go with the flow" also enables you to take control of a situation by choosing the path that affords the most benefits for improvement and progress. By realizing that there are always choices available (regardless of the change situation), you do not limit yourself by letting fear paralyze you into inaction. You choose **not** to become a 'victim' of change, but rather an active participant in positive restructuring.

> *"Optimism is essential to achievement and is also the foundation of courage and of true progress."*
> Nicholas Murray Butler

Choose to adopt a positive attitude toward the changes that occur in your life. Be willing to invest a little work toward self-improvement, and you **will** see the rewards and benefits that result from learning to apply a forward-looking attitude. More importantly, be aware that your attitude and actions will always have an effect on others. The Customer Service Specialist knows that maintaining and presenting a positive attitude is essential to effective customer service.

Making The Transition

Adapting to change is not always an easy transformation to make; it requires conscious effort, unflagging dedication, and a real commitment to personal growth and improvement. However, the rewards are definitely worthwhile and will be immediately evident.

The first step is to realize that change is inevitable and necessary for personal growth.

However, complicated and/or major changes can often leave us feeling overwhelmed. The fear of being "lost in a maze of too many transitions" will usually lead to inaction, simply because we do not know where to begin. (If you've ever had to clean out the junk room, prepare an itemized tax return, or compose a thesis, this feeling will be all too familiar!)

Don't Sweat the Small Stuff

A sure-fire way to bring things to a grinding halt is by allowing too many specifics to confuse and overwhelm you. As you make new plans and strategies for your personal adjustment to change, don't let the 'small stuff' sneak in and cloud your thinking. There is a good possibility that this will cause you to abandon your blueprints for change.

> *"It is the little things that fret and worry us; you can dodge an elephant, but not a fly."*
> Josh Billings

To avoid getting bogged down by the 'big picture,' take things one step at a time. Start with a basic plan of what you want to accomplish. Keep it simple, and keep moving. Devoting too much time and energy to minor details can be counterproductive.

You will have taken an important step in the transition to accept change by realizing that the 'small stuff' also consists of uncertainty, confusion, worry, and doubt--all of which are born of fear. With a little practice, however, you will find that by seeking positive change you'll be able to conquer these anxieties and turn them to your advantage.

Change and The CSS

Customer service is exactly that—your goal is to *serve the customer*. Customer service know-how does not happen overnight. These skills take time, practice and patience (emphasis on the latter two). In order to be an effective Customer Service Specialist, you must first be a willing and sensitive listener. (One of the first skills you'll need to master is to always remember the customer's name.) Your attentiveness to detail says, "I care."

Be open to what the customer is trying to explain to you. Too often we fall into a pattern of forcing our own opinions upon others. If you find yourself

Chapter 28. Handling Resistance to Change

insisting that the other person conform to your beliefs, you will usually encounter resistance. Resistance ultimately leads to conflict, which brings you back to square one. Pursuit of this vicious cycle is not only pointless, but it may cost you an important customer.

> **INSISTENCE = RESISTANCE**
> **RESISTANCE = CONFLICT**

For example, a customer requests help in choosing a VCR. He explains that he's looking for a unit having just the standard features. "I don't want anything complicated or expensive," he says, "just the basics will do. What do you suggest?"

"Well, this model includes the standard factory options. They're pretty basic, but you'd probably enjoy this other VCR instead. It comes with all of these extra features and doesn't cost much more."

"No, all I'm looking for is just something that's affordable, simple and..."

"...easy to operate? Yeah, I know. It's very easy to learn how to operate this advanced model, too. The user's manual contains detailed instructions along with plenty of color photos. I've got one just like it at home. I really think you'd like this one."

"No, I don't think I'll be using it enough to justify the extra expense. Now, can you give me some information about this VCR, explain how it works and how much a basic model will cost?"

"But this one is really on the cutting edge of technology. Don't you know that the type of VCR you're interested in will probably be outdated before you even get it home?"

"Hey, I already told you what I'm looking for. Now can you help me with this or not?"

"Sure, if that's what you *really* think you want. But, like I was trying to tell you, this new technology is what you..."

"Listen, I'm, uh, running late. I might check back with you later."

In the above example, it's obvious that the sales representative's approach to lead the customer toward technological change didn't work. He allowed himself to become frustrated by the customer's lack of interest and cooperation. Nor did he realize that his 'pushy' approach was alienating the customer instead of convincing him that newer technology was rapidly replacing the older VCR model. What was the rep's first mistake? He wasn't listening to his customer's request for something simple, easy to use, and economical.

You cannot browbeat the customer into accepting your way of thinking. What may be right for you may not always be right for someone else. The customer expects your help, not your personal opinion, regardless of how beneficial you may think it to be. It's not a cardinal sin to voice your own opinion occasionally, but try to limit yourself. Use a little discretion and common sense, and always stick to the facts. One fact will mean more than ten opinions. When opinions do clash, you'll find yourself in the middle of a battle of wills. It's helpful to remember that *it's not about **who** is right, but **what** is right*. This is an important basic of customer service. Adopt this practice and you'll avoid customer conflict.

How could a Customer Service Specialist have handled the above situation differently? Let's take a look at how this conversation might have resulted had he used the aforementioned skills to help the customer handle resistance to change:

Introducing himself, the CSS says, "Good afternoon, I'm John Smith. How may I help you?"

"I'm looking for a VCR with just the standard features. What do you suggest?", says the customer.

"I'm sorry, I didn't get your name."

"I'm Mr. Jones."

"Alright, Mr. Jones, we carry several models that have just the factory options. I'd be happy to show you any of these. Do you have a particular model, specific feature or price range in mind?"

"No, all I'm looking for is just something that's affordable, simple and easy to operate."

John Smith, CSS, then shows Mr. Jones a line of low-priced, basic VCRs that he has in stock and says, "I understand that you wish to combine savings and simplicity. If this is all you need, Mr. Jones, then these standard, economical units may be suitable. However, there are a few other things you may want to consider when shopping for a VCR."

"Is there something I've overlooked that you can tell me about?"

"Before buying any consumer electronics item, you may want to keep in mind not only economy and simplicity. Product quality, warranty, and parts/service availability are points you may also want to consider.

"Is the product user-friendly? Are the instructions easy to understand? Are troubleshooting techniques included? Is technical support available?

"Another important feature to look for is whether the item's technology is compatible with the electronics equipment you'll be using it in conjunction with, such as a TV, DVD player, or satellite/cable

Chapter 28. Handling Resistance to Change

equipment. If the VCR's technology is dated, you may want to consider choosing a more technologically current product. This may be a bit more expensive, but it will save you money in the long run by not having to replace a cheaper and dated model."

Remember, the customer's needs must take priority. The customer also deserves your attention, respect, and courtesy. Start by communicating in this manner. You will be setting a good example—one the customer will, in most cases, follow. Only after you have established this kind of rapport will you be able to introduce, explain and lead the customer toward positive change when needed.

Regardless of how this scenario ended, whether the customer did or did not take the Customer Service Specialist's advice, the important point of these illustrations is that the Customer Service Specialist in the latter example implemented several of the communication skills as outlined in the following section. But first and foremost, he supported his information with facts, not personal opinion. Facts will add validity to any argument.

Tips to Remember:

Change may be difficult for the customer due to:

- Fear of the unknown, due to a lack of information.
- Loss of trust due to past problems.
- Belief that there is no need to change.

Address and overcome fear by explaining:

- Existing situation.
- Why change was needed.
- New factual information.
- How the change *positively* affects the customer.

Overcome fear by "putting it in its place":

- Acknowledge fear; face it head-on.
- Make the conscious choice to become *unafraid*.
- Don't be overwhelmed—the best progress will be made by taking things one step at a time.

Ways to help the customer:

- Smile!
- Maintain a POSITIVE ATTITUDE.
- Present a relaxed and *confident* manner. Remember, if you don't have confidence in what you're saying, neither will the customer. Relax, and the customer will too.

- Use positive body language.
- Be supportive and understanding.
- Show encouragement.
- Show sensitivity to emotional responses such as fear, loss, anxiety and grief.

Start with good communication skills. Attitude is everything!

USE POSITIVE LANGUAGE:

- Align yourself with the customer.
- Use positive phrases such as, "I understand how you feel."
- Avoid negative phrases such as, "You don't understand what I'm trying to tell you."

BE A GOOD NEGOTIATOR:

- Start with an attitude of humility, and be willing to yield to the customer's point of view.
- Include the customer by welcoming his opinions.
- Begin by letting the customers know that you are willing to deal with them on their own terms.

BE A GOOD LISTENER:

- Be patient. Allow the customers an opportunity to express their emotions and vent their concerns.
- Don't interrupt.
- Don't finish the customer's sentences for him/her.

BE A GOOD ROLE MODEL:

- Set a good example. The customer will usually follow your lead.
- Show respect.
- Have patience.
- Be tolerant of views other than your own.
- Be HONEST with the customer.

In Closing...

"The service we render others is the rent we pay for our room on earth." Wilfred Grenfell

Once you understand the principles of natural resistance to change and are able to apply positive change in your own life, you will then be armed with the tools needed to assist the customer in dealing with his/her resistance to change. It has often been said that the best way to learn a new skill is by teaching it to someone else. The Customer Service Specialist wears many hats in addition to that of teacher: he/she may also play the

Chapter 28. Handling Resistance to Change

part of assistant, negotiator, role model, communicator, mediator, mentor and confidante. You will discover that your CSS skills will be useful in more areas than just the workplace. These techniques can be applied in your relationships with your family, friends and neighbors—and you'll be amazed at the

> *"Simply give others a bit of yourself; a thoughtful act, a helpful idea, a word of appreciation, a lift over a rough spot, a sense of understanding, a timely suggestion. You take something out of your mind, garnished in kindness out of your heart, and put it into the other fellow's mind and heart."*
> Charles H. Burr

positive results you receive. In a nutshell, the Customer Service Specialist embraces the tenet of "doing unto others as you would have them do unto you."

Chapter Quiz:

1. _____ is usually the biggest obstacle with the least validity.

   a. Happiness
   b. Anxiety
   c. Fear
   d. Depression

2. Which of the following "resistant" types is the easiest to identify?

   a. Passive
   b. Aggressive
   c. Apathetic
   d. Passive-aggressive

3. Which type of resistance is the most difficult to identify because of false impressions of support and agreement?

   a. Apathetic
   b. Passive
   c. Materialistic
   d. Resistant

4. The _____ type can always find an excuse for his/her inaction, saying "I'll be happy to cooperate, just as soon as I finish…"

   a. passive-aggressive
   b. competent
   c. denial
   d. neutral

5. When _____ is introduced, we feel threatened, or fearful.

   a. resistance
   b. attitude
   c. emotion
   d. change

6. "Fear of the unknown" is usually a learned emotion, based solely on a/an _____ of past experiences.

   a. avoidance
   b. generalization
   c. ignorance
   d. deficiency

7. When approaching the decision to deal with change, what simple phrase must you keep in mind?

   a. "It's All In Your Mind."
   b. "Change Can Be Mandatory."
   c. "Attitude Is Everything."
   d. "Remember The Alamo."

8. Existing habits and_____ ___ , based on past experiences, may direct some to cling to old practices that don't work anymore.

   a. belief systems
   b. established patterns
   c. bad manners
   d. consistent ideas

9. In making the transition to positive change, the first step is to realize that change is _____and necessary for personal growth.

   a. important
   b. available
   c. frequent
   d. inevitable

10. The customer will usually follow your lead if you do what during communication?

    a. Remember his name
    b. Set a good example
    c. Offer sound information
    d. Shake his hand

Answers:

1-c, 2-b, 3-b, 4-a, 5-d, 6-b, 7-c, 8-a, 9-d, 10-b

Chapter 29

Listening and Activating a Listener
Give and Take in Conversation

Barbara Kirkland

Barbara Kirkland is a customer service/front-line service provider instructor at the Area Technical Trade Center in Las Vegas, Nevada. She has been teaching for six years. She has been married for 31 years, has three children, and two dogs. Prior to becoming a teacher she worked in the service industry for thirty plus years. Her experiences include retail clothing sales, inside sales manager for an aluminum extrusion company, cost accounting clerk, and a career as district sales manager and countersignature agent for a major national insurance company in Nevada. Listening and communication skills have been major contributors to her success. She feels very strongly that listening and communication skills are core requirements for success in any occupation, especially service related positions.

"You never listen to me."
"Didn't you hear what I said?"
"How many times do I have to tell you?"

Sound familiar? We have all heard these comments. Listening is more than hearing. To hear you don't have to concentrate; hearing occurs naturally. Listening, on the other hand, is learned and it's harder. Think back to your years of education. Did you ever have a course in listening? Do you daydream, plan what you want to say next, or stop listening altogether because you assume what the speaker is going to say? How about interrupting, talking while others are talking, or waiting for a lull in the conversation so you can jump in with your ideas?

Characteristics like these cause people to listen only about 25 percent of the time. That is why people misunderstand, fail to follow directions, and make mistakes in their work and personal lives. In any service industry you must have good listening skills to be successful. With listening comes the need to sense, interpret, and evaluate what you hear.

Listening is a mental process. Mental participation is the critical part of the listening skill. The mind must be engaged with the content of what is being discussed. Listening is a process that begins with a speaker, travels to a listener, and is returned to the speaker in the form of a question or a response from the listener. A number of things complicate a person's ability to be a good listener. Individuals interpret information differently, depending on age, gender, ethnic group, education, economic status, religious background, and other characteristics known as filters.

Everyone brings his or her own set of listening filters into every conversation. What you hear may be different from what the speaker intended because your filters change the meaning. Each person possesses a set of unique filters that affects his or her listening skill. As a listener, you accept some comments as presented, but you run others through mental filters where the message is adjusted by your experiences and attitudes.

Examples of some listening filters are discussed below.

Memories – Good and bad memories of past experiences cloud your thinking. If a customer reminds you of an ex-boss who was mean and unfair, your listening will be colored by the memory.

Values – All information you receive filters through your personal value system, and you interpret what you hear based on these values. If your parents taught you to always speak quietly and politely, then a rude and loud customer may not receive your full attention.

Interests – Subjects that interest you get your attention. If you are not interested, you may ignore important information.

Strong feelings & beliefs – Strong feelings on a subject directly relate to listeners' objectivity. A lifetime of beliefs, some taken from family and cultural background, influence what a listener hears. A worker who comes from a family that believes in honesty above all else, may lose his/her objectivity when he/she finds out the virus was caused by illegal software.

Expectations – When the performance expectations of the speaker and the listener don't match, the listener tends to hear the words that satisfy his or her need. If you try to upgrade a customer's computer and he/she feels it does the job he/she needs, what you are saying may be ignored.

Past and future images – Good and bad past experiences play a part in what is heard. If the customer has had two other computer techs try to fix his/her computer, he or she may listen skeptically when you try to explain what is wrong.

Improving listening also means identifying and eliminating any bad habits you may have acquired. The five

Chapter 29. Listening and Activating a Listener

most common poor listening habits are:

Interruptions – These tell a customer that what he/she is trying to say is not important to you. Do not sort through paperwork or type while he/she is talking. Don't allow co-workers to interrupt.

Fear of not having all the answers –This bad habit causes you to miss the real question. No one has all the answers. Concentrating on what is being said will help you understand the real question. You may have to research or get help to answer correctly, but understanding the question fully is essential to resolving the issue.

Believing you know where the conversation is headed – Before the customer can get the words out, you jump in with an answer. Consider the computer tech who suggests a number of reasons for the computer problems before the customer has a chance to explain the problem. This results in offending the customer.

Overreacting – We all have "hot buttons." Sometimes a customer's choice of language or style of explanation causes you to stop listening and mentally disagree.

Pseudo-listening –Pretending to listen when actually focusing our attention elsewhere. I think this is one of the most common habits. We have all learned this from child-hood and expertly fine-tuned it during our teenage years.

**How many of these have you been guilty of?
How many have you dealt with while helping a customer?**

> **"Nothing is quite so annoying as to have someone go right on talking when you keep interrupting."**
>
> **-Unknown**

To improve your listening skill, concentrate on the words being spoken. This means giving your full attention to the speaker and discontinuing other activities. If you feel like talking or interrupting, take a deep breath. Make a conscious decision to listen. Look for interesting and useful comments in the conversation. Mentally paraphrase what is being said. Maintain eye contact. This is called the hitch-hiking theory; where your eyes focus, your ears follow.

Effective listeners focus on more than the speaker's words. They rely on non-verbal communication as well as the spoken word. Non-verbal communication refers to body language.

This can be more reliable than spoken words. Body language occurs subconsciously when messages are being transmitted through eyes, face, hands, arms, legs, and posture. It is very hard for the average person to hide true feelings and attitudes.

As a skilled listener, you need to observe facial expressions and body movements to gain insight into what is really being communicated by the speaker. Listed below are some tips for interpreting body language:

Eyes – Eyes are wonderful communicators. Rolling of the eyes indicates boredom or disbelief. Raising of the eyebrows shows surprise, and staring emphasizes a point. Winking is used to flirt or to let others know when you agree or support them, and constant eye contact or staring shows interest in what is being said. Eye gestures are the easiest to interpret because they are used often.

Face – The face is an excellent indicator of a person's true thoughts or emotions. When a customer approaches with a frown or clenched jaw, it is pretty obvious he/she is upset. This observation enables you to approach with a neutral or pleasant comment to reduce tension. On the other hand, the customer who wears a smile communicates a positive attitude and encourages a positive approach and conversation.

Hands – Hands are used for emphasis, and to give directions. When used in combination with facial expression and eyes, they express surprise, shock, and pleasure. A customer who has clenched hands, a frown and narrow eyes is definitely not having a very good day.

Arms and Legs – Crossed arms and legs can be negative communication signals. Crossed arms indicate resistance, fear, control, the need for protection, or guardedness. A customer with arms crossed while the salesman is trying to convince him or her to upgrade his computer is probably not going to buy.

Posture – When you sit, stand, and walk, you convey important clues about how you feel and what you think. Would you rather consult a service tech who stands tall and erect, or one who slouches and slumps his shoulders? The technician who stands tall and erect conveys confidence and self-assurance. Slouching sends a message of low self-esteem and low enthusiasm or interest.

Being aware of your own body language is one step to becoming a better listener. A customer uses your non-verbal feedback to know whether his/her message is being understood. Good listeners give nonverbal feedback often and consistently so the speaker can change or adjust the message based on the feedback. Remember to face the speaker, make eye contact, use facial expressions, display good posture and take notes. Decide what communication you want to send and concentrate on sending it so that your non-verbal and verbal messages match.

Good listeners ask questions. As a listener, you have a responsibility to try to understand what is being said. Asking the customer to repeat information, give examples, or provide further explanation are all good questioning techniques. Asking questions means you are a smart listener. But timing is everything. Remember not to interrupt your speaker until his or her thought has been explained. Write down your questions so you can ask them at the appropriate time. Keep your questions pertinent to the topic being discussed. Ask questions if the speaker uses terms or acronyms you are not familiar with. Ask speakers to repeat and explain any area of the problem you do not understand. By asking for further explanation, you can avoid confusion, misunderstandings, and unhappy customers.

RING RING – Can you hear me?

A telephone conversation requires the use of the same techniques used while listening to a speaker face to face. However, their intensity should be increased during telephone conversations since non-verbal feedback is missing. Techniques for effective telephone listening are listed below:

Concentrate - This means giving your full attention to the speaker and discontinuing other activities.

Listen for main ideas - Good telephone listeners focus on the main idea and avoid unnecessary details and side comments.

Ask questions - Make sure you understand what the caller is saying. If not, ask open-ended questions that cannot be answered "yes" or "no." This encourages the customer to explain further.

Repeat what you hear - Clarify what you hear by repeating the information. Rephrase the message in your own words and relay it back to the customer. This not only helps you understand what is being said, but also provides the customer with feedback.

Write it down – To avoid confusing, inaccurate, or missed messages, take notes about what is said.

Since non-verbal communication is not present during telephone conversations, your voice reflects your mood and attitude. Employers, business callers, and customers expect you to be cheerful and pleasant. The following tips can help activate a listener and create a give and take conversation:

1. Be warm and pleasant.
2. Smile while speaking.
3. Use a natural tone.
4. Avoid a monotone.
5. Be alert and interested.
6. Use a normal volume.
7. Speak at a moderate rate.

Now you can speak!

The companion skill of listening is speaking. When both are effective, time is not wasted. You can activate and increase the customer's level of listening by carefully choosing your words and asking the appropriate questions. Certain groups of words can dramatically change the image you're trying to give your customer.

Listed below are common negative comments and their positive replacements:

Negative	Positive
I can't do it	Lets see what I can do
I won't do it	This is what I can do
I shouldn't	I would be happy to do the following for you
We don't do	This is what I can do for you
That could not have happened	I have not come across this problem before
Avoid using 'but'	Use closed-end sentences

In order to activate a customer's level of listening and generate give and take in conversation, it is important to understand the different types of questions you should be asking.

Open-ended questions don't require specific answers. They are used to get the customer talking. Example: "What happens when you turn your computer on?" They are used to obtain detailed information. This type of question is used most often at the beginning of the service call.

Chapter 29. Listening and Activating a Listener

Closed-end questions require specific yes/no type answers. Their primary focus is to determine very specific information or to clarify a customer's perceptions, wishes, or responses. Closed-end questions get you further into the discovery process. For example: "Was your computer turned on or off when the problem occurred?"

Status questions are asked at the beginning of the service call to obtain information necessary for resolving a problem. For example: "What is your name, serial number and account number?"

Illustrative questions are open-ended questions that require a customer to paint as complete a picture as possible about their experience. For example: "Please describe for me what happened next."

Clarification questions are probably the least asked and the most important. Example – "Mr. Customer, when you say you want your computer to run faster, please describe for me what speed you would consider to be fast."

Consequence questions tell you how the problem is affecting your customer. Example – "What will happen if you need to send us your computer and not have it for a while?"

Desires questions are asked at the end of the conversation to let the customer know you really care about them. Example – "Is there anything else we can help you with?"

People feel good when others listen to them. Information gets reported accurately; more work gets done; coworkers trust each other, and teams interact more effectively. If listening is not one of your strong points, it is time to develop the skill. You probably will find yourself in the minority because most people are not good listeners.

Hello, do you understand me?

Another powerful element of listening is getting others to listen to you when you speak so that they become activated in order that results can be accomplished.

The skills of listening and speaking are closely related. When both are well developed, few of the problems often seen with oral communications at work will arise.

There are frequent occasions at work when you must speak with others and when you must listen to what is being said. Being responsive and attentive to the basic listening and communication skills is critical, for such communica-

tions will be invaluable in your overall effectiveness in handling responsibilities and customers.

> "Every person I work with knows something better than me. My job is to listen long enough to find it and use it."
>
> -Jack Nichols

In the business world there are two types of customers: external and internal. The external is the paying customer, while the internal customer is your boss, coworkers, suppliers, delivery people, or anyone you come into contact with in order to deliver a finished product to the paying external customer. Understanding two important steps in communication will help you keep both of these customers actively involved while communicating with them.

Step 1: Show sincerity

The first step to gaining a listener's attention is to be a good listener yourself. When you listen attentively to others, they sense your sincerity. When your turn comes to speak, they will listen – if not out of desire, then out of respect.

Step 2: Identify your barriers

The second step is to identify any of your behaviors that make you a bad speaker. Before people can listen, you must have their attention. You can use words, behavior, voice, attitude, questions, and feedback to gain attention.

The choice of words you use contributes to the listener's desire to hear your message. In order to be an effective speaker, use positive words as shown in the chart below.

Negative Flag Words	Positive Replacement
Problem	Challenge
Mistake	Overlooked a point
Poor	A few changes needed
Negligent	Pay attention to detail
Unacceptable	Redo

Your tone of voice communicates more than your words. Adjust your tone to fit the situation. Use a warm

Chapter 29. Listening and Activating a Listener

friendly tone when greeting someone and a stronger, confident tone to make a point.

By showing a positive attitude, you encourage people to trust you. They will want to hear what you have to say. Be sincere. Say what you mean and mean what you say.

When you speak, ask your listener a question from time to time to ensure that he/she understands what you are saying and to obtain ideas and draw out concerns.

Look for feedback from your audience. How you use the feedback determines whether your listener continues to participate in the conversation. If you ignore the feedback and continue to talk about your views instead of altering the message to address the listener's concerns, you will lose the individual's trust.

For example: You want to present a new idea to your coworkers which, you feel will eliminate a technical problem that has been occurring. You ask their opinion. They input a few suggestions, but you ignore them and continue with your own ideas. By doing this, you communicate that you really do not want their input or ideas, and you make them feel foolish.

The table below can help you become an effective speaker so your listeners will listen.

Talking Do's	Talking Don'ts
Deal with facts	Don't state opinions as facts
Stick to the facts	Don't participate in gossip or rumor
Describe the situation – "He talks loudly."	Don't use judgmental descriptions- "He is a loudmouth."
Be clear and concise	Don't drag things out
Be specific	Don't generalize
Say what you mean	Don't use idle threats or make false promises
Eliminate or control distractions	Don't be the cause or source of distractions.

Effective listeners focus on the speaker's words along with their body language. Effective speakers modulate the

tone of their voice, watch their listener's body language, ask for feedback and respond to it.

> "Opportunities are often missed because we are broadcasting when we should be receiving."
>
> **Author Unknown**

The companion skill of listening is speaking. When both are effective, there is little wasted time. No matter what area of service or sales you are in, good listening and speaking skills are essential to your success.

> "There are four ways, and only four ways, in which we have contact with the world. We are evaluated and classified by these four contacts: what we do, how we look, what we say, and how we say it"
>
> **- Dale Carnegie**

Chapter 29. Listening and Activating a Listener

Chapter Quiz:

1. **With listening comes the need to sense, interpret, and evaluate.**

   a. True
   b. False

2. **Listening is a sense most people are born with.**

   a. True
   b. False

3. **Listeners provide feedback to the speaker through their nonverbal messages.**

   a. True
   b. False

4. **People listen through filters.**

   a. True
   b. False

5. **Individuals interpret information the same way.**

   a. True
   b. False

6. **Which of the following is NOT a technique for effective telephone listening?**

   a. Body language
   b. Ask questions
   c. Repeat what you hear
   d. Take notes

7. **Which of the following can activate a listener and create a give and take conversation?**

   a. Use a monotone voice.
   b. Use a faster than normal rate to keep their attention.
   c. Smile while speaking, be alert and interested.
   d. Speak louder than normal to ensure they understand.

8. **Which of the following statements reflects a positive image to the customer?**

   a. I shouldn't.
   b. Let's see what I can do.
   c. That could not have happened.
   d. But....

9. **The following is an example of an internal customer.**

   a. Customer with a billing problem
   b. Customer with a technical problem
   c. Co-worker
   d. Customer with a complaint

10. **In order to be an effective speaker, you should do which of the following?**

    a. Use judgmental descriptions.
    b. Generalize.
    c. State opinions as facts.
    d. Stick to the facts. Don't use gossip or rumor.

Answers:

1-a, 2-b, 3-a, 4-a, 5-b, 6-a, 7-c, 8-b, 9-c, 10-d

Chapter 30

Encouraging Customer Feedback

Darrel W. Wilson, a native of Crowley, Texas has worked with PRIDE of Florida since July, 1995. While beginning his employment as a Laboratory Technician, he moved to the Customer Service Department where he maintains a Master rating. With a major in mathematics, Darrel possesses a very analytical mind that has helped to assist many customers. Darrel recognizes that customers are the "lifeblood" of any company and a happy customer is a loyal customer. Darrel earned the coveted CSS certification in January of 2002.

Darrel W. Wilson, CSS

Chapter Objectives

- Identify areas of feedback affecting customers.

- Understand why customer feedback is essential to the operation of a company's objective of total customer satisfaction.

- Learn the methods of encouraging customer feedback and the formats used to collect the data.

- How to document customer feedback for easy analysis and action.

Customer feedback is your customers' opinions, criticisms and *perceptions* of your company, its product, and the overall experience of your company's service. A CSS belongs to only a single department within the company, yet is responsible for overseeing all aspects of his or her company that affect customers. Why? Because when customers call with a problem or need assistance, they speak to Customer Service. Therefore, a CSS represents all aspects of the company within the eyes of the customer, making the collection of feedback the responsibility of the CSS.

Feedback is important information that a CSS gathers and ultimately uses as a guide to better service individual customer needs. Have you – as a customer – been asked for feedback? Did you *perceive* that the company was specializing their service to fit your needs? If so, then the goal of that company to utilize your input was half realized. The other half would be actual implementation.

A CSS can encourage customer feedback during routine phone calls, personal visits, electronically, or by written surveys. Even with a small sampling of customer responses, a broad outline of your company's projected image can be ascertained.

With this information, your company can construct a continuous improvement framework of customer satisfaction. And the CSS who initiates, collects and analyzes customer feedback becomes a dynamic force on any Customer Service team!

Areas Open to Customer Feedback

Because of the many industries and their specializations, there are a myriad of specific areas open to customer feedback. This chapter will cover the general areas common to most companies:

- Marketing
- Products*
- Customer Service
- Telecommunication Systems
- Company Image

*Products refer to manufactured goods as well as services throughout this chapter.

Note: *Even if your company satisfies 100% of its customers 100% of the time in four of the categories but fails consistently in just one, they will lose that customer 100% of the time.*

Marketing

The greatest widget ever invented that's *"Guaranteed to save you MONEY! Guaranteed to save you TIME! Guaranteed to make your company more PRODUCTIVE and PROFITABLE!"* is worthless if nobody buys it because of poor marketing.

Conversely, after a slam-bang marketing campaign, what is your customer's opinion of your truth-in-advertising? Does the product perform as claimed?

GUARANTEED!!

Chapter 30. Encouraging Customer Feedback

Effective marketing and truth in advertising is vital to the future health of any company. Understanding why new customers are beating down the doors to buy their products or why they see very few repeat customers is determined with feedback.

Companies typically engage in multi-media marketing strategies at the same time. If a company is employing three media strategies – say: radio, newspaper and TV, but decides it can only afford two, which one is eliminated? The most expensive? How would the company know if the costliest one actually brings in more revenue per advertising dollar?

The company can cancel the most expensive marketing strategy, then sit back and watch the effects on their revenue stream. Or they can proactively – and simply – ask their customers which media influenced their buying decisions. A company that monitors and understands its marketing effectiveness can weed out the losers and focus on its strengths.

Products

There are two types of feedback involving products:

1. Solicited
2. Unsolicited

Solicited feedback is when a CSS initiates the customer contact. One form of unsolicited feedback is casual customer comments made during everyday business transactions. Both of these will be covered in depth later in this chapter. In this section we will identify the most common form of unsolicited feedback: complaints.

There will be many days a CSS will experience workday harmony, a smooth, easy day with no problems. Then there are the days filled with phone calls, faxes and e-mails of customer complaints.

Unfortunately, complaints happen; they just seem to happen *all on the same day*. This then consumes the next several days while the CSS pounds the pavement investigating, tracks the troubleshooting efforts, documents the corrective actions, and coddles the customers throughout the process.

Sound like fun? Maybe not (except the resolution), but it's an opportunity for the company to improve. So a complaint is a form of feedback called *negative feedback*.

Therefore, complaints are good. Keep that thought in mind the next time an irate customer is giving you the business about how your product failed. The customer may be trying your patience, but convince him or her that you appreciate the input, and then the experience for both you and the customer may not be so unpleasant.

Complaints are not hard to deal with. Reread chapter 10 "Communications With Customers" and chapter 29, "Listening and Activating a Listener" with your mind tuned to extracting customer feedback using the chapters' techniques and lessons for handling customers. Within those two chapters you will learn *how* to handle customer situations. This chapter will teach you how to *use* the information to your company's advantage.

Handling an unsatisfied customer positively and correctly can reverse the customer's perception of your company. It will also improve your supervisor's perception of your skills.

Keep in mind that only a minority of customers will complain. Most unsatisfied customers just take their business elsewhere. It's the job of the CSS to prevent the loss of customers. Take a proactive approach by asking customers what they like and dislike about your company's product, what improvements they suggest, and what new products they would like to buy from your company. Advance knowledge of potential problems will avert potential loss of customers. Remember, your customers are your products' end users; they are the field experts.

Customer Service

Bringing in new customers through marketing or introducing new products creates new revenue so that a company can grow. However, a CSS must maintain the established, repeat customers that represent the foundation on which a company can expand its sales.

Dealing with this customer base for an extended period of time, a rapport is naturally built between the CSS and the customer. That rapport can range from business-like and efficient to relaxed, like an old friendship. Either extreme, or the ones that fall in between, present an opportunity to receive feedback from the users of your *company's system.*

The company's system is any aspect of a company that a customer comes in contact with while dealing with that company — in other words, usually dealing with customer

Chapter 30. Encouraging Customer Feedback

service.

A formal survey need not be used to extract information about the customers' experience with your service, but is recommended (formal surveys will be covered later). Asking questions by listening to customer's verbal cues about themselves or their business can seem like friendly banter, but it provides a dual purpose. First, it makes the customer feel important and shows that you're interested. Second, sometimes revealing and important information can be gleaned that you can use to better serve the customer.

The following is an example of feedback I received from a customer by listening, as well as an example of un-solicited feedback. The company I work for does business with some government agencies. One customer, who treats me as if we were longtime friends (we've never met), fre-quently jokes with me about the hoops he has to jump through just to order the supplies he needs.

During one particular phone call the customer was noticeably upset. He told me his supervisors had instructed him to purchase certain items from other businesses that he had previously purchased from my company. He was upset because he liked our products and preferred to deal with one vendor.

All I did was listen and sympathize. However, I took this information to my supervisors. They investigated and found that my customer could still purchase his supplies through my company if we met certain criteria. My company then implemented the changes necessary to meet the criteria.

I then called the customer and informed him that a memo was sent to his supervisors outlining the changes we made. The customer was immensely pleased because it saved him time and paperwork.

It also saved a significant portion of my company's sales because it affected more than just that one customer. My supervisors commended me for my action. Also, the customer wrote an unsolicited letter to my supervisors praising my effort and dedication to his account.

The above is just one example of feedback experienced in the area of Customer Service. A CSS is the company's liaison with the customer—a customer advocate, so to speak. The success or failure of your CSS career may hinge on the content of the feedback.

Telecommunication Systems

The increase of customer utilization of the Internet for commerce has companies paying close attention to, and paying big money for, building and maintaining an e-store that is user-friendly and easily accessible. If a company has hired web designers, consultants and web masters for their home page, do not think customer feedback is unnecessary. The e-store users are *your* customers, not the consultants.

It would be a good idea (actually, it should be *mandatory*) for the CSS to become an expert at using their company's website. They must not only assist customers in how to use it, but be able to ask the appropriate questions to collect insightful feedback for its improvement.

The other traditional telecom systems are:

- Answering systems
- Voicemail
- E-mail
- Wireless phones
- Faxes
- Land line phone systems

An example is the automated answering system. Most companies use them today instead of human operators to cut costs. They are undoubtedly the most irritating, frustrating, asinine answering systems ever invented.

Did you agree with that assessment? If so, then you have experienced the time consuming, multi-branched sequencing tree monstrosity that some companies employ *and believe are efficient and helpful.* How efficient are customer hang-ups? People grudgingly accept automatic answering systems because they are so ubiquitous, but keep it simple. What are your customers experiencing?

The following are brief questions for you to consider about the other telecom systems your company employs:

Voicemail: Do you keep your voicemail message up to date? Do your customers encounter your voicemail frequently?

E-mail: Do you check your e-mails every hour? Do you answer promptly? Do you have a simple address?

Wireless phones: Are your batteries charged all the time? Do customers complain about reception?

Fax: Do customers indicate they get "communication

Chapter 30. Encouraging Customer Feedback

errors"? Or busy signals?

Land line phones: Does your company need multiple phone numbers? Are the phones reliable?

The method a customer uses to contact a company is unimportant. What *is* important is that he/she encounters a system that works. "Works" in this context means: A system customers can use and *want to use.*

Company Image

How much sales revenue is generated at your company by word-of-mouth? Do your customers trust your company? Customer opinions of company image are the most vital aspect of customer feedback because they base their buying habits on experience or perception.

Company image involves everything from individual employee attitudes toward customers to customer perceptions of a company's action or stance on social issues. If just one of your coworkers is rude to your customers, it will have a huge negative impact on customer perception. There are many diverse social and environmental issues important to numerous groups and activists that can influence customer's opinions. What are your customer's opinions of the many aspects of company image?

Unfortunately, company image is probably the hardest to quantify because there are so many intangibles outside the company which can influence customer perception. For instance, polls show a lack of trust for corporations in general after the high-profile accounting fraud scandals and bankruptcies of 2002.

Why Encourage Feedback?

To Meet Customer Expectations

Encouraging feedback allows customers to participate in "building" the kind of personal service and products that meet customer expectations. *Customer expectations* are a set of preconceived notions about a company's image, its products' performance, and the overall experience the customer encounters while interacting with any aspect of the company.

Encouraging feedback asks the customer the question, "How can we make our company better for *you*?" Feedback gives customers the "power" to shape how a company can better serve them. An example came to me in the form of a survey from one of my customers:

The customer had been receiving her regular shipments for months with no complaints or questions. I mailed her a survey at random and received quite a surprise when she mailed it back. Overall, her marks for the company were good. However, in the comment section she wrote, "I would like to see lift gates on delivery trucks because I don't have a loading dock... ."

I was stunned. Not only because some of our trucks are equipped with lift gates, but also because I had failed to provide such a simple service to her. I should have inquired if she had any special requirements for her shipments the first time she placed an order. I later learned she didn't complain because our truck drivers graciously unloaded her orders for her. Her next order was delivered with a lift gate.

Customer expectations are as varied as people's personalities. It is impractical to assume that expectations from one customer will work for all customers. Soliciting feedback from as many customers as practical will give you the insight to provide personalized service over the broadest range of customers.

Resolving/Preventing Customer Problems

Inevitably, customers experience difficulties with products, personnel or the company's system. However, fewer than 5% of customers call to complain. What do the other 95% do? That depends on the customer's experience with the product or company. First-time buyers almost always take their business elsewhere because of a negative first impression.

Buyers who have a good working history with a company or its products tend not to allow an isolated, negative incident to influence their purchasing patterns. These are the customers a CSS can mine data from to unearth patterns of the company's failures or weaknesses. With this data, preventive measures are incorporated to shore up weak areas and eliminate errors that drive away new customers and aggravate existing ones.

Another advantage of collecting and documenting feedback is that the entire CSS team and any new employees will benefit from the knowledge already gained without having to experience it directly. For example, if a customer calls in with a problem, a CSS can check that problem against the records. If a similar problem had occurred, the document will show its cause and resolution, thereby eliminating the investigative work and speeding up the solution.

Chapter 30. Encouraging Customer Feedback

Research and Development

Have you ever had a call similar to the following?

"Good morning. Swee' Peas' Broom Company, Customer Service, Darrel speaking. How can I help you?"

"Hi, Darrel. This is Janet from Janet Oriole's Cleaning Service."

"Hello Janet. What can I do for you today?"

"I would like to place an order for 12 push brooms and 12 corn brooms. But, I was wondering if you sell dustpans, too? I don't see it in your product catalog."

"No ma'am, we don't sell dustpans. But that sounds like a good idea. Why don't I check on that, then get back with you…"

CLICK! A light bulb should have come on in your head: *Brooms...Dustpans...Makes sense!*

This is an example of complementary products – which are products that are used or purchased with the other. However, these items may take different and expensive machinery to manufacture. Don't run to your supervisor with a great idea if only one customer suggests it. Call other customers and ask if they would purchase a new product if your company offered it, document their answers, then take your proposal to your supervisor.

The purpose here is to see why customer feedback is important. The customer, Janet, asked an unsolicited, simple – but logical – question about what *she* thinks your company can do for *her*. A CSS who actively pursues this kind of feedback gives his/her company a better idea of what products will improve on their customers' service – and increase company sales.

The other (subtle) purpose here is: Don't let unsolicited feedback pass over your head. In other words, listen and recognize what your customers *mean*. If Janet says, "Do you sell dustpans, too?" Don't answer, "Nah, we don't sell those. Just brooms." That kind of admission gives customers the impression you are not interested in their needs.

Knowing Your Customers

Feedback on a consistent basis underscores companies' strengths and weaknesses; exposing areas that need improvement and highlighting departments or personnel that demonstrate exemplary work. By encouraging feedback, even if customers don't answer, you at least enhance customers' perception of better service.

However, a CSS needs information on what customers like and dislike about any aspect of their company and of any problems in order to provide the individual service customers expect. Managers need the information to make informed decisions that will steer their company in the same direction as the market. Without feedback, a CSS has no information or customer history to *prevent* problems or provide service which the customer expects. Without it, a CSS gives only *reactive* service, which is always too late.

How to Encourage Feedback

There are various formal and informal methods of soliciting feedback, but there is no best way that fits all customers. The rule here is to offer several options.

Phone Surveys

The trick with using phone surveys successfully is to wait until the customer calls you. If you initiate the call for the purpose of soliciting feedback, *you* are interrupting *his/her* workday. Some customers may find the time to answer your questions, but do not exceed two or three minutes. That is enough time to ask eight to ten short-answer questions or four to six questions requiring detailed answers.

Listen to the customer's tone of voice. If you detect a little impatience in his/her voice, then the information he or she gives could be useless. At that point, all the customer wants to do is to get rid of you. Your best strategy is to oblige.

The CSS who has experience with some of his/her customers' accounts has the advantage to initiate calls because they have built a solid working relationship — in other words, trust.

Another way to get feedback when initiating calls is to target customers who have experienced recent problems. After a complaint has been rectified, call the customer to see if they are satisfied with the resolution. It would be a good idea to allow about a week to elapse to let bad memories fade. Then ask questions such as:

Chapter 30. Encouraging Customer Feedback

"I don't want to see you experience these kinds of problems again. Tell me, is there anything specific we can do to improve our overall service to you?"

Or, use other questions specific to the customer's problem that will provide the information needed to prevent such problems in the future.

But when the customer calls, and after his/her business has been taken care of, you can ask directly for feedback or take a subtle approach. For example:

The direct approach:

"...Your order is logged in our system, Mrs. Franklin."

"Great. Can I expect delivery on Friday?"

"Yes, ma'am. Your delivery instructions are noted and you can expect your order on Friday. Oh, Mrs. Franklin, can you spare a few moments to answer a few survey questions about the service my company provides you?"

"Sure, I can spare a few minutes."

In this example, permission has been granted, but with a time restriction. Listen carefully for customer instructions and *stay within the boundaries of the instructions.*

What questions should you ask? A good rule is to have a list of general questions by the phone. However, Mrs. Franklin's verbal cues give emphasis to her concern for the company's delivery schedule. Direct your questions in that area to learn the object of her concern.

Or the subtle approach:

"...Your order is logged in our system, Mrs. Franklin."

"Great. Can I expect delivery on Friday?"

"Yes, ma'am. Your delivery instructions are noted and you can expect your order on Friday. Mrs. Franklin, out of curiosity, how has your experiences with our deliveries been in the past?"

Or: "...Mrs. Franklin, have you experienced any problems with our deliveries?"

From that starting point, you may find customers who are willing to sacrifice more than a few minutes when they are telling you how they would like things to be done for them. Take notes of what your customers say to mold the customer's service to their expectations.

Face to Face

This method is probably the least used because it is too time consuming and cost intensive. A CSS who has his/her supervisor's trust to visit his/her customers shouldn't be going for feedback alone. If a visit is scheduled for other purposes, then allotting time for feedback may be productive. However, will you be prepared to look a dissatisfied customer in the eye? It is recommended that a CSS be prepared and well-versed in the customer's account and personality.

Written Survey

This is the most used method in business today because it is the most effective at soliciting responses. Regardless of method of delivery to the customer – Internet, fax, or postal service, the written survey provides ease of use and the privacy to answer as honestly as possible. All mailed surveys should include a self-addressed stamped envelope.

On the next page are examples of types of written surveys.

Form A-1, A-2, & A-3 - Questions Requiring Written Answers

Note that each survey has only seven questions. That is by no means the optimum number; nor are the questions designed to supply all the specific answers for each individual company. However, the number of questions were tested and found to take no more than five minutes to answer, which is the optimum time a customer spends on a survey without losing interest.

How can a CSS learn very much with only seven questions? For one, there is a place for comments on each one. This allows each customer to voice his/her most pressing concern which may not necessarily be covered by the questions. And two, there are three different types of Form A. Two of the forms cover a specific area and the third combines the two. Obviously, the CSS must develop as many forms as necessary to cover all company areas.

Send only one questionnaire to a customer at any one time period. Depending on how many customers your company has and how many responses are needed to present a broad sampling of customers will determine how many surveys should be sent. Don't send the same customer a questionnaire more than once every six months, or as determined by management.

Chapter 30. Encouraging Customer Feedback

Form A-1

WIDGET INC., CUSTOMER EXPECTATION QUESTIONNAIRE

DATE:
CUSTOMER NAME:
CUSTOMER ADDRESS:

CUSTOMER PHONE #:

1. What criteria do you use in choosing a vendor? (Technical assistance, reputation, etc.)

2. Which vendor criteria does WIDGET, Inc., best exemplify? Which is the worst?

3. What criteria do you use in choosing a product? (Price, delivery, quality, etc)

4. Which product criteria does WIDGET, Inc., best exemplify? Which is the worst?

5. What is going well with WIDGET Inc., as your vendor? What should we keep doing?

6. What are we not doing that we should be doing?

7. Is our advertising campaign (radio, TV, newspaper) useful to your purchasing decisions? If so, which media?

Do you plan to continue to purchase from WIDGET Inc?

    Yes   No

COMMENTS:
Thank you for taking the time to assist us by answering our questionnaire. We are sincere in our desire to provide the best possible service to our customers and look forward to fulfilling your future needs.

Form A-3

WIDGET INC., CUSTOMER EXPECTATION QUESTIONNAIRE

DATE:
CUSTOMER NAME:
CUSTOMER ADDRESS:

CUSTOMER PHONE #:

1. What criteria do you use in choosing a product? (Price, delivery, quality, etc)

2. Which product criteria does WIDGET, Inc., best exemplify?

3. Which product criteria does WIDGET Inc., least exemplify?

4. Please describe the best experience you have had with a WIDGET Inc., product.

5. Please describe the worst experience you have had with a WIDGET Inc., product.

6. What products would you like to see WIDGET Inc., supply that we do not at this time?

7. Is our advertising campaign (radio, TV, newspaper) useful in your purchasing decisions? If so, which media?

Do you plan to continue to purchase from WIDGET Inc?

    Yes   No

COMMENTS:

Thank you for taking the time to assist us by answering our questionnaire. We are sincere in our desire to provide the best possible service to our customers and look forward to fulfilling your future needs.

Form A-2

WIDGET INC., CUSTOMER EXPECTATION QUESTIONNAIRE

DATE:
CUSTOMER NAME:
CUSTOMER ADDRESS:

CUSTOMER PHONE #:

1. What criteria do you use in choosing a vendor? (Technical assistance, reputation, etc.)

2. Which vendor criteria does WIDGET, Inc., best exemplify?

3. Which vendor criteria does WIDGET Inc., least exemplify?

4. Please describe the best experience you have had with WIDGET Inc.

5. Please describe the worst experience you have had with WIDGET Inc.

6. What are we not doing that we should be doing?

7. Do you plan to continue to purchase from WIDGET Inc.?

       Yes   No

COMMENTS:

Thank you for taking the time to assist us by answering our questionnaire. We are sincere in our desire to provide the best possible service to our customers and look forward to fulfilling your future needs.

Form B

WIDGET INC., CUSTOMER EXPECTATION QUESTIONNAIRE

	Excellent	Good	Fair	Poor
1 How would you rate our customer service department?				
2 How would you rate our sales department?				
3 How would you rate our products?				
4 How would you rate our delivery time?				
5 How would you rate our drivers?				
6 How would you rate our telephone etiquette?				
7 How would you rate our telecommunication systems?				
8 How would you rate our response to complaints?				
9 How would you rate our price competitiveness?				
10 How would you rate our paperwork administration? (Packing slip, invoicing, etc)				
11 How would you rate our R & D efforts? (ability to introduce new products to meet your needs)				
12 How would you rate our radio advertising?				
13 How would you rate our television advertising?				
14 How would you rate our newspaper advertising?				
15 How would you rate our company overall?				

COMMENTS:

Form B - Questions with Pre-provided Answers

These surveys allow more flexibility in the number, subjects and specific quality of questions. As you can see, the questions cover a wide range of areas. Some of the sample questions ask for an evaluation that covers a broad area, and others ask more specific questions. The question format can be as specific or as general as deemed necessary. However, customers should still be able to complete the survey in five minutes or less.

This survey format gives a good mathematical representation of the areas covered in the survey. However, interpreting the numbers is up to the discretion of the company. A more in-depth look at how the numbers are used will be discussed in the next section.

Another form (not pictured) is using a combination of Form A and Form B. Again, the survey should be one that can be finished in five minutes or less.

How to Use Feedback

Few companies can satisfy all of their customers all of the time or solve all the problems to the customer's satisfaction. Utilizing a feedback system is one more tool companies use to increase overall customer satisfaction. But how is feedback used?

A working feedback system consists of three parts:

1. Gathering information.

2. Documentation.

3. Analysis and Action

We've covered the how and why of the first step. Now we will look at the last two steps that show us how to use the information we gathered.

Using Form A-2 and A-3 is the easiest for documenting because it focuses on one area or department. When these forms are returned, they can be stored for later review in one area or file that corresponds to the subject area. Form A-1 needs to be filed in a central area that is easily accessible by all departments involved in the survey. It would be a good practice to assign a unique identifying number to each of the different forms for easier tracking.

After the surveys have been collected and filed, a supervisor, or the personnel assigned, collects the surveys, reviews them, and prepares notes for later presentation during analysis and action. The notes should highlight customer concerns, suggestions and comments – both positive and negative (praise is just as important at improving an employee's job expertise).

When steps one and two have been completed, all personnel from the departments affected by these surveys should be assembled. Included also should be *the CSS team*. A facilitator leads the meeting, using the notes taken earlier, discussing all points raised by customers, and offering solutions or requesting suggestions from the personnel affected. When the solutions have been reached, it is only a matter of implementing the changes to start the process of improvement. However, it is easy to talk about the changes. Actually applying the solutions is not only a matter for management put in motion; *it is in the interest of the CSS as well*. After all, the CSS is the one who faces the customers and their concerns. That is why the CSS team should be present in all department meetings on feedback to learn the details of the survey's action so it can be passed on to the customer, which closes the loop of the feedback process.

Documentation of Form B is purely mathematical. On a master copy of the form (see below) is placed the arithmetical results.

The survey questions:

1. How would you rate our customer service department?

2. How would you rate our sales department?

3. How would you rate our products?

4. How would you rate our delivery time?

5. How would you rate our drivers?

6. How would you rate our telephone etiquette?

7. How would you rate our telecommunication systems?

8. How would you rate our response to complaints?

9. How would you rate our price competitiveness?

10. How would you rate our paperwork administration? (packing slip, invoicing, etc)

Chapter 30. Encouraging Customer Feedback

11. How would you rate our R & D efforts? (Ability to introduce new products to meet your needs)

12. How would you rate our radio advertising?

13. How would you rate our television advertising?

14. How would you rate our newspaper advertising?

15. How would you rate our company overall?

	EXCELLENT	GOOD	FAIR	POOR
1.	20	70	10	0
2.	10	50	35	5
3.	60	30	10	0
4.	50	30	20	0
5.	55	35	10	0
6.	75	20	5	0
7.	10	55	30	5
8.	55	30	15	0
9.	75	20	5	0
10.	35	35	25	5
11.	70	20	5	5
12.	20	20	10	5
13.	25	25	10	5
14.	15	35	10	0
15.	40	40	20	0

But what do these numbers mean? They must be taken in relation to the question to get the broadest sense of what customers as a group feel. This table's numbers show a majority of Excellent and Good responses compared to Fair and Poor. For example, Question #1 shows an overall 90 out of 100 Good or Excellent. That's a 90% success rate in most companies' assessment. However, only 20% are Excellent, which means this area still needs a lot of improvement.

Review which customers gave Fair and Poor ratings to determine why. It may be an isolated incident. But ask your team if these incidents were resolved to the customer's satisfaction. If no clear answer can be ascertained, then call the customer and ask. Then, use the feedback to improve overall service to all customers.

Review the comment section on Form B as well the Form A surveys that pertain to Customer Service to find any reasons why Customer Service is not performing to the highest standard and implement a corrective action plan based on what the customers say.

Take a look at Questions #3 and #9. Both of these are very strong areas of the company. Customers feel that the products and their prices are superior to the competition. The bar chart (below) gives a better idea of what Question #3 looks like.

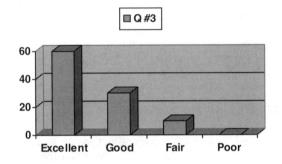

In contrast to Question #3, compare it to the bar chart below for Question #1:

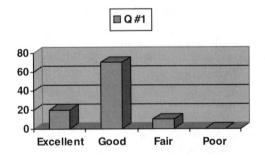

As you can see, bar charts are a good visual tool to show the affected employees the overall rating of their area in customers' eyes.

You now have the what, why and how of customer feedback, and how to use it to improve customer service, not only in the area of customer service, but of the company as a whole. A proactive customer service team can produce the information directly from customers, and good leaders in management can formalize plans from the information to continuously improve their teams to be a world-leading supplier of the best customer service.

Chapter 30. Encouraging Customer Feedback

Chapter Quiz:

1. **Which is the most proactive way to prove the effectiveness of an advertising campaign for a product?**

   a. Scrutinize changes in revenue streams closely and frequently.
   b. Form a team to experience the advertising firsthand to see if they feel compelled to purchase the product.
   c. Ask customers how they rate the advertising and if it influenced their decision.
   d. Hire consultants to form focus groups to give feedback on commercial's appeal.

2. **The term *experiencing the company's system* means what customers encounter of any aspect of a company when they contact the company to do business.**

   a. True
   b. False

3. **Listening to a customer's verbal cues and asking questions for feedback based on those cues provides two advantages. One of those advantages is that it makes the customer feel he/she is receiving special service. What is the second?**

   a. Customers learn more intimate details about the CSS.
   b. The CSS learns intimate details from customers worthy of gossip with another CSS.
   c. The CSS makes customers perceive he is sweet talking him or her.
   d. The CSS learns details about customers that can be used to provide better service to that customer.

4. **What are customer expectations?**

   a. What customers expect a CSS to do for them.
   b. What customers expect products to do for them.
   c. What customers expect a company to do for them.
   d. A customer's preconceived perceptions of company image, its products and the service they expect.

5. **Why encourage customer feedback?**

   a. To meet customer expectations, prevent problems, develop new products, and provide better service by knowing the customers.
   b. To build customer relationships by spending a lot of time chatting with them.
   c. To use phone, electronic and written surveys to gather important information on each customer.
   d. Relieves the boredom a CSS experiences in the day.

6. **Why is the written survey the best format to use to solicit feedback?**

   a. Customers desire to become novelists and like to write.
   b. It is the most effective in amassing the responses from customers.
   c. Customers will not use any other method.
   d. It is the least effective in amassing responses from customers.

7. **How many questions should a written survey requiring long written answers have and why?**

   a. 5; because it takes one minute per question to answer.
   b. Unlimited; because customers will answer as many as they feel like.
   c. 7; because this amount can be completed in five minutes or less.
   d. 15; because the more answers the CSS gets, the more information can be used to improve service.

The following chart is a simulated customer response tabulation. Use the chart for the next two questions:

	Excellent	Good	Fair	Poor
Question #1	25	50	25	0
Question #2	50	40	10	0
Question #3	10	20	30	40
Question #4	75	15	10	0
Question #5	40	30	10	20

8. **Which two of the questions' customer responses show the most strength?**

   a. Question #1 and Question #4.
   b. Question #1 and Question #4.
   c. Question #2 and Question #4.
   d. Question #1 and Question #2

9. **Which two questions' customer responses show the most weakness?**

   a. Question #3 and Question #5
   b. Question #1 and Question #3
   c. Question #1 and Question #5
   d. Question #3 and Question #4

10. **Which of the following is <u>not</u> a good question for a customer feedback survey?**

    a. How would you rate our on-time delivery?
    b. Does our product wrapping machine wrap enough products per hour to justify the number of packers per machine?
    c. Does our Super Deluxe Widget meet your expectations of that product?
    d. Do you experience any problems with our automated answering system? If so, please explain.

Answers:

1-c, 2-a, 3-d, 4-d, 5-a, 6-b, 7-c, 8-c, 9-a, 10-b

Chapter 31

Interpersonal Relationships – Coworkers and Other Employees

Carolyn Carson

Carolyn Carson first joined ETA's staff in 1994, just one week after retiring from the U. S. Department of Agriculture. She later left ETA to become a mortgage loan officer, then retired again, but has been back with ETA for five years. Carolyn and her husband John have owned a successful marketing business for many years. Carolyn has three daughters and eight grandchildren.

Coworkers—Let's Get Along

If you can master the art of good interpersonal relationships, especially with coworkers and other employees, life will be much more pleasant for you. Getting up and going to work each day will be an easier task, and you might even look forward to getting there.

Obviously, with the recent rash of workplace shootings, we can see that there is still a lot to be learned about this subject. Many places of employment still haven't got it right.

Ideally, the workplace should function like a family unit, but not so closely that you live in each other's pockets. As with the family unit, Aunt Tillie might not be your favorite person, but you respect her and treat her well because you are in the same family. That doesn't mean that you invite her over to dinner every week.

The same is true in the workplace. It is wise to show respect to every coworker, whether you agree with everything he or she does or not. If you are not on the same page politically and don't go to the same church, it's probably best just not to discuss those subjects. You can work together amicably during the day and go your separate ways when you leave work. It's not necessary for you to agree on personal matters. To be fair to your employer, your work time needs to be centered on work, anyway.

There's no hard and fast rule about socializing with other employees outside the workplace, but don't overdo it. If your dog bites their child, or your child gives theirs a black eye, and they're upset about that, then you have to contend with that resentment in the workplace. We all know couples who socialize all the time that end up having disagreements because they spend too much time together. Why add that pressure to your work life?

Let's look at some of the reasons people are dissatisfied with their jobs, and then let's discuss what can be done to improve matters.

Hovering

There are still some unenlightened employers who feel that they must treat their employees as school children and hover over them every minute. This certainly doesn't give the employees a sense that they are valuable to the company. Automation has allowed some employers to track every minute of the employee's workday, and some help-desk and airline-ticketing employees are frequently criticized by their employer for spending too much time on a call. Who pays for the employees' feeling that they have to rush through a call? The end-user—the customer!

Big Brother

A friend told us that he had been contacted by the post office, and they wanted to put a bar code on his mail box so that they could track their postman's movements and know exactly what time he reached that house. Our friend refused to allow it and told them that he thought they were going way too far—that the postman had a hard enough job without that pressure.

If at all feasible, employees should be given as much autonomy as possible to complete the work expected of them. Whenever possible, give the tasks to employees and let them complete them in the way that works best for them. You just might find that they have a way to complete the job that is much more efficient than "the way it's always been done." The more control an employee has over his/her job, the happier that employee will be. Joe does not do his best work if he feels he's being treated like a first-grader,

174

Chapter 31. Interpersonal Relationships – Coworkers and Other Employees

and Susie is much more likely to make a mistake if someone is peering over her shoulder all the time.

If you are in this situation, it might be worth your while to sit down with the boss and suggest that you be allowed to take a task and use your own methods to accomplish it. If he/she is concerned that might not work, maybe both of you could agree to a trial for a set period of time. As long as you are dealing with a reasonable person, and you approach it with the right attitude, you might be able to establish better working conditions for yourself and your fellow employees.

Reasonable Rules

Of course, employees must understand what is expected of them, and what company policy is, overall. If something your company does is regulated by law and must be done in a certain manner, everyone must understand that thoroughly. I have always felt that if employees knew WHY something had to be done a certain way, they would do it.

Most employees would take less money for a job where they feel appreciated, rather than work for more money on a job where they have no sense of satisfaction. Many times, just the ability to have some control over their job will cause employees to turn down more lucrative offers and stay with their present employer.

The Electronics Technicians Association (ETA) is a good example of an employer allowing employees to manage their own work. Some of the workers have school-age children, and they appreciate the fact that they can work flex-time and be home when their children are home. Some days the lights come on pretty early because someone is already in there working. Because the employees appreciate this aspect of working for ETA so much, they are very conscientious about their jobs. They schedule their work and take responsibility for getting it done, even arranging for someone else to take over necessary tasks when they go on vacation.

 It's very important that the rules are the same for all employees. If Mary is chastised for doing something that Bill is allowed to do, stress and dissatisfaction are the certain result. Unhappy employees are not efficient employees. They are also much more likely to be the ones out on sick leave battling ulcers, depression, headaches and all sorts of stress-related conditions.

The List

Here are some ideas that might help to create a more efficient, stress-free workplace.

1. Take responsibility for doing your job well. Be at work during the hours you're expected, and do what is assigned to you.
2. Be pleasant and friendly to everyone at your workplace, but don't make it your social life.
3. Keep your feelings to yourself, for the most part. Hold your temper, and don't have a tantrum if things aren't going the way you think they should.
4. Keep your nose out of the other person's business. If your opinion is needed, someone will ask you for it.
5. Please don't gossip or pass on rumors. A lot of harm can come from that—to you and to the business.
6. Practice honesty—not the "that dress is ugly" kind—but don't take credit for something you didn't do, and if you have made a mistake, own up to it. Don't furnish your home office with supplies from work, and be sure to give an hour's work for an hour's pay.

Rules in the Workplace

Unfortunately, in today's litigious environment, one has to be very careful not to cross the line legally. Watch out for actions that could be classified as "offensive" to other employees. This could include telling a sexually implicit joke, showing offensive pictures, unwanted touching, or even continuing to ask another employee for a date after you've been turned down once.

It's even possible to be sued for sexual harassment if employees once had a relationship, and when one wanted to break it off, the other used his/her power in the workplace to try to continue the relationship. Dating in the workplace between unequal employees can be a recipe for disaster.

Charges of discrimination can arise because of perceived harassment due to reasons of race, ethnicity, religion or national origin. For the sake of everyone concerned, don't pass on those crude stories and jokes, even if they seem funny to you on first reading. Remember that they might be very hurtful to someone else.

We now have a very multicultural workplace. Don't let

that be a problem for you. Learn to appreciate people's differences. Every culture has something to offer that is of value, and the more we know about those differences, the more well-rounded we can become.

Style of Communication

The way we say something can be just as important as what we say. *Perception* is everything. Miscommunication is one of the largest problems in our culture. Even your body language can affect how your message is received. Whether verbal, written, or non-verbal, be sure that your communications are clear enough that there is no chance of them being misunderstood.

When composing a memo, an e-mail, or a letter, go back over your written words two or three times before you send them. Check for wording that could be misinterpreted, and make whatever changes are necessary to be sure that your meaning is crystal clear.

When discussing something face-to-face, watch for signs that you are being misunderstood—even asking questions to be sure that the correct message is being sent.

If you are taking a message or an order over the phone, ask enough questions to get the information you need. Repeat the request back to the person on the other end of the line to be sure that you both agree on the information you are taking down. It's much more professional to get it right the first time than to have to call back or re-send an order because you misunderstood.

Etiquette

Successfully working with other people really boils down to the basics your mother tried to teach you even before you started to school. Be polite, say Please and Thank You, Don't interrupt, etc. If you've never read Robert Fulghum's book, *All I Really Need to Know I Learned in Kindergarten*, you might want to do so. He calls it "uncommon thoughts on common things." Here's one paragraph from his book that says it all.

Share everything.
Play fair.
Don't hit people.
Put things back where you found them.

Clean up your own mess.
Don't take things that aren't yours.
Say you're sorry when you hurt somebody.
Wash your hands before you eat.
Flush.
Warm cookies and cold milk are good for you.
Live a balanced life—learn some and think some and draw and paint and sing and dance and play and work every day some.
Take a nap every afternoon. (*If only!!*)
When you go out into the world, watch out for traffic, hold hands and stick together.

Maybe other than the nap, most businesses would see an improvement if their employees would just follow these principles.

People Power

Some people never learn that their success at their job depends on how they interact with other people. It's not enough to keep the boss happy. In today's business climate, it's very possible to come to work on Monday morning and find that your boss has been transferred two states away, and someone new is in his/her place. Let's hope that the new boss is someone that you have always treated politely. In my career, I've certainly seen new managers arrive on the scene with old scores to settle. Some of them didn't waste much time getting even with someone who treated them badly in the past. Also, never underestimate the power a secretary has with the boss. ALWAYS treat the secretary and the receptionist well!

Gossip

If we're honest, we'd all have to admit that some time in our lives, we've passed on gossip. I doubt that any of us are proud of that fact. Gossip in the workplace is a cancer. No good can come from it, and much harm can result. Even if the story you are passing on is true, you may not know all of the circumstances, and it's probably none of your business anyway. Once a rumor is passed on, it takes on a life of its own, and you can never call it back. People can be hurt beyond repair. Don't do it!

Handling Criticism

Criticism hurts, especially when you think you've done your best. Try to look at it objectively. Let's hope that your boss is enlightened enough to know that criticizing you should be done privately, face-to-face. If this is the case, listen carefully and remain calm. Then evaluate what he/she has said. Is it correct? If not, explain why it isn't accurate. If it is correct, ask what you need to do to improve. Try not to take it personally. A person who cannot handle criticism will probably never be able to move up in the company. Yes, it may hurt your feelings, but look at it as a way to improve yourself.

If the criticism comes from a coworker, take time to sit down with him or her and find out what the problem is. The same theory applies. If the criticism is accurate, try to come to an agreement on how to remedy the situation. If it is not correct, try to discover why the other person perceives it to be a problem. It's best to "head these problems off at the pass" rather than to let them fester.

Conclusion

Let's face it, most of us are never going to win the lottery (especially if we don't buy a ticket), and work is going to remain a fact of life with us for at least forty years. That can be a long forty years or a short forty years, depending on your relationships with your coworkers. Make an effort to become an expert at inter-personal relationships. Be courteous to your coworkers and expect them to treat you accordingly. Remember to be fair and ethical and to do your job as professionally as possible. There's no rule that says you can't enjoy your job. Life will be more fun if you can look forward to going to work each day.

Chapter Quiz:

1. **An excellent way to get ahead at work is to socialize with your coworkers.**

   a. True
   b. False

2. **One way an employer can increase employee satisfaction is:**

   a. criticize the employee in public for mistakes.
   b. scrutinize every facet of the work assigned.
   c. give the employee leeway to complete the job as he/she sees fit.
   d. provide a list of instructions that must be followed for each step of the task.

3. **Only the boss needs to be concerned about harassment and discrimination laws.**

   a. True
   b. False

4. **If you have asked a subordinate employee for a date and been turned down, you should:**

   a. continue to ask until he/she says yes.
   b. try a different brand of cologne.
   c. give up and move on.
   d. ask his/her coworker to help you get a yes answer.

5. **Manners are very important at work.**

   a. True
   b. False

6. **One reason for giving employees some autonomy on the job might be:**

   a. the workers will feel better about their jobs.
   b. the employer wouldn't have to come in to work.
   c. they might expect you to do their work.
   d. they will expect more money.

7. **It's not worth your time to be nice to anyone except the boss.**

   a. True
   b. False

8. **One reason to be nice to the boss' secretary is:**

   a. so you will be invited to the boss' next party.
   b. you might like to ask her for a date some day.
   c. she signs the paychecks.
   d. secretaries usually have a lot of power with the boss.

9. **Workplace gossip is:**

   a. inevitable, so just join in.
   b. just good, clean fun.
   c. a recipe for disaster.
   d. something that is expected of you.

10. **Pay is not always more important than working conditions to employees.**

    a. True
    b. False

Answers:

1-b, 2-c, 3-b, 4-c, 5-a, 6-a, 7-b, 8-d, 9-c, 10-a

Chapter 32

Customer Service Specialist Practice Examination and Answers

Introduction

Included here are over 150 questions typical of what a prospective Customer Service Specialist might find on ETA's Customer Service Specialist exam covering the soft skills needed to interact with the public and co-workers. The answers are provided at the end of this chapter.

1. **Because Customer Service is a complex and demanding field, it requires the successful CSS to possess all of the following except:**

   a. intelligence.
   b. stunning good looks.
   c. technical skills.
   d. judgment.

2. **When a CSS has the technical skills, discipline, intelligence, and judgment required for the job, he/she can fail their customers with a lack of:**

   a. exact change.
   b. popular cologne.
   c. desire.
   d. appealing storefront.

3. **To become a successful leader, it is mandatory that you have a compulsive drive to succeed.**

   a. True
   b. False

4. **The mind of a successful person is:**

   a. usually in a lower I.Q. range.
   b. smarter than others.
   c. hard to understand because it comes naturally.
   d. on call at all times.

5. **The following traits are shared by top Customer Service professionals except:**

   a. viewing getting ahead as a goal.
   b. working hard.
   c. viewing success as relational to salary.
   d. not being afraid to put themselves on the line.

6. **Every business decision we make should be geared toward holding firm for our employer's sake?**

   a. True
   b. False

7. **If we display traits of honesty and candor, we are demonstrating the concept of:**

   a. integrity.
   b. fairness.
   c. diligence.
   d. incompetence.

8. **Some companies pay those with CSS certificates more than ordinary workers.**

   a. True
   b. False

9. **Company loyalty requires an employee to:**

   a. establish friendships inside the competitor's company to discuss work ideas.
   b. stay on the same page with shifting company goals.
   c. argue with customers (if necessary) to get your company's position across.
   d. volunteer for an assignment at the company picnic.

10. **Effective customer service operations will:**

    a. increase customer loyalty and retention.
    b. increase overall sales revenues.
    c. provide competitive advantage.
    d. All of the above.

11. **A complaint is called what kind of feedback?**

    a. Unwanted
    b. Negative
    c. Positive
    d. Not called feedback at all

12. If a company's website is maintained by an outsourced company of web designers and consultants, then the CSS will not be troubled with customer feedback concerning the web site. All feedback should be directed to the consulting firm.

    a. True
    b. False

13. What is customer feedback?

    a. A customer relating their opinions and perceptions of your company, its products, and their experience with the company.
    b. Incessant nagging.
    c. Complaints.
    d. Sales created by customer word-of-mouth .

14. Why is a CSS concerned with all aspects of customer feedback to the company?

    a. If a CSS wants a promotion, he/she has to know it all.
    b. The CSS is the first contact with a caller and must know enough about the company to route the call to the person who can handle it.
    c. A CSS is not responsible for all aspects of customer feedback.
    d. A CSS is not responsible for all aspects of their company.

15. What is the most important reason for an employer to recognize the personality types of employees?

    a. To place an employee in the position where he/she can be the most effective.
    b. To place an employee where he/she can make the most friends.
    c. To keep an employee 'out of your hair.'
    d. To prevent discord.

16. It is not necessarily helpful for you to know your own personality type.

    a. True
    b. False

17. To keep your emotions from controlling your decisions, it is a good idea to:

    a. ask someone else to make the decision for you.
    b. make a chart listing assets and liabilities of all possible decisions.
    c. toss a coin.
    d. go with the decision that "feels" best.

18. If you are dating someone at your work place, it is best to:

    a. share your happiness with the other employees.
    b. pretend you don't know each other at work.
    c. be discreet and don't discuss the situation with other employees.
    d. rehash last night's date with your co-workers.

19. If your day becomes too stressful, you should take a minute to relax and think of something peaceful.

    a. True
    b. False

20. If your coworker is dealing with a tragic situation, your best bet is to:

    a. ignore the situation.
    b. be helpful without prying into his/her affairs.
    c. do nothing. He/she didn't help you when you were having a bad time.
    d. give him/her advice on 'rising above' the problem.

21. If your coworker takes charge and starts to order you around, you know you're dealing with a Phlegmatic personality.

    a. True
    b. False

22. A person with a Sanguine personality is ideally suited for a sales job.

    a. True
    b. False

Chapter 32. Customer Service Specialist Practice Examination and Answers

23. The CSS testing program was started in:

    a. 1980.
    b. 1990.
    c. 2000.
    d. 2002.

24. The concept of offering a customer service skills program was originally proposed by:

    a. military educators.
    b. mass merchandiser companies.
    c. independent service shop owners.
    d. large manufacturing companies in Washington state.

25. Customer service problems were shifted around in the 70's and 80's as a cost cutting policy by many major companies.

    a. True
    b. False

26. Soft skills such as those taught in CSS courses can't be learned.

    a. True
    b. False

27. Including CSS type training concepts in technical training programs usually short-changes CSS and soft skills.

    a. True
    b. False

28. You work for a mass merchandiser. After parking in the large parking lot, you could take one of the shopping carts back into the building and put it in the cart pickup area, but you don't. This is not an example of a pro-profit employee.

    a. True
    b. False

29. Cold telephone calls are classified as a _____ marketing tool.

    a. premium and incentive
    b. outdoor
    c. telemarketing
    d. discount program

30. To ensure products and services reach intended customers, _____ is required.

    a. analysis
    b. follow-up
    c. comparison
    d. meeting

31. Effective customer service operations will:

    a. increase customer loyalty and retention.
    b. increase overall sales revenues.
    c. provide competitive advantage.
    d. all of the above.

32. Continuous improvement in the customer service picture means:

    a. using customer feedback to improve the overall operations of the company, its products and services.
    b. using customer feedback to increase customer call backs and recalls.
    c. using customer feedback to extend overall company bureaucracy, its products and services.
    d. using customer feedback to avoid empowerment, discussion groups and exchanges.

33. If your company doesn't seem to be paying you as much as you feel you are worth, there is no reason to devote your best efforts to your work.

    a. True
    b. False

34. Since a public library is usually a tax-supported service, the idea of being a pro-profit employee does not apply to that type of employee.

    a. True
    b. False

35. ROI means:

    a. Reduce Our Inventory.
    b. Return On Investment.
    c. Returned On Invoice.
    d. Reduced Overtime Income.

36. **Which of the following might be considered pro-profit actions?**

   a. Making sure service literature or product catalogs are filed in proper order.
   b. Smoking in the rest room, rather than at your bench.
   c. Taking a bundle of ball point pens (which advertise the company's products) home for personal use.
   d. Stopping work in plenty of time to be prepared to clock out right at quitting time.

37. **Which of the following would be considered pro-profit activities?**

   a. Building relationships with fellow workers by discussing last evening's bowling.
   b. Submitting an employee suggestion to improve efficiency or safety.
   c. Leading your coworkers in asking management to relieve your department workers of clean-up details.
   d. Calling in sick because you can't be at your best with a hangover.

38. **If you have poor handwriting, you should:**

   a. always type your messages.
   b. speed up in order to hurry through the unpleasant task of writing longhand.
   c. slow down and try to improve the legibility.
   d. ask others to do your writing.

39. **If you aren't a good writer because of bad grammar, spelling, or punctuation, you should:**

   a. avoid writing any more than necessary.
   b. ask someone else to write it for you.
   c. tell people what you want, thus avoiding the embarrassment of not knowing the English language.
   d. write as often as possible.

40. **Asking clients to demonstrate what they under stand, is not a good policy.**

   a. True
   b. False

41. **Pencil and paper are great tools for organizing your thoughts.**

   a. True
   b. False

42. **Developing routines is a bad idea because you can get stuck in them.**

   a. True
   b. False

43. **Using a sophisticated phone message system can simplify office communications.**

   a. True
   b. False

44. **Most office/service center software is too costly to be effective.**

   a. True
   b. False

45. **Preparing to unload the service van, you back up to a loading area. Unfortunately, you also back over another worker, who claims you were negligent. Most likely:**

   a. the injured worker has no claim as he or she should have been watching out.
   b. the company will have to pay the injury claim.
   c. you, the driver of the van, will be held personally responsible for the accident.
   d. the injured worker will have health and accident insurance and that will cover the costs of the accident.

46. **It is unfair for a company to refuse to hire you, just because you have a history of drug abuse.**

   a. True
   b. False

Chapter 32. Customer Service Specialist Practice Examination and Answers

47. **You know some of the employees are stealing small items from the company you work for. The best thing for you to do is:**

    a. ignore these activities. It is none of your concern.
    b. call the police.
    c. bring the activity to the attention of management.
    d. plead with the workers to quit stealing.

48. **If the company is paying you less than comparable workers in similar businesses, it is fair to steal a few things or to take care of personal business while on duty.**

    a. True
    b. False

49. **Wasting time, or taking care of personal business while being paid to take care of company business, is stealing, just as if you were taking a tool or product of the company for yourself.**

    a. True
    b. False

50. **Not offering to give the customer a receipt, with the intent of not including the income in sales for the day, is a criminal act.**

    a. True
    b. False

51. **Tech support is an expense for a company. If a company claims to have technical support for the products it sells, but then knowingly hires fewer help desk workers than it needs, it is shifting these costs to the purchaser of its products and is defrauding the customer.**

    a. True
    b. False

52. **A good way to punish a deadbeat customer who didn't pay his service bill is to:**

    a. take him or her to small claims court.
    b. post the unpaid invoice in plain view for future customers to see.
    c. publish a notice naming that customer in the local newspaper.
    d. take several big guys, go back to the home and take your parts back.

53. **Which of these rules might be considered a BAD rule?**

    a. No sexual harassment
    b. No parking in the boss's spot
    c. No pay checks till 4 PM
    d. Only one trip to the water fountain each morning

54. **Which of these rules might be considered a GOOD rule?**

    a. Keep lights off unless absolutely necessary.
    b. Keep food and drink away from your key board.
    c. It is mandatory that you attend a certain church.
    d. All employees must wear crew-cuts.

55. **One way to build trust with coworkers is to:**

    a. cheat if you find one or more of them cheating.
    b. show them you will report them if you suspect they might be doing some thing detrimental to the company.
    c. help an employee resist the temptation to cheat.
    d. secretly report all violations to management.

56. **Showing your boss a way to save time or money for the company is a good way to gain trust.**

    a. True
    b. False

57. **The company inadvertently pays you for over time hours which you did not put in. What should you do to gain trust?**

    a. Go to the payroll department and show them the mistake.
    b. Accept the windfall.
    c. Act as if you didn't notice the mistake.
    d. Explain that you thought you had worked the overtime.

Chapter 32. Customer Service Specialist Practice Examination and Answers

58. Company policies are rules within the company that govern how the business and employees are expected to behave.

   a. True
   b. False

59. Company policies protect the company and employees from:

   a. fraud.
   b. liability.
   c. sanctions.
   d. bankruptcy.

60. Noncompliance to company policies does what?

   a. Creates a fun workplace.
   b. Creates a burden on others.
   c. Destroys businesses.
   d. Makes the day more enjoyable.

61. Who usually creates company policies?

   a. Corporate executives
   b. Corporate attorneys
   c. Managers
   d. All of the above

62. What factor is considered when forming company policies?

   a. Organizational vision
   b. Corporate culture
   c. Industrial climate
   d. All above factors

63. Policies are implemented from the bottom of the organizational structure.

   a. True
   b. False

64. Corporate policies are based on what?

   a. Competitor's policies
   b. Mission statement
   c. Strategic goals
   d. b and c

65. Company policies should be:

   a. locked away.
   b. available.
   c. disposed of.
   d. read daily.

66. Who is responsible for complying with company policies?

   a. Everyone
   b. Employees only
   c. Officers and managers
   d. Customers

67. The most important company policies are:

   a. those that affect you.
   b. those that are issued by the corporate office.
   c. those issued by direct supervisors.
   d. all company policies.

68. When communicating, we use symbols such as:

   a. words.
   b. gestures.
   c. personal appearance.
   d. All of the above are correct.

69. Which of the following terms would be the most appropriate to use when speaking about your new secretary?

   a. My Girl Friday
   b. My administrative assistant
   c. My male administrative assistant
   d. My female administrative assistant

70. By saving just five minutes a day for five days per week you would:

   a. not make much difference in managing your time.
   b. be able to finish a tough project.
   c. have saved and gained 21 hours by the end of the year.
   d. none of the above.

Chapter 32. Customer Service Specialist Practice Examination and Answers

71. It is always best to use technical language when dealing with a customer.

    a. True
    b. False

72. Potential customers responding to your marketing campaign are called _____ sales.

    a. involuntary
    b. voluntary
    c. incidental
    d. general

73. Talking and communicating are the same thing.

    a. True
    b. False

74. Using the "You Attitude" when communicating with customers is:

    a. unethical.
    b. unnecessary.
    c. dishonest.
    d. building goodwill.

75. Universal remote controls are simple for everyone to understand.

    a. True
    b. False

76. If you cannot help a customer with a request, you should:

    a. suggest where he/she might find help.
    b. tell him or her it is not your department.
    c. never mention a competitor.
    d. call the boss.

77. Communication and customer service go hand-in-hand because:

    a. communicating can help solve problems.
    b. good communication promotes respect.
    c. a company is judged by the ability of its employees to communicate.
    d. All of the above are correct.

78. Telephone conversations give the participants a greater understanding of the intended message because they give the listener a feeling of the caller's:

    a. mood.
    b. height.
    c. weight.
    d. marital status.

79. Your best opportunity for success in dealing with a customer's problem begins:

    a. after you've had plenty of time to consider the situation.
    b. when you come across a solution.
    c. when you answer the phone.
    d. before the phone rings.

80. Before you can solve a customer's problem, you need to find out:

    a. who he/she is.
    b. what is the nature of his/her situation.
    c. when the problem occurred.
    d. All of the above.

81. Letting the customer know that he or she has made a mistake is good because:

    a. it shows that you know more than he/she does.
    b. it makes you feel better about your own knowledge.
    c. it keeps the customer in his/her rightful place.
    d. None of the above.

82. The following information needs to be included in all faxes.

    a. The company's quarterly report.
    b. A cover sheet.
    c. A notation of how much time you spent on this fax.
    d. Your lunch order.

Chapter 32. Customer Service Specialist Practice Examination and Answers

83. The best way to make certain a fax was transmitted properly is to:

    a.   come back later and see if the machine has produced any error code messages.

    b.   wait for the customer to call and let you know if it was received.

    c.   'babysit' your fax until the machine has confirmed it transmitted.

    d.   allow another coworker who is already at the fax machine to send it after his/her fax is done.

84. During an interview, which of the following would probably be LEAST considered?

    a.   Your attitude
    b.   Night school electronics classes
    c.   Your personal appearance
    d.   You're "always on the job."

85. A disadvantage of formal training of employees is:

    a.   the employee is away from his job place.
    b.   the employee will be more knowledgeable.
    c.   most employees do not like homework.
    d.   all of the above.

86. Which of the following packing scenarios is cause for concern that the job is not satisfactory?

    a.   Corrugated box sides are bowed out.
    b.   Shaking the box lets inside objects move back and forth and rattle.
    c.   The masking tape used to secure the box flaps appears to be tearing.
    d.   All of the above.

87. Which of these is most susceptible to damage from permanent magnets?

    a.   Credit cards
    b.   Cellular telephone antennas
    c.   Polarized power connectors
    d.   AA batteries

88. If you are having computer hardware problems that you are not sure how to repair, you should:

    a.   unplug the equipment and attempt the service yourself.

    b.   contact a computer repair specialist since you aren't trained in such repair.

    c.   leave the problem to be found by someone who might know more.

    d.   while wearing safety goggles, use a fairly large sledge hammer to beat the computer into very small pieces, sweep them into the trash and ask for a new system.

89. So long as a worker sets his own work hours at a company, he can be classified as 'contract labor' even if he does operate out of a company truck.

    a.   True
    b.   False

90. So long as a worker uses company-owned test equipment and tools and the company vehicles to perform his work, he is not allowed to also use some of his own private test equipment or tools.

    a.   True
    b.   False

91. One negative result of an employer hiring a worker, but treating him or her as 'contract labor' might be:

    a.   the employee resents not being an employee, knowing he legally should be.

    b.   the employee doesn't trust management in its other activities since it is cheating on him.

    c.   the worker may file a complaint with the wage-hour agencies, thus costing the company far more than it would have paid operating legally.

    d.   All of the above are correct.

Chapter 32. Customer Service Specialist Practice Examination and Answers

92. Records management involves:

a. planning record keeping activities.
b. training users of records.
c. controlling records.
d. All the above.

93. Responsible companies use records for:

a. selling data to other companies.
b. performing quantitative and qualitative analysis.
c. spying on the customer.
d. identifying competitors.

94. We pass information to higher levels to:

a. let the boss know we are working.
b. divide areas of specialty.
c. answer the next call.
d. pass the responsibility.

95. You demonstrate company loyalty by:

a. supporting company policies.
b. constantly looking to change company policies.
c. checking to see how your company ranks with competitors.
d. all of the above.

96. An organization may be required by law to keep what kind of data?

a. Employee records
b. Hazardous waste disposal
c. Customer income levels
d. a and b

97. Complete destruction of records stored on magnetic media involves:

a. shredding.
b. emptying the recycle bin.
c. throwing it away.
d. degaussing.

98. What is a Career Path?

a. A plan and map for your career
b. The progression of jobs you have held
c. A training plan
d. A company hierarchy

99. Which of the following could be a valid e-mail address?

a. Richardnixon@sneaky
b. Bobknighttemper.com
c. Jeffgordon@racing.net
d. Frank.sinatra.com

100. Ethical values of right and wrong can be influenced by reason and changed?

a. True
b. False

101. In a confrontation who should "come out on top?"

a. Customer Service Representative
b. Employer
c. Customer
d. All of the above

102. Trade organizations are beneficial because they foster:

a. communications among professionals.
b. common solutions among competitors.
c. practices and standards that benefit everyone.
d. all the above.

103. Teams exist to:

a. make life easier for us and others.
b. combine the efforts of several people.
c. let others do our work.
d. report the actions of workers.

104. Who is responsible for the success of the team?

a. Only the team leader
b. The entire team
c. The project leader
d. The C.E.O.

Chapter 32. Customer Service Specialist Practice Examination and Answers

105. An effective team leader would deal with conflict by:

a. immediately disciplining those involved.
b. making a report and filing it with Human Resources.
c. yelling and screaming.
d. immediately rectifying it.

106. What is the first step in the problem-solving process?

a. Report the problem
b. Solve the problem
c. Collect and analyze data
d. Identify the cause

107. A person who acts as a bully in the work place is often that way because:

a. of his or her superior ability with the job at hand.
b. of his or her feeling of incompetence.
c. it's the only way to get subordinates to work.
d. management will notice his or her ability to work with people.

108. The person with a Sanguine personality is very shy.

a. True
b. False

109. If you need someone to fill a position that requires a lot of planning, meeting deadlines, and attention to detail, your best bet is a:

a. Sanguine.
b. Phlegmatic.
c. Melancholy.
d. Choleric.

110. Never Criticize, Condemn or _____.

a. Castigate
b. Compliment
c. Cauterize
d. Complain

111. If a customer asks you to spend a few minutes as he brags about his expensive duck hunting dog, you should explain that you are too busy to play with dumb animals.

a. True
b. False

112. Practicing etiquette while performing service work or talking to people on the help line may be nice, but it is a wasteful use of time.

a. True
b. False

113. Which of the following would be an effective way to check for punctuation errors?

a. Use a writer's manual.
b. Use grammar-check on your computer.
c. Have a colleague proofread the letter.
d. All of the above are correct.

114. The customer has what appears to be a vicious dog which seems determined to attack you as you approach the house. What might you do?

a. Spray the dog with Mace and warn the customer that your firm will not make further service calls until the dog is killed.
b. Yell at the customer and tell them to get that *$#%@*& animal restrained or face a (&%$#@ lawsuit.
c. Call from your vehicle and ask that the dog be tied or penned up.
d. Call the dog catcher.

Chapter 32. Customer Service Specialist Practice Examination and Answers

115. What is the ETA Solution?

   a. Evaluate the problem, Troubleshoot/Test the problem, Authenticate/Answer question, Ignore the problem

   b. Evade the problem, Troubleshoot/Test the problem, Authenticate/Answer question, Solve the problem

   c. Evaluate the problem, Troubleshoot/Test the problem, Authenticate/Answer question, Solve the problem

   d. Evaluate the problem, Troubleshoot/Test the problem, Authenticate/Answer question, What is the problem?

116. To ensure that you are giving the customer exemplary services you should:

   a. play, "You and Me" against the company.

   b. be "more than fair" and give away the store.

   c. use the ETA Solution.

   d. both A and B are correct.

117. How should you answer the telephone?

   a. Answer with your own stylized greeting reflecting your personality

   b. Answer the telephone by the third ring.

   c. Write down whatever information they give you, without asking any questions.

   d. As soon as the phone rings, answer and say **"Please Hold."**

118. In order to manage your time, you must first:

   a. prioritize your tasks.

   b. use an agenda or diary.

   c. make a "to-do" list.

   d. none of the above.

119. A Priority Matrix designed for one department:

   a. can be used by other departments.

   b. cannot be used by any other department.

   c. is all that is needed for one company.

   d. needs to list all appointments and schedules.

120. Real multi-tasking is only possible:

   a. with one person.

   b. with the first computer.

   c. with a team.

   d. none of the above.

121. One way an employer can increase employee satisfaction is:

   a. criticize the employee in public for mistakes.

   b. scrutinize every facet of the work assigned.

   c. give the employee leeway to complete the job as he/she sees fit.

   d. provide a list of instructions that must be followed for each step of the task.

122.. It is usually good practice to just write-off debts incurred by deadbeat customers as the cost of taking them to court outweighs the possible amount recovered.

   a. True

   b. False

123. It is not the responsibility of workers to prevent or reduce incidents of cheating. That is management's job and a reason they get paid more.

   a. True

   b. False

124. Running a credit check on a customer is usually illegal.

   a. True

   b. False

125. People who have no telephone may be more likely to have bad credit than those who do.

   a. True

   b. False

Chapter 32. Customer Service Specialist Practice Examination and Answers

126. A business which offers a help-desk service for buyers of its products, then reduces the help-desk pool so that callers must be on hold for long periods of time is:

    a. more efficient than others.
    b. cheating the public and their customers.
    c. not legally liable for fraud.
    d. simply taking advantage of the fact that their employee's time is much more valuable than that of a servicer or the public.

127. Professional organizations are:

    a. technical only.
    b. non-technical only.
    c. technical or non-technical.
    d. tax-exempt.

128. One reason to be nice to the boss's secretary is:

    a. so you will be invited to the boss' next party.
    b. you might like to ask her for a date some day.
    c. she signs the paychecks.
    d. secretaries usually have a lot of power with the boss.

129. Holding membership in important organizations usually results in a pay raise or promotion.

    a. True
    b. False

130. You may have the opportunity for a leadership position in an organization if:

    a. you are the most important member.
    b. you are a CEO or Vice-president in your day job.
    c. you make a generous donation.
    d. you make an important and valuable contribution.

131. Membership in a professional organization may be absolutely required for some jobs.

    a. True
    b. False

132. _____ is usually the biggest obstacle with the least validity.

    a. Happiness
    b. Anxiety
    c. Fear
    d. Depression

133. Which of the following "resistant" types is the easiest to identify?

    a. Passive
    b. Aggressive
    c. Apathetic
    d. Passive-aggressive

134. Which type of resistance is the most diffi cult to identify because of false impressions of support and agreement?

    a. Apathetic
    b. Passive
    c. Materialistic
    d. Resistant

135. The _____ type can always find an excuse for his/her inaction, saying "I'll be happy to cooperate, just as soon as I finish…"

    a. passive-aggressive
    b. competent
    c. denial
    d. neutral

136. When _____ is introduced, we feel threatened, or fearful.

    a. resistance
    b. attitude
    c. emotion
    d. change

137. "Fear of the unknown" is usually a learned emotion, based solely on a/an _____ of past experiences.

    a. collection
    b. generalization
    c. variety
    d. abundance

Chapter 32. Customer Service Specialist Practice Examination and Answers

138. Listing habits and_____ , based on past experiences, may direct some to cling to old practices that don't work any more.

    a. belief systems
    b. established patterns
    c. bad manners
    d. consistent ideas

139. In making the transition to positive change, the first step is to realize that change is _____and necessary for personal growth.

    a. irritating
    b. available
    c. frequent
    d. inevitable

140. The customer will usually follow your lead if you do what during communication?

    a. Compliment his clothing
    b. Set a good example
    c. Offer sound information
    d. Shake his hand

141. With listening comes the need to sense, interpret, and evaluate.

    a. True
    b. False

142. Listeners provide feedback to the speaker through their nonverbal messages.

    a. True
    b. False

143. People listen through filters.

    a. True
    b. False

144. Which of the following is NOT a technique for effective telephone listening?

    a. Body language
    b. Ask questions
    c. Repeat what you hear
    d. Take notes

145. The following is an example of an internal customer.

    a. Customer with a billing problem
    b. Customer with a technical problem
    c. Coworker
    d. Customer with a complaint

146. In order to be an effective speaker, you should do which of the following?

    a. Use judgmental descriptions.
    b. Generalize.
    c. State opinions as facts.
    d. Stick to the facts. Don't use gossip or rumor.

147. Voltage can be thought of as:

    a. a pressure that moves electrons from one point to another.
    b. the amount of electrons per second that pass through a point.
    c. current flow from an AC source.
    d. a and b above.

148. A store display is a good distance from the wall receptacle that is to be used. The best extension cords to use would be:

    a. a 50 foot #14 cord.
    b. two 25 foot #16 cords.
    c. one 50 foot #12 cord.
    d. one 50 foot #10 cord.

149. The term "experiencing the company's system" means any aspect of a company that a customer encounters when they contact the company to do business.

    a. True
    b. False

Chapter 32. Customer Service Specialist Practice Examination and Answers

150. Which is the most proactive way to prove the effectiveness of an advertising campaign for a product?

a. Scrutinize changes in revenue streams closely and frequently.
b. Form a team to experience the advertising first hand to see if they feel compelled to purchase the product.
c. Ask customers how they rate the advertising and if it influenced their decision..
d. Hire consultants to form focus groups to give feedback on a commercial's appeal.

151. What are customer expectations?

a. What customers expect a CSS to do for them.
b. What customers expect products to do for them.
c. What customers expect a company to do for them.
d. Customers' preconceived perceptions of company image, its products and the service they expect.

152. Why is the written survey the best format to use to solicit feedback?

a. Customers desire to become novelists and like to write.
b. It is the most effective in amassing the responses from customers.
c. Customers will not use any other method.
d. It is the least effective in amassing responses from customer.

153. An excellent way to get ahead at work is to socialize with your coworkers.

a. True
b. False

154. One reason for giving employees some autonomy on the job might be:

a. the workers will feel better about their jobs.
b. the employer wouldn't have to come in to work.
c. they might expect you to do their work.
d. they will expect more money.

155. Workplace gossip is:

a. inevitable, so just join in.
b. just good, clean fun.
c. a recipe for disaster.
d. something that is expected of you.

156. Manners are very important at work.

a. True
b. False

Chapter 32. Customer Service Specialist Practice Examination and Answers

ANSWER KEY

1.-b	51.-a	101.-d	151.-d
2.-c	52.-a	102.-d	152.-b
3.-b	53.-d	103.-b	153.-b
4.-d	54.-b	104.-b	154.-b
5.-c	55.-c	105.-d	155.-c
6.-b	56.-a	106.-c	156.-a
7.-a.	57.-a	107.-b	
8.-a	58.-a	108.-b	
9.-b	59.-b	109.-c	
10.-d	60.-c	110.-d	
11.-b	61.-d	111.-b	
12.-b	62.-d	112.-d	
13.-a	63.-d	113.-d	
14.-b	64.-b	114.-c	
15.-a	65.-b	115.-c	
16.-b.	66.-a	116.-c	
17.-b	67.-d	117.-b	
18.-c	68.-d	118.-c	
19.-a	69.-b	119.-b	
20.-b	70.-c	120.-c	
21.-b	71.-b	121.-c	
22.-a	72.-b	122.-b	
23.-b	73.-b	123.-b	
24.-d	74.-d	124.-b	
25.-a	75.-b	125.-a	
26.-b	76.-a	126.-b	
27.-a	77.-d	127.-c	
28.-a	78.-a	128.-d	
29.-c	79.-d	129.-b	
30.-b	80.-d	130.-d	
31.-d	81.-d	131.-a	
32.-a	82.-b	132.-c	
33.-b	83.-c	133.-b	
34.-b	84.-d	134.-b	.
35.-b	85-.a	135.-a	
36.-a	86.-d	136.-d	
37.-b	87.-a	137.-a	
38.-c	88.-b	138.-a	
39.-d	89.-b	139.-d	
40.-b	90.-a	140.-b	
41.-a	91.-d	141.-a	
42.-b	92.-d	142.-a	
43.-a	93.-b	143.-a	
44.-b	94.-b	144.-a	
45.-b	95.-a	145.-c	
46.-b	96.-d	146.-d	
47.-c	97.-d	147.-a	
48.-b	98.-a	148.-a	
49.-a	99.-c	149.-a	
50.-a	100.-a	150.-c	

ETA Testing Sites for FCC and CET Examinations

CAs—Certification Administrators

The following listed examination administrators are the heart of the CET and FCC testing program. Without them there would be no professional certification for electronics technicians. Finding a test site to take FCC Commercial License exams would require traveling long distances and being there on specific dates. We all owe a lot to the CAs.

When you are nearly ready to attempt either type of exam, contact the closest CA. Understand that some CAs are electronics instructors in schools who cannot just drop what they are doing and administer an examination for you. Ask the CA when it might be convenient for he/she and the institution to monitor your exam. Be sure the CA knows which exams you want to take. If you are in the military service, your education office and the DANTES TCO will obtain exams and set a time for you to take the exams, either CET or FCC. Bear in mind that military education offices are usually less aware of the details of the CET and FCC programs than civilian electronics technical schools, thus you should be aware of the rules and options of the program and help to make sure you are taking the correct exam and abiding by the other criteria of the FCC and CET program.

Many public libraries offer to administer exams. If there is no listed CA above, contact your local public library, get agreement to administer your exam(s) and call ETA with the library official's name, address, phone, etc. You do not have to register in advance for ETA exams, and you pay the exam fee at the time of sitting for that exam. A money order, or your charge card numbers are the preferred method of exam payment.

You can help your CA and the ETA Testing Staff by making sure you include the examination number on your information sheet as well as on each answer sheet. Be sure every word you write on the information form is legible. If your school teaches electronics and is not an established CA site, have the school contact ETA: 800-288-3824, or e-mail us at eta@eta-i.org .

APO/FPO
Academia, Edgardo, CST, Mann, HHC, 7th Signal Brigade, chiefacademia@yahoo.com
Dewey, Jody, FPO, 095242875, USS HARRY S TRUMAN, 7574437885
Stout, Terry, FPO AA, Onboard Maritime Training, 9546552182, terrystout2000@yahoo.com
Alabama
Duck, Barry, Alexander City, Central AL CC, 2562154403, bduck@cacc.edu
Lockhart, James, Bessemer, ITT,2054975799, jlockhart@itt-tech.edu
Taylor, Roderic, CET, Bessemer, ITT, 8004887033, rptaylor@itt-tech.edu
Butler, Elbert, CET, Childersburg, Central AL CC, 2563782074
Robbins, Mary, CST, Birmingham, Herzing, 2052714265,maryb@bhm.herzing.edu
Middlebrooks, Stan, CETsr, Homewood, 352094816, Herzing, 2059162800, smiddlebrooks@bhm.herzing.edu
Tucker, Lee, CET, Tuscaloosa, Shelton State, 2053912450, ltucker@sheltonstate.edu
Banks, Sherman, Decatur, Calhoun CC, 2563062972, smb@calhoun.edu
Rose, Mark, Muscle Shoals, Muscle Shoals Ctr, 2563892660, mrose@mscs.k12.al.us
Atnip, James, Huntsville, Priest Electronics, 2566536505, atnipj@bellsouth.net
McNair, Barry, Attalla, Etowah Co CTC, 2565383312, barry_mcnair@ecboe.org
Ashley, Julie, Rainsville, NE AL CC, 2566382325, ashleyj@nacc.edu
Cohen, Julie, Rainsville   AL, NE AL CC, 2562286001,cohenj@nacc.edu
Griggs, Nancy, Rainsville, NE AL CC   2562286001, griggsn@nacc.edu
Rogers, Fred, Rainsville, NE AL CC, 2562286001, fred@nacc.edu
Thomason, Pat, CET, Montgomery, Trenholm, 3344204374, pthomason@trenholmtech.cc.al.us
Paramore, Thomas, Ozark, Enterprise-Ozark CC, 3347545113, tparamore@eocc.edu
Bundrick, Tracy, CETsr, Opp, LB Wallace CC, 3344935348, tbundrick@lbwcc.edu
Harder, Gerald, Mobile, Remington Coll, 2513438200, gerald.harder@remingtoncollege.edu
Jones, Carlton, Opelika, Southern Union CC, 3347498678, cjones@suscc.edu
Jones, Douglas, Opelika, Southern Union State CC, 3347456437,djones@suscc.edu
Arkansas
Cook, Jerry, N Little Rock, Union Pacific, 5013732808, gpcook@up.com
Rushing, William, Forrest City, Crowley's Ridge Tech Inst, 8706335411
Duggan, Paula, Harrison, N Arkansas Coll, 8703913533
Baker, Larry, Fort Smith, U of AR-Fort Smith, 4797887712, lbaker@uafortsmith.edu
Arizona
Dominique, Jeffrey, FOT, Phoenix, NT, 6024140606, office@f-n-t.com
Gardoski, Bradley, Phoenix, FNT, 6024140606, brad@f-n-t.com
Wallace, Paul, Phoenix, FNT,6024140606, office@f-n-t.com
Smith, Richard, Tempe, US Dept of Energy, 4807073579, rlandmithsmith@yahoo.com
Gelman, Harold, FOI, Yuma, Advanced Tech Inst, 9283739300,skills@votectraining.com
Phelan, Stuart, Yuma, KOFA HS, 9287265750, sphelan@yumaed.org
Russo, Joseph, Surprise, Light Brigade (Fiber Only), 6238761458, vzn05uai@verizon.net
Daskam, Richard, CET, Tucson, ITT, 5204089277, RDaskam@itt-tech.edu
Nichols, Kimberly, MBA, Tucson, S AZ Instit, 5205737399
Nicks, Tad, Tucson, Pima CC,5207471170,tnicks9309@aol.com
Sena, Emory, FOI, Tucson, S AZ Instit, 5205737399, emorys@cox.net
Wood, Carol, FOI, Kingman, Light Brigade,9287536773, sales@lightbrigade.com
Bahamas
Josey, Patrick, Nassau, Bahamas Tech, 2423932804, patrickjosey@msn.com
McFarlane, Colin, Nassau, Bahamas Tech, 2425026382, colinbmc@hotmail.com
California
Chavez, Eric, Los Angeles, LA Trade Tech, 2137633789, chavezel@lattc.edu

Runas, Arnulfo, CETsr, Torrance, ITT, 3103801555, arunas@itt-tech.edu
Atarodi, Abe, Sylmar, ITT, 8183645151, aatarodi@itt-tech.edu
Rivera, Kenneth, Chino, JM Fiber Optics, 9096283445, krivera@jmfiberoptics.com
Franceschi, George, FOI, Spring Valley, KITCO, 7572162224, george.franceschi@navy.mil
Barbee, Steven, Carlsbad, APT, 8004318488, sbarbee1@aol.com
Cawley, Thomas, B-VoIP, Carlsbad, APT,8004318488, tcawley@aptc.com
Cruickshank, Debra, Carlsbad, APT, 8004318488, djcruic@starstream.net
Meyers, Warren, Carlsbad, APT, 8004318488, meyerswarren@hotmail.com
Rasmussen, Jerry, Carlsbad, APT, 8004318488, thomasryan@math.com
Uribe, Xavier, FOI, Carlsbad, APT, 8004318488,xuribe@aptc.com
West, Everette, Carlsbad, APT, 8004318488
Wolf, Timothy, Carlsbad, APT, 8004318488, tawolf2@hotmail.com
Zmarthie, Kevin, Carlsbad, APT, 8004318488, zmarthie@yahoo.com
Sullivan, James, Carlsbad, APT, 8004318488
Tennell, Craig, Carlsbad, APT, 8004318488
Villaman, Jose, El Cajon, Advanced Training, 6195962766, tony@advancedtraining.edu
Mikesell, Richard, CETa, Oceanside, AESA, 7604331577
Julian, Fred, San Diego, San Diego City, 6193883720, fjulian@sdccd.net
Wolford, Gerald, San Diego, Associated Tech Coll, 6192342181x206, gwolford@atcmil.com
Moreno, Antonio, CET, Rebasar Sys, 7603550968, amoreno@rebasar.com
Faro, Tom, CETma, Victorville, 923925849, 7602454271, t.faro@verizon.net
Lowell, Carl, San Bernardino, ITT, 9098064600, clowell@itt-tech.edu
Barot, Harsh, Anaheim, ITT, 7145353700, hbarot@itt-tech.edu
Kennington, Kay, Brea, Underwriters, 7142233658, kay.kennington@us.ul.com
Noury, Mohammad, Oxnard, Modern Inst Techn, 8059832444, mitvocationeducation@yahoo.com
Montanez, Pedro, CETsr, Point Mugu, US Navy, 8054885961, psm0169@cablerocket.com
Payne, Daniel, Fresno, Cable Links, 5592778555, slummyclc02@cs.com
Slumberger, Sandy, Fresno, Cable Links, 5592778555, sslumberger@clcinc.us
Shahin, Paul, Milpitas, Heald Coll, 4089344900, paul_shahin@heald.edu
Spinale, Vincent, CETa, San Jose, 951311230, UL, 4088762150, vincent.s.spinale@us.ul.com
Trebino, Marjorie, Valley Springs, Chuck Trebino A & P, 2097721694
Thompson, William Brian, FOI, Auburn, MT&E, 5302681108, brian@psyber.com
Krempin, Robert, Vacaville, The Lighthouse, 7073229410
Blubaugh, Jonathan, Colfax, AESA, 8003452742
Lightfoot, Herbert, Colfax, AESA, 8003452742
Pinkney, Calvin, FOI, Colfax, AESA, 5303466792
Solomito, Sharon, Colfax, AESA, 5303466792
Teeters, Dennis, Dutch Flat, MT&E, louzypher@earthlink.net
Bugarin, Richard, FOT, Roseville, ETA-I, 9163003192, kf6wmf@hotmail.com
Bellamy, Rudolph, Elk Grove, AESA, 9166846601
Kovacs, Michael, Sacramento, Kovacs Eng, mike@kovacsengineering.com
Rodriques, John, FOI, Sacramento, AESA, 8003452742, jrhugger@aol.com
McLeod, Dean, FOI, Grass Valley, MT&E, 5302748365, ldm115@netzero.net
Reddekopp, Wayne, CET, Grass Valley, MT&E, 309131552, wreddekopp@a-m-t-c.com
Banghart, Brad, CET, Redding, Shasta Coll, 5302253948, bbanghart@shastacollege.edu
Canada
Ing, Robert, CESma, Toronto, Ontario, King's Markham, 4168840893, ring549@yahoo.co.uk
Montroy, Tim, CES, Thunder Bay, ONT, AKA Enterprises, 8076232488
Nordal, Allan, Ctech, Pr George, BC, Coll of New Caledonia, 2505622131
Labelle, Michel, Trois-Rivieres, Queb, CEGEP, 5149230817, michel.labelle@cegeptr.qc.ca

Appendix A - ETA Worldwide Certification Administrator Listing

China
Ho, Yiu Kwong, CET, Hong Kong(SAR), China Amateur Radio, ykho2k@yahoo.com.hk
Chong, Norman, SIPIVT, nmchong2001@yahoo.co.uk
Colorado
Holmes-Smith, David, Aurora, Georgetown Inst of Technology, 3033442900, david@culdee.org
Janca, Tom, CETsr, Centenial, Power Eng, 3037711621, trjanca@halfwavelength.com
Berkes, Albert, CET, Denver, Trent Schools, 3033211812, admissions@theschools.com
Cross, Gene, Thorton, Bollman Tech Educ
Hoover, John, Colorado Springs, Tech Education Coll, 7195978446
Bixler, Bob, CETsr, Durango, 9702597727, handibob@earthlink.net
Eubanks, Stanley, Cortez, San Juan Basin Tech Coll, 9705658457,seubanks@sjbtc.edu
Showalter, Leonora, Nucla, TriState Training, 9708647316, lshowalter@tristategt.org
Koch, Gordon, CETma, Grand Junction, Mesa State, 9702552607, gkoch@mesastate.edu
Yon, Jack, Grand Junction, ETA - UTEC, 9702552609, Jyon@mesastate.edu
Counts, Richard, Grand Junction, IntelliTec Coll, 9702458101, rcounts@intelliteccollege.edu
Huisman, George, Grand Junction, IntelliTec Coll, 9702458101, synthrok2a@aol.com
Sakala, Rob, CETa, Fruita, Olde STAR School, 9708588972, star@acsol.net
Meyers, Jerry L, Craig, Tri-State G&T Training, 9708244411, jermey@tristategt.org
Connecticut
Cottone, Gary, Rocky Hill, Automated Technologies, 8607210799, marty@autotechinc.com
Baker, Dolores, CSS, Milford, CT Computer Service, 2038744546, dolores@ctcomp.com
Trela, Kim, Plantsville, CT Computer Service, 8602761285
Houston, Corey, Southbury, Southbury Sch, 2034052587, corey.h@southburyaeronautics.com
Jacobi, Karl, Southbury, Southbury Sch of Aeronautics, 2035567966
Strong, Douglas, Southbury, Southbury Sch, 2034052587, doug.s@southburyaeronautics.com
Delaware
Longwood, Ben, CST, Newark, 3024559445, LongwoodBR@Comcast.net
Burroughs, Karen, Georgetown, Delaware Tech & CC, 3028555982, kburroug@dtcc.edu
Stevens, Richard, Georgetown, DE Tech & CC, 3028555931, rstevens@college.dtcc.edu
Fiji
Goundar, Sam, Raiwaqa, Suva, Univ of the South Pacific, 6793309866, sam.goundar@ag.gov.fj
Jith, Ameet, Lautoka, Australia Pacific Tertiary Inst, 6796652620, aptiltka@connect.com.fj
Florida
Fulbright, Neill, CETsr, Daytona Beach, Embry-Riddle, 3862266651, neill.fulbright@erau.edu
Travis, Glen, CETsr, Daytona Beach, Embry-Riddle Aeronautical, 3862266651
Janik, Louis 6600, Jacksonville, ITT Tech, 9045739100, ljanik@itt-tech.edu
Landry, Robert, CETma, Neptune Beach, ETA, 9042468108, markaman2040@comcast.net
Spraggins, Don, Tallahassee, Lively Tech Ctr, 8504877460, spragginsd@mail.lively.leon.k12.fl.us
Allen, Joe, CET, Panama City Beach, MERCOMMS, 9042237739, Mercomms@aol.com
Cannon, Gary, CETma, Fort Walton Beach, 2cold4me@gmail.com
Conley, Edward, Milton, Locklin Tech Ctr, 8509835700, conleye@mail.santarosa.k12.fl.us
Bonner, Thomas, FOT, Apopka, JDS Uniphase, 4074642145, orbia11@embarqmail.com
Skoczek, Louis, CET,CS, Maitland, Wireless, 4076448907, lou.skoczek@wtecmss.com
Abel, J. Randall, CETsr, Orlando, Wireless Tech, 4078438631, jr.abel@wtecmss.com
Rice, Brian, CETsr, Cocoa, 3216371298, brice10778@cfl.rr.com
Page, John, Dania, RTM Star Ctr, 9549203222, jpage@star-center.com
Farinas, George, CETma, Hialeah, ETA, 3056200911
Bartoszewicz, Paul, CETma, Islamorada, ETA, 3058522443, kab1271@earthlink.net
Lopez, Hector, Coconut Creek, Atlantic Tech, 7543215100, hector.lopez@browardschools.com
Dabbas, Mohammad, CET, Coconut Creek, Broward CC, 9542012429, mdabbas@broward.edu
Weintraub, Neil, CSS, Miami, ITT, 3054773080, nweintraub@itt-tech.edu
Morales, Robert, Miami, George Baker Aviation Sch, 3058713143, gtba@dadeschools.net
Ali, Shaikh, Davie, City Coll, 9544925353, Sali@intelliplans.net
Tehrani, Atoussa, Fort Lauderdale, ITT, 9544679300, ahosseini-tehrani@itt-tech.edu
Huse, Scott, Port Charlotte, Charlotte Tech Ctr, 9412557500, scott_huse@ccps.k12.fl.us
Schrock, Steve, Port Charlotte, Charlotte Tech Ctr, 9412557500, steve_schrock@ccps.k12.fl.us
Panayiotou, Chrys, CET, Ft Pierce, Indian River CC, 7724624386, cpanayio@ircc.cc.fl.us
Georgia
Eichenlaub, Bruce, CETma, Covington, DeKalb Tech, 7707869522, eichenlb@dekalbtech.edu
Lindstrom, Harry, Lawrenceville, Light Brigade (Fiber Only), 7703381647, harryoh@bellsouth.net
Palmer, Greg, Acworth, N Metro Tech, 7709754067, gpalmer@northmetrotech.edu
Lewis, Jim, Statesboro, Ogeechee Tech Coll, 9128711644, jlewis@ogeecheetech.edu
Linebarger, Phillip, CETa, Vidalia, SE Tech Coll, 9125383102, pline@southeasterntech.edu
Bennett, Lamar, Commerce, Royston Business Products, Inc, 7062460477, rbpinc@bellsouth.net
Roberts, Ken, CETa, Athens, Athens Tech Coll, 7063555068, kroberts@athenstech.edu
Thurman, Lamar, CETsr, Rock Spring, NW Tech, 7067643710, lthurman@northwesterntech.edu
Mayo, David, CETsr, Cordele, South Georgia Tech, 2292714057, dmayo@southgatech.edu
Miller, Cecile, Dublin, Heart of Georgia Tech, 4782747643, cecilem@hgtc.org
Willcox, Chester, Dublin, Heart of Georgia Tech, 4782747928, chesterw@hgtc.org
Cardwell, LaVerne, Waycross, Okefenokee Techt, 9122875859, bcardwell@okefenokeetech.edu
Hires, Eric, Jesup, Altamaha Tech Coll, 9125882520, ephires@altamahatech.edu
Teston, Chuck, Jesup, Altamaha Tech Coll, 9125882520, cteston@altamahatech.org
Smith, Jerry , Valdosta, Valdosta Tech Coll, 2292595187, jsmith@valdostatech.edu
Mockalis, George, Albany, Albany Tech Coll, 2297242118
Castongia, Joseph, Albany, Albany Tech Coll, 2294306614, jcastongia@albanytech.edu
During, Donald, Fitzgerald, East Central Tech Coll, 2294682061, dduring@eastcentraltech.edu
Warren, Roy, Fitzgerald, East Central Tech Coll, 2294682061, rwarren@eastcentraltech.edu
Clark, Andrew, Moultrie, Moultrie Tech Coll, 2292174173, atclark@moultrietech.edu
Straws, Demetrice, East Point, United Medical & Business, 4047612335, dstraws@umbi-edu.com
Ghana
Mumuni, Fuseini, CSS, Obuasi, Engineering Training, fabdulmumuni@yahoo.com

Guam
Alicto, Alfred, FOI, Barrigada, Coradi (Telecom Training), 6713445194, alicto@spawar.navy.mil
Hunter, Matthew, Barrigada, Hunter's Inst of Technology, 6714721829, matter2k@hotmail.com
Limtiaco, John, FOI, Barrigada, Guam CC, 6717353033, anital@vzpacifica.net
Tyquiengco, Ricky, FOI, Dededo, Guam CC, 6716320515, rictye@excite.com
Hawaii
Shortsleeve, Alexander, Honolulu, Hawaii Business Coll, 8085244014, admin@hbc.edu
Langenbacher, Mark, Honolulu, Remington Coll, 8089421000, malekospin@yahoo.com
Glass, Randy, CST, Honolulu, Hawaii Business Coll, 8085244014, eta@rjglass.com
Iowa
Salmons, Cliff, CETma, Mason City, NIACC, 6414224283, salmocli@niacc.edu
Philpott, Ian, Cedar Rapids, Kirkwood CC, 3193985899, ian.philpott@kirkwood.edu
Goudy, James, CET, Fairfield, Indian Hills CC, 3194984200, joe.goudy@elpaso.com
Laughead, Robin, CETsr, Davenport, Hamilton Tech Coll, 5633863570
Idaho
Brusse, Glenn, CETma, Boise, Micron, 2083683139, gbrusse@micron.com
Robertson, Michael, Boise, ITT, 2083228844, mrobertson@itt-tech.edu
Siddall, Dan, CETsr, Boise, Hewlett-Packard, 2083774252, siddall@cableone.net
Douglas, Mikel, CETa, Boise, Boise State Univ, 2084264087, mdouglas@boisestate.edu
Jansson, Paul, CET, St. Maries, ETA-I, 2082450113, p.jansson@verizon.net
Illinois
Pierson, Donald, Antioch, USMSS, 8476503002, dpierson55@hotmail.com
Wolfe, Glen, CET, Elk Grove Village, Traces Services, 8479859800, gw1966@hotmail.com
Shen, Steve, Mt Prospect, ITT, 8473758800, sshen@itt-tech.edu
Lee, Sang, Addison, DeVry, 6306528269, lee@dpg.devry.edu
Lauck, Steve, Orland Park, ITT, 7083263200, slauck@itt-tech.edu
Chin, Jerry, Burr Ridge, ITT, 6304556470, jchin9@aol.com
Oczkowicz, Sara, Darien, J&S Power Solutions, 6304349388, jandspower@yahoo.com
Fleeman, Stephen, Rock Valley Coll, 8159213060, sfleeman@ednet.rvc.cc.il.us
Perry, William, CETsr, Monmouth, Fishnet Comm Grp, 3097346756
Lane, Eddie, CET, Weldon, ETA-I, 2177362203, elane@uiuc.edu
Beavers, Michael, Mattoon, Lake Land Coll, 2172345341,mbeavers@lakeland.cc.il.us
Long, Glenn   , Menard, MCC Sch District 428, 6188265071
Leonard, David, Quincy, Quincy AVTC, 2172243770
Dalman, Richard, Centralia, Kaskaskia Coll-Crisp Ctr, 6185453405, rdalman@kaskaskia.edu
Fleming, George, Forest Park, 7084889500, gfleming@usmss.net
India
Baby, Tom, CST, Kuthuparamba, Keral, ETA, 914902364447, babyktom@rediffmail.com
Lazar, Joseph, Kannur, Keral, Nirmalagiri Coll, 049023644472365, ngc_edu01@rediffmail.com
Manamkuzhi, Asok, Calicut, MULTISOFT, 9104952260634, multisoftclt@rediffmail.com
Nair, Naveen Kumar, Mumbai, MAQ Software LLC, 919870160483, navi_n_nair@yahoo.com
Indiana
Lewis, Leon, Pendleton, T. White HS, 7657782107, na9y@arrl.net
Miller, David, Indianapolis, Ivy Tech, 3179214548, DMiller@ivytech.edu
Glass, Tom, CET, Indianapolis,
Heller, Don, CETsr, Indianapolis, ITT, 3178758640, dheller@itt-tech.edu
Arney, Ernest, Indianapolis, ITT, 3178758640, earney@itt-tech.edu
Hughes, Gary, Indianapolis, ITT, 3178758640, ghughes@itt-tech.edu
Kenning, David, Valparaiso, Porter Co Career Ctr, 2195313170, dkenning@mail.valpo.k12.in.us
Ferguson, J. Douglas, CET, Elkhart, ETA-I, 5749702959, dougferguson@comcast.net
Negahban, Rahim, CET, South Bend, Ivy Tech, 5742897001, rnegahba@ivytech.edu
Nahrwold Mike, Ossian, ETA, 2606227912, mnahrwold@aol.com
Preest, Joyce, Fort Wayne, ITT, 2604976257, jpreest@itt-tech.edu
Walker, Kent, CST, Fort Wayne, ITT, 2604844107, kwalker@itt-tech.edu
Baker, Jackie, Sellersburg, Ivy Tech, 8122463301, ebaker@ivytech.edu
Riley, Michael, Columbus, Columbus Area Career, 8123764240, rileym@bcsc.k12.in.us
Ramey, Mary, Richmond, Ivy Tech CC, 7659662656, mramey@ivytech.edu
Millen, Thomas, Bloomington, Ivy Tech, 8123306055, tmillen@ivytech.edu
Jones, David, CET, Bedford, N Lawrence Voc-Tech, 8122793561, jonesd@nlcs.k12.in.us
Long, James, Washington, Fiber Camp, Inc, 8122543488, seamasL@msn.com
Norris, Kent   , Washington, Fiber Camp, Inc, 8122543488, kent@fibercamp.com
Burden, Dennis, CET, Newburgh, ITT, 8128581600, dburden@itt-tech.edu
Smith, James, Lafayette, Ivy Tech CC, 7652695151, jgsmith@ivytech.edu
Jamaica
Morris, Rohan, Kingston, Vector Technology Inst, 8769241129, rohmor@cwjamaica.com
Jordan
Barakat, Samer, Jubaiha-Amman, ICECC ME, 96265160131, sbarakat@go.com.jo
Alfitiani, Yahya, Amman, AEMA-Arab Eng, 9626462647, iedtc@yahoo.com
Kansas
Hoffsommer, Gary, Topeka, TFM Comm, 7852332343, ghoffsommer@tfmcomm.com
Thomas, Donald, Wichita, ETA, 3166861414, w0pea@cox.net
Kentucky
Pozgay, Walt, CET, Bardstown, Mitsuba, 5023483100, w-pozgay@mbt.americanmitusba.com
Yost, Paul, CET, Louisville, ITT, 5023277424, Paul_2000_37@yahoo.com
James, Paul, CETsr, Lexington, ETA, 8592253035, paulkjames@insightbb.com
Maggard, Mary, Lexington, Bluegrass Comm & Tech, 8592466671, mary.maggard@kctcs.edu
Elsener, Glen, CET, Highland Hts, Gateway Comm, 8594424112, glen.elsener@kctcs.edu
Ritchie, Lamarr, CET, Hazard, Hazard Comm, 8002467521, lamarr.ritchie@kctcs.edu
Adair-Weber, Robin, CET, Columbia, Better Reception, 2703786842, dulca@duo-county.com
Louisiana
Little, William, FOI, Metairie, LTC, 9856466430
Grant, Jacques, St. Rose, ITT, 5044630338, gjgrant@itt-tech.edu

194

Lowry, Krystal, Golden Meadow, Abdon Callais Offshore, 9854757111, acokl@mobiletel.com
Shellenberger, Craig, Golden Meadow, Abdon Callais, 9854757111, acosecurity@mobiletel.com
Lemmons, Stephen, Houma, ETA, 9853813459, lcdrdata@bellsouth.net
Bruce, Ken, Houma, Fletcher Tech CC, 9858573658
Ghirardi, Glen, Morgan City, Ghirardi Marine, 8002982419, ghirardi2@juno.com
Brissette, Lawrence, Morgan City, LTC-Young, 9853802436
Ellis, Patricia, Morgan City, LTC, 9853802436, pellis@theltc.net
Granger, Joan, Morgan City, LTC, 9853802436, jgranger@theltc.net
McGrath, Helen, Morgan City, LTC, 9853802457, helen.mcgrath@theltc.net
Moore, Carl, Morgan City, LTC, 9853802436, cmoore@theltc.net
Creel, Frank, CET, Bogalusa, LTC, 9857326640, fcreel@sullivan.tec.la.us
Bowers, Robert, CCNA, Franklin, LTC, 3378281448, rbowers@theltc.net
Fruge, Wayne, Ville Platte, Port Barre HS, 3375857256
Merryman, James, Barksdale AFB, 3184564918, james.merryman@barksdale.af.mil
Walker, Andrew, CETma, Reston, MT&E, 3185644832
Massachusetts
Cathcart, John, Woburn, ITT, 7819378324, jcathcart@ittech.edu
Edmunds, Brock, Woburn, ITT, 7819378324, bedmunds@itt-tech.edu
Makem, Robert, Haverhill, Whittier Reg HS, 9783734101, rmakem@whittier.tec.ma.us
Rondeau, Robert, Whittier Reg HS, 9783734101, rrondeau@whittier.tec.ma.us
Houghton, Tom, Norwood, ITT, 8008798324
Emmanuel, Axell, Somerville, Network Technology Acad, 6176280277, axell@ntai.net
Hickey, Robert, FOI, Somerville, Professional Training, 6172837195, wire.tech@verizonmail.com
McLaughlin, B, CET, Wellesley Hills, Telecomm Trng, 6177841844, barry@barrymclaughlin.com
DiMauro, Michael, Hyannis, MJD Comms, 5087718665, mdimauro@comcast.net
Gagne, Michael, CETa, Fairhaven, Woods Hole Oceanic, 5082892233, gagnes@comcast.net
Guay, Ronald, Fall River, Diman Reg Vo Tech, 5086782891
Rapoza, Kenneth, Fall River, Diman Reg Vo Tech, 5086782891, ken@dimanregional.org
MacLeod, Ralph, Rochester, Old Colony Reg Vo Tech, 5087638011, rmacleod@oldcolony.us
Malaysia
Chua,Theresa, Asia City, Sabah, MasterCom, 6088316819, mccis@tm.net.my
Maryland
Havens, Gregory, Patuxent River, Naval Air Warfare Ctr, 3013421210, gregory.havens@navy.mil
Manders, Paul, Beltsville , Teltronic, Inc, 3104686500, paul.manders@teltronic.com
Miller, Carl, Laurel, Woodland Job Corps Career, 3017257900, cfmiller@comcast.net
Williams, Bruce, CETsr, Capitol Hts, ETA, 3018089455
Warren, Robert, CETsr, Upper Marlboro, 3015998953, warrcetsr@earthlink.net
Ganescu, Virgil, Owings Mills, ITT, 8774116782, vganescu@itt-tech.edu
Vahedi, Edward, Baltimore, TESST Coll, 4106446400, arshya@msn.com
Tyndall, William, Cambridge, Charter Captain Courses, 4102280674
Miles, David, Salisbury, Parkside HS-CTE, 4106775144, damiles@wcboe.org
Jacobs, Jack, North East, Mergenthaler VTHS, 4103966496, jjacobs128021@comcast.net
Maine
Whitten, Charles, Brunswick, Embry-Riddle Aeronautical, 2077210664, whitten@maine.rr.com
Hersey, April, S. Portland, Sheppard AFB, 2077564872, april.hersey@mebngr.ang.af.mil
Michigan
Wilbourn, Richard, Southfield, Everest Inst, 2487999933, rwilbour@cci.edu
Fugate, Robert, Troy, ITT, 2485241800, rfugate@itt-tech.edu
Langdon, Donald, CETsr, Dearborn, 6163648464
Sweet, Donald, Monroe, Visual Technology, 3134782894, visualtec@yahoo.com
Golshan, Rahmatollah, Taylor, Wayne Co CC, 7343743204, rgolsha1@wcccd.edu
Powers, Michael, Canton, ITT, 7343977822, mpowers@itt-tech.edu
Smoot, Wayne, Canton, ITT, 7343977800, wsmoot@itt-tech.edu
Udanoh, Charles, Detroit, Breithaupt Career & Tech, 3138669550, cudanoh@yahoo.com
Jankowski, Allan, FOI, Sterling Heights, Diversified Wire, 5862646500, ajankowski@dw-c.com
Bocksch, Gary, CETsr, Flint, Mott Coll, 8102327315, gbocksch@mcc.edu
Csondor, Dennis, Eaton Rapids, Lansing CC, 5176633936
Betzer, Steven, Lansing, Lansing CC, 5172675936, sbetzer@lcc.edu
Schmitt, Philip, CET, Plainwell, MI Career&Tech Inst, 2696649249, schmittp@michigan.gov
Toth, Ken, Holland, Careerline Tech Ctr, 8777028461, ktoth@oaisd.org
Hudson, Lee, Grand Rapids, Olympia Career Training, 6163644854
Buhler, Max, Grand Rapids, ITT, 6169561060, mbuhler@itt-tech.edu
Koole, Michael, CET, Grand Rapids, ITT, 6169561060,mkoole@itt-tech.edu
Palanisamy, Aravindan, Grand Rapids, ITT, 6169561060, apalanisamy@itt-tech.edu
Ufer, John, CETsr, Sault St. Marie, EUP Workforce, 9066354217, onsiteedu@earthlink.net
Highum, Mark, CET, Escanaba, Bay de Noc CC, 9067865802, bayelex@yahoo.com
Linderoth, Karl, Escanaba, Bay Coll, 9067865802, linderok@baycollege.edu
Beckwith, Robert, Flint, MT&E, 8102400123, BobBeckwith@comcast.net
Minnesota
Baldwin, John, CETsr, Faribault, ETA, 5073312308, jbaldwin@myclearwave.net
Bartholow, Clayton, CETsr, Minneapolis, Dunwoody, 6123840659, cbartholow@dunwoody.edu
McShannock, John, Minneapolis, Dunwoody Coll, 6122818111, jmcshannock@dunwoody.edu
Kalis, Marc, Winona, MN State Coll Southeast, 5074532674, mkalis@southeastmn.edu
Gordon, Charles, Willmar, Ridgewater Coll, 3202317660, joe.gordon@ridgewater.edu
Johnson, H Dean, Moorhead, MN State Comm, 2182996520, h.dean.johnson@minnesota.edu
Missouri
Abatgis, George, Arnold, ITT, 6364646600, gabatgis@itt-tech.edu
Janjua, Gulam, CET, Earth City, ITT, 3142987800, gjanjua@itt-tech.edu
Paynter, Robert, CETma, Webster Groves, 3149630226, rpaynter@swbell.net
Boldwyn, Scott, St Louis, Missouri Tech, 3145693600, sboldwyn@motech.edu
Kightlinger, Ronald, CET, Park Hills, ETA-I, 5735181319
Wadsworth, Luke, Kansas City, BreakThru Training, 8165848177, lwadsworth@btstraining.com

Aber, Max, Raytown, Herndon Career Ctr, 8162687100, maxxedout@excite.com
McKlosky, John, Kansas City, BTS-Training Solutions, 8165848177, jmcklosky@BTStraining.com
Weyer, John, Kansas City, BTS-Training Solutions, 8165848177, jweyer@BTStraining.com
Stephens, Richard, CETsr, NW Tech Sch, 6605624128
Corcoran, Nancy, Rolla, Univ of Missouri, 5734264189, nancyc@fidnet.com
Schallon, Keith, Rolla, Rolla Tech Inst, 5734580150, kschallon@rolla.k12.mo.us
Van Camp, Andrew, CETma, Bourbon, Thistle Seed, 5734683379, evancamp@fidnet.com
Gustad, Robert, CETsr, Springfield, Ozarks Tech CC, 4174478149, gustadr@otc.edu
Mississippi
Joy, William, Clinton, Irby Construction, 6019240626, wjoy@jam.rr.com
Thompson, Michael, Natchez, Copiah-Lincoln CC, 6014461160, michael.thompson@colin.edu
Cerniglia, Vic, Poplarville, Pearl River CC, 6014031108
Montana
Carson, Joy, Kalispell, Flathead Valley CC, 4067563883, jcarson@fvcc.cc.mt.us
North Carolina
Billings, Darrin, Dobson, Surry CC, 3363868121, billingsd@surry.edu
Shelton, Shelia, Dobson, Surry CC, 3363863352, sheltons@surry.edu
Burcham, Steve, CET, Dobson, Surry CC, 3363863302
Kateeb, Ibraheem, Jamestown, Guilford Tech CC, 3363344822, IAkateeb@gtcc.edu
Blackburn, Norman, CETsr,F, Kernersville, ECPI, 3366651400, dblackburn@ecpi.edu
Morgan, William, Kernersville, Weaver Academy, 3363708282, morganw2@gcsnc.com
Campbell, Edwin, Greensboro, ECPI, 3366651400
Cook, Sam, CST, Greensboro, ECPI, 3366651400, ccook@ecpi.edu
Johnson, Johnny, Cary, NC Elite Career Service Ctr, 9197406972
McGoogan, Laura, FOI, Raleigh, ECPI, 9195710057, lmcgoogan@ecpi.edu
Willett, Donald, FOI, Raleigh, ECPi, 9195710057, dwillett@ecpi.edu
McSwain, Mike, Shelby, Cleveland CC, 7044844000, mcswainm@cleveland.cc.nc.us
Cauble, Gary, CETma, Charlotte, ECPI, 7043991010, gcauble@ecpi.edu
Hamby, Michael, CET, Charlotte, ECPI, 7043991010
Hickman, Walter, Fayetteville, ETA, 7049481110, hickmanfy@aol.com
Estrada Ochoa, Mario, Hope Mills, E&Z Sch of Aeronautics, 9102619797, vini8a@gmail.com
Brown, Eldon, CETsr, Wilmington, Cape Fear CC, 9103627400
Stokes, William, CET, Wilmington, Cape Fear CC, 9103627285
Pritchard, Herman, Wilmington, ETA, 9102792486, fishinstructor@aol.com
Gonzalez, John, CETsr, Carolina Beach, ETA-I, 9104585553
Gray, Mark, CETma, Castle Hayne, Cape Fear CC, 9103627391, mgray@cfcc.edu
Jones, David, CET, Kinston, Lenoir CC, 2525276223, djones@lenoircc.edu
Zarra, Rodney, Spur Hubert, Bear Creek Computer, 9105549524, rodzarra@gmai.coml
Garten, Ronald, Jacksonville, Coastal Carolina CC, 9109386105, gartenr@coastal.cc.nc.us
Miceli, Frank, Asheville, Ashville-Bucombe Tech, 8282541921, fmiceli@abtech.edu
North Dakota
Hendrickson, Rick, Wahpeton, N Dakota State, 7016712315, rick.hendrickson@ndscs.edu
Nebraska
Martin, Thomas, Elkhorn, Prime Comms, 4022181620, temartin2@cox.net
Pulte, William, Omaha, Metropolitan Tech, 4027384727
Cripe, Eugene, FOI, Beatrice, AESA, 8003452742
Gharzai, Karim, Lincoln, NE Inst, 4024648484, dr.gharzai@polytecusa.org
Roeser, Fredrick, CETsr, Grand Island, Central CC, 3083987478, froeser@cccneb.edu
Gompert, Dan, CET, Hastings, Central CC, 4024612486, dgompert@cccneb.edu
Arensdorf, Berva, North Platte, Mid-Plains CC, 3085353618, arensdorfb@mpcc.edu
Spikes, Monte, Omaha, ITT, 4023312900, mspikes@itt-tech.edu
New Hampshire
Abbott, Bryant, Keene, Cheshire Career Ctr, 6033527100
Wesolowski, J, CET, Portsmouth, Prtsmth HS, 6034367100, j.wesolowski@portsmouth.k12.nh.us
New Jersey
Frankunas, Nicholas, Turnersville, SEPTA Training, 2155805190, nfrankunas@septa.org
Kamran, Jamshed, CETma, West Orange, 9733255753, successful_55@msn.com
Krutsick, Michael, Newark, ETA, 9735895619, Phantom01@att.net
LaGanga, Joseph, Glenwood, Motorola Glen Rock, 2014477549, joe.laganga@motorola.com
Dale, Bob, Hackensack, ESS, Inc, 2014882292, bdale@gotoess.com
Sniffen, Paul, Rumson, Aerospace Test Technologies, 7327419460, paulsniffen@yahoo.com
Bauer, Jacqueline, CSS, Cherry Hill, Medical Consultants Instr, 8563178300, jbcpc@verizon.net
Celona, Joseph, Blackwood, Camden Co Coll, 8563744955, joeinstructor_2000@yahoo.com
Kozachyn, Karen, CSS, Blackwood, Camden Co Coll, 8563744955
Nastasi, Anthony, CWS, Blackwood, Camden Co Coll, 8563744955, anastasi@camdencc.edu
Ewert, William,CETma, Clementon, MT&E, 8564357843, w.ewert@att.net
Harris, Steven, CWS, Cherry Hill, Camden Co Coll, 8568746000
Miller, Robert, CET, Pitman, DTI Publishing, 8562187893, bmiller@dtipublishing.com
Byrd, Trina, Pleasantville, T.Byrd Computer Training Inst, 6074849356, tbyrd@bellatlantic.net
Shehata, Osama, Pleasantville, Technology Force Inst, 6092729996, lcdrdata@bellsouth.net
Miller, Robert, CET, Jackson, Miller Training, 7328334973, robert.lawrence.miller@us.army.mil
Orlowski, Lynn, Trenton, Mercer Co Tech, 6095865144, lmfo@mctec.net
George, William, Toms River, OCVTS, 7324733100, bgeorge@mail.ocvts.org
New Mexico
Dudley, Melody, Albuquerque, Integrated Training. 5058834113, melodyd@itc4u.com
Kinney, Robert, Albuquerque, Integrated Training, 5058834113, btkinney@itc4u.com
Sutton, William, CET, Albuquerque, ITT, 5058281114,bcsutton@itt-tech.edu
Bussey, Jennifer, Clovis, Clovis CC, 5057694019, jennifer.bussey@clovis.edu
Nutt, James, CET, Alamogordo, New Mexico State, 5054393786, jim88310@yahoo.com
Nevada
Stage, Edward, Henderson, ITT, 7025585404
Reilly, Edward, Las Vegas, CC of Southern, 7022293872, edrcet@cox.net

Appendix A - ETA Worldwide Certification Administrator Listing

Kirkland, Richard, CETsr, Las Vegas, ETA, 7027998300, rbkirk@interact.ccsd.net
Morehouse, Jerry, Reno, CCNV, 7758562266, jerry@rmcomputers.com
New York
Harry, Davanan, CET, New York, TCI, 2125944000, davananh@yahoo.com
Lau, Roy, CNST, New York, TCI, 2125944000, rlau@tcicollege.edu
Maybar, Stephen, FOI, New York. TCI, 2125944000, smaybar@tcicollege.net
Bachrach, Scott, New York, Mobile Training & Education, 2122030989, scottb@mtande.com
Giordano, Steven, New York, NY Inst of Technology, 2122611618, sgiordan@nyit.edu
Hinds, Edwin, CETsr, Brooklyn, E. NY Transit Tech H.S, 7186475204, ehinds6062@aol.com
Gleans, Alan, Brooklyn, 7182287785
DelliCarpini, Michael, Fresh Meadows, Coll of Aeronautics, 7182291562
Maiuri, Vincent, Jamaica, Thomas Edison HS, 7182976580, vinnyelectron5@aol.com
Di Liberto, James, Amityville, Island Drafting, 6316918733, dilibertoj@islanddrafting.com
Klein, Nancy, West Babylon, Katharine Gibbs, 5168491363, purple71871@hotmail.com
Dymond, Wm, Medford, ETA, 6312891968, wmdymo@aol.com
Woomer, Patrick, Queensbury, Adirondack CC, 5187432332, pwoomer1@nycap.rr.com
Corey, Anthony, FOI, Ticonderoga, 7574441262, anthony.corey@navy.mil
Dixon, Donna, Plattsburgh, Clinton CC, 5185624232, donna.dixon@clinton.edu
Flick, Connie, Plattsburgh, CV-TEC, 5185610100, cflick@cves.org
Keeler, Steven, Auburn, Cayuga CC, 3152551743, keeler@cayuga-cc.edu
Bechtold. Charles, Dryden, Tompkins CC, 6078448211, bechtoc@sunytccc.edu
Fellows, James, LCET, East Syracuse, ISCET, 31544533314, jfellows@unitedradio.com
Fairbanks, Carl, Liverpool, ITT, 3154618000, mfairbanks@itt.edu
Lackey, Clifton, CET, Liverpool, ITT, 3154618000, clackey@itt-tech.edu
Wahl, Heinz, CETma, Watertown, Jeff-Lewis, 3157797200, heinz@frenchcreekmarina.com
Smith, Paul, CET, Getzville, ITT, 7166892200, pasmith@itt-tech.edu
Gullo, Peter, CETsr, Getzville, ITT, 7166892200, pgullo@itt-tech.edu
Ashman, Alvin, Williamsville, Erie CC, 7168511509, ashman@ecc.edu
Smith, Arlyn, CETsr, Wellsville, Alfred State Coll, 6075873137, SmithAL@alfredstate.edu
Casler, Cindy, Plattsburgh, Clinton CC, 5185624143, cindy.casler@clinton.edu
Ohio
Poole, Dennis, Delaware, Delaware Area Career Ctr, 7405480708, poolej@delawareareacc.org
Morrison, Charles, CETsr, Ashville, ETA, 7409833338, sippencoffee@columbus.rr.com
Karr, Steve, Fremont, Terra CC, 4195592453, skarr@terra.edu
Campbell, Jack, Toledo, RTM Star Ctr, 4192553940, campbellbt@aol.com
Molenaar, Tom-jan, Toledo, RTM Star Ctr, 4192553940, tj_mlnr@hotmail.com
Dudas, Matthew, Zanesville, Mid-East Career, 7404540101, mdudas@mid-east.k12.oh.us
Alexander, Harold, Cadiz, Jefferson Co Joint Vocational, 7409428245, halexander@eohio.net
Todd, Mark, Concord Twp, Auburn Career Ctr, 4403577542, mtodd@auburncc.org
Arcaro, Jim, CETsr, Wickliffe, 440922030, 2163628104, jgarcaro@juno.com
Heidenreich, James, Cleveland, Cuyahoga CC, 2169874006, james.heidenreich@tri-c.edu
Carlton, Christopher, CETa, Brooklyn, Kaplan Career Inst, 2164850900, ccarlton@ttinst.com
Yager, Edward, Middleburg Heights, Polaris Career Ctr, 4408917625, eyager@polaris.edu
Bowers, Richard, Brooklyn Heights,Comms, 2166351313, rickcatcwa@hotmail.com
Smith, Kelly, CETa, Strongsville, Honeywell Intl, 4408264331,kelly.smith@honeywell.com
Huston, Donald, Solon, Bird Technologies Group, 4405192228, dhuston@bird-technologies.com
Pinkava, Rick, Brecksville, Cuyahoga Vlly Career, 4407468344, rick.pinkava@cvcc.k12.oh.us
D'Alessandro, Dan, CETma, Brook Park, Philips, 2165386027, Dan@Dalessandro.com
Kushner, Robert, CETsr, Brooklyn, Kaplan Career Inst, 2164850900, rkushner@ttinst.com
Delio, Joseph, CSS, Broadview Heights, ETA, 4402305394, joedelio@cox.net
Dulik, John, Broadview Heights, Vatterott Coll, 4405261660, john.dulik@vatterott-college.edu
Swan, Donna, Medina, Medina Co Career Ctr, 3307258461, swan@mccc-jvsd.org
Weiss, Fred, RESI, Akron, East HS, 3307944116, fweiss@akron.k12.oh.us
Magnoski, Robert, Niles, ETI Tech Coll, 3306529919
Woods, Curtis, Niles, ETI Tech Coll, 3306529919
Brett, David, CET,CS, Youngstown, ITT, 3302701600, dbrett@itt-tech.edu
Ballinger, Robert, Massillon, Perry HS, 3303773486, ballingr@perry1.stark.k12.oh.us
Karam, Ted, Ravenna, Maplewood Career Ctr, 3302962892, karamte@mwood.cc
Vogel, Steve, CETsr, Bucyrus, Columbus District HQ, 6144663933
Gladish, Jeffrey, Norwood, ITT, 5135318300, jgladish@itt-tech.edu
Hochwalt, Glenn, CETma, Dayton, P&R Comms, 9375128100, glenn.hochwalt@prcdayton.com
Frey, James, St. Marys, Joint Township District Memorial, 4193949500
Oklahoma
Cradduck, Kaye, Norman, Moore Norman Tech, 4053645763, kcradduck@mntechnology.com
Watson, Doyl, CET, Oklahoma City, ITT, 4058104100, dlwatson@itt-tech.edu
Cook, James, Lawton, Cameron Univ, 5805812200, jamesco@cameron.edu
Moffett, Wesley, Lawton, ETA
Kechter, Greg, Alva, NWOSU/RSI Educational, 5803278139
Walz, Steve   , Alva, NWOSU/RSI Educational, 5803278140, stevew@rsicorp.com
Gremler, William, CETma, Broken Arrow, American Airlines, 9184612929, gremler@cox.net
Bowles, James, Tulsa, Spartan Sch, 9188318607, jim@bowlesonline.com
Gann, William, CET, Poteau, Carl Albert State Coll, 9186471215, bgann@carlalbert.edu
Oregon
Allenbrand, James, CET, Portland, ITT, 8002345488, jallenbrand@itt-tech.edu
Jezeski, Daniel, CET, Milwaukie, Comcast, 5036546078, d.jezeski@comcast.net
Pennsylvania
Hinkle, Shannon, Jefferson Hills, Steel Ctr AVTS, 4124693200, shannon.hinkle@scavts.net
Karlowsky, Richard, Jefferson Hills, Steel Ctr AVTS, 7248406562, r.kar@verizon.net
Fisher, Dennis, CETsr, Donora, Pittsburgh Inst. of Aeronautics, 4123462106, dfisher@pia.aero
Dings, John, CETa, Oakdale, Pittsburgh Tech Inst, 4128095399, Dings.John@pti.edu
Mueller, James, Oakdale, Pittsburgh Tech Inst, 4128095156, mueller.james@pti.edu
May, Margaret, NCT, West Newton, May Consulting, 7248725795, maypcmom@aol.com

Parady, Edward, CET, Pitcairn, Pittsburgh Job Corps Ctr, 4124010846, eepar@aol.com
Golofski, John, Monroeville, ITT, 4128565920, jgolofski@itt-tech.edu
Rumbaugh, Harvey, Pittsburgh, ITT, 4129379150, hrum@itt-tech.edu
Delso Jr, Joseph, Somerset, Somerset Co Technology , 8144433651, jdelso@sctc.net
Lohr, John, Latrobe, Eastern Westmoreland CTC, 7245399788, jlohr@wiu.k12.pa.us
Broker, James, New Stanton, Central Westmoreland CTC, 7249253532, jbroker@wiu.k12.pa.us
Simons, PE   , Allan, Youngwood, Westmoreland Co CTC, 7249254118, simons_4@hotmail.com
Elliott, Glen, CETsr, Johnstown, PA Highlands CC, 8142626412, gelliott@pennhighlands.edu
Hittle, Brenda, Mercer, Mercer Co Career Ctr, 7246623000, Bhittle@mccc.tec.pa.us
Patt, Brian. Mercer, Mercer Co Career Ctr, 7246623000, bpatt@mccc.tec.pa.us
Ryan, Paul, Mercer, Mercer Co. Career Ctr., 7246623000, pryan@mccc.tec.pa.us
Keys, Robert, FOI, Adrian, TBK Technologies, 4126008185, rkeys@gpsx.net
Lyons, Timothy, Oil City, Venango Technology Ctr, 8146773097, tlyons@vtc1.org
Burchill, Guy. Meadville, Crawford Co Vo-Tech, 8147246024, gburchill@ccvts.org
Mientkiewicz, Timothy, Erie, Erie Co Tech Sch, 8148640641, tmientkiewicz@ects.org
Peters, Joseph, Clearfield, Clearfield Co Career & Tech, 8147655308, jpeters@ccctc.org
Harman, Larry, Cumberland Perry Vol Tech, 7176970354, lharman@cpavts.org
Skamangas, Louis, Mechanicsburg, ITT, 7176919263, lskamanagas@yahoo.com
Jacobs, Dean, Harrisburg, Dauphin Co Tech. 7176523170, dakajacobs@netrax.net
Eckenrode, Harry, CET, Chambersburg, Franklin, 7172639033, shawn@fcavts.tec.pa.us
Ferrell, Thomas, CETsr, York, YTI Career Inst, 7177571100
Baran, Candace, Williamsport, Penn Coll, 5703202400, cbaran@pct.edu
Paulhamus, Jonathan, CNST/N, Williamsport, PA Coll, 5703274775, jpaulam@ltsd.k12.pa.us
LaBonge, Chris, Breinigsville, FiberOptic.com, 8775299114, clabonge@fiberoptic.com
Cary, Paul, CET, Allentown, Lincoln Tech, 4847672936, pfcary@verizon.net
Samsell, David, CETsr, Moscow, ETA-I, 5708427053, glowfuel@verizon.net
Holmes, Thomas, Tobyhanna, Army Depot, 5708957156, thomas.b.holmes@us.army.mil
Fornes, Richard, Scranton, Johnson Coll, 5703426404, rfornes@johnson.edu
Hessmiller, Wm, CET, Dunmore, Editors & Training, 5703422889, hessmiller7@netscape.net
Lettieri, Ronald, CETma, Dunmore, 5708958390
Rutkowski, Mark, P.E., Nanticoke, Luzerne Co CC, 5707400646, mrutkowski@luzerne.edu
Dyckman, John, CET, Aston, Penn State, 6104971689, wa3kft@arrl.net
Hartman, Linda, Bensalem, ITT, 2152448871
Muir, Ferdinand, CETa, Bensalem, ITT, 2152448871, Fmuir@itt-tech.edu
Crotts, James, CETsr, Fairless Hills, Bucks Co Tech High, 2159491700, BCTS1@aol.com
Phillips, Cully, CET, Fairless Hills, Transcor Plymouth Radio Shop, 2152950310, n3htz@fast.net
Maduzia, Stephen, CET, Willow Grove, Steven & Sons' Electronics, 2156575317
Agard, Richard, FOI, Philadelphia, Philadelphia Fiber Optic, 2159289960, RAgard@aol.com
MacLean, John, CETsr, Philadelphia, Fire Dept HQ, 2156861151, ATLAS8569@yahoo.com
Jones, Ellis, Philadelphia, Murrell Dobbins CTE HS, 2152274421, ime2jj@hotmail.com
Krug, Leonard, Leesport, Berks Career & Technology, 6103744073, lakrug@berkscareer.com
Zidik, Michael, Sinking Spring, ETA, 6106782091, mjzidik25@intergate.com
Philippines
Martinez, Jose, Pasig City, ICS, 6326375587
Puerto Rico
Colombani, Dan, CET, Aguada, Universal Technology Ctr, 7878681483, dcolombani@prtc.net
Delgado, Edwin, Aguadilla, 7878821646, edwind@caribe.net
Valdes, Ramon, CET, San Juan, ETA, 7877240182
Cortes-Vazquez, Rafael, San Juan, Caribbean Forensic, 7877670548, rcortes@prw.net
Diaz-Torres, Abner, CETsr, Hortencia, Carolina, ETA
Rhode Island
Cardoso, Stephen, Lincoln, William M. Davies Jr. Career, 4017281500, scardoso1@cox.net
Carpentier, Real, Wood River, Chariho Career, 4013646869, Real.Carpentier@Chariho.k12.ri.us
DiFazio, Albert, Cranston, Cranston Area Career & Tech, 4012708070, adifazio@cpsed.net
Saipan
Masilungan, Marcelo, FOI, Tanapag Vlg, White Coconut, 6703229442, mar@whitecoconut.com
Shankweiler, Jason, Saipan, Marine Tech International Corp, 6702872420, jwad@vzpacifica.net
South Carolina
Eaton, Richard, Newberry, Newberry Co Career Ctr, 8033212674
Gilliard, Sylvia, Charleston, Naval Consolidated Brig, 8437430306, sylvia.gilliard@navy.mil
Dugan, Timothy, FOI, N Charleston, ECPI, 8434140350, eznet@bellsouth.net
Harrelson, James, Goose Creek, Hanahan HS, 8435729834, harrelsonj@wwdb.org
Taylor, Larry, Conway, Horry-Georgetown Tech, 8433495256, Taylor@hor.tec.sc.us
Smith, Ernest, CETma, Wallace, Smith's Radio-TV, 8435377880, ernest2165@aol.com
Mao, Leei, Greenville, Greenville Tech Coll, 8642508427, maolm@gvltec.edu
Edens, Robert, CET, Greenville, ECPI, 8642882828, redens@ecpi.edu
Jones, Roy, CETsr, Aiken, Aiken Tech Coll, 8035939231, rjones@atc.edu
Overton, Stewart, Hilton Head Island, Light Brigade, 8432272028, stuoverton@aol.com
South Dakota
Koenig, David, CNST, Sioux Falls, ETA, 5052801353, ran111@onebox.com
Hoffmann, Bob, CET, Sioux Falls, SETech Inst, 6053674741, bob.hoffmann@southeasttech.com
Adams, Clark, CETsr, Watertown, Ideal Power, 6058869611, stuff@dailypost.com
Berger, Christine, Watertown, Lake Area Tech Inst, 6058825284, bergerch@lakeareatech.edu
Geffre, Martin, Watertown, Lake Area Tech Inst, 6058825284
Reyelts, Jeffrey, Watertown, Lake Area Tech Inst, 6058825284
VerSteeg, David, CET, Mitchell, Mitchell Tech, 6059953095, dave.versteeg@mitchelltech.edu
Sweden
Westberg, Staffan, Hudiksvall, Lansenutbildningar, 4665019685, staffan.westberg@hudiksvall.se
Tennessee
Haggard, Larry, CET, Shelbyville, Larry's Electronics, 9316955334, lhaggard@united.net
Butler, Norma, Nashville, TN Technology, 6157411241, nButler@nashville.tec.tn.us
Carr, Christie, Nashville, TN Technology, 6154255525, act@ttcnashville.edu

Harper, Barbara, Nashville, TN Technology, 6154255525, bharper@nashville.tec.tn.us
Que, Sarah, CST, Nashville, ITT, 6158898700, sque@itt-tech.edu
Cofer, Charles, Chattanooga, Chattanooga State TTC, 4236973238, charles@cofer.com
Ramsey, John, Sevierville, TN Technology, 8654535644, leeramsey49@hotmail.com
Keith, Doug, CETa, Knoxville, Fountainhead, 8656889422, doug.keith@fountainheadcollege.com
Kohlmeyer, C, Knoxville, Fountainhead, 8656889422, charles.kohlmeyer@fountainheadcollege.
Sullivan, Patrick, Knoxville, Fountainhead, 8656889422, patrick.sullivan@fountainheadcollege.co
Smith, Jeffrey, CETsr, Knoxville, Central Comms, 8658090969, service@mssenger.com
McMillan, Cecil, CETsr, Knoxville, ITT, 8656712800, cmcmillan@itt-tech.edu
Day, Sally, Knoxville, Pellissippi State Tech, 8656946454, saday@pstcc.edu
Edmonds, Nancy, Knoxville, Pellissippi State Tech, 8656946454, njedmonds@pstcc.edu
Maher, Stuart, Knoxville, Pellissippi State Tech, 8656946454, wmaher@pstcc.edu
Morin,Patrick, Knoxville, Pellissippi State Tech, 8656946454, plmorin@pstcc.edu
Newman, Joan, Knoxville, Pellissippi State Tech, 8656946752, jnewman@pstcc.edu
Walker, Thomas, CETsr, Knoxville, Pellissippi State Tech, 8656946752, tewalker@pstcc.edu
Hajibeigy, Mohammad, CETma, Cordova, ITT, 9013810248, moham21@hotmail.com
Wiseman, Freddrick, CET, Cordova, ITT, 9017620556, fwiseman@itt-tech.edu
Carter, Carlton, Memphis, TN Technology, 9015436140, ccarter@memphis.tec.tn.us
Lewis, Tom, McKenzie, TN Technology, 7313525364, tlewis@mckenzie.tec.tn.us
Skelton, Richard, Jackson, Jackson State CC, 7314243520, rskelton@jscc.edu
McDougal, Mark, Hohenwald, TN Technology, 9317965351, mmcdougal@hohenwald.tec.tn.us
Pritchard, Michael, Crossville, TN Technology, 9314847502, pritchard.mike@gmail.com

Texas

Shirk, Brian, FOI, Allen, Amphenol Fiber Systems, 2145472415, bshirk@fibersystems.com
Breland, Darwin, Irving, DFW Comms, Inc, 9727304339, dbreland@dfwcomm.com
Kohr, Alvin, Richardson, ITT, 9726909100, AKOHR@ITT-Tech.edu
Matsumoto, Patrick, CETsr, Sherman, TX Instruments, 9038685691, p-matsumoto1@ti.com
Burnett, Barton, Duncanville, Duncanville HS, 9727083801, bburnett@ducanvilleisd.org
Clark, Patty, Mesquite, Eastfield Coll, 9728608318, pmc4705@dcccd.edu
Oliver, Verlon, Dallas, ATI Career Training, 2149028191, oliver1812@comcast.net
McFadden, Rickey, Paris, Paris Junior Coll, 9037820722, rmcfadden@parisjc.edu
Cantu, Mario, Marshall, Texas State Tech Coll, 9039233372, mario.cantu@marshall.tstc.edu
Williams, Kevin, CETma, Arlington, ITT, 8177945100, captkmwilliams@comcast.net
Davis, Elliott, Ft. Worth, Aviation Courses, Ltd, 8175212063, skip@aviationcoursesltd.com
Sims, James, Sheppard AFB, Cable Install, 9406765543
Baker, Steven, Sheppard AFB, Cable/Antenna, 9406765545, steven.baker@sheppard.af.mil
Jackson, Mark, Sheppard AFB, FO Cable Install, 9406765551
Kerr, Robert , Sheppard AFB, FO Cable Install, 9406765551, robert.kerr@sheppard.af.mil
Merritt, Melvin, Sheppard AFB, Cable/Antenna, 9406765548, les.merritt@sheppard.af.mil
Siverling, Wayne, FOI, Sheppard AFB, 9406765545, wayne.siverling@sheppard.af.mil
Hankins, Mike, CET, Belton, Texas Attorney General, 2548994922, mikeandrea@sbcglobal.net
Lenox, Misty, Killeen, Killeen HS, 2545010400, misty.lenox@killeenisd.org
Gray, Renelle, FOI, Waco, Texas State Tech, 2548672909, renelle.gray@tstc.edu
Herinckx, Sandra, FOI, Waco, Texas State Tech, 2548672903, sandra.herinckx@tstc.edu
Anderson, Jesse, Goodfellow AFB, 3256543988, jesse.anderson@goodfellow.af.mil
Brittain, Michael, FOI, Houston, Cricket Inst of Tech, 7137229988, michael@selricocomm.com
Eriksen, Walter, CETsr, Houston, ITT, 2814862630
Meadows, Jon, CETsr, Houston, ITT, 7139522294, jmeadows@itt-tech.edu
Boden, David, FOI, Conroe, The Ctr for Business, 9362716033, david.r.boden@nhmccd.edu
Groves, JB, FOI, Richmond, Wharton Cty. Jr Coll, 2812391554, jbgroves@wcjc.edu
Fenn, William, CETsr, Lake Jackson, Brazosport Coll, 9792303261, wfenn@brazosport.edu
Cranek, Koehl, FOI, League City, Inst of Robotics, 2815353030, lourobotics@yahoo.com
Gertson, Matthew, FOI, League City, Inst of Robotics, 2815353030, lourobotics@yahoo.com
Williams, Pat, FOI, League City, Inst of Robotics, 2815353030, lourobotics@yahoo.com
Rider, Erik, CST, Seabrook, etrider@verizon.net
Rainer, Anita, Bryan, Turek's Computer, 9798227305, anita_break5@hotmail.com
Turek, Beverly, CST, Bryan, Turek's Computer, 9798227305, crazytureksrb@msn.com
Getkin, Terry, College Station, TEEX, 9794580415, terry.getkin@teexmail.tamu.edu
Stansbury, William, College Station, TEEX, 9798456566, bill.stansbury@teexmail.tamu.edu
Smith, Joe, FOI, College Station, TEEX-TAMUS, 8006450686, joe.smith@teexmail.tamu.edu
Elliott, Thomas, Victoria, Victoria Coll, 3615822506, tom.elliott@victoriacollege.edu
Stroud, Rayford, CETma, Schertz, MT&E, 2105689428
Crawford, Mary, Seguin, Seguin HS, 8303725770, mcrawford@seguin.k12.tx.us
Aguilera, Alejandro, San Antonio, Everest Inst, 2107327800
Funderburk, Eric, CETma, San Antonio, Everest Inst, 2107327800, k5iii@arrl.net
Holmes, Clyde, CETsr, San Antonio, Everest Inst, 2107327800, cholmes283@hotmail.com
Turner, Michael, San Antonio, Texas Careers, 2103088584, turnertwenty@hotmail.com
Gibson, Robert, San Antonio, B & R, 2105088733
Prasse, Tere, CST, San Antonio, San Antonio Coll
Turner, Harold, CNST, San Antonio, ETA, 2106331024, hturner848@yahoo.com
Pedraza, Trino, San Antonio, ITT, 2106944612
Blankenship, Ed, FOI, Ingleside, ECPI, 3617752976, eblankenship@ecpi.edu
Diehl, James, FOI, Corpus Christi, Del Mar Coll, 3616981728, jdiehl@delmar.edu
Erickson, Timothy, FOI, Corpus Christi, ETA, 3617262400, terickson@ecpi.edu
Stewart, Kenneth, Corpus Christi, Flour Bluff HS, 3616949153, kstewart@flourbluffschools.net
Keyes, Angie, McAllen, SACMDA-McAllen, 9566301499
Villarreal, Juan, Harlingen, Texas State Tech, 9563644843, juan.villarreal@harlingen.tstc.edu
Roose, Howard, Austin, SW Inst of Technology, 5128922640, droose@timberline1.com
Cloud, Tom, Austin, Austin CC, 5122234849, cloud@austincc.edu
Harrell, James, Levelland, South Plains Coll, 8068949611, jharrell@southplainscollege.edu
Dean, Marshall, El Paso, El Paso CC, 9157555367, mhd@elp.rr.com
Villarreal, Rik, El Paso, Western Tech Coll, 9155669621, rvillarreal@wtc-ep.edu
Arias, Fernando, El Paso, Ctr for Career and Technology, 9155455900, farias@episd.org

Trinidad/Tobago

Mendoza, Celia, Champ Fleurs, School of Bus & Computer, 8686638787, celiam@sbcstnt.com
Peters, Ancil, Tunapuna, Advanced Solutions Inst, 8686620996, education@asitt.com
Reid, Fitz, Marabella, Caritech, 8686582453, cari62@hotmail.com
Tinto, Maureen, Champ Fleurs, School of Bus & Computer, 8686638787, maureent@sbcstnt.com
Khan, Lazim, CNST, Arouca, Digital Architects, 8687026651, lazim_khan@hotmail.com

Utah

Labonte, Thomas, CETsr, Riverton, ETA, 4358317440, thomas.labonte@us.army.mil
Maxfield, Leslie, CETsr, Murray, ITT, 8012633313, lmaxfield@itt-tech.edu
Ulibarri, Gilbert, Salt Lake City, Salt Lake CC, 8019573274, Gilbert.Ulibarri@slcc.edu
Belliston, Ward, Logan, Utah State Univ, 4357971801, ward@cc.usu.edu
Paskett, Curtis, CETsr, Salem, ETA, 8013673260, njpcmp@yahoo.com

Virginia

Warnecke, Brian, Manassas, ECPI, 7033305300, bwarnecke@ecpi.edu
Dunnington, Ian, Falls Church, Knowlogy Corp, 7035321000, idunnington@knowlogy.com
Webster, Arnold, CET, Arlington, Homeland Security, 7038922152, arnold_webster@hotmail.com
Curran, Kristine, CSS. Alexandria, GPS-Education Ctr, 7039210200
McGraw, Stephanie, CSS, Alexandria, Global Prof Solut, 7039210200, smcgraw@gps-hq.com
Sullivan, Edward, Spotsylvania, Spotsylvania Career, 5408982655, eesulliva@aol.com
Browder, William, FOI, Glen Allen, ECPI, 8049340100, mbrowder@ecpitech.edu
Taha, Khalid, CETsr, Glen Allen, ECPI, 8049340100, ktaha@ecpitech.edu
Bellibas, Mehmet, Gloucester, Gloucester HS, 8046937961, mbellibas@gc.k12.va.us
Nunn, Steven, FOI, Toano, ECPI, 7572254242, steve.nunn2@langley.af.mil
Ludgate, Gary, Bon Air, Dept of Trans, 8043783403
Neuhaus, Jerrel, Richmond, 232355270
Jackson, Allen, CETa, Richmond, ECPI, 8043305533, ajackson@ecpitech.edu
Malbon, Iantha, Richmond, ECPI, 8043305533, ifinley@ecpitech.edu
Mclaughlin, William, CETma, Richmond, ECPI, 8045211009, wmclaughlin@ecpi.net
Seddon, Robert, CNST, Richmond, ECPI, 8043305533, rseddon@ecpitech.edu
Hogan, John, Chesapeake, Priest Electronics, 7574362466
Woodward, Wm, FOI, Chesapeake, Ursa Nav Sols, Inc, 7573120790, wwoodward@ursanav.com
Ralston, William, CETsr, Chesapeake, ECPI, 7576719202, wralston@ecpi.edu
Greene, Theodore, FOI, Chesapeake, ETA, 7576216397, tedgreene@hotmail.com
Floyd, John, Melfa, Eastern Shore CC, 7577891779, jfloyd@es.vccs.edu
Cagni, David, Virginia Beach, Tidewater Tech, 7573402121, cetttv@tidetech.com
Stover, Robert, TCM,FO, Virginia Beach, Advanced Tech, 7574688960, rstover@vbschools.com
Faison, Marian, Virginia Beach, VA Beach Tech, 7574275300, marian.faison@vbschools.com
Nowell, James, Virginia Beach, VA Beach Public Schools, 7575632018
Fain, Dennis, FOI, Virginia Beach, FiberTrain Corp, 7576357340, dennis@fibertrain.com
Barks, Kevin, FOT, Virginia Beach, KITCO, 7575188100
Berg, Hans, FOT, Virginia Beach, KITCO, 7572162222, hansb@kitcofo.com
Burch, Glenn, FOI, Virginia Beach, KITCO, 7575188100, glennb@kitcofo.com
Casbeer, Charles, FOD, Virginia Beach, ECPI, 7572132729, ccasbeer@ecpi.edu
Dadaian, Scott, FOT, Virginia Beach, KITCO, 7572162222, scott.dadaian@kitcofo.com
Dallas, James, FOT, Virginia Beach, KITCO, 7572162227, jdallas@kitcofo.com
Guadalupe, Felipe, FOT, Virginia Beach, KITCO, 7572162226, fguadalupe@kitcofo.com
Kruer, Gregg, FOI, Virginia Beach, KITCO, 7575188100, kruer@cox.net
Mooney, Thomas, Virginia Beach, KITCO, 7572162221
Morris, Dan, Virginia Beach, KITCO, 8885482636, dmorris@kitcofo.com
Salice, William, CETsr, Virginia Beach, ECPI, 7576719202, wsalice@ecpi.edu
Sisson, John, FOI, Virginia Beach, ECPI, 7572132729, jsisson@ecpi.edu
Smith, William, CETsr, Virginia Beach, ECPI, 7576717171, wesmith@ecpi.edu
Stone, Donald, FOT, Virginia Beach, KITCO, 7572162224, dstone@kitcofo.com
Blevins, Lance, FOD, Virginia Beach, ECPI, 7576717171, lblevins@ecpi.edu
Heggan, Sean, FOT, Virginia Beach, ETA, 7573482673, lamort@cox.net
Milling, Dorian, CETsr, Norfolk, ITT, 7574661260, dmilling@itt-tech.edu
Marques, William, CET, Newport News, ECPI, 7578389191, bmarques@ecpi.edu
Gibb, Lawrence, FOT, Newport News, ECPI, 7578389191, lgibb@msn.com
Rich, Charles, Newport News, Tidewater Tech, 7578742121, cettp@tidetech.com
Lee, Ronald, FOI, Chesterfield, ECPI, 8045210154
Zava, Robert, Farmville, Prince Edward Co Career, 4343152142, rgzava@pecps.k12.va.us
Steinmetz, Robert, CETma, Goodview, ECPI, 5408904439, BSTEINME@verizon.net
Dollar, Stephen, FOI, Montvale, 5408190334, stevedollar@verizon.net
Ferguson, Colin, Martinsville, Patrick Henry CC, 2766560349, cferguson@ph.vccs.edu
Chamberlain, Jeramè, CET, Radford, Nippon, 5406330704, jchamberlain@nipponpulse.com
Vasudeva, Sunil, CETma, Radford, ECPI, 5405638080, svasudeva@ecpitech.edu
Parton, Jane, Big Stone Gap, Mountain Empire CC, 2765232400, jparton@me.vccs.edu
Newman, David, Hillsville, Carroll Co HS, 2767282125, NA4L@PSKNET.COM
Jarvis, Alton, Lexington, Rockbridge Co H.S, 5404635555, ttjarvis@rockbridge.net
Casey, Bryan, CETa, Richmond, ECPI, 8043305533, bcasey@ecpitech.edu

Vermont

Renard, Jeff, Springfield, River Valley Tech Ctr, 8028858358, jrenard@springfield.k12.vt.us

Washington

Eckard, Charles, Everett, ITT, 8002723791, ceckard@itt-tech.edu
Gryniuk, Joe, CETsr, Kirkland, Lake Washingtonl, 4257398343, joe.gryniuk@lwtc.ctc.edu
Fawcett, Michael, Auburn, Auburn Mountainview HS, 2538044539
Masiker, Kathleen, Seattle, ITT, kmasiker@itt-tech.edu
Cameron, David, FOI, Tukwila, Light Brigade, 2065750404, sales@lightbrigade.com
Fulton, William, FOI, Tukwila, Light Brigade (Fiber Only), 2065750404, sales@lightbrigade.com
Gilbert, Albon, Tukwila, Light Brigade (Fiber Only), 7063679623, sales@lightbrigade.com
Johnson, Larry, Tukwila, Light Brigade (Fiber Only), 2065750404, sales@lightbrigade.com

Karch, Cameron, Tukwila, Light Brigade (Fiber Only), 2065750404, sales@lightbrigade.com
Lee, Christopher, Tukwila, Light Brigade (Fiber Only), 2065750404, sales@lightbrigade.com
Morse, David, Tukwila, Light Brigade, 2065750404, techs@lightbrigade.com
Shoemaker, Phil, FOI, Tukwila, Light Brigade (Fiber Only), 2065750404, sales@lightbrigade.com
Sloan, Jason, FOI, Tukwila, Light Brigade (Fiber Only), 2065750404, techs@lightbrigade.com
Wheeler, Larry, Tukwila, Light Brigade, 2065750404, lawrence@lightbrigade.com
Hopkins, Jason, FOI, Arlington, ETA, 4257782710, Jason.D.Hopkins@us.ul.com
Swartos, James, Bellingham, Bellingham Tech Coll, 3607528412, jswartos@btc.ctc.edu
Bratley, Melvin, FOI, Mount Vernon, Skagit Valley Coll, 3604167634
Horak, Ray, Mount Vernon, Context Corp, 3604285747, ray@contextcorporation.com
Gudden, Donald, Bremerton, Naval Air Station, 3604750095, nuddge1@yahoo.com
Latimer, Mark, FOT, Shelton, AESA, 4253080501, mtlat@hotmail.com
Childers, Thomas, Camas, Underwriters Lab, 3608175629, thomas.r.childers@us.ul.com
LaSarge, Candi, Camus, Workforce Learning, 3609072647
O'Connor, Michael, Longview, Lower Columbia Coll, 3604422744, moconnor@lcc.ctc.edu
Hortin, William, Vancouver, Light Brigade (Fiber Only), 3062543910, hortin@pacifier.com
Eley, Robert, CET, East Wenatchee, 2068783710
Smith, Michael, Yakima, Perry Tech Inst, 5094530374, mikes@perrytech.edu
Wisconsin
Cross, Jimmy, CETma, Milwaukee, ETA, 4148717609, jcross@wi.rr.com
Hahn, Kenneth, CETsr, Greenfield, ITT, 4142829494, khahn@itt-tech.edu
Kirchner, Herbert, Greenfield, ITT, 4142829494, hkirchner@itt-tech.edu
Petroff, Robert, CETma, Greenfield, ITT, 4142829494
Landmark, Susan, Madison, Herzing, 6086630843, slandmark@msn.herzing.edu
King, Debra, Superior, Wisconsin Indianhead Tech, 7153946677, drking@witc.edu
Fleischman, Terry, Appleton, Fox Valley Tech Coll, 9207352553, fleischm@fvtc.edu
Evans, Jazzmar, Milwaukee, MT and E, 4142344481, jazzywizkid@gmail.com
West Virginia
Gump, Terry, CET, Leroy, Roane-Jackson Tech Ctr, 3043727335, tgump@verizon.net
Soule, Jennifer, S Charleston, S Charleston Public Library, 3047446561, souleja@scpl.wvnet.edu
Ransom, Gary, Charleston, Charleston Job Corps, 3049253200, gsransom714@hotmail.com
Gosnay, Greg, FOT, Hamlin, Yeager Career Ctr, 3048245449
Toler, Jerry, Logan, Ralph R. Willis Career & Tech, 3047524687, inetnurd@yahoo.com
Evans, Richard, CET, Wilkinson, ETA, 3047527267, snuffy_hillbilly@yahoo.com
Clay, Mark, CET, Huntington, ETA, 3046970527, wylcradio@hotmail.com
Zawatski, Ed, New Cumberland, J.D.Rockefeller, 3045643337, ezawatsk@access.k12.wv.us
House, Roger, Clarksburg, United Tech Ctr, 3046243280, csacannon@aol.com
Spurling, James, Keyser, Mineral Co Tech Ctr, 3047884240, jspurlin@access.k12.wv.us
Wyoming
Bjork, Christine, Rawlins, Carbon Co. Higher Ed, 3073289274, cbjork@cchec.org
Arndt, David, Casper, Casper Coll, 3072682521, darndt@caspercollege.edu
Blesi, Jonathan, CET, Casper, Casper Coll, 3072682459, jblesi@caspercollege.edu
Patterson, N. Joe, Rock Springs, Western Wyoming CC, 3073821782, jpatters@wwcc.cc.wy.us

A current list of Certification Administrators and testing locations is available on our website at www.eta-i.org.

The Electronics Technicians
Code of Conduct

1. I will improve my own technical proficiency for the sake of my own firm and country.
2. I will conduct myself in a professional manner - admitting and accepting errors when proven wrong - and refraining from changing the facts in an attempt to justify my position.
3. I will never encourage, directly or indirectly, any gratuity, commission, tip or other financial benefit in connection with any work I perform.
4. I will avoid any conflict of interest or appearance of conflict of interest.
5. I will assist fellow technicians in understanding the technical, as well as the financial needs of the firm I am a part of, as I know that teamwork is the key to success.
6. I will respect the fact that my customers, clients, and non-technician fellow workers may not easily understand the highly technical and complex nature of my work. Therefore, I will have patience and will do my best to allow them to maximize understanding of the difficulty and the need for each of my procedures, and within reason, when requested, explain use and/or operation of the products I service.
7. I will display my license, certification and other diplomas as marks of professionalism for public recognition.
8. I will undertake only the assignments for which I have been properly trained and qualified, and will request help, without hesitation, for those which I am not qualified.
9. I will not misrepresent my firm or my own credentials or qualifications, nor will I downgrade those of my fellow technicians or competitors.
10. I will perform the duties of my job with complete fidelity and honesty.
11. I will safeguard trade secrets, never revealing facts, data, or information obtained in connection with services rendered, without prior consent of the client or my employer, except as authorized by law.
12. I will not improperly offer to, or obtain work, by way of commissions, or otherwise make an offer to pay a client or prospective client in order to obtain work.
13. I will have due regard for the physical environment, public safety, health and public well being. If my decisions are overruled, I will notify my employer, client and/or such other authority as may be appropriate.
14. I realize I must give back some of what others have given me. Where feasible I will accept cheerfully, to the best of my ability, positions on advisory committees of my school, membership in my professional association, or in other activities, doing my share to raise the level of income, knowledge, proficiency, skills, and public understanding and respect for my profession.
15. When I can no longer abide by these principles, I shall consider seeking a different profession.

Glossary

Answering machine A telephone device that uses RAM or tape to automatically answer the telephone and record incoming messages during times when no one is available to answer the phone.

Battery The common term referring to a component made up of two or more voltage storage cells, used to supply DC voltage. See *Cell*.

Brown-out An event that occurs when power demand in a utility service area exceeds supply capabilities.

Business card A small, 2" x 3.5" card, personalized for you, showing your company name, your name, addresses, phone numbers and special credits, titles and interests you have. It is distributed freely.

Cable
1) A group of two or more wires or fiber optics bundled together to carry electric current or electronic signals.
2) The popular term used when referring to a TV signal distribution network connecting signal sources such as antennas, satellite dishes and telephone to consumer televisions.
3) Coaxial - A cable, comprised of a center conductor surrounded by an insulation material, an outer shield conductor and outside insulation.
4) Fiber Optic - A cable, comprised of one or more fiber optic conductors. These conductors are made of ultra-pure fiberglass, capable of conveying light.

Caller ID The combination of a decoding machine and a telephone company service that allows display of calling party information to the recipient before they answer the phone.

CD (CD-ROM) The common term identifying a disk (compact digital disk), laser encoded with music or data in a digital format. It currently is able to be both read and written to with recording equipment.

Cell (electronic)
1) One of many types of voltage storage devices used to provide DC voltage. Some common ones would be: carbon, lead/acid, alkaline and nickel/cadmium. See *Battery*.
2) An area some miles in diameter, serviced by a transceiver for the purpose of providing telephone service to special telephones.

Cellular telephone Portable telephones that can be connected to the worldwide telephone network via "cell" transceivers that cover small areas (cells) of the countryside.

Certified Customer Service Specialist A technician or service support person who has been trained and tested in customer handling techniques and business relations and who has passed the ETA-I examination.

Charge-Coupled-Device (CCD) A memory type used in computers and cameras capable of storing charges of voltage representing data on microscopic materials.

Coaxial (cable) See *Cable*.

Cordless telephone Telephones that use radio frequency signals between the base unit and the hand unit. Operating radius is approximately 100 feet.

Customer Service Using general or technical support to tend to the desires and needs of customers in order to keep them as loyal customers.

Dot-Matrix The term used to identify a printer that uses combinations of tiny wires acting against ribbon and paper to imprint information on that paper.

Electricity AC, DC or static, is the flow of electrons (current) through conductors and devices (resistances) as a result of pressure (voltage) being applied, thus dissipating energy (power).

Electronics The technology that uses specially designed components to process signals (voltage and current) to accomplish a wide assortment of special tasks.

Electrostatic Discharge (ESD) The discharge of static voltage off of one body onto another. This is a point of serious concern when working with modern semiconductor types of devices, as many of them can be destroyed by charges a human might not be able to feel.

Feedback A part of the marketing effort that solicits and retrieves information from customers after sales efforts in order to measure the marketing, sales and service efforts against designed standards.

Fiber optic Optical quality fiberglass shaped into wires or special shapes for the purpose of conveying light.

Follow-up Direct contact after a sales or service effort for the purpose of insuring customer satisfaction with the intent of protecting the customer base.

Fuse A current-carrying component, used to protect electric circuits and devices by self-destructing, to open the circuit when current or heat exceeds a certain level.

Identification card A wallet-sized card, possibly including your photograph. Will show information about you such as company name, address, phone number. Might be required, or just helpful when dealing with government, business or home associates.

Ink-Jet A type of printer that sprays ink on paper according to microprocessor controlled concepts so as to imprint information on paper with a high degree of definition.

Integrity Uncompromising adherence to moral and ethical principles

Interlock A switch or connection that breaks the flow of current to a device when certain events occur, such as the removing of a cover, or opening an access door.

Laser A light emitted by a special source, such as excited ruby, that can be modulated and introduced into fiber optic wire and light sensitive devices.
Or; a printer that uses LED or Laser technology to encode a light sensitive drum with information that then causes toner to be picked up and applied to paper.

Light Emitting Diode A diode designed to emit light of a given frequency when voltage is applied. This light might not be visible to humans.

Marketing The process of promoting and preparing a product or service so as to be available for purposes of sale.

Media Means such as TV, radio, print, disk, tape and general advertising to convey information.

Microwave oven (microwave) An appliance that utilizes a radar frequency magnetron tube to generate an RF signal capable of cooking food.

Monitor
1) A device used to display operational conditions, such as liquid-crystal power line meter.
2) The common name for the CRT display unit for a computer.

Polarized plug A connector that is misshaped or mis-matched so as to insure connections are properly matched.

Productivity A measurable process of determining what is accomplished during a period of time by a person or shop.

Purchase Order A permanent paper log used to record material needs as they arise, including pertinent information related to them, and used to order those materials. Most will have a numbering system that allows the shop and the vendor to have a common reference.

Sales The final execution process of a marketing effort - passing a product or service to a buyer in exchange for money, services or some other product.

Satellite The common name used when referring to dish-type antenna systems capable of receiving radio-TV signals from earth orbiting satellites.

Service Bill A paper record, possibly multi-part, that is used to record all information concerning a customer, his problem, the faulty device and the parts and servicing efforts expended in the servicing effort.

Software Programs of several levels used by computers, processors and microprocessors to cause the device to perform a task.

Spike An instantaneous change in signal level on a conductor. May be caused by lightning or extreme changes in equipment connected to that line, such as when heavy loads are turned on or off.

Static electricity A charge of voltage developed in a physical body as the result of friction with another body. It can be dissipated by contact or near contact with another body.

Support Maintaining contact with clients for the purpose of completing old or creating new services and products so that the client's desires and needs might be satisfied.

Surge A short period variation in voltage on a line. Is usually caused by variations in supply voltage or load.

Technology The science of electro-mechanics that continually provides new products and services.

Telemarketing The use of blanket advertising using telephone.

Video Cassette Recorder (VCR) A device that receives television channels and records them on magnetic tape. It also plays recorded magnetic tapes and outputs the signal to television.

Voice mail Use of computers or answering machines to automatically answer telephones and record messages for later review. May be single-or multi-user.

Wire A single-strand metal electrical conductor or a combination of strands of metal bound together to make a larger conductor.

ISBN: 1-891749-04-8

Printed in U.S.A.

Index

Customer Service Specialist Credentials

The CSS certificate is beautiful, as are all of the other C.E.T. and Specialty certification recognition forms by ETA. Both the CSS wall certificate and wallet card samples shown here are laminated, suitable for framing, signed, dated, and personalized. Holding the CSS credential is an instant plus when interviewing for employment. Many companies offer advancement and higher compensation to CSS's.

The CSS Certification Certificate

The CSS Wallet Card